Aesthetics and Arts Education

Published with the assistance of the Getty Center for Education in the Arts, a program of the J. Paul Getty Trust.

Aesthetics and Arts Education

EDITED BY

Ralph A. Smith and Alan Simpson

UNIVERSITY OF ILLINOIS PRESS
Urbana and Chicago

This book is printed on acid-free paper.

Library of Congress Cataloging-in-Publication Data

Aesthetics and arts education / edited by Ralph A. Smith and Alan
Simpson.
    p.   cm.
    Published with the assistance of the Getty Center for Education in
the Arts.
    Includes bibliographical references and index.
    ISBN 0–252–01752–8 (cloth : alk. paper). ISBN 0–252–06141–1 (paper : alk. paper)
    1. Arts—Study and teaching. 2. Aesthetics—Study and Teaching.
I. Smith, Ralph Alexander. II. Simpson, Alan, 1933– . III. Getty
Center for Education in the Arts.
NX294.A38 1991
700′.7—dc20
                                         90-10986
                                           CIP

Acknowledgments

*The editors are grateful to the writers and their publishers
for permission to reprint the following:*

"The Questions of Aesthetics" by Donald W. Crawford was originally published under the title "Aesthetics in Discipline-based Art Education" in the *Journal of Aesthetic Education* 21, no. 2 (Summer 1987): 227–39. © 1987 by The J. Paul Getty Trust. Reprinted by permission of the author and The J. Paul Getty Trust.

"Types of Aesthetic Theory" by Harold Osborne is an excerpt from his *Aesthetics and Art Theory: An Historical Introduction*. Reprinted by permission of the publisher, E. P. Dutton, an imprint of Penguin Books, USA, Inc.

"Recent Aesthetics in England and America" by Roger Scruton is from his *The Aesthetic Understanding* (London and New York: Methuen, 1983), pp. 3–13. © 1983 by Roger Scruton. Reprinted by permission of the author and the publisher.

"Case Problems in Aesthetics" by Margaret P. Battin was originally published under the title "The Dreariness of Aesthetics (Continued), with a Remedy" in the *Journal of Aesthetic Education* 20, no. 4 (Winter 1986): 11–14. Reprinted by permission of the author and the University of Illinois Press.

"Versions of Creativity" by R. K. Elliott is from the *Proceedings of the Philosophy of Education Society of Great Britain* 5, no. 2 (1971): 139–52. Reprinted with minor editing by permission of the author and the Society.

"Aesthetic Experience" by Monroe C. Beardsley is from his *The Aesthetic Point of View: Selected Essays,* ed. Michael J. Wreen and Donald M. Callen (Ithaca: Cornell University Press, 1982), pp. 285–97. Reprinted by permission of the publisher.

"Interpretation" by Marcia Muelder Eaton is an excerpt from her *Basic Issues in Aesthetics*. © 1988 by Wordsworth, Inc. Reprinted by permission of the author and the publisher.

"Assessment and Stature" by Harold Osborne is from the *British Journal of Aesthetics* 24, no. 1 (Winter 1964). © Oxford University Press. Reprinted by permission of Oxford University Press.

"When Is Art?" by Nelson Goodman is from his *Ways of Worldmaking*. © 1978 by Nelson Goodman. Hackett Publishing Company, Indianapolis and Cambridge, 1978. Reprinted by permission of the author and the publisher.

"The Arts as Basic Education" by Harry S. Broudy is from the *Journal of Aesthetic Education* 12, no. 4 (October 1978): 21–29. © 1978 by Harry S.

Broudy. Reprinted by permission of the author and the University of Illinois Press.

"Philosophy and Theory of Aesthetic Education" by Ralph A. Smith is from *Dialectics and Humanism* 15, nos. 1–2 (Winter-Spring 1988): 31–45. Reprinted by permission of the author.

"Aesthetic Literacy" by Maxine Greene is an excerpt from "Aesthetic Literacy in General Education," in *Philosophy and Education,* ed. Jonas F. Soltis, 80th Yearbook, National Society for the Study of Education, Part 1 (Chicago: University of Chicago Press, 1981), pp. 121–41. Reprinted by permission of the author and the publisher.

"Why Teach Art in the Public Schools?" by E. F. Kaelin is from the *Journal of Aesthetic Education* 20, no. 4 (Winter 1986): 64–71. Reprinted by the permission of the author and the University of Illinois Press.

"The Usefulness of Aesthetic Education" by Alan Simpson is from the *Journal of Philosophy of Education* 19, no. 2 (1985): 273–80. Reprinted by permission of the author and the *Journal of Philosophy of Education.*

"Questions" by David Best is an excerpt from his *Feeling and Reason in the Arts.* © 1985 by David Best. Reprinted by permission of the author and Unwin Hyman Ltd.

"An Excellence Curriculum for Art Education" by Ralph A. Smith was published as "Excellence in Art Education" in *Art Education* 40, no. 1 (January 1987): 8–15. Reprinted with some editing by permission of the author and the National Art Education Association.

"Justifying Music Education" by David N. Aspin is an excerpt from "The Place of Music in the Curriculum: A Justification," *Journal of Aesthetic Education* 16, no. 1 (Spring 1982): 46–55. Reprinted by permission of the author and the University of Illinois Press.

"Literature as a Humanity" by Albert William Levi is an excerpt from "Literature as a Humanity," *Journal of Aesthetic Education* 10, nos. 3–4 (July-October 1976): 50–60. Reprinted by permission of the Levi estate and the University of Illinois Press.

"Discipline-based Art Education: Becoming Students of Art" by Gilbert A. Clark, Michael D. Day, and W. Dwaine Greer is an excerpt from "Discipline-based Art Education: Becoming Students of Art," *Journal of Aesthetic Education* 21, no. 2 (Summer 1987): 130–36, 180–83. © 1987 by The J. Paul Getty Trust. Reprinted by permission of the authors and The J. Paul Getty Trust.

"Defining the Aesthetic Field" by Peter Abbs is from his *Living Powers: The Arts in Education.* © 1987 by Peter Abbs. Reprinted by permission of the author and Falmer Press Ltd.

"Language, Literature, and Art" by Alan Simpson is from the *Journal of Aesthetic Education* 22, no. 2 (Summer 1988): 47–53. Reprinted by permission of the author and the University of Illinois Press.

"Developing and Checking Aesthetic Understanding" by H. Betty Redfern is an excerpt from her *Questions in Aesthetic Education.* © 1986 by H. B. Redfern. Reprinted by permission of the author and Unwin Hyman Ltd.

"Toward More Effective Arts Education" by Howard Gardner is from the *Journal of Aesthetic Education* 22, no. 1 (Spring 1988): 157–67. Reprinted by permission of the author and the University of Illinois Press.

"Principles of Critical Dialogue" by E. Louis Lankford is from the *Journal of Aesthetic Education* 20, no. 2 (Summer 1986): 59–65. Reprinted by permission of the author and the University of Illinois Press.

"Levels of Aesthetic Discourse" by David W. Ecker and E. F. Kaelin is an excerpt from "The Limits of Aesthetic Inquiry: A Guide to Educational Research" in *Philosophical Redirection of Educational Research,* ed. Lawrence G. Thomas, 71st Yearbook, National Society for the Study of Education, Part 1 (Chicago: University of Chicago Press, 1972), pp. 268–74. Reprinted by permission of the authors and the publisher.

"Teaching Aesthetic Criticism in the Schools" by Ralph A. Smith is an excerpt from "Teaching Aesthetic Criticism in the Schools," *Journal of Aesthetic Education* 7, no. 1 (January 1973): 39–49. Reprinted by permission of the author and the University of Illinois Press.

"Ten Questions about Film Form" by George Linden is an excerpt from "Ten Questions about Film Form," *Journal of Aesthetic Education* 5, no. 2 (April 1971): 63–73. Reprinted by permission of the author and the University of Illinois Press.

"Criteria for Quality in Music" by Bennett Reimer was published as "Choosing Art for Education: Criteria for Quality" in *Design for Arts in Education* 85, no. 6 (July-August 1984): 4–10. Reprinted with the permission of the author and the Helen Dwight Reid Education Foundation. Published by Heldref Publications, 4000 Albemarle St., N.W., Washington, D.C. 20016, © 1984.

"Useful Imaginings" by Vernon A. Howard is an excerpt from "Music as Educating Imagination," in *The Crane Symposium: Toward an Understanding of the Teaching and Learning of Music Performance,* ed. Charles C. Fowler, pp. 29–35. Potsdam College of the State University of New York, 1988. Reprinted by permission of the author and the publisher.

"The Aesthetic Transaction" by Louise Rosenblatt is from the *Journal of Aesthetic Education* 20, no. 4 (Winter 1986): 122–28. Reprinted by permission of the author and the University of Illinois Press.

"The Analysis of Dance" by Janet Adshead, Valerie A. Briginshaw, Pauline Hodgens, and Michael Robert Huxley is an excerpt from "A Chart of Skills and Concepts for Dance," *Journal of Aesthetic Education* 16, no. 3 (Fall 1982): 51–61. Reprinted by permission of the authors and the University of Illinois Press.

"Stages of Aesthetic Development" by Michael J. Parsons is from the *Journal of Aesthetic Education* 20, no. 4 (Winter 1986): 107–11. Reprinted by permission of the author and the University of Illinois Press.

For Chris and Jane

Contents

Introduction

This anthology was originally intended to be a second edition of *Aesthetics and Problems of Education* (University of Illinois Press, 1971), which was part of a series of volumes published by an Office of Education–University of Illinois Philosophy of Education Project (see Bibliographic Note). But as selections were being made for a second edition it soon became apparent that the growth of the literature of aesthetic education since 1971 necessitated an entirely new volume, one which had a more descriptively accurate title and reflected the interest in aesthetic education in both the United States and Great Britain. In further contrast to the earlier volume, this collection concentrates solely on arts education and features a number of British contributions. Appropriately, then, Alan Simpson of Manchester Polytechnic, one of the leading figures in the development of the idea of aesthetic education in Great Britain, is coeditor. Over the last decade he has been instrumental in organizing a number of important conferences in England which have brought together creative and performing artists, academic specialists, government officials, and school teachers to discuss problems of aesthetic education. His own contributions and the other British selections give this volume an Anglo-American character which the editors hope will further cross-cultural communication.

Over twenty years ago when I was selecting essays and excerpts for *Aesthetics and Criticism in Art Education: Problems in Defining, Explaining, and Evaluating Art* (Rand McNally, 1966), there was no literature of aesthetic education, only scattered statements that had not been systematically identified or placed in some kind of coherent context. It was also apparent that most writers about arts education continued to be influenced by images of the learner as a creative or performing artist. In 1966 it was thus important to draw attention to a range of disciplines that were being neglected but which nonetheless are relevant to a theory of arts education, for example, aesthetics, the history of art, and art criticism. There was also a need to move thinking about arts education beyond a tendency to construe the goals and objectives of learning in the arts in principally extra-aesthetic terms, that is, to place the socialization of the child or art's general therapeutic benefits above distinctively aesthetic understanding and appreciation.

A new generation of arts education theorists sought to rectify this situation, and *Aesthetics and Problems of Education*, the progenitor of this collection, revealed a substantial new literature from which one could make selections. Several conditions and developments influenced this state of affairs, chief among which were the establishment of the National Endowment for the Arts (1965), which gave a national recognition to the arts they had not previously enjoyed; the continuing influence of Jerome Bruner's *The Process of Education* (1959), which stimulated theorists of arts education to ponder whether or not art education was a subject and what its structure and key ideas might be; the founding of the *Journal of Aesthetic Education* (1966), which provided a major outlet for theoretical writings about arts education; the inauguration of Harvard Project Zero (1967), which lent the prestige of a major university to the conduct of basic research in the arts; and the activities of the CEMREL (Central Midwestern Regional Educational Laboratory) Aesthetic Education Program (1968), which provided opportunities for persons interested in advancing aesthetic studies in the schools to combine their efforts. Since 1971 the growth of the literature of aesthetic education has been exponential, and many of the tendencies in the field of arts education (at least visual-arts education) have been endorsed and further extended by the Getty Center for Education in the Arts, an operating entity of the J. Paul Getty Trust. Indeed, the literature has grown to such an extent that we could have assembled an anthology twice the size of the present one. To our considerable regret, therefore, we were obliged to omit numerous worthwhile discussions, an extensive reference section, and a section on issues. We nonetheless think that a good sense of the important ideas and topics of aesthetic education is conveyed by the contents of this collection.

The opening section of *Aesthetics and Problems of Education*, which was devoted to historic ideas of aesthetic education, has been replaced in this volume by one on aesthetics as a discipline and another on some typical topics of aesthetic analysis. This is not to say that we have completely slighted historical references; they are amply represented in the selections of Donald Crawford, Roger Scruton, and Harold Osborne. The section on the aesthetic dimensions of teaching and other subjects has also been omitted. While such dimensions are certainly worth some thought, they are less important for substantive discussions of arts education than writings which address questions about the meaning, nature, value, and function of art. Indeed, discussions of the aesthetic dimensions of education are now beginning to compete with writings about aesthetic education proper and are distorting the right relations of aesthetic theory to education. Otherwise, the selections in this volume address, as they must, the problem areas of aims, curriculum, and teaching and learning.

While the essays themselves make clear that aesthetics is an important resource for aesthetic education, some of the major ways in which aesthetics can be used in teaching art should be mentioned. Before proceeding, however, we should point out that for purposes of this volume we use "aesthetics" and "philosophy of art" synonymously, although, strictly speaking, aesthetics may range farther in its concerns than with inquiries into the creation, appreciation, and judgment of art. Aesthetics may ponder the character of practically anything considered from an aesthetic point of view, for example, the qualities of the natural environment, of sports activities, and even of well-wrought arguments.

One way to show how aesthetics is relevant to the teaching of art is to indicate how it can provide important subject matter. Such subject matter takes two forms. There are, first, comprehensive philosophies of art which go beyond the analysis of particular topics and concepts in attempts to find an important place for the arts in the life of man. In the modern era, the writings of Friedrich Schiller, Herbert Read, John Dewey, and Susanne Langer come to mind. Large-scale philosophies of art provide broad justifications for the study of the arts and help to underline the importance for the human career of a fundamental form of human culture. The major theories of arts education typically appeal to writings of this kind.

A second kind of subject matter that aesthetics provides consists of the results of conceptual analysis. Microscopic or small scale in comparison, conceptual analysis attempts to clarify the meanings and uses of such concepts as art itself, as well as a cluster of others such as aesthetic object, aesthetic experience, imagination, style, form, content, artistic expression, artistic intention, interpretation, aesthetic judgment, and so forth. Teachers of art are well served by such analyses, especially when knowing the different senses of words can keep them from talking at cross-purposes. Educators are further well served by R. K. Elliott's scrutiny of the concept of creativity, Monroe C. Beardsley's analysis of aesthetic experience,

Osborne's classification of standards of critical evaluation, and Nelson Goodman's articulation of an aesthetic symbol system. From the standpoint of providing subject matter for teaching art, then, aesthetics as a resource yields important insights into the nature, meaning, and value of the arts, which in more technical terminology constitute the ontological, epistemological, and axiological concerns of aesthetics. Discussion of such concerns, moreover, often leads into the study of the social and institutional relations of art, as the selections by Crawford and E. F. Kaelin reveal. Once again, teachers of art are less well prepared to instruct the young in the proper engagement of works of art if they have little understanding of the peculiar mode of being of a work of art (the ontological concern), what or how art means (the epistemological concern), and what art's value is (the axiological concern). The more such philosophical or theoretical knowledge informs the teaching of art, the more teaching becomes a professional rather than a merely intuitive activity. We believe that one of the weaknesses of education in the arts has been the insufficient attention paid to aesthetics by the field.

The conclusions of aesthetic inquiry constitute only one important way that aesthetics functions as a resource for aesthetic evaluation. The methods of aesthetics, whether those of philosophical speculation or conceptual analysis, also help the teacher and learner to come to grips with some of the puzzling aspects of the arts. As important as the conclusions they reach are the ways writers such as Elliott, Beardsley, Osborne, Goodman, Broudy, Best, Aspin, Rosenblatt, and Eaton address their topics. Prospective teachers of the arts who read such analyses will also develop respect for the rational and reasoned discussion of topics that are often written about in excessively florid prose. They will develop, as Louis Lankford puts it, an appreciation of the principles of critical dialogue.

To reiterate, as a resource for teaching art aesthetics provides both subject matter and methods for thinking about art. These two uses of aesthetics are brought to bear when, as so often happens, a student poses a question that invites recourse not only to the conclusions reached by philosophical analysis but also to the method used to arrive at them. Consider that perennial question "What is art?" For all that has been written about the pedagogical importance of eliciting questions, it is disappointing to observe how seldom teachers can field this query in a way that reaps the greatest educational benefit. Yet this deficiency is not surprising if teachers have neither a grasp of the principles of critical analysis nor knowledge of relevant disciplines, in the instance at hand, of aesthetics. What is more, teachers who have some familiarity with the logic of the concept of art can better understand the nature of other puzzling concepts, for example, the concept of education itself and its sub-concepts of teaching, learning, and curriculum. It was Israel Scheffler in his *The Language of Education* (1960) who pointed out the resemblance between the logic of the concept of education and that of art. An assessment of the growth of aesthetic understanding, in other words, should pay some attention to the ways young people think and reason about art and not rest content with determining whether they can merely state the conclusions reached by philosophical analysis.

Another value of the study of aesthetics derives from what may be called its integrative capacity. When aestheticians analyze a concept—for example, when they try to clarify what is involved in taking up the aesthetic point of view toward an object—they typically compare and contrast the aesthetic with other points of view and in so doing sharpen our understanding of nonaesthetic realms of experience as well. For instance, it is David Best's contention that once relevant criteria of assessment are taken into account, objective critical judgment is possible not only in scientific but in aesthetic contexts as well. Goodman, moreover, believes that art and science both share the goal of promoting human understanding and that aesthetic experience, like scientific inquiry, is inherently cognitive. And, as Albert William Levi and George Linden indicate, moral considerations apply across the disciplines and are brought to bear in aesthetic, social, political, and religious contexts. In short, the study of aesthetics inevitably leads into those other segments of what Ernst Cassirer in his classic *An Essay on Man* calls the circle of human understanding.

So much for some uses of philosophical aesthetics. What about scientific or empirical aesthetics? Empirical aesthetics receives little space in this collection not only because in the modern era aesthetics has come to be understood as a branch of philosophy but also because empirical aesthetics tends to focus less on the tangible aspects of artworks and our overt commerce with them than on underlying psychological mechanisms of behavior or imputed social relations. Emphasis on the former tends to draw attention away from the qualities and import of works of art while preoccupation with the latter often dissolves works of art into their social circumstances. However, as there are counterexamples to most generalizations, it should be mentioned that the cast of mind that informs

Michael Parsons's and Howard Gardner's empirical studies reflects both philosophical and psychological interests, and their observations gain significantly from this breadth. Still, empirical aesthetics is a more heterogeneous field than philosophical aesthetics, and its problems and methods demand separate consideration. The same might also be said of environmental aesthetics; the number of disciplines relevant to addressing its concerns range far beyond aesthetics.

A final word is in order about reading the literature of aesthetics from Plato and Aristotle to Kant, Dewey, Langer, and contemporary writers. Courses in aesthetics are usually offered by departments of philosophy in higher education where the content varies depending on the interests of instructors. In some classes students read the classics of aesthetics and thus receive something of a survey of historical aesthetic opinion. Beardsley's *Aesthetics from Classical Greece to the Present* (1966) is the standard short history of such opinion. Other courses place emphasis on the conceptual analysis of aesthetic concepts. The third edition of Joseph Margolis's *Philosophy Looks at the Arts* (1987) and the second edition of George Dickie, Richard Sclafani, and Ronald Roblin's *Aesthetics: A Critical Anthology* (1989) reflect this stance. Margaret Battin's contribution to this collection exemplifies another kind of philosophical literature, the use of a range of puzzles the solving or clarification of which can often be accomplished with the use of aesthetic theory.

All of these kinds of aesthetic literature have merit, but not all aesthetic writings bear directly on the theory and practice of aesthetic education. This necessitates the making of a judicious selection for educational purposes. We have tried to do this in selecting representative examples of the literature that address aesthetic topics. But the more teachers of art know about aesthetics in general the better they will be able to cultivate aesthetic percipience. For example, though teachers of art would be ill advised to assign, say, Kant's *Critique of Judgment* to adolescents, they would do well to know something about the importance of Kant in the history of modern aesthetics. Similarly, teachers can become more adept at handling questions about people's experience of art if they have a grasp of the complexities of aesthetic experience even though they may not assign certain writings on the topic. There is a difference, in other words, between what teachers think with and what they teach explicitly in class; it is the difference between what Harry S. Broudy calls pedagogical and repertory content. When aesthetic theory is brought to bear on educational problems we might speak of it as applied aesthetics, an effort to interpret in pedagogically useful ways the insights and methods of philosophical scholarship. This volume then is one example of applied aesthetics.

Since the British contributions to this volume refer to organizations and developments that may be unfamiliar to American readers, a few remarks by Alan Simpson about the British educational system and recent developments in arts education in Great Britain follow.

Ralph A. Smith

State education in Britain is not one system but two, in that Scotland has its own system quite separate from that in England and Wales; but although there are important differences of detail, the broad pattern of provision is similar. There is also the schooling offered by the private sector, the most well known being that in the inappropriately named "public schools"; but these remarks apply only to the provision for the vast majority of children in England and Wales. We are thus talking of an area roughly similar to, say, New York State, and where, as it happens, the major concentration of wealth and power also lies in the southeast corner.

For the most part in Britain there is the traditional division between primary (age five to eleven, corresponding to the American "elementary") and secondary schools (eleven to sixteen, or to eighteen), although a small number of areas have the primary, middle (nine to thirteen), and secondary or senior high schools. Primary schools are usually relatively small, with no more than a few hundred children, and it is not uncommon to find separate infant (age five to seven) and junior schools (seven to twelve). In these the children's education is in the hands of classroom teachers; specialists are rare, although there has been increasing development toward "semi-specialism" in which certain teachers take leadership roles in various areas of the curriculum. Secondary teaching is very largely through subject specialists in a highly differentiated curriculum. Without doubt it is in the primary sector that the effects of progressive thinking are most manifest and where the greatest innovation has taken place, from the design and furnishing of the school buildings to the content, methods, and organization of teaching. Secondary teaching, in contrast, is still to a great extent dominated by traditional, didactic methods, and developments in this sector have been largely in the area of logistics and organization.

Education is controlled both by central and local government. Each locally elected body is responsible for the provision of schools, staffing, and so on, in its area, while a government ministry, the Department of Education and Science (DES), headed by the Minister of State for Education, is responsible for education overall. Like all government ministries, the DES is staffed by members of the apolitical civil service, and the most visible in this case are the professional educators, Her Majesty's Inspectors of Schools (HMI). It is from these sources that official publications concerning directives on national policy, reports, and discussion documents emanate. These are invariably published by Her Majesty's Stationery Office (HMSO), and come in some profusion. As a result, many of the articles and extracts by my fellow countrymen and women contain responses and references to this near-constant flow of documentation and its implications for teachers in schools. It is unusual to find a British author who in some way or other does not feel obliged to make reference to an HMI paper or DES report.

In addition to the foregoing, there is also an independent source of reports and advocacy of policies for the arts that is worth noting: the Calouste Gulbenkian Foundation. Although it has numerous studies to its credit, probably the Gulbenkian's most politically effective and influential report is *The Arts in Schools*, published in 1982. Dealing broadly with "principles, practice, and provision" and culminating in some thirty-two recommendations, this report may be criticized for its generality. But it has nevertheless provided a persuasive case for the arts in general education, and its value in this respect should not be overlooked.

Over the last ten years, educational debate in Britain has probably been dominated by two themes: "The Curriculum" and "Standards"; or, in plain politician's terms: Are children learning what they should be taught in schools, and are they learning it well? Discussion of the curriculum has increasingly been concerned with the educational diet that *all* children should receive during the years of compulsory, general education—from age five to sixteen. For some time this has been known as the "core curriculum" and most recently has become the "national curriculum." The political attractiveness of this notion is apparent from the fact that *both* the present Conservative government and the Labour opposition see it as highly desirable; but, of course, they differ sharply over the ways in which it should be brought about. Increasingly, the ingredients of the curriculum pie are simplistically listed in terms of subjects. There was a time when HMI tried to loosen and broaden this trend with talk of "areas of learning and experience," but this seems to have faded away. The debate and its political, socioeconomic background provide a context in which the position of the arts is often felt to be under threat, but by dint of unstinting and clamorous effort they have so far managed to cling onto a slender slice of the curriculum.

Allied to the curriculum debate has been that over standards, in particular consideration of the feasibility of the monitoring of achievement on a national scale, and secondly, the overhauling of the public examination system. It is not too much to say that concern with assessment and examination is something of a British obsession. The movement toward national monitoring developed through the establishment by the DES of its Assessment of Performance Unit (APU). This body, initially launched over a decade ago, set up working groups which were to inquire into the feasibility of national monitoring of children's development across broad areas of the curriculum. The group for the area of "Aesthetic Development" eventually produced a disappointing document in 1983. However, we have now reached the stage where the government has enacted legislation which prescribes a highly specific national curriculum and testing for *all* children at the ages of seven, eleven, fourteen, and sixteen. Currently these tests are in the newly designated "core" of English, mathematics, and science, but it seems unlikely that the original intention of testing in all ten subjects of the national curriculum at each of the specific ages will be carried out. The testing at sixteen remains, for the present, dominated by the General Certificate of Secondary Education (GCSE), a national public examination which has recently been introduced to bring some unity to the previously complex and uneven system.

The foregoing are two examples of developments that raise fundamental educational issues and are likely to have more radical effects throughout the whole of schooling than any of the changes that have taken place over the past twenty years. It is against such a theoretical and ideological background that the day-to-day problems of teaching are set. Just one of the many concerns that teachers have (and not only those in the arts) is that the imposition of such extensive testing will reinforce the limiting and reductive effects of a rigidly determined curriculum.

Paranoia is an occupational hazard of which arts teachers in Britain are rarely free, and in the present climate it is likely to provoke an even more acute outbreak than the one evident over the last few years. One of the contributing factors might be that until very recently the arts each held to their quite separate, individual domains and enjoyed as little interrelation with each other as they did with, say, the sciences. In a variety of ways and for a variety of reasons, from clearly argued theoretical standpoints to those of pragmatic expediency in the face of government pressures, the arts have developed much more group cohesion since the late 1970s, and one of the strongest indicators of this trend is the aforementioned Gulbenkian Report. So far, however, attempts to form a Council for Arts Education, independent of government, have foundered on the inability of the potential member associations to reconcile their individual loyalties with allegiance to the arts as a whole.

The art forms vary in the strength and security of their position within the curriculum, and the anxieties are most acute in secondary schools. Of course, English language is absolutely secure, but how far its creative and appreciative aspects can develop is another matter. The visual arts are generally strong and music too appears likely to survive, but drama and dance seem to have prospects only for existing within some composite arts grouping or for being reabsorbed into English and physical education. Insofar as the arts do survive within a national curriculum of general education, it will probably be in an attenuated form; for example, should one area such as the visual arts gain strength through association with what is known as "craft, design, technology," it may well do so at the expense of one or more of the other arts.

Whatever the outcomes of current proposals, it is important for anyone not wholly familiar with general education in Britain to realize the extent to which it is becoming increasingly centralized. The power and independence of local authorities are being eroded as central government, through the DES and its other agencies, seeks to dictate and control all aspects of educational policy and provision. Ostensibly liberal moves to give greater authority to headteachers (school principals), parents, and school governors are offset by the requirement that they must adhere to the prescribed national curriculum. On the other hand, it should be recognized that some local authorities have themselves sought to impose certain political views and policies upon educational administrators and teachers in schools. In short, although the assumption that education has ever been free of politics is illusory, education is probably more fully embroiled in the political arena at the present time than ever before.

Finally, as political debate about the role of the arts in education takes place it is important to realize that questions about the value or the usefulness of aesthetic education, like those of the humanities as a whole, concern the capacity of the individual to participate in and contribute to his society's culture in its richest and broadest sense, and within that context to the quality of life. It is not for nothing that Harry S. Broudy distinguishes between an impoverished and a cultivated imagination, or that H. Betty Redfern remarks that to limit young people to the experience of their own and their peers' artistic creations and deny them acquaintance with great art is to "leave them imprisoned within the straightjacket of their own necessarily limited experience." Insofar as aesthetics is concerned with the quality of experience, with questions of excellence, worth or stature, and with human expression and creativity in the arts, such concerns must provide the regulative principles which underlie the fundamental goals of arts education and inform its curriculum design and its styles of teaching and learning. We examine these areas in diverse ways and from differing perspectives in various sections of this volume.

Alan Simpson

PART ONE

Aesthetics
as a Field of Study

Introduction

The relevance of aesthetics to the problem areas of aesthetic education cannot be appreciated without some understanding of the typical concerns, theories, and methods of aesthetics itself. In "The Questions of Aesthetics" Donald W. Crawford writes that in the modern period aesthetics has become an essentially philosophical discipline less concerned with analyses of beauty and nature than with attempts to answer or clarify a number of questions that bear on our experience and understanding of works of art. Such questions are about the nature of the art object and the character of its creation, the appreciation, interpretation, and evaluation of art, and the relations of art to society, all of which can be examined at different levels of complexity. The scrutiny of such questions proceeds in the spirit of reflective inquiry, the basic disposition of philosophy.

Crawford believes that the educational value of aesthetics as a branch of philosophy lies in its potential for clarifying basic human interests and values—our interest, for example, in the creation and appreciation of works of art—and as such it contributes to personal development and self-fulfillment. Crawford further distinguishes the typical work of philosophical aesthetics from the kinds of inquiry characteristic of art history, art criticism, and art production, the conclusions and products of which all provide material for philosophical discussion and analysis. This is why Crawford calls aesthetics a second-order discipline; its work begins when other disciplines have completed theirs.

Believing that the formal literature of aesthetics should not be introduced to young people until the secondary years, Crawford nonetheless thinks that teachers should have some knowledge of aesthetic theories and their dialectical mode of thinking and reasoning in order to be able to guide the activities of students at any level. One might say that teachers should be able to apply aesthetic principles to particular situations even though the subject being taught is not aesthetics per se. Or, it might be said that a teacher should be able to use aesthetics as a resource to achieve the purposes of aesthetic education while realizing that teaching aesthetics is not *the* central purpose of aesthetic education.

Whatever else aesthetics may be, it has traditionally been devoted to the formulation of systematic aesthetic theories which typically feature definitions of art, beauty, aesthetic experience, and critical evaluation. Harold Osborne, who until his death was the dean of British aestheticians, classifies the types of interest which have preoccupied theorists from antiquity to the present under the three rubrics of instrumental, naturalistic, and formalistic theories. He fails to mention institutional theories which have influenced recent aesthetic writing, but a sense of that interest may be gained from reading E. F. Kaelin's essay in Section 3. For the most systematic and comprehensive account of aesthetic theories yet published, readers may turn to Francis Sparshott's *The Theory of the Arts* (1982).

Although Crawford's references are not exclusively to analytical aesthetics, this type of aesthetics and its method of conceptual analysis has tended to characterize American philosophical writing. Roger Scruton, a British philosopher who has called attention to modern philosophy's neglect of aesthetics, assesses the efforts of both American and British aesthetic writing and finds that though its formulations are often ingenious, it fails to address adequately questions regarding the humanistic significance of art. Accordingly, he thinks that no sufficiently substantive conclusions are forthcoming from analytical, Marxist, phenomenological, psychoanalytical, or semiotic aesthetics. We must therefore, says Scruton, return to the kinds of concerns and distinctions typically favored by writers of an earlier period. When we do this we will address with renewed interest questions regarding the nature and value of aesthetic experience and the irreplaceable value of art in the lives of human beings. We will further ensure that aesthetic understanding, though it is not without practical and moral dimensions, will be distinguished from moral and scientific understanding. Objections will be made to some of Scruton's assertions, but there is little doubt that aesthetics invites charges of irrelevance and dreariness when it becomes analytical scholasticism or favors mystification.

In what might be called a Deweyan spirit, Margaret P. Battin approaches the teaching of aesthetics by concentrating on puzzling problems and cases. In instances of the sort Battin describes, the aim of aesthetic inquiry is not to build systematic theories for their own sake—a case of aesthetics being theory-driven—but to use theory to clarify and solve aesthetic puzzles. Battin's samples of puzzles are appropriate for even young children to ponder and they illustrate some of the questions that Crawford says aesthetics typically asks; for example, questions about the nature of representation, the beautiful, and the objectivity of critical evaluation. Readers who conceive teaching and learning in terms of problem solving and dialectical thinking should find Battin's approach quite congenial. It is also apparent that it is possible to discuss problem cases at different levels of complexity and thus they can be part of instruction during both earlier and later phases of schooling.

Donald W. Crawford

The Questions of Aesthetics

Although the term *aesthetics* was first used by the German philosopher Alexander Baumgarten in 1744 to mean "the science of the beautiful," philosophical reflections on the nature of beauty date from the earliest of classical times. The word itself comes from the Greek root *aesthetikos*, "pertaining to sense perception." This link between the perceptual and the beautiful was clearly expressed in the thirteenth century by Saint Thomas Aquinas in his remarks that "the *beautiful* is that whose very apprehension pleases" (*id cujus ipsa apprehensio placet*) and that "beautiful things are those which please when seen" (*pulchra enim dicuntur quae visa placent*).[1] And even as late as the turn of the last century, aesthetics was defined as the philosophy of the beautiful.[2]

Today, however, aesthetics is conceived somewhat more broadly and tends not to concentrate exclusively on the concept of beauty, although that idea is still explored.[3] As a philosophical discipline, aesthetics is the attempt to understand our experiences of and the concepts we use to talk about objects that we find *perceptually* interesting and attractive—objects that can be valued not simply as means to other ends but in themselves or for their own sake. As a teacher of mine once said, the best answer to the question What is painting good for? is: It's good for looking at! Traditionally aestheticians have inquired into the nature of our experiences of the beautiful in art and in nature and into the nature of the objects of these experiences—particularly works of art. In recent years aesthetic inquiry as a philosophical discipline has become essentially the philosophy of art, being concerned primarily with the nature of the work of art as the product of artistic creative activity and as the focal point of aesthetic appreciation and art criticism. And in ordinary use today, the term *aesthetic* sometimes simply means "having to do with art" rather than "pertaining to sensory contemplation and its objects," its broader and etymologically more proper meaning.[4] The central question of philosophical aesthetics is often considered to be What is art?, although some have questioned whether a simple, clear question is thereby being asked.[5] Many different styles of philosophy are represented in the work of contemporary aestheticians. Some writings are systematic and synthetic— theoretical attempts to demonstrate interrelationships between some or all of the arts; others focus on the developments of twentieth-century art, though still at a highly abstract level; others, including most journal articles, exemplify analytic philosophy by concentrating on the analysis of specific aesthetic concepts or problems.

Rationale for Aesthetics in the Public Schools

Except at the graduate level, aesthetics is not taught with a mind to training students to become philosophical aestheticians. Rather, it is part of a liberal arts education designed to broaden perspectives and to develop critical skills. As such, it is as applicable to primary and secondary education as it is to higher education, although it does not usually form part of the structured curriculum of the former. Although philosophers perennially disagree on the nature of their discipline and its proper methods, in general they concur that philosophy is a reflective or deliberative inquiry rather than a historical investigation or a series of scientific experiments aiming to acquire new facts. As Sparshott remarks, "A philosopher tries by argument to reach and guide decisions about what it would be best to say and how it would be best to think."[6] Philosophy, then, is not simply reflection but *critical* reflection, the assessment of chains of reasoning (or "arguments," as they are called) in the attempt to gain insight into our beliefs and values. It aims at understanding our ideas, clarifying them for ourselves and others. Thus Hospers introduces the problems of aesthetics by stating that philosophical inquiry or reflection on the arts is concerned "to clarify the basic concepts we employ in thinking and talking about the objects of aesthetic experience."[7]

The basic presupposition of aesthetics as a branch of philosophy is that our experiences of art—creating, appreciating, criticizing— involve basic human values and, as such, are worthy of serious inquiry. Philosophical inquiry, being both reflective and critical, always begins by taking one step back from the phenomena it seeks to understand. To take a simple example: I visit a local art gallery and look at a number of different sculptures, but I am continually drawn back to one in particular. Suppose at some point I notice what has happened; I become aware that my behavior indicates a preference. When I ask why this is the case, I am beginning to engage in philosophical reflection. In seeking to understand my own experience, to explain it to myself, to integrate it with other things I know about myself, I am engaged in critical reflection. I might simply ask, Why am I drawn to this particular sculpture? I may get a very simple answer (such as that it reminds me of my cousin) and think little more about it. Or I may be led to ask whether there is something about that sculpture—its aesthetic quality—that makes it seem better to me. And in doing so, I am raising one of the central questions of philosophical aesthetics: Is there a distinction between my mere preferences and aesthetic values? In asking about the nature of my experience, stepping back from simply enjoying viewing the sculptures, I have initiated a philosophical inquiry into aesthetics. This can happen naturally, in the ordinary course of events, alone or in dialogues with others, or it can be induced through educational planning—even built into the curriculum of an art education program.

Aesthetics is that branch of philosophical activities which involves the critical reflection on our experience and evaluation of art. Critical reflection consists in part of conceptual analysis and the formulation of principles of interpretation, of critical reasoning, and of evaluation. Art-historical concepts such as style and innovation provide material for analysis, and art criticism affords examples of interpretation and evaluation. Thus the subject matter for aesthetic inquiry comes not only from creative and appreciative activities in the arts themselves but also from the disciplines of art history and art criticism. The present discussion seeks to identify the concepts and skills about aesthetics that should be part of young people's education and to discuss how these concepts and skills interrelate with the disciplines of art production, art history, and art criticism.

The issues of aesthetics are quite various. One major concern is with aesthetic values and our standards for the interpretation and criticism of particular works of art. Another major focus concentrates on the many ways in which artworks can come to have significance or meaning. In particular, many works of visual art become meaningful by straightforwardly *representing* the real world (such as a painting that depicts how the coast of Maine looks on a stormy winter day.) But often the meaning of a representational painting is not exhausted by its representing the way the world looks. Its meaning goes beyond mere representation, and by means of representing an object in the world, it comes to symbolize other thoughts or ideas. For example, the boots in van Gogh's painting *Pair of Boots with Laces* take on a significance that goes well beyond their material and formal features. Artworks may be significant by virtue of somehow reflecting the inner life of the mind, the realm of emotions and feelings, and we find ourselves led to describe these works as *expressive* rather than representational. In short, in reflecting on our experience of works of art, aesthetic inquiry ponders the nature of value and significance as it arises in the arts—being embodied in works of art by creative artists and imaginatively reconstructed through the experience of appreciators. Some of these problems will be described in more detail below, but first let us address the more general question of the rationale for philosophical inquiry into the arts.

A preliminary question, of course, is Why philosophize at all? What can be gained from philosophical reflection and inquiry? More specifically, why structure an educational curriculum that encourages students to engage in it? Why not simply promote the enjoyment that can come from the aesthetic experiences available to us and educate our children so that they can enlarge the range of their enjoyment and maximize the pleasure to be obtained from art? Why is critical reflection desirable? These are old questions, and many answers have been suggested over the course of history. Socrates, the intellectual father of philosophy, maintained that the unexamined life is not worth living. Implicit in his claim is the view that our actions and attitudes are guided by our beliefs, our principles, and our values and that the rigorous, critical examination of these is an important part of what it is to be a *human* being. Socrates believed that self-knowledge is the highest type of knowledge, without which one can never be truly happy. In a more contemporary vein, one can say that the critical reflection that constitutes philosophical inquiry relates to our personal development and our happiness, since it "helps us to clarify issues, discriminate among options, and make better decisions."[8]

Applying these general rationales for philosophy to the discipline of aesthetics, we reach three conclusions: First, coming to understand the nature of art, our experience of it, and the basic concepts we employ in talking about it are part of understanding who we are and what values we have.[9] Second, the critical examination of our beliefs about art in general can increase perceptual sensitivity in the approach to individual works, thereby helping us to become more discriminate and to make better decisions in what art we choose to appreciate and preserve, as well as create. Third, through the aesthetic activities of analyzing the nature of art and formulating principles of interpretation and evaluation applicable to works of visual, plastic, and tactile art, the study of aesthetics becomes an introduction to the study of philosophy. These are values for art education programs generally; they are not restricted to specialized programs in art production.

The next question concerns the ways in which aesthetic inquiry can help in the education of those who wish to specialize in the arts. The most general answer is that for these students aesthetic experiences will constitute an important part of their lives, so the greater the understanding they have of the principles and values that underlie their experiences of art, the better informed about themselves they will be. But there are many, more specific answers as well, and these can best be explained through a discussion of the various concepts treated by aesthetics as a discipline.

To summarize, philosophical aesthetics is the critical reflection on our experience of art, whether from the standpoint of creators, appreciators, or critics. It aims at understanding the components of these experiences and the bases of the values we find there, as well as at gaining insight into how these values integrate, or sometimes conflict, with other values (such as those in the moral, economic, political, and religious realms). Thus the subject matter for aesthetic inquiry comes not only from creative and appreciative activities in the arts themselves but also from the disciplines of art history and art criticism.

Concepts and Skills in Aesthetics

There are five main clusters of concepts to which aestheticians direct their attention and which thus serve to define the discipline: (1) the art object, (2) appreciation and interpretation, (3) critical evaluation, (4) artistic creation, and (5) the cultural context. The following analyses of these clusters are intended to be representative, not exhaustive. Obviously these concepts can be discussed at various levels of complexity, but every young person's education should include the challenge of an exposure to some questions concerning each of these basic clusters.

The Art Object

The first cluster of concepts revolves around the created object, the work of art. The issues here concern how we identify it and describe its form, its content, and its meaning. Some questions address the nature of the art object's existence. Traditionally the artwork was considered an imitation or representation of something else, real or imagined. But many contemporary works of abstract art seem to be real things in their own right and not imitations of real things.[10] Is the work always a physical object, or is it primarily a creation of the mind, existing in conception or thought? Some have suggested that artworks partake of both worlds by being physical embodiments of our mental states, in much the way that gestures reveal our personality and thoughts.[11] This suggestion leads to the interesting concept that in important ways artworks are like persons, with qualities that reveal themselves more fully and become more or less interesting as we get to know them better.

There are further questions concerning how we identify individual artworks. In some art forms, such as painting, an artist creates just a single work; in other art forms, such as etching, there is an original plate as well as a number of prints made from that plate. We consider the prints works of art, but why do we not ordinarily consider the original plates works of art? From the standpoint of artistic appreciation, we are usually no more interested in the plate itself than we are interested in the mold in which a sculpture was cast. By discussing similarities and differences between various art forms, such as painting and printmaking, students can discover important features of the arts in general and thereby expand their appreciation of the place of the arts in history and culture.

Another traditional goal of aestheticians has been to discover and clarify key concepts used to describe a work's artistic form, such as unity, balance, harmony, rhythm, theme and variation, development, and tension.[12] But since these concepts are now well covered in art education curricula, attention to the special treatment of them by aestheticians is probably not necessary. Finally, in recent years aestheticians have devoted considerable attention to the analysis of concepts we use to discuss the various types and levels of meaning we believe artworks convey: subject matter, representation, symbolism, metaphor. It is not as easy as one might think to explain what is taking place when we claim that a work of visual art represents something in the real world—past, present, or future.[13] There are difficult questions here concerning the relation of the artist's intentions to what an artwork represents or means. This is another area in which the disciplines of aesthetics, art history, and art criticism interrelate.

Similarly, aestheticians have inquired into the conditions under which we can know what a work of art expresses. Is it determined by what the artist feels in creating the work, by what the individual viewer feels when looking at the work, or by other factors as well?

Tolstoy's challenging essay "What Is Art?"[14] can still be read with profit today by beginning students in aesthetics. Tolstoy held that true art only arises when an artist expresses a genuine feeling that the viewer is also able to experience—that is, that art is the transmission of feeling by means of movements, lines, colors, sounds, or forms. Recent authors have challenged Tolstoy's view and attempted new analyses of the concept of artistic expression as a property of the work itself.[15]

Appreciation and Interpretation

A second cluster of concepts relates to the appreciation and interpretation of works of art. First, with respect to appreciation, aestheticians have asked whether there are any special conditions required in order to have an aesthetic experience. Many traditional aesthetic theorists suggested that there is a unique aesthetic attitude or point of view of disinterested contemplation we need to adopt in order to appreciate art.[16] Others do not believe that our approach to art differs from our normal way of dealing with things in the world.[17] Furthermore, there is the question whether there is a unique aesthetic experience that is different in quality or intensity from nonaesthetic experiences.[18]

The appreciation of an art object usually goes beyond simply enjoying looking at it and involves coming to understand its meaning as well. Consequently, in talking about a work of art, we are often not content simply to describe its physical or visual characteristics. A good description of Brancusi's *Bird in Flight*, for example, would not simply report what one sees but would also involve an interpretation of what is seen—an explanation of the work's meaning. It may be based on what is readily seen in the work but often goes beyond that by making use of information about the artist's intentions, the social or cultural context of the work, and so on. Art history and art criticism are both essentially interpretive activities directed to specific artworks, artists, styles, and movements. Aesthetic inquiry often makes use of the interpretations of art critics and historians, but the issues of philosophical aesthetics are, once again, one step removed: What makes one interpretation better than another? Is an understanding of the artist's intentions either necessary or useful to interpret a work correctly? How do we decide between competing interpretations of a work? These questions arise naturally in art education contexts when competing interpretations are discussed. Students can explore not only differences in their perceptions but also differences in what they find important in a given work of art. Involving students in a discussion of how to decide between competing interpretations is a way of helping them understand the value of art.

Critical Evaluation

The experience of works of art is often immensely satisfying and enjoyable. For some this is the primary raison d'être for art. For others, art is valuable because it expresses or reflects important truths or provides us opportunities to learn about ourselves and others. In either case, we find these experiences valuable, and in time most of us come to believe that some works of art are truly better than others. Art criticism is seldom purely descriptive but is almost always concerned to evaluate the quality of a work. Art historians strive for objectivity in their analyses, avoiding explicit critical evaluations, but to the outside reader they often seem to make implicit judgments or comparative assessments of the quality of the works they study, as well as describing and identifying the work and tracing influences and sources. A major concern of aestheticians is whether the evaluative judgments they make are legitimate claims to knowledge—as opposed to mere expressions of personal preference or reflections of contemporary opinion. Aestheticians ask whether critical judgments about art can be supported by sound reasons, whether there are objective standards or criteria for determining if a work of art is good. Immanuel Kant[19] pinpointed the difficulty that the facts present for our clear thinking on these issues: On the one hand we believe we must judge each work of art for ourselves, see it with our own eyes—we cannot be forced by reasoning or argument alone to conclude that an artwork is good or successful. On the other hand, when we ourselves find a work good, we think that we have discovered something objectively true about it, that we have good reasons for our judgment, and that others ought to agree with us. The fact that controversy still abounds on the issue of the objectivity of aesthetic judgments[20] should not dissuade teachers of the arts from directly confronting the issue of the objectivity of aesthetic values. The distinction between an explanation as to why I like a painting and a justification of why I think it is good (and hence why I think you ought to find it good, too) is fundamental to the discipline of aesthetics.[21] Teachers can be sensitive to the educational level at which this distinction can be recognized and a discussion of it helpful to students. Even if the philosophical issue of the objectivity of value judgments remains unresolved, having students articulate and discuss their varying reasons—both subjective and objective—can reveal the levels of meaning and value embodied in one and the same artwork.[22]

Artistic Creation

Philosophy is said to begin in wonder, and who among us has not wondered what makes one person a creative artist while a second person, who might try just as hard or have the same amount of training, always remains at best an imitator? During consideration of the individual artist and the creative process of making art, questions of aesthetics naturally arise. How does the making of art differ from idle activity, such as doodling? At an early age students can come to appreciate that art is goal-directed and that one can get better at it, as is not the case with doodling. And yet art making is usually not goal-directed or purposive in the strict way that simply following a recipe to make bread is. Creating art differs from completing a paint-by-number painting. So it seems that in some ways the making of art requires learning rules and techniques—following the examples or instructions of others—while in other ways it requires innovation and imagination.[23]

At higher levels of aesthetic education, students can come to realize that creative artists, unlike paint-by-number painters, develop their own individual styles. Although in early grades there is unlikely to be discussion of the concept of style in abstract philosophical terms, students do recognize and can begin to talk about similarities and differences in the works of different artists, and this sensitivity and verbalization are the bases for later, more sophisticated aesthetic inquiry into how we identify an artist's style and what we mean when we say that one artist is more expressive, imaginative, or original than another.[24] When this inquiry is accompanied by studies in art history and criticism, further difficult but fascinating issues emerge; these include the relative aesthetic worth of originals versus copies and replicas and the even more vexing question of what, if anything, is *aesthetically* wrong with a forgery of a work of art.[25] These deeper philosophical questions, which may be too difficult for students in the early years, should prove challenging for high school students.

Other questions focus on the creative experience itself in an attempt to understand why people find creating art a valuable activity. At a prereflective level, students might simply be asked the question Why do you like to draw? and subsequent discussion of the various answers can sensitize them to one another's motives and sources of satisfaction. At a more advanced level, answers to the same question could become the data for some preliminary aesthetic theorizing. Is there a general answer to the question of why artists create? Is the creation of art best described by analogy to language—that is, in terms of the artist trying to say something visually, as one would use words to tell a story? Or is it more a matter of the artist expressing his or her feelings? Or sometimes one and sometimes the other—or even a mixture of the two? Even at the most advanced levels, discussion of these issues will benefit from a focus on specific examples, perhaps those suggested by the students themselves. And this can lead to the overriding question of what makes the process of creating art valuable to the creator. Is it always enjoyable, or is it valuable in other ways?[26]

The data for aesthetic reflection and theorizing about artistic creation become even more complicated when one considers not simply individual artists and their works but also cooperative or multistaged artistic ventures. What are the various ways in which artistic cooperation occurs? Are those who do not execute works of art but help implement them, such as the gallery curator who decides how to hang a painting, to be appreciated in the same way as creative artists?[27] Exploring these complications can help illuminate what we find valuable in the artistic process as a whole, as well as the place of the arts in society.

Cultural Context

Art does not exist in a vacuum. Its origins and its acceptance or rejection are intimately tied to other aspects of society and culture. The cultural context often interacts with the key subconcepts listed above to enlarge the scope of the aesthetician's inquiry. For example, the levels of meaning we attribute to works of art may be determined within a cultural setting by religious and ideological forces, and whether a work is viewed as primarily expressive or formal may depend upon the conditions of the time during which it is created or appreciated. Indeed, even whether something (a quilt, for example) is viewed as a work of art depends upon cultural conditions. There are also questions concerning the kind of cultural institution "the art world" is and how it relates to other cultural institutions. Finally, there are broad questions concerning the relationship between art and the social or moral order. What higher values, moral or religious, does or should art aim to achieve? Can propaganda or advertising also be good art? Can there be art that is immoral? If so, should it ever be censored or subjected to other kinds of control? Many issues concerning the arts in society reveal themselves in the products of the disciplines of art history and art criticism—another example of the interrelatedness between these disciplines and aesthetics.

In summary, the concepts and subconcepts of aesthetics generate inquiry ranging from the most general question about the nature of art to more specific issues, such as consideration of what is aesthetically wrong with a forgery.

Aesthetics in the Public Schools

Aesthetic inquiry can occur at various levels of sophistication and complexity; the extremes seem clear enough, however: First-graders can begin to reflect on their reasons for liking the things they make. Twelfth-grade students, assisted by a teacher familiar with some of the basic literature in aesthetics, should be able to appreciate the significance of most of the subconcepts discussed above.

The question of how best to introduce aesthetic inquiry into the classroom at first might appear to be difficult, since aesthetic issues often seem quite abstract, and philosophy is not regularly taught at a precollege level. The techniques of philosophical inquiry can be characterized in general as *dialectical*, in the sense that they are methods of exposition that weigh competing and possibly incompatible ideas with the aim of resolving them into a coherent viewpoint. The views that challenge the student may be drawn from textual material or hypothetical examples, although they may be elicited from the past experience of students themselves. The teacher may directly request the students to state their views and then challenge them with opposing views—thereby engaging them, singly or as a group, in Socratic-style dialogues, elucidating the reformulation of views, which are in turn tested by the critical scrutiny of the teacher or the students themselves. Alternatively, the teacher may choose a particularly poignant example (real or imaginary) that presents a puzzle and simply ask the students to try to reach some conclusions. The techniques of teaching aesthetics are not unique to the discipline. As in all teaching, one of the most difficult decisions concerns at what level particular issues can be introduced and still be challenging. The caricature of philosophers arguing about how many angels can sit on the head of a pin has a point: Younger students may fail to respond to a subtle issue, such as whether there are relevant aesthetic differences between an orig-

inal work and an exact replica, while older students may be stimulated to relate this to actual cases or to imagine a wide range of
possible scenarios in which the world of art as we know it is
slightly altered. In any event, we must rely on the sensitivity and
good sense of the individual teacher. The brief of this discussion is
that the art educator will benefit from a familiarity with some of the
basic issues of the discipline of aesthetics, which can enrich students' awareness of the value of art.

Aesthetics and Discipline-based Art Education

Some of the more specific interrelations between aesthetics and
the other disciplines of discipline-based art education have been indicated above; here we will simply make a few generalizations. Although the aims, methodologies, and vocabularies of aesthetics, art
history, and art criticism differ, the boundaries among them are
somewhat artificial and frequently overlap. Consequently, it is likely
that the similarities and differences among these disciplines will be
characterized differently by members of the different disciplines. An
aesthetician is likely to believe that both art criticism and art history
seek knowledge of specific works of art and thus are less theoretical
than aesthetics, which deals with specific works (or critical evaluations or interpretations of them) only by way of examples, to test
theories or to analyze concepts. Further, aestheticians see themselves seeking to understand the conceptual underpinnings of the
claims of knowledge about art made by art critics and art historians.
They recognize that art historians describe, analyze, compare, and
interpret individual works, collections of works, and styles, but see
themselves as inquiring into the categories used for these descriptions and comparisons. They see art critics engaged in uncovering
specific meanings to be found in individual works and making evaluative judgments about those works, but view themselves as engaged in the attempt to understand the criteria employed in these
interpretive and critical judgments.

NOTES

1. Monroe C. Beardsley, *Aesthetics from Classical Greece to the Present*
(New York: Macmillan, 1966; reprint, University, Ala.: University of Ala-
bama Press, 1975), pp. 101–2.
2. Bernard Bosanquet, *A History of Aesthetic* (London: S. Sonnenschein,
1892; reprint, New York: Macmillan, 1932).

3. Guy Sircello, *A New Theory of Beauty* (Princeton: Princeton University Press, 1975); Mary Mothersill, *Beauty Restored* (Oxford: Clarendon Press, 1984).

4. Francis Sparshott, *The Theory of the Arts* (Princeton: Princeton University Press, 1982), p. 468.

5. W. F. Kennick, ed., *Art and Philosophy: Readings in Aesthetics*, 2nd ed. (New York: St. Martin's, 1979), pp. 4, 117–19.

6. Sparshott, *Theory of the Arts*, p. 12.

7. John Hospers, ed., *Introductory Readings in Aesthetics* (New York: Free Press, 1969), p. 2. Cf. Kennick, ed., *Art and Philosophy*, p. xii.

8. S. M. Honer and J. C. Hunt, *Invitation to Philosophy: Issues and Options*, 4th ed. (Belmont, Calif.: Wadsworth, 1982), p. 5.

9. Melvin Rader and Bertram Jessup, *Art and Human Values* (Englewood Cliffs, N.J.: Prentice-Hall, 1976).

10. Arthur Danto, *The Transfiguration of the Commonplace* (Cambridge, Mass.: Harvard University Press, 1981).

11. Joseph Margolis, "Works of Art as Physically Embodied and Culturally Emergent Entities," *British Journal of Aesthetics* 14, no. 3 (Summer 1974): 187–96; idem, *Art and Philosophy* (Atlantic Highlands, N.J.: Humanities Press, 1980).

12. Stephen C. Pepper, *Principles of Art Appreciation* (New York: Harcourt, Brace and World, 1949) [parts of chapters 2 and 3 are in Hospers, ed., *Introductory Readings in Aesthetics*]; J. F. A. Taylor, *Design and Expression in the Visual Arts* (New York: Dover, 1964).

13. E. H. Gombrich, *Art and Illusion: A Study in the Psychology of Pictorial Representation*, A. W. Mellon Lectures in the Fine Arts No. 5, 1956, Bollingen Series 35 (London: Phaidon, 1960); H. Gene Blocker, *Philosophy of Art* (New York: Scribner's, 1979); John Hospers, *Understanding the Arts* (Englewood Cliffs, N.J.: Prentice-Hall, 1982).

14. Leo Tolstoy, *What is Art?* and *Essays on Art* (1898), trans. A. Maude (London: Oxford University Press, 1955).

15. John Hospers, "The Concept of Artistic Expression," *Proceedings of the Aristotelian Society*, n.s. 55 (1954–55): 313–44; Alan Tormey, *The Concept of Expression: A Study of Philosophical Psychology and Aesthetics* (Princeton: Princeton University Press, 1971); Guy Sircello, *Mind and Art: An Essay in the Varieties of Expression* (Princeton: Princeton University Press, 1972).

16. Jerome Stolnitz, *Aesthetics and Philosophy of Art Criticism* (Boston: Houghton Mifflin, 1960). [The chapter "The Aesthetic Attitude" is in Hospers, ed., *Introductory Readings in Aesthetics*.]

17. George Dickie, "The Myth of the Aesthetic Attitude," *American Philosophical Quarterly* 1, no. 1 (January 1964): 56–65. [Also in Hospers, ed., *Introductory Readings in Aesthetics*, and in W. F. Kennick, ed., *Art and Philosophy: Readings in Aesthetics*, 2nd ed. (New York: St. Martin's, 1979).]

18. John Dewey, *Art as Experience* (New York: Capricorn Books, G. Putnam's Sons 1934); Monroe C. Beardsley, "Aesthetic Experience Regained,"

Journal of Aesthetics and Art Criticism 28, no. 1 (Fall 1969): 3–11 [also in Michael J. Wreen and Donald M. Callen, eds., *The Aesthetic Point of View: Selected Essays of Monroe C. Beardsley* (Ithaca: Cornell University Press, 1982) and in Kennick, ed., *Art and Philosophy*]; Kingsley Price, "What Makes an Experience Aesthetic?" *British Journal of Aesthetics* 19, no. 2 (Spring 1979): 131–43; Michael Mitias, "What Makes an Experience Aesthetic?" *Journal of Aesthetics and Art Criticism* 41, no. 2 (Winter 1982): 157–69.

19. Immanuel Kant, *Critique of Judgment* (1790), trans. J. C. Meredith (Oxford: Clarenden Press, 1952).

20. Mothersill, *Beauty Restored.*

21. Arnold Isenberg, "Critical Communication," *The Philosophical Review* 58, no. 4 (July 1949): 330–44. [Also in Kennick, ed., *Art and Philosophy.*]

22. Monroe C. Beardsley, *Aesthetics: Problems in the Philosophy of Criticism* (1958), 2nd ed. (Indianapolis: Hackett, 1981), pp. 454–70; Dewey, *Art as Experience*, chap. 13.

23. Monroe C. Beardsley, "On the Creation of Art," *Journal of Aesthetics and Art Criticism* 23, no. 3 (Spring 1965): 291–304. [Also in Wreen and Callen, eds., *The Aesthetic Point of View*, Kennick, ed., *Art and Philosophy.*

24. Beryl Lang, ed., *The Concept of Style* (Philadelphia: University of Pennsylvania Press, 1979).

25. Dennis Dutton, ed., *The Forger's Art: Forgery and the Philosophy of Art* (Berkeley: University of California Press, 1983).

26. Albert Rothenberg and Carl R. Hausman, eds., *The Creativity Question* (Durham, N.C.: Duke University Press, 1976).

27. Nelson Goodman, "Implementation of the Arts," *Journal of Aesthetics and Art Criticism* 40, no. 3 (Spring 1982): 281–83.

Note: The American Philosophical Association has an active Committee on Pre-College Instruction in Philosophy. Information about its activities and publications may be obtained from the Association's national office, University of Delaware, Newark, DE 19716.

HAROLD OSBORNE

Types of Aesthetic Theory

A reasonably dispassionate survey of Western cultural history reveals three basic categories of interest in the fine arts, manifested by
social practice and conventions and by the fluctuations of taste as
well as the ways in which people have been accustomed to talk
about art and artists. With each of these kinds of interest is associated a characteristic group of art theories and critical criteria,
though historically these have not been entirely exclusive or rigidly
distinct but may often be seen interacting and simultaneously or
even sometimes inconsistently assumed.

First there is the pragmatic interest, which gives rise to a large
and complicated group of *instrumental* theories of art. In the most
general terms this involves a practical interest in the purposes
which works of art are considered or intended to serve and the effects which are believed to flow from them. Since through the
greater part of human history the so-called "fine arts" were regarded as handicrafts among others, not distinguished as a class,
and since art objects like other products of human industry were
designed to serve a purpose recognized and approved by the society in which they arose, this practical interest in the purposes of the
arts is the most general and in a sense the most natural of all. The
purposes of the arts have been extraordinarily various: works of art
have been religious implements, symbols for the glorification of rul-
ers or institutions, memorials, and a hundred and one other things.
But until the notion of the fine arts as a class of handicrafts whose
sole or main purpose was to serve aesthetic contemplation established itself from the eighteenth century onwards, no special group
of "aesthetic" attitudes was consciously called into play in talking
and thinking about the fine arts. The pragmatic interest in the arts
as handicrafts, products of workshop industry, found its earliest
and still interesting theoretical expression in the writings of the
Greek philosophers, who discussed the arts within the context of a
wider theory of Manufacture, and in the Greek socioeconomic theory of the arts. But the attitude of mind which tends to think of the

fine arts as one group of human artifacts among others is by no means obsolete or without influence. As an example of its persistence today the art historian George Kubler begins his book *The Shape of Time* (1962) as follows: "Let us suppose that the idea of art can be expanded to embrace the whole range of man-made things, including all tools and writing in addition to the useless, beautiful, and poetic things of the world. By this view the universe of man-made things simply coincides with the history of art."

The sort of criteria which are germane to this pragmatic attitude of interest are: the value of the purpose served or thought to be served by a work of art; the effectiveness of the artwork for this purpose; and the quality of its workmanship. These are not *aesthetic* criteria as we understand the matter today and in this context of ideas the aesthetic motive is not deliberate—which is not to say that an aesthetic motive may not have been active both in the manufacture and in the assessment of artworks long before it was consciously recognized.

Among the uses of the arts to which the highest social importance has often been attached are their uses as instruments of education or edification. The powerful emotional appeal of the arts and the intimate connections which they have often had with moral conventions and with religious belief and ritual have rendered their functions in these fields particularly prominent to theorists. Therefore moralistic theories of art—that is theories which justify, condemn, or assess art products in terms of their educational, edificatory, and propaganda uses and the effects, controlled or uncontrolled, which they are seen to have on human behavior—form a special group of instrumental theories. During classical antiquity the moralistic outlook was predominant in discussions of the literary and musical arts. During the medieval period in the West the moralistic outlook was very prominent with regard to the visual arts also. In modern times a strong interest in the social effects of the arts, judged by political or moral rather than by aesthetic standards, has been characteristic of Marxist theories and of theories such as those of Tolstoy. In one form or another the relation of art and morality has remained a persistent theme of interest and is debated today particularly in literary theory, and in connection with such practical social issues as the rights or wrongs of censorship. The discutients in all such debates are precluded from making fruitful contact with one another unless there is agreement whether an instrumental or some other basic interest in the arts is to be presupposed for the purposes of the discussion.

A rather separate group of instrumental theories came to prominence during the Age of Romanticism and is still prevalent in the
language of contemporary art criticism. These theories arose from
 interest in the arts as a means for the expression of emotion (in a
wide and indefinite sense of that word), as a means for the communication of emotion and feeling, and as a means of edification by the
vicarious expansion of experience. In the context of these theories
art objects are, characteristically, valued and appraised for their effectiveness in furthering these purposes. The criteria which they
impose are not aesthetic criteria. Works of art are not the only
forms of self-expression, the only ways of communicating emotion,
or the only ways of expanding experience beyond the confines of a
man's real-life experience. It does not make nonsense to ask of an
artifact (a novel, a psychotic's drawing, a volume of photographs)
which does any of these things whether it is also a work of art in
the aesthetic sense. Even more insidiously than in the case of some
other types of instrumental theories, these Romantic modes of interest conduce to the substitution of pragmatic for aesthetic criteria in
the theories of art to which they give rise.

The second basic category of interest with which we shall be
concerned is interest in the work of art as a reflection of a reality
other than itself. Like a mirror, the work of art is assumed to represent, reflect, or somehow copy a section of reality, which is its
subject or theme. The characteristic group of theories which presuppose an interest in the subject or theme, rather than an interest
in the artwork for itself, we call *naturalistic*. They do not always or
necessarily preclude an instrumental interest; but neither do they
imply it. They arise from a different attitude of mind towards the
art object. It is not incumbent on naturalistic theories to speculate
why we are interested in having copies, though suggestions about
this have sometimes been given. Aristotle, for example, spoke of a
natural human instinct for mimicry which finds an exalted outlet in
the arts, and also suggested that our liking for representations derives from an intellectual pleasure in recognizing what they are copies of. Others have assumed that we value copies because they
remind us of, or help us to experience vicariously, sections of reality
which it is inconvenient to contact directly—the reason why people
bring back souvenir postcards from their holidays. Our interest in
the subject or theme of a representation may also be an aesthetic
one: we may find it beautiful and therefore take pleasure in experiencing its beauty vicariously by means of a statue or painted picture of it. In such case the naturalistic attitude has affinities with

the aesthetic interest which is the third basic type. Naturalism as such, however, is the attitude of mind which deflects attention away from or *through* the art object towards that of which the art object is a representation.

The attitude of interest from which Naturalism derives is more restricted than the pragmatic interest which underlies instrumental theories. For example it applies less obviously to the nonfigurative arts of music, architecture, and decoration of the sort which preponderated in Islamic art than to the representational and literary arts—even though in classical antiquity music was regarded as a "mimetic" art. Naturalism as an artistic aim probably emerged with the painting and sculpture of the Greeks in the fifth century B.C., in striking contrast to the still highly conventionalized character of their drama. With regard to the visual arts naturalistic assumptions were basic to the art theory of classical antiquity and continued to be preponderant in the West until about a century ago. By comparison Naturalism has been of comparatively minor significance for Chinese and Oriental art theory. Its importance in Europe from the end of the Middle Ages until about the middle of the nineteenth century accounts for the prominence it must be given in any handbook of aesthetics. Indeed in Western countries artistically unsophisticated persons still tend automatically to assume that it is the job of a picture to provide a reasonably accurate reflection of the external reality which is its subject.

The characteristic criteria of Naturalism are correctness, completeness, and vividness (or convincingness) of representation. We find "correctness" assumed as the standard when the reflected reality can be independently known. It is replaced by "convincingness" when the depicted reality is imaginary or ideal. The technical skill of the artist in representing something in a different medium is usually associated with both these as a secondary criterion of value.

Naturalism of one sort or another expresses the attitude of interest in the subject of the work of art rather than the work itself. The same sort of interest may apply to Realistic art (which represents what is actual) or to Idealistic art (which represents the actual improved and embellished) or to Imaginative art (which represents fancied reality or fiction). Both the Realistic and the Idealistic attitudes have had a strong influence on art theory—and of course on our ways of appraising art works in practice—from classical antiquity onwards into the present day. The value of imaginative fiction for its own sake had little recognition before the Romantic Age. The various sorts of naturalistic art have their different uses and practical

effects. Realistic art may teach and inform, as Aristotle noticed. As
was recognized in the second half of the nineteenth century, by emphasizing social ugliness and injustice it may touch men's feelings,
awake their conscience, and stir indignation, thus operating as an
influence towards social amelioration. Idealistic art may edify and
inspire: indeed this has often been alleged as its main function.
Thus Naturalism ties up with the moral and practical interest in art
and links with instrumental theories. Again, Realism may be
thought of as the representation of the actual as it appears to the
particular temperament of this or that artist—a version of the theory which also came to the fore in the second half of the nineteenth
century—and in this way Naturalism ties in with the Expressionist
group of instrumental theories.

The third basic attitude towards works of art, ancient or modern,
involves interest in them as furthering deliberate cultivation and enjoyment of aesthetic experience. From this attitude derive *formalistic*
theories of art, which express the aesthetic outlook most characteristic of the last fifty or a hundred years. Presupposed in this outlook
is belief in a mode of apprehending the world around us which,
although not wholly separable from our ordinary everyday commerce with our environment, differs from the latter in the emphasis
it lays on direct perceptual or intuitional awareness without consideration of practical implications. This way of commerce with the
world in which we live is called "aesthetic experience" or "aesthetic
contemplation" and although it has probably been practiced by
most peoples at most periods of history, it first began to emerge as
a deliberate value to be cultivated in the course of the eighteenth
century. But in contrast to the attitudes which prevailed in the eighteenth century the outlook which is more typical of our own day
involves an assumption that the exercise of our perceptive powers
in this mode of apprehension needs no justification of an instrumental kind; it is worthwhile for its own sake and for the sake of
the heightened awareness of the world which it brings.

The value ascribed to aesthetic experience rests not entirely and
perhaps not primarily in the knowledge of the world around us
which it imparts; it is not a kind of cognition which can be formulated in terms of theoretical knowledge. The value derives partly
and perhaps mainly from full exercise of a trained and mature sensibility extended to maximum capacity. It is further recognized that
although we can take up an aesthetic attitude towards anything at
all, not all things are equally adapted to sustain aesthetic contemplation at a high pitch. Contrary to the eighteenth-century preferences

for natural beauty, it is characteristic of contemporary outlook in aesthetics to assume that on the whole art objects are most adapted for expanding and sustaining mature sensibility. Consistently with this works of art are thought of as things created in their own right rather than as copies of other sections of reality, as objects with their own autonomous values rather than as things intended primarily to be bearers of values extraneous to the furtherance of aesthetic experience. The critical criterion germane to this attitude of interest is therefore the aptness of a work of art for appreciation, the degree in which an artwork is adapted to sustain aesthetic contemplation in a suitably trained and prepared observer.

The sort of interest in works of art which we are now discussing invites a *formalistic* theory of art since by definition it is what are called the formal properties of things rather than their practical or scientific significance which make them more or less adapted to aesthetic apprehension. Furthermore attention tends to be directed towards those "emergent" properties of things—sometimes called "field" properties or "gestalt" properties—which belong to rich and closely knit complexes of perceptual material but not to the smaller constituents into which they can be broken up. These qualities are particularly interesting to nondiscursive, aesthetic contemplation. Some advocates of a formalistic type of art theory (among whom I number myself) have thought that fine works of art are the most successful examples of a special class of perceptual objects, called "organic wholes," which by the subtlety and complexity of their emergent properties and the intricate hierarchical relations among them are outstandingly adapted to evoke and sustain aesthetic contemplation.

Many people who have now adopted this characteristic aesthetic outlook believe that the aesthetic motive has been operative throughout history to control the making and appraisal of those artifacts which we now regard as works of art even though it has been latent and unconscious. Though there was no explicit theory of aesthetic experience in classical antiquity or in the Middle Ages or at the Renaissance, works of art were fashioned meet for appreciation; and from the earliest human periods artifacts were made with formal qualities enabling us now to appreciate them aesthetically although these formal qualities—often far from easy to achieve—were redundant to their practical utility or to the religious, magical, or other functions which they were designed to fulfill. This unconscious operation of a natural aesthetic impulse which became self-conscious only recently forms one of the recurrent themes of this book.

Western art theories may therefore be schematized as follows in relation to the basic interests from which they derive.

1. *Pragmatic Interest: Instrumental theories of art*
   (1) Art as manufacture
   (2) Art as an instrument of education or improvement
   (3) Art as an instrument of religious or moral indoctrination
   (4) Art as an instrument for the expression or communication of emotion
   (5) Art as an instrument for the vicarious expansion of experience
2. *Interest in art as a reflection or copy: Naturalistic theories of art*
   (1) Realism: art as a reflection of the actual
   (2) Idealism: art as a reflection of the ideal
   (3) Fiction: art as reflecting imaginative actuality or the unachievable ideal
3. *The aesthetic interest: Formalistic theories of art*
   (1) art as autonomous creation
   (2) art as organic unity

ROGER SCRUTON

Recent Aesthetics in England and America

Aesthetics owes more than its name to Greek philosophy. Nevertheless it is a peculiarly modern discipline. Its rise and fall (as we presently perceive them) have been contemporaneous with the rise and fall of Romanticism. Now that art looks back to the upheavals which created the "modern" consciousness, philosophy stands at its shoulder, discoursing on their common loss of faith. To understand the state of contemporary aesthetics, we must therefore reflect on its romantic origin. We then find a peculiar synthesis of British empiricism and Leibnizian idealism, achieving systematic statement in Kant's *Critique of Judgement*. It was Kant who gave form and status to aesthetics. And it was Hegel who endowed it with content. In the light of those facts, we should not be surprised at the difficulties which analytical aesthetics has experienced in attempting to make sense of its inherited subject-matter.

Kant put forward a threefold division of rationality: aesthetic judgment was distinguished from morality (practical reason) and from science (understanding), to be united with them only through a general theory of agency the details of which Kant did not disclose. Hegel offered to reveal the details of this as of everything. He found that it was not possible to discuss aesthetics without advancing a theory of art. Kant, who had preferred real flowers to painted flowers, thereby suffered a radical transformation. Both philosophers were convinced, however, that aesthetic judgment is no arbitrary addendum to human capacities, but a consequence of rationality, a bridge between the sensuous and the intellectual, and an indispensable means of access to the world of ideas.

Anyone interested in a subject will be attracted by the theories which make it seem important. Until the advent of analytical philosophy, therefore, those with an interest in aesthetics were invariably tempted by idealism. As an illustration it is useful to consider the last systematic work of English aesthetics to appear before the advent of linguistic analysis. R. G. Collingwood's *Principles of Art* was published in 1938, and, despite its influence upon art and criticism, was soon to be regarded as anachronistic. Collingwood presented in a novel idiom the distinctions through which idealist aesthetics had created its subject. He distinguished imaginative understanding from subjective association, artistic insight from scientific belief, expression from representation, seeing as an end from seeing as a means. Following Croce (*Estetica*, 1902) he advocated a version of "expressionism," according to which art is the expression of the inner life. "Expression" (which displays the "particularity" of its subject) is contrasted with "description" (which, in employing concepts, must abstract from the particularity of what it describes). It is integral to this theory that we must see art as end and not as means: we must see it, in Kant's words, "apart from interest." True art is therefore to be distinguished from craft, from magic, from evocation, and even from representation. This is the final residue of the idealist doctrine, that art does not advise, describe, or moralize, but gives immediate, and therefore sensuous, embodiment to its "idea."

A corollary of most idealist theories of art is that the distinction between "form" and "content" is thrown in doubt. It is in the nature of a work of art to give expression to the uniqueness of its subject-matter. At the same time, the work of art—being neither a description, nor a technique—must also exemplify the uniqueness which it expresses. All features of a work of art are bound up with its "particularity," and any change in the form brings with it a corresponding change in subject-matter. If form and content always change together, it seems problematic to claim that they are distinct.

Analytical philosophers are quick to observe a paradox, and it was not long before expressionism began to suffer from their assaults. To say that a work of art expresses something is to imply the existence of a relation, and of the two terms that are joined by it. But are there *two* things here—the work of art and its content? And is there a real relation between them? To assert a relation between *a* and *b* is to suggest that we can identify *a* and *b* independently. But that is what idealism denies. If the only answer to the question What does Beethoven's fifth symphony express? is The content of Beethoven's fifth symphony, then the term "express" can no longer be taken to refer to a genuine relation. Moreover, the theory that we understand a work of art by grasping what is "expressed" by it becomes entirely empty. At such a point, idealists lean on the doctrine of "internal relations," but it was an early achievement of contemporary British philosophy to show that doctrine to be unintelligible.[1]

In the light of such difficulties it is not surprising to find that the first articles of analytical aesthetics (gathered together as *Aesthetics and Language* [1954] edited by W. Elton and *Collected Papers on Aesthetics* [1965] edited by C. Barrett) show a fairly consistent hostility towards idealist thought. Their tone is not entirely negative. Under the influence of modern logic the authors ask questions which are to some extent new to the philosophy of art—questions about the identity and ontological status of the work of art, and about the structure of critical argument. Nevertheless, it is fair to say that these early essays subtract from the subject far more than they add to it. Analytical philosophy lays great emphasis upon logical competence, and is apt to be unadventurous in searching for the comprehensive standpoint from which aesthetics can be surveyed. This failing has persisted in the articles published in the two leading journals—the *British Journal of Aesthetics*, and the American *Journal of Aesthetics and Art Criticism*—which have been at their best when devoted to detailed analysis of critical argument, and not when attempting to explore the philosophical foundations of the subject.

It is a popular view that analytical philosophy is nothing but a devious repetition of old empiricist prejudices, expressive of an unnatural isolation from cultural life, and an ahistorical view of man. Unlike idealism, it seems to occupy itself exclusively with questions of meaning, conceding to science the sole authority to determine how things are. How, then, is it to provide its own substantive conclusions? By contrast, it has seemed that other ways of thought—literary criticism, for example, or speculative phenomenology—provide a perspective on the world which renders it intelligible in a way that science does not. They seem to generate an understanding of art that goes beyond the analysis of critical terminology.

In response to those sentiments, aesthetics has tended to move in two contrasting directions—in the direction of criticism, and in the direction of more speculative schools of philosophical enquiry. I shall consider each of these movements in turn.

In focusing his attention on criticism, a philosopher might take one of two attitudes. There is an obscure realm where criticism and philosophy coincide, the realm, as one might put it, of applied aesthetics, where the concepts of philosophy are used to stretch and embellish the speculative conclusions of critical argument. Since I am not sure about the nature or the value of such an enterprise, I shall simply refer to the most important analytical philosopher who has engaged in it. This is Stanley Cavell, whose essays *Must We Mean What We Say?* (2nd ed. 1976) contain extended discussions of

music and literature. It may well be true that these essays add
something considerable to the understanding of art. Cavell is also
noteworthy for an analysis of the cinema, *The World Viewed* (1974),
written in a style that conceals (from this reader at least) the nature
and importance of the ideas which it is designed to convey.

A clearer, and more orthodox, way of taking inspiration from
criticism is to engage in the philosophical analysis of critical ideas.
As an example I shall consider John Casey's *The Language of Criticism*
(1966), which sets out to examine certain philosophical preconcep-
tions embodied in the procedures of Anglo-American criticism. Casey shows a particular interest in F. R. Leavis who, for all his
rejection of universal premises, represents in a striking way the
deep longing of the English mind, oppressed by its own compulsion
towards empiricist scepticism, for the intellectual framework of idealism. This framework comes to Leavis not from philosophy, but
from the literary tradition of which Coleridge and Arnold are the
most distinguished representatives.

Leavis had shown, in a now famous analysis of Thomas Hardy's
poem "After a Journey,"[2] that sincerity in literature is not simply a
matter of truth-telling. Echoing a thought of Croce's (*Estetica*, p. 60),
he argued that sincerity is a property of the whole manner in which
a poet's feeling finds expression, being inseparable from a detailed
attention to the outer world and a concrete realization of the objects
·there presented. (Here is the idealist doctrine, that expression in art
is connected with the "particular," the "concrete," and so irreplaceable by the abstractions of any discursive science). Sincerity therefore necessitates thought, is incompatible with sentimentality, and
reflects a mode of understanding of the world which, while not of a
"scientific" (or theoretical) kind, is nevertheless more important to a
man than any understanding that a scientific training might have
brought to him.

Writers like Casey argue that the connections here—between sincerity, reality, thought, and emotional quality—are not merely connections of fact. It does not just so happen that the sincere
expression of emotion coincides with an attention to and realization
of attendant circumstances, or that a sentimental emotion is one
that outruns the control of any justifying thought. Leavis's conclusions are, if true, necessarily true, and reflect an insight into the
concepts of sincerity and sentimentality. Thus it seemed that, properly interpreted, criticism would be an extension of conceptual analysis, covering those important but elusive areas of the human mind
which art makes peculiarly vivid to us.

Whatever the merits of such an approach, it cannot in the nature of things lead us to a general aesthetics. On the contrary, it redeems art for philosophy through bypassing the questions of aesthetics altogether, and seeing in criticism only instances of more general philosophical concerns. It discusses problems relating to emotion, culture, and practical knowledge. But—while these may obtain vivid exemplification in the criticism of art—they are not problems of aesthetics. Of course, it is not an accident that literary criticism forces its practitioners to confront, in this way, fundamental questions in the philosophy of mind. Nevertheless, we need a philosophical account of art that will explain why that is so. Moreover, problems remain which seem to be peculiar to the traditional subject of aesthetics and which are not, and perhaps cannot be, solved by rewriting literary criticism in philosophical terms. It is from a desire to solve such problems that writers disillusioned with the minutiae of linguistic analysis turned to other styles of philosophical reflection. It has been said, and with considerable truth, that contemporary analytical philosophy has deprived philosophy of its status as a humanity. An informed understanding of society and culture, an acquaintance with art and literature, a consciousness of history and institutions—all these seem to have no place in the studies undertaken in English and American philosophy departments. And this reluctance to engage in the activity which Matthew Arnold (noting its overwhelming importance for the German mind) called "criticism," is rightly to be condemned as philistine. By contrast, neither phenomenology nor Marxism has, in our century, incurred that charge. Both have a large appetite for culture, and both promise to incorporate art directly and centrally into their conceptions of philosophical method. Major schools of aesthetics on the Continent—Russian formalism, Parisian semiology, the *Rezeptionsästhetik* which has recently emerged in Germany—all claim to be indebted either to Marxism or to phenomenology. Methods which seem to add so many results to a subject that is otherwise without them, naturally arouse curiosity. It seems to me that, in fact, the results proclaimed by many of these continental schools are, like the methods which create them, illusory. The attempt to translate them into English has led to a great proliferation of jargon, and a massive edifice of scholastic disputation. But it is very hard to extract a theory of aesthetics from the result. Nevertheless the claim is still frequently made that Marxism, at least, provides an indispensable clue to art, and to the mystery posed by modern man's intimate relation to it.

It is difficult to give any general assessment of that claim. But there are, I believe, grounds for scepticism. Consider the Marxist theory of history, which divides base from superstructure, hoping thereby to achieve a scientific view of both. Such a theory confines art to the superstructure, explaining its character in terms of the economic conditions under which it is conceived. Even if true, it is uncertain what such a theory can contribute to our understanding of art. It is one thing to assign causes to a work of art, another thing to understand its content or value. If this kind of explanation can generate criticism, then we shall want to know why: hence we shall need a theory of what it is to understand and appreciate art. Which means that we shall need an independent aesthetics, relying on precisely those philosophical reflections that the theory of history sought to replace. The theory can therefore neither solve the problems nor preempt the solutions of philosophical aesthetics. Of course, there have been more subtle models of historical determinism, conceived within the broad spirit of Marxian materialism. But it is not *subtlety* that is required in order to make the theory of history relevant to aesthetics; the question of its relevance can be decided only from the standpoint of aesthetics, and is not a question for the theory itself to answer. It is not surprising therefore, if the attempts to give a "subtle" version of the theory fail to make an impact on philosophical aesthetics. For example, the fairly representative discussion contained in Raymond Williams's *Marxism and Literature* (1977) proves wholly unilluminating both as criticism and as analysis. It says nothing persuasive about the nature of realism, about literary truth, about the value of literary expression, or the nature of our interest in it. It presents no method for the interpretation of texts, and casts no light on the crucial critical concepts—expression, imagination, form, and convention—which it is constantly forced to employ. Indeed, the author at one point expressly rejects "Aesthetics," as a study which mystifies what he purports to explain.

A Marxist will hasten to point out that there is more to Marxism than the materialist theory of history. In particular, there is a Marxian philosophy of action, according to which it is man's essence to create his own nature in production. Partly because of the influence of Lukács, partly because of the residual Hegelianism that all modern criticism betrays, this thought has commanded considerable attention among artists and their critics. But it is again difficult to see how it can either generate or replace philosophical aesthetics. Suppose it is true that the nature of man is self-created, and has its origin in productive activity. How does that enable us to understand the results of that activity? Such a theory does not tell us how the active nature of man is distilled in art or science, or why he stands in need of these activities, or what the difference is between them. The traditional problems remain. It seems reasonable to suppose that this deficiency will attend every application of Marxist doctrine. For it is characteristic of this doctrine that it will always deny the autonomy of any activity to which it is applied, while the subject of aesthetics arises directly from the perception that the significance of art is inseparable from its autonomy—inseparable, that is, from our disposition to treat art as bearing its significance within itself. If we are to argue that art has no autonomous value, no peculiar place in the spectrum of human interests, then we shall require a philosophy that demonstrates the point, not one that merely assumes it. It is for some such reason, perhaps, that Marxist criticism so often ends in futile and scholastic battles over matters which seem irrelevant to the works of art which it discusses.

Phenomenology seems better placed to generate the answers to the questions of aesthetics. It deals directly with mental data, and seeks to explore what is essential to consciousness, without either representing it as the product of some economic "base" or leaning on some premature "science" of the mind. Adopting a phenomenological standpoint it therefore seems possible to inquire into the nature of aesthetic experience, and into the manner in which the world is represented through it. Sartre, in exploring such questions, had been led to a theory of imagination, in terms of which to explain not only the character of aesthetic representation, but also the deep relation between aesthetic and ordinary perception (*L'Imaginaire*, 1940). Sartre concealed his theory in extended metaphor and parenthesis. The style was characteristic of a philosopher for whom rhetoric has always been an important value: as a result it was some time before the nature of the theory was adequately perceived in the English-speaking world. Those with an interest in phenomenology stayed with the more pedestrian and commonplace thoughts of Ingarden and Dufrenne. When interest was at last aroused by Sartre's work, it was partly because its conclusions were seen to resemble those of Wittgenstein, whose posthumous *Philosophical Investigations* (1952) changed the course of analytical philosophy. One of Wittgenstein's most persuasive and original arguments, however, also seems to have the consequence that there can be no such thing as phenomenology.

Wittgenstein had argued that I cannot acquire insight into the essence of my mental states from the investigation of my own case alone. The first-person standpoint can provide no knowledge of the nature of any mental process. To suppose otherwise is to assume, however covertly, the possibility of a "private language"—a language intelligible to one person alone. Such a language, Wittgenstein argues, is logically impossible. To suppose the possibility of a "pure" phenomenology, a study in depth of the "meanings" contained in every mental phenomenon, without reference to any external circumstances, is, however, to suppose the possibility of just such a language. Wittgenstein's argument was presented together with many complex and elaborate illustrations of the need for a "third-person" standpoint in the philosophy of mind. And in the course of his discussion, Wittgenstein recognized the existence of what he called "phenomenological problems." In particular he was interested in problems in the philosophy of aesthetic appreciation, such as those discussed by Sartre. For example, there is the important question of the relation between perceiving an object in the street and perceiving it in a painting. In understanding a painting I see something that I know not to be there. What are the peculiarities of this kind of perception? Wittgenstein suggests an answer which, while it shares some of the spirit of Sartre's, does not stray from the third-person standpoint. He also suggests that there is an important relation between perceiving paintings and understanding music. For some time Wittgenstein's readers did not perceive that many of his reflections were directly relevant to aesthetics. Only now are philosophers beginning to appreciate that Wittgenstein's philosophy of mind enables us to take up the subject of aesthetics at the point where idealism left it.

The first major philosopher to produce work in general aesthetics that showed the influence of the later Wittgenstein was Richard Wollheim, whose *Art and Its Objects* appeared in 1968. In this work, and in a series of essays collected in 1973 under the title *On Art and the Mind*, Wollheim has attempted to advance a philosophical account of the nature of art which will guarantee its central place in human experience, and so translate into the terms of modern analytical philosophy the spirit of Romantic aesthetics. He has tried to explain the concepts of representation and expression while avoiding the paradoxes which bedevil the idealist theories of their nature. Wollheim draws on Wittgenstein's remarks about "seeing as": the concept vital to his own and to Sartre's theory of imagination. The peculiarity of "seeing as" is that it is neither an illusion (since it involves no tendency to mistake), nor a perception of what is there. In exploring this experience Wollheim shows his debt to, and his rejection of, the work of Sir Ernst Gombrich, who, in *Art and Illusion* (1960) and *Meditations on a Hobby Horse* (1963), had discussed, from the standpoint of the psychology of art, the nature of representation and expression. But the more powerful influence at work in Wollheim's writings is Freud, both directly, and also indirectly, through the writings of Melanie Klein and the Kleinian art critic, Adrian Stokes. This leads Wollheim to speculations that are far at variance with the arguments of Wittgenstein (who rejected psychoanalysis as confusion and pseudo wisdom). Moreover it is difficult to gather from the result either a consistent theory of aesthetic experience, or a satisfactory description of art. It seems odd, in retrospect, that anyone should seek to combine a Wittgensteinian approach to consciousness with a Freudian theory of the unconscious mind, while thinking that it is the latter, and not the former, which will generate the most plausible description of aesthetic experience.

But Wollheim abstains from generalities, and invites us to see his work as providing suggested answers to suggested questions. In this, at least, he follows the convention of analytical philosophy. There is one analytical philosopher who has been bold enough to reject this convention. Nelson Goodman's *Languages of Art* (1969) was the first work of analytical philosophy to produce a distinct and systematic *theory* of art, and for this reason it has attracted considerable attention, the more so in that the theory turns out to be an extension of a more general philosophical perspective, expounded in works of great rigour and finesse, which embraces the entire realm of logic, metaphysics, and the philosophy of science.

Goodman's methods and outlook are highly idiosyncratic. But his project is a familiar one. He seeks for the nature of art in symbolism and for the nature of symbolism in a general theory of signs. This project has been promoted, both on the Continent and in certain branches of the humanities in the English-speaking universities, under the name of "semiology." But unlike the semiologists, Goodman advances rigorous foundations for his "semantic" theory of art. The theory derives from the uncompromising nominalism expounded in his earlier work, a nominalism developed under the powerful influences of Carnap and Quine, but showing certain affinities with the later philosophy of Wittgenstein (in its results, if not in the methods by which it arrives at them). A major difference—crucial to the kind of aesthetic theory that each philosophy generates—is that, while both Goodman and Wittgenstein represent the relation between language and the world as largely inscrutable, and draw striking metaphysical conclusions from this, Wittgenstein's central interest

is in the philosophy of mind. It is this which provides the Wittgensteinian vision of consciousness, as constituted by its outward expression, in language, in culture, and in the available "forms of
life" under which these are subsumed.

According to Goodman's general theory of signs the relation between signs and the world can be described, like any relation, in
terms of its formal structure—in terms of such logical categories as
symmetry, reflexivity, and transitivity—and in terms of the objects
related (in this case signs and things). But apart from that formal
analysis, there is nothing to be said. Words are labels which attach
to things, but the attempt to describe that relation of attachment
must, in using words, presuppose what it seeks to explain.

A corollary of this view is that relations of identical logical structure are one and the same. Thus, if we assume paintings, like
words, to be signs, then portraits stand to their subjects in the same
relation as proper names stand to the objects denoted by them.
Hence representation and denotation are the same relation. We
should not worry if that leads us to no new understanding of the
relation—for example, that it leads to no procedure for "decoding"
the painted sign. For what we are being told is that there is nothing
to be understood, or rather, to put the point in Wittgensteinian idiom, that "understanding" is what is *given*. That is what nominalism says.

Goodman proceeds to generalize his theory of symbolism, using
the word "reference" to express the relation between word and
thing (the relation of "labeling"). Denotation is the special case of
reference exemplified by proper names and portraits—the case
where a symbol labels *one* individual. When a single label picks out
a class of things, then we have, not a name, but a predicate. (To
speak of "properties" is both redundant and, in Goodman's view,
metaphysically vicious, since it implies that there are things which
are not individuals. Even to employ the term "class" is to encourage
illegitimate metaphysical expectations.)

Sometimes the process of "labeling" goes both ways. A color
sample is a sign for the color which it possesses—the color red, say.
It therefore "refers" to the label "red," which in turn refers to the
sample. In this case the predicate "red" and the sample mutually
label each other. Goodman calls this relation "exemplification," and
analyzes expression as a special case of it, the case where the exemplification of a predicate proceeds by metaphor.

The economy and elegance of Goodman's theory are matched only
by its extreme inscrutability. On the surface, it seems to provide di-

rect and intelligible answers to all the major problems of aesthetics. What is art?—a system of symbols. What is representation?—denotation. What is expression?—a kind of reference. What is the value of art?—that it symbolizes ("displays") reality. What is the distinction between art and science?—a distinction between symbol systems, but not between the matters which they display. And so on. And yet at every point we feel at a loss to know what we are learning about art in being told that its essence is symbolic.

The fashionable works of semiology that have succeeded Barthes's *Éléments* of 1964 leave the reader without any method for attaching "meanings" to the literary and artistic "codes" which are supposed to exemplify them: the reader is offered only a battery of useless technicalities. By contrast, Goodman bases his analysis of art in a serious philosophy of symbolism. Nevertheless it is also true that if one describes the forms of art as "symbol systems," while refusing to answer all epistemological questions concerning the nature of symbolism, the subject is made more, and not less, obscure. We need to know how we would *discover* that something is a symbol, and how we would *know* what it says about its subject. Moreover, the semantic theory seems to have implications that are extremely counterintuitive. In particular it seems to imply that the relation of a work of art to its expressive content is, like any semantic relation, a matter of convention. It is true that expression in art requires convention—but it is not determined by convention. If you could achieve expression by following conventions, then art becomes a matter of skill. It requires only facility to rival Mozart. But that is implausible. To achieve artistic expression is to use rules only to transcend them, to act as much in defiance of convention as in obedience to it.

What, then, should we put in the place of the view that all art is language? Is there any theory which so successfully combines range of application with apparent explanatory power?

NOTES

1. G. E. Moore, "Internal and External Relations," 1920; reprinted in *Philosophical Studies* (Cambridge and Atlantic Highlands, N.J., 1922).
2. "Reality and Sincerity," *Scrutiny* 19 (1952–53); reprinted in F. R. Leavis, ed., *Selections from Scrutiny*, 2 vols. (Cambridge and New York, 1968), vol. 2.

MARGARET P. BATTIN

Case Problems in Aesthetics

In 1951, J. A. Passmore shamelessly titled an essay "The Dreariness of Aesthetics."[1] Drawing on John Wisdom's earlier complaints, he denounced aesthetics' dullness, its pretentiousness, and the fact that it was "peculiarly unilluminating." What Passmore had in mind were the vapid abstractions and metaphysical hyperbole involved in "saying nothing in the most pretentious possible way"; he thought aesthetics wasn't in touch enough with the real world of the specific, different arts. He was right. But while in the intervening years aesthetics has changed course and this complaint has largely been heeded, Passmore's uncompromising title can still provoke a ripple of embarrassment among aestheticians who suspect that the accusation might be true.

Indeed, aesthetics is still dreary, at least in one major respect. To be sure, since it deals with art and beauty, aesthetics has an incomparably interesting subject matter. And it has for the most part abandoned the empty generalizations to which Passmore attributed its dreariness. But it is still dreary anyway, at least in one central feature, though it need not be this way.

What makes aesthetics so dreary has to do with its format, or rather, its modus operandi as a discipline, the characteristic way in which it operates. It is not the content of its theories that makes aesthetics dull, but the way in which it makes use of those often rather exciting theories. The root problem is that aesthetics is for the most part *theory-driven*, rather than *driven to theory*; the issues with which it is concerned are a product of the demands and deficiencies of its theoretical constructions, not issues made pressing by the subject matter itself. If aesthetics as a discipline sometimes seems impenetrably arcane and stultifyingly dull—just more hot air from the philosophers—this may be why.

The long and ornate history of aesthetics consists in a series of theoretical formulations, each of which purports to provide a principled account of art or beauty as well as related artistic and aesthetic phenomena. Later theoretical constructions in this ongoing historical discussion typically work to amend or supersede earlier theories: so, for instance, Tolstoian expression theory tries to unseat the imitation theory handed down from Plato and Aristotle; Clive Bell's views about significant form attempt to dismiss expression theory, and so on throughout most of the history of aesthetics. To be sure, there is something these thinkers see in art that leads them to develop these revolutionizing views, but what these thinkers characteristically emphasize in presenting and defending their views is a function of the previous ones.

The introduction of a new theory typically involves a three-part process: (1) itemizing the defects of the earlier theories, especially where they are inconsistent, incomplete, or unclear; (2) articulating a new theory to supplant the old ones; and (3) pointing to works of art, or kinds of experiences, in order to confirm the new claims. In this way, aesthetics seems to contain destructive, constructive, and confirmatory elements. But notice that this process is almost entirely theory-directed: new theories are proposed because of deficiencies in the old, and works of art or examples of beauty are pointed out to confirm the new. Thus the discipline is consigned to a kind of distanced, remote position vis-à-vis art and beauty themselves: in its overriding concern with theory, it never really seems to quite get around to addressing the *problems* art and beauty themselves present. Theory is constructed to answer theory, and art and beauty are dragged in only to illustrate those points.

Of course, not all work in aesthetics follows this pattern, especially in contemporary writing. There is much in aesthetics that is richly informed by sensitivity to specific cases of art and beauty, and much that is motivated by these puzzles. But where it does follow this pattern, aesthetics finds itself engaged in a largely unsuccessful process. Since aesthetics, unlike macrolevel natural science, does not have a range of uniform, comparatively stable entities to describe, theory is often precarious; aesthetics must deal with a range of continuously shifting and developing entities or states of affairs which are only sometimes said to count as art or occasions of beauty and thus to fall within its realm. Then, too, the strategy of pointing to works of art or experiences of beauty to confirm new theoretical claims is flawed: since this process is always selective (unless done at random), it is inherently biased in favor of the theory being advanced and can do no more than illustrate or explain, not prove. Thus aesthetics' condition is an unfortunate one: it is largely theory-driven, but this very theory-drivenness makes it in the end unsuccessful in advancing its claims. This is dreary indeed.

It is not quite the same sort of dreariness Passmore lamented, of course, but it is a dreariness just the same: aesthetics never quite approaches the real problems raised by beauty and art. It *says* things about art, to be sure, and sometimes interesting things, but always from the little distance its theory-driven stance imposes.

The remedy for this dreariness, I'd like to suggest, is to start at the other end of aesthetic discussion: not with theory, but with actual cases, practical dilemmas, and puzzle problems about beauty and art. These are problems of the sort that specific, individual, concrete examples of beauty and art present: "Is this stick of driftwood on display in this gallery, exhibited by this well-known artist, actually *art?*" "Could that bleak landscape be beautiful, and what would we have to know about it or its viewers to determine whether it is?" "Is this piece of music really *about* what its title says?" Some slightly more extended examples, posed as philosophers' puzzle cases, display the kinds of problems which seem trivial at first but can be seen on reflection to harbor much more fundamental problems. For instance:

1. Al Meinhardt paints a portrait of art dealer Daffodil Glurt. The resulting canvas is a single solid color, chartreuse. Meinhardt hangs the canvas in the Museum of Modern Art, labeled *Portrait of Daffodil Glurt*. Daffodil is not amused. But has she actually been insulted?

2. The Louvre is on fire. You can save either the *Mona Lisa* or the guard who stands next to it, but not both. Which do you do?

3. We regard the Cycladic votive figurines, with their flat, oval faces and elongated bodies, as beautiful. We surmise that they were used as fertility goddesses in household shrines, and we believe that the culture in which they arose did not have a conception of "fine arts." Have these figurines always been beautiful, or have they come to be so only now?

Case problems of this sort have been very effectively used in various areas of normative ethics during the last decade or two, particularly in professional ethics fields like bioethics, business ethics, and the ethics of the practice of law; they have also been used in teaching law since the case method was introduced at Harvard early in the century. Their specific virtue is that while they address conflicts and points of tension within a field, they do not invite unrestrained theory construction beyond what is required to examine the case critically. They do not invite "saying nothing in the most pretentious possible way," as Passmore criticized aesthetics, since

saying nothing will not resolve a case; and they do not rely on selectively biased pointing out of works of art to prove a point, since
the troublesome case is already at hand. They may seem deceptively
simple, even artless; but a little reflection will reveal that the issues
these sorts of puzzle cases can raise are not simple at all.

Indeed, the issues these little problems raise are fundamental to
the concerns of aesthetics. Deciding whether the chartreuse portrait could insult Daffodil Glurt, for instance, requires saying something about the assertoric properties of nonobjective art; deciding
whether one ought to rescue the *Mona Lisa* or the guard requires
determining the relative weight of aesthetic and ethical values; saying whether the Cycladic figurines were beautiful all along requires
addressing the issue of the subjectivity or objectivity of beauty. The
major aesthetic theories each have something to say, either directly
or by implication, about each of these issues. But, generally, as long
as we approach the world of art and beauty from the perspective of
antecedent theoretical commitments—that is, in a theory-driven
way—we may not even really see the issues at hand. So, for instance, traditional imitation theory would presumably hold that the
chartreuse portrait of Daffodil Glurt cannot "say" anything and
hence cannot insult her; indeed, a featureless canvas can hardly
count as a *portrait* at all. On the other hand, most forms of expression theory will hold just the reverse: they will point to the negative
emotions evoked by the bilious color of the chartreuse and the flat-
ness of the canvas. But does the work insult Daffodil or not?
As long as we start from the top down with a given theory and
simply point to the case, we do not see the issue; and if we do not
see the issue this common sort of case presents, aesthetics remains
quite dull.

Starting with the cases does not mean that aesthetics ought to try
to jettison those theoretical structures with which it has been concerned. Appeal to theory will still ultimately be required to address
and resolve the issues which concrete puzzle cases raise, though it
is appeal to theory motivated by the problems actually arising in
our experience with beauty and art, not just problems generated by
other theories alone. It is true that it is the theory-drivenness of
aesthetics that makes it dreary, but this hardly recommends a retreat to noncritical judgment; it is simply to suggest that aesthetics
ought not let theory lead it around by the nose. Aesthetics ought
not and cannot discard theory nor the sophisticated discussion that
the analysis of theory brings; rather, what it may hope for in the
end is the kind of "reflective equilibrium" between theoretical

claims and judgments in specific, concrete cases concerning art and beauty so effectively recommended in ethics.[2] But this kind of balanced position is hardly possible if aesthetics starts top-down to impose its theoretical constructs upon art and beauty; it is when we *also* start bottom-upwards with the kinds of puzzle cases art and beauty pose for us everywhere, and use them to press the theoretical issues that might allow their resolution, that aesthetics finally begins to be a genuinely exciting discipline, no longer very dreary at all.

NOTES

1. J. A. Passmore, "The Dreariness of Aesthetics," *Mind* 60, no. 239 (July 1951).

2. See John Rawls, *A Theory of Justice* (Cambridge, Mass.: Harvard University Press, 1971), pp. 20ff and elsewhere.

PART TWO

_Some Problems of
Aesthetics_

Introduction

In order to convey the flavor of aesthetic topics and the philosophical methods used to analyze them, this section presents analyses of the concepts of creativity, aesthetic experience, interpretation, critical evaluation, and art itself.

In "Versions of Creativity" the British philosopher R. K. Elliott suggests that creativity can be a meaningful concept provided we trace some of its underlying aspects and dimensions. He distinguishes between the traditional concept of creativity that features the myth of divine creation and the modern concept that emphasizes imaginativeness or ingenuity in any kind of pursuit, for example, in both art and science. Once we are aware of some of its ambiguities, says Elliott, we are in a better position to deploy the concept in expressing important human aspirations, not least of which is the need to transform our material environment and human life itself. In brief, Elliott provides an exemplary examination of a concept on which further analysis may build.

Monroe C. Beardsley, who until his death was the dean of American aestheticians, does likewise with the concept of aesthetic experience by trying to identify five criteria of the aesthetic. Beardsley sets out just what it is we are looking for when trying to identify aesthetic experience, how and where we can expect to discern it, and the degree of clarity we can expect in our descriptions of it. He appreciates, in other words, the difficulty of understanding something so seemingly intractable as human experience in its various strands. Important to Beardsley's analysis is his belief that aesthetic experience is both compound and disjunctive; it consists not of one but of a number of features and, though its features may occasionally be found in other kinds of experience, it is sufficiently distinct to warrant its own label. Beardsley is careful to qualify his assertions, and he states that his intention is not to close but to open up a line of discussion. Ever alert to new forms of artistic expression, Beardsley further indicates how a theory of aesthetic experience can also help us come to terms with new forms of aesthetic value.

Part of our experience of art is an interpretation of its meaning or significance, although just what interpretation entails or how we can distinguish it clearly from description and evaluation are far from being obvious. In "Interpretation" Marcia Muelder Eaton distinguishes interpretation from criticism. Interpretation involves describing or explaining the meaning of a work and its properties and characteristics whereas criticism attempts to estimate its value. But interpretation, she points out, is also evaluative "not because it concerns evaluation of particular works but because it concerns how we think we should look at works." Can our interpretations be correct, or true or false? Can we give good reasons for our interpretive judgments? Moreover, is objectivity possible (a) when we don't have all the facts we need to do the job of interpretation, (b) when we agree about the facts but interpret them differently, or (c) when we disagree about what the basic facts are? Eaton discusses the variously interpreted *The Turn of the Screw* by Henry James to help thread her way through these questions.

It will be said that there is more to a work of art than the aesthetic experience it is capable of affording. Of course, but Beardsley's analysis, carefully read, reveals just how powerful, informative, and stimulating aesthetic experience can be. Harold Osborne agrees and thinks that the preeminent value of aesthetic experience lies not so much in providing aesthetic gratification or understanding but in stimulating mental faculties for their own sakes; that is, the value of aesthetic experience rests in its strengthening of the powers of percipience. In "Assessment and Stature," however, Osborne is concerned to describe the different kinds of judgment that can be made of works of art, only one of which is of a work's capacity to sustain interest in the aesthetic mode. There are, he thinks, three principles of assessment, two aesthetic (artistic excellence and aesthetic satisfaction) and one nonaesthetic (stature). The pedagogical usefulness of Osborne's analysis should be obvious. It is helpful in the same way that Elliott's and Beardsley's essays are: knowing the kinds of value works of art possess enables teachers to guide the young more coherently toward an appropriate understanding and judgment of art.

In one aspect, all of the essays discussed thus far in this section have had to contend with the problem of definition, e.g., the definition or at least characterization of such terms as creativity (Elliott), aesthetic experience (Beardsley), interpretation (Eaton), and critical evaluation (Osborne). In "When Is Art?" Nelson Goodman faces head-on the problem of defining art itself. His approach is typically novel in asking not "What Is Art?" but *"When* Is Art?"—and his answer is "Whenever something functions efficaciously as a character in a symbol system of a particular kind." Goodman thus means us to understand that art has an essentially cognitive character and function. He accordingly finds a common function in the activities of art and science: both seek enlightenment and contribute to human understanding. After reviewing briefly earlier efforts to define the essence of art, Goodman concludes that something functions as a work of art if five symptoms of the aesthetic are present, where, once more, "the aesthetic" refers to the cognitive functioning of the object and not to the felt qualities of experience. Although both Beardsley's and Osborne's theories have a cognitive aspect, the preponderantly cognitive emphasis in Goodman's theory, grounded as it is in interpretations of human understanding and worldmaking, distinguishes his from theirs. In section 3, Smith discusses further differences and similarities among Beardsley's, Osborne's, and Goodman's ideas of aesthetic experience.

R. K. ELLIOTT

Versions of Creativity

There are two main concepts of creativeness (or creativity), which I shall call the "traditional" and the "new" concept, respectively. The myth of divine creation is central to the traditional concept, since analogy with the creative activity of the myth has been a criterion for the use of "creative" as an evaluative expression; but because the creation of the world has traditionally been conceived on the model of that of a work of art, the notion of artistic creation is even more fundamental to the concept. Consequently the traditional concept, which is firmly embedded in the uses and usages of our ordinary language, fairly readily allows creativeness to be attributed to makers, but resists its ascription to persons who bring no new thing into being. Scientists have been regarded as men of wisdom who have discovered truths concerning things which already exist, but have not been called "creative." But in recent times creativeness has been attributed to certain "revolutionary" scientists because they have re-created or re-constructed the world as we conceive it. Furthermore, according to the myth the divine creation is even more significantly that of man than that of the world, and though for reasons of piety people during the Christian centuries would not have spoken of self-*creation*, yet they would not have denied the importance of fashioning the self. Notions of self-becoming and self-realization are of considerable antiquity and have had a continuous history. I shall therefore regard the emphasis recently placed on self-creation by such philosophers as Nietzsche and Gabriel Marcel not as a departure from but as a development within the traditional concept of creativeness. This development is probably one cause of the confusion in which the whole notion now stands, but the confusion is due far more to the appearance of a new concept of creativity which has not been clearly distinguished from the traditional one. According to this new concept, it is not necessary to make or create anything in order to be creative. Creativity is imaginativeness or ingenuity successfully manifested in any valued pursuit, and the paradigms of creativity are located not in art but in science and practical activity. Accounts of the new concept (which is in some ways antithetical to the traditional one) have been received—and sometimes even put forward—as if they were characterizations of the traditional concept. No philosophical analysis of the concept of creativity will be fully satisfactory unless it uncovers the factors which make for confusion in this area, or if it fails to do justice to the powerful appeal which the concept has for us.

The Traditional Concept

Though we speak of certain valued objects—a poem, for example—as having been created, we also apply the term to objects which we regard as unreal and undesirable. Falstaff was a creator of lies, Houdini of illusions. But on most occasions of its use the word does not strike us as ambiguous or ironical. It is straightforwardly pejorative, or honorific, or it is neither. Ambiguity does arise, however, when we use the word "creative" to describe scientists and scholars. If we call someone a "creative" historian it is virtually impossible, no matter how we load the context, to avoid the suggestion that he makes up his stories instead of deriving them from the historical evidence. "Creative critic" has a rather similar connotation. "Creative biologist" suggests a breeder of new germs; "creative anatomist" a Dr. Frankenstein; "creative chemist" an alchemist. "Creative engineer" has no ironical undertone, but its sense is not clear. Does it mean a person who *makes* machines rather than runs or maintains them? The emergence of these ambiguities indicates that scholarly and scientific achievement is *not* a paradigm of creativeness as we ordinarily conceive it. On the other hand, there would be no point in calling someone a "creative poet" or a "creative novelist" since so far as artists are concerned the epithet is redundant, save for the purpose of distinguishing artists in general from performers. Creativeness is part of the concept of an artist, but it is not part of the concept of a scholar or a scientist, and even resists being predicated of them.

This state of affairs exists because, traditionally, coming to know and causing to exist have been sharply distinguished, and being a creator has been regarded as a condition of being creative. The knower does not create the pre-existent reality which he comes to know or the truth which is the end of his activity. He discovers truth by discovering what is really the case, and thereby he acquires, obtains, gains, gets, attains, or achieves knowledge. It is as if knowledge were an object which we can lack, come into possession of and lose, but which cannot be created or destroyed. It seems to share the pre-existent objectivity of the reality which is known. We do not even create the adjustment of our mind to the realities known, for to suppose that would be to suppose that we create our insights, whereas we are passive relative to them. It would be as paradoxical to say of someone that he created his discovering as it would be to say that he created what he discovered.

Against this somewhat archaic epistemological background embodied in our ordinary use of words, the scientist's claim to creativeness hardly shows up at all. To establish his claim we have to be able first to represent him as a creator, but his business is not creation but discovery. If we think of him as creating hypotheses we are embarrassed because when scientific hypotheses have been sufficiently confirmed they are regarded as truths. When the scientist achieves success he becomes again a discoverer and ceases to be a creator. If we adopt an instrumentalist view of science, then we can represent the scientist as a maker of powerful and useful predictive devices, which we refuse to convert into truths. But even if we are willing to pay this price, the scientist will not attain the creative rank of the artist, for we call the production of novel useful objects not "creation" but "invention." Invention has its place in the hierarchy of creativeness, but its place is not at the top. To say that Sir Frank Whittle *created* the jet-engine is to speak just a little grandiloquently, giving him rather more than is his due; yet there is nothing in the least excessive in saying of Milton that he created *Paradise Lost*, or of a chef that he created a sauce, an actor a role, a hairdresser a style, a producer a star, or the practitioners of *haute couture* creations.

Because it is embodied in the uses and usages of ordinary language, the traditional concept of creativeness still influences even those who have no knowledge of its old-fashioned rationale; and in this case we cannot gain a satisfactory understanding of the concept merely by looking to see how the relevant expressions are actually used. Blind to the history of the concept, we discover only a tissue of uses and usages for which there seems to be no integrating principle. There is such a principle, however, namely the mythical archetype, which can be specified approximately as follows: Either instantaneously or by process of making, God freely brought into being, *ex nihilo* or from some pre-existent indefinite material, a concrete, infinitely rich, perfectly ordered and beautiful world, the most wonderful of all created objects save man himself. He made it for man, not only as his environment and to sustain him, but, more importantly, for him to contemplate and wonder at, a perpetual occasion for him to praise his Maker.

Our ordinary concept of creativeness is still dominated by this myth. Instances of creating are arranged in a hierarchy, from accidental production and mechanical fabrication through simple originative making (as when a schoolchild makes something of his own choice out of clay) to production which involves uniqueness or originality and is further classified as invention or artistic creation. The closer the analogy between any human activity and the mythical paradigm, the more confidently we attribute creativeness to the agent. This is why the artist's claim to creativeness is unassailable. At least he produces a concrete, well-ordered object for us to contemplate, and we cannot wonder at its beauty without at the same time paying tribute to its maker. But very often the artist makes not just an object but a world, and in supreme instances it is a world which compares in richness, order, and beauty with the world of the Creation myth. We are accustomed to thinking of great poets like Dante and Shakespeare, and great novelists like Tolstoy and Dostoevsky, as having created worlds, but great painters and composers have achieved the same. Furthermore, artistic creation is preeminently free activity. The scientist must submit himself always to the control of reality which, no matter what concepts he uses, functions always like a pre-existent pattern to which his statements must conform. The artist is under no such limitation.

In seems clear that the myth envisages the creation of the world *on the model* of artistic creation. It is hardly surprising, therefore, that the artist's activity resembles the paradigm most closely.

The knowledge that an aesthetic notion underlies the Creation myth enables us to understand uses of words which would otherwise remain puzzling. We speak of "creation" in connection with chefs, actors, hair stylists, and fashion designers because they produce objects not so much for use as for perception—to be contemplated and admired. The film producer is said to "create" a star because a star is thought of as a resplendent object to be gazed upon and wondered at. When we say that someone "creates a scene" we are thinking of the event as an object for aesthetic contemplation— again, as something to be wondered at. A hurricane which "creates havoc" produces an astonishing devastation. Other usages are connected with other features of the mythical paradigm. If someone "creates a job" he brings it into being out of nothing, so to speak;

and we talk of creating panic or a traffic jam because these things seem to spring into being suddenly, fully formed, but as if out of nothing or from nowhere.

These usages show how the concept of creation feels the pull of the mythical paradigm. It is usual to speak of certain activities and processes as "creation" because they resemble the activity of the mythical Creator in a certain respect, even though they are unlike this activity in other and, one would suppose, more important ways. But to create something is simply to bring it into being, and an object does not have to be excellent or valuable or even an object of aesthetic interest for us to be able to speak of it correctly as having been created. We talk of a machine creating so many cigarettes per hour or so many copies of a newspaper. The Creation myth is necessary for understanding the concept of creativeness, but it presupposes the concept of creation.

To our modern mind it may seem that the traditional concept of creativeness does less than justice to scientific and scholarly achievement. But the scientific discoverer and the *savant* have never been regarded as having a status inferior to that of the artist. They have not been called "creative," but their understanding of nature, of the scriptures, and of the classical past have usually been valued much more highly than the artist's creativeness. It has never been forgotten that the worlds created by artists are unreal, and there has been a persistent tendency to place the creation and enjoyment of such objects outside the really serious business of life. By comparing him with the Creator, the traditional concept of creativeness honors the artist but at the same time belittles him. Traditionally, scientist and scholar have not felt themselves unjustly deprived of the equivocal title which is proper for the artist.

A major difficulty in offering an account of a concept with an eventful history is that the analysis tends to fit the concept as it predominantly was at one time but not as it was at another; or, to put the same matter in a different way, it tends to explain certain present tendencies in our use of the relevant words but to leave other, perhaps opposite, tendencies unaccounted for. So far I have mentioned only aspects which I believe to have been part of the concept of creativeness for a very long time, but comparatively recently the concept has undergone quite momentous developments. Although nowadays most educated people do not think of the practitioners of normal science as creative, they do regard *revolutionary* scientists—men like Newton, Darwin, Einstein, and Freud—as creative, and, what is more, believe them to have been creative to an exceptionally high degree. I think this is because it has been recognized that these men, though of course they cannot be said to have re-created or re-structured *the* world, have quite radically restructured *our* world, which is *the* world as we conceive—and even perceive—it.[1] They have fundamentally and extensively changed our lived environment. At the same time each has reconstructed the "world" or "language" of his particular science. We see these men as having given their various disciplines a new beginning—as having re-created them.

As regards Art and Science, the traditional concept is still strikingly asymmetrical: *all* successful artists—including even savage and child artists—are incontestably creative; and so are a few of the greatest scientists, namely those whom we regard as having transformed our world and/or the worlds of the sciences. Our regarding these scientists as creative does not depend upon our being able to conceive their discoveries as if they were a kind of making. We call them creative, without prejudice to their status as discoverers, because of the reconstruction effected by their discoveries. But we still call them creative because of an analogy between their achievement and that of the mythical Creator.[2]

In the past century the traditional concept has been subject to various further influences. Among the most important of these has been the philosophy of Nietzsche, and the concept is coming under increasing pressure from this quarter as relevant features of Nietzsche's doctrine become more and more widely accepted. In his *Zarathustra* Nietzsche calls upon man to recognize that the concept of God is now obsolete, and to assume the role of creator of values. In effect Nietzsche demythologizes the concept of creativeness. But he does not reject the Creation myth absolutely. Rather, he transforms the idea of an actually accomplished creation of man and the world into that of a still-to-be-accomplished transformation of the moral and spiritual life-worlds, and of man himself, since in becoming the originator and sustainer of values man will surpass his previous mere humanity. Thus Nietzsche retains a notion of totality in the idea of creation, yet succeeds in adapting the idea to man conceived as creator. But the re-creation of man depends upon the re-creation of the individual self.

The traditional concept embodies a good deal of respect for creativeness, but this scarcely accounts for the great prestige which creativeness enjoys nowadays. Nietzsche's understanding of creativeness as the overcoming of what our world seeks to impose on us as necessity[3] is probably a contributory cause of the Promethean atmosphere which now surrounds the concept, but our modern feeling that creativeness is a matter of the very highest importance owes at least as much to the stress Nietzsche laid on self-creation. This is a dimension of creativeness which the traditional concept is able to absorb. Since the autonomous self is a valued object which is brought into being by deliberate endeavor, there is no real reason why it should not be said to be created, or why the person who achieves autonomy should not be regarded as creative in this respect.

The New Concept

What I have called the "new" concept of creativity came into prominence in the first two decades after World War II, when the space and nuclear research projects presented a wide variety of theoretical and technical problems which required imagination for their solution. It is possible to distinguish two main versions of this new concept of creativity. According to the first of these, a problematic situation is defined as one for which no adequate response is available in terms of existing knowledge, methods, and techniques, and creativity is taken to be the capacity to resolve situations of this kind. The second version identifies creativity with getting novel ideas and making something of them. By "making something of" an idea is meant either solving some existing problem by means of it, or putting it to some other acceptable purpose, or just making it available to others who actually do or might well find some such employment for it.

Though not identical, these two versions are closely related. The first "problem-solving" version does not allow everything which we would ordinarily call problem solving to count as an exercise of creativity, and since it makes the need to get a novel idea in order to resolve a problematical situation a condition of the situation's being problematical in the required sense, it makes the getting of a novel idea a condition of creativity. The first version of the "new" concept is therefore a special case of the second. The second version differs from the first in that it does not tie creativity to problem solving. It recognizes that someone might hit on a valuable idea during a free play of fancy rather than under the pressure of a need to solve some problem, and that the value of a novel idea may not lie chiefly in its usefulness for problem solving. Though in certain contexts the differences between these two versions become significant, it will for the most part be convenient, without being misleading, to speak of the two versions collectively as "the new concept of creativity."

Since the new concept allows that a person is creative simply by having and making use of novel ideas, it is nothing but a part of our existing concept of imaginativeness. In terms of the traditional concept, to be creative a person had to produce some object of a sufficiently impressive kind, not merely come to know something or get someone to do something, but under the new concept to proceed imaginatively is *ipso facto* to be creative. All creativity is creative (i.e. imaginative) thinking. The contention that a good scientific hypothesis is either a truth or a merely useful object ceases to be relevant so far as the attribution of creativity is concerned, and no longer prevents us from regarding many of the achievements of normal science as creative. Hitherto we might have said of a scientist or scholar that he had performed original work in which he had used imagination to solve his problems, but we would not also have called him creative. Under the new concept he qualifies for this latter title. Now when creativity is manifested it may be that all that happens is that a truth gets expressed or a practical purpose accomplished. Under the new concept expressions like "creative historian," "creative critic," etc., lose their ambiguity and others, like "creative salesman," acquire a meaning.

It would not have been possible for a part of our concept of imaginativeness to have begun to take the place of our ordinary concept of creativeness if that concept had not already fallen into a state of obscurity, in which it lives in uses and usages of words but, for the great majority of language-users, lacks anything like a satisfactory account, definition, or rationale. A concept in such a state is extremely vulnerable to a sort of "takeover." Someone supplies what seems to be the missing account—as the psychologists have done for creativity—but the account is in fact an expression of contemporary interests, not a *logos* of the traditional concept. Naturally, it will not perfectly fit the uses and usages which embody the ordinary concept, but if when there is conflict we begin to adjust uses and discount usages then a new concept is taking the place of the old one, perhaps without our being fully aware of what is happening. Even if we take alarm at the situation, if we lack an explicit understanding of the ordinary concept which is being supplanted we scarcely know what it is that we feel ourselves inclined to defend.

So far as creativity is concerned, however, it might be said that we have inherited a concept whose rationale depends on a myth which is no longer a living force in our lives, and which separates art too sharply from science, scholarship, and *praxis*. But the acceptability of the new concept to the artist and lover of art depends on whether artistic activity can be adequately conceived in terms of problem solving or getting novel ideas, i.e., in terms derived from the analysis of scientific enquiry. The danger is that by assimilating art to science we shall misconstrue the nature of art.

An immediate objection to the proposal to conceive artistic creation as problem solving is that whereas very many scientific achievements can be seen as solutions to pre-existing, formulated problems there is not reason for supposing that artists are normally stimulated to create by some problem of which the work constitutes a solution; and sometimes they claim not to have been aware of any problem in the course of making the work, but to have created the whole work in an inspired or spontaneous manner. If it is maintained that nevertheless the work can be understood as the solution to a problem or set of problems, without reference to the artist's empirical state of mind, this involves our understanding *Othello*, for example, as the solution to the problem of which *Othello* was the solution. The case is no better if we try to think of the work as the solution to a set of lesser problems. If what counts as a problem has no reference to what the artist experienced as a problem, any and every element in the work can be regarded as the solution of a problem. But since none of these problems is specified independently of its own solution, each is no more than an echo of the work itself. The case is not materially altered if we declare each aesthetically valuable quality of the work to be the solution to the problem of producing a quality of the relevant general kind. These "problems" are simple transformations of general descriptions, still no better than echoes of the finished work. Though it has analogies with scientific enquiry, artistic creation also proceeds differently, within a different encompassing form of life. Consequently, the new concept of creativeness may not be so well suited to art as the traditional concept was. If we assume or presuppose that it *is* well suited to art, this may lead us to analyze artistic creation in a manner which distorts our understanding of it.

The view that artistic creativity is a matter of getting and making use of novel ideas is open to a rather different objection. This view identifies artistic creativity with inventing novel techniques or new methods of composition or exploiting the medium in new ways—in a word, with changing the language of the relevant art. But the traditional concept allows creativeness to be ascribed to those who produce beautiful objects, whether or not they make innovations in the language of their art. Eliot has contributed more than Yeats to the language of twentieth-century poetry, yet many critics would want to say that Yeats is the greater and more creative poet. Such cases, where criteria of creativeness conflict, are incomprehensible if we think in terms of the new concept alone. It has often been said that since World War II the tendency to identify artistic creativeness with the invention of new techniques and transformations of the language of Art has had very regrettable consequences, since no style has acquired the authority and stability which are virtually necessary for the emergence of a great masterpiece. Here, again, it is not obvious that so far as Art is concerned the new concept is likely to be an improvement on the traditional one.

Even more important, the new concept cannot assimilate the "subjective" dimension of creativeness. Though the autonomous self is unique it scarcely makes sense to call it "novel," and novel ideas are not necessary for its formation. Furthermore, the standard of autonomy is not a competitive one: we do not necessarily have to do better than most people in order to be autonomous. Lacking this notion of self-creativeness the new concept reveals its orientation towards entirely external, mundane efficiency and success.[4] It is not surprising that some young people will have nothing to do with the creativity which is a matter of achieving success in the recognized disciplines and professions, but want to transform society, or go off to the Himalayas seeking self-realization. They are not looking for novel ideas, but dream of putting some very old ideas into practice. So far as creativity is concerned they are reactionary rather than progressive, since, in effect, they have rejected the new concept in favor of the traditional one.

Conclusion

The concept of creativity brings together a number of matters which are of great importance for us, yet because for a long time we have felt the concept to be in a state of profound confusion we have come to mistrust its pretensions. It is hoped that the grip of this sceptical attitude can be eased, and a large measure of freedom from confusion attained, simply by setting out the various different lines of force which come together in the concept as it is at present. It would be unrealistic to think that we shall be able to alter the language, but we do not need to do this in order to become at home in the conceptual situation. The most necessary thing is that the individual teacher should discover what creativity (or creativeness) means for him; and that when he knows what he takes to lie within the concept he should consider what degree of importance he attaches to each of the various aspects or dimensions of creativity, relative to the others and to things which lie outside the concept altogether. If we are clear about the causes of the present confusion and have reflected on the values involved in the concept, it will hardly matter exactly how the words "creativity" and "creative" are applied by different individuals and groups of people. These variations will no longer perturb us and will have lost the power to lead us astray.

We should not suppose that because our present concept of creativity collects together a number of highly important matters it must be pretentious or inflated. It is simply a focus of human hopes and aspirations. In reflecting upon it from an educational point of view we relate the ideas of freedom, founding, innovation, progress, and autonomy to education. It reminds us that education is concerned with the development of energies which will transform the material and moral environments, yet it suggests also that education is for the sake of the individual soul—that it is not in the students' interest for them merely to gain the world. It proclaims the strength of the spirit against necessity. If we allow it to become associated with narrow unimaginative aims and with achievements which are too exclusively materialistic it has the power to call us back from our error. Its chief values lie in its inspirational force and its capacity to make us reflect on the connection between the nature of education and the meaning of life. Despite its "unfinished" character it functions as a regulative idea for education. Hence it would be short sighted of us to complain that it does not reveal *how* we are to accomplish the various ends it envisages and is therefore empty. Its role is not that of an educational encyclopaedia or a handbook of method.

Even the present confusion of the concept, once we have charted its contributory features, can be seen as a fair reflection of our human situation. If the concept yokes together real or apparent incompatibles, by doing so it presents us with problems which we have to face in any case in life. We have to decide concerning the relative values of the arts and sciences; we have to choose between or find a way of reconciling achievement in the recognized disciplines and the care of the soul; how far to seek innovation, how far to be content with success within a stable convention. Getting the concept of creativity finally and satisfactorily arranged will involve more than decisions concerning the uses of words.

For this reason stipulative general definitions of creativity are undesirable. They incorporate preferences for conservation or innovation, art or science, self or society, etc., but the teacher does not need the philosopher to make these choices for him. Equally unacceptable are accounts of creativity which entirely ignore the "ideal" or "romantic" aspects of the concept, since they assume that what most requires elucidation is unworthy of notice. Eventually we must get down to details, of course, but it would be a mistake to adopt a dogmatic account of creativity just to be able to hurry on to deciding what is to be done in the classroom. I hope I shall be forgiven for repeating that the value of the concept of creativity is chiefly a value for the imagination and the reflective spirit, and that we shall not realize that value if we impatiently thrust the concept aside or arbitrarily clip or reshape it.

NOTES

1. See T. S. Kuhn, *The Structure of Scientific Revolutions* (Chicago: University of Chicago Press, 1962).

2. The traditional concept is not applicable only to artists and scientists. A statesman who founds or reconstitutes a nation is properly called creative. So is a stateman who liberates a nation or a people, when the achievement of political autonomy can be regarded as a new beginning. Someone who founds or reconstructs and reinvigorates an institution may be called creative, also. But we distinguish between creation and preservation. A statesman like Churchill, who holds a nation together in time of peril, is not a *creative* statesman, but a hero or savior.

3. See H. Corbin, *Creative Imagination in the Sufism of Ibn 'Arabi* (London: Routledge and Kegan Paul, 1969), p. 180.

4. The new concept has a real imaginative life when it incorporates the notion of overcoming what the world seeks to impose on us as given. Then creativity appears in unconfinable spiritual energy, the power to break free or break through. Some people easily interpret and apply the concept in this light, even when the relevant achievements are of an everyday or trivial kind. Others, who find this easy creativity absurd, are willing to apply the new concept only to recognized achievements in art, science, management, etc. But, as we have noted, some people consider these later achievements to lack the freedom which characterizes true creativity.

MONROE C. BEARDSLEY

Aesthetic Experience

Though some members of each opposing party would impugn so balanced a judgment, it is in my opinion still an open question whether it is possible—or, if possible, worthwhile—to distinguish a peculiarly aesthetic sort of experience. The question of possibility involves the debatability of the claim that there is a common character that is (1) discernible in a wide range of our encounters with the world and (2) justifiably called "aesthetic." The question of worthwhileness involves the debatability of the further claim that, once distinguished, this character is sufficiently substantial and noteworthy to serve as the ground for important theoretical constructions. . . .

Before we begin our own search for this character, or inquire whether it has already been found, we ought to consider carefully what it is we are searching for, and how we shall know that we have found it. Our hope is to end up justified in saying that some experiences are marked by aesthetic character and some are not; and of those that have it, that some have it more markedly than others. Experiences with such character need not be universally associated with objects that belong to familiar artistic categories. (It is convenient to have the term "artkind instance" to cover poems, paintings, sculptures, musical compositions, dances, and so on, without—at this stage—raising or begging questions about the definition of art in general.) But to deserve the epithet "aesthetic," such experiences ought (1) to be obtainable commonly through, or in, the cognition of artkind instances, (2) to be obtainable in their most pronounced character from artkind instances that have been judged to be outstanding examples of their kind, and (3) to be obtainable in some degree from other objects or situations (especially natural objects) that are often grouped with artkind instances in respect to an interest we take in them.

It is not surprising that it has proved very difficult to distinguish and articulate an aesthetic character of experience. Accurate phenomenological description, especially of common strains in so richly varied a class of phenomena, requires more care and effort than (I am afraid) many of us have been willing to make, and perhaps were too easily discouraged because we often had unreasonable expectations of exactness in our results. It is also, and consequently, not surprising that there has been a good deal of honest difference of opinion about what the aesthetic character is, even among those who agree that there is such a thing. But here we must not follow those who have magnified and emphasized these differences in order to cast doubt on the whole inquiry. Some features very widely and frequently found in experiences of artkind instances have been noted by perceptive aestheticians, and very often their divergent descriptions, when carefully analyzed in relation to the examples offered, turn out to be quite close in meaning. Moreover, if we do not insist a priori that the aesthetic character must be a single and simple one, but look instead for a set of central criteria, we may find that we can accommodate and reconcile insights and discoveries from several quarters.

This last conclusion, I must confess, is one that I have come to only over a long period of intermittent reflection on the problem and after a gradual recognition that my earlier attempts to capture the aesthetic character were defective and incomplete in ways that either became apparent to me as I tried to apply them and work out their consequences or were thoughtfully called to my attention. My struggles with the problem have taken two forms, which are not utterly hopeless, but which have not managed to satisfy me fully.

For some time I tried working with the concept of *aesthetic experience*, trying to make the most of Dewey's inspiring ideas (as they have always struck me) by sharpening them and seeing how they can actually be applied to concrete artkind instances. In my *Aesthetics*,[1] I made a somewhat sketchy attempt to fix this concept usably, and ten years later . . . I tried to revive and renew it, after it had wilted somewhat in the intervening climate of opinion. I must say that I am still a partisan of aesthetic experience; I don't fully understand how anyone could deny that there are clear and exemplary cases of such experience, described in Dewey's words (at least as supplemented and qualified by mine!). And if there are such experiences, I do not understand how anyone could reasonable refuse to call them "aesthetic." But I have come to see that, even so, only a very limited account of our aesthetic life can be given in such terms. Aesthetic experiences—one of Dewey's most insistent and most eloquently made points—have an unusually high degree of unity in the dimension of completeness, and when you listen, for example, to an entire string quartet, the experience has this character to a very marked degree. But even if you tune in the quartet in the middle, and listen for a minute or two before you are torn away, there is no doubt that something aesthetic has happened to you—without completeness or consummation. During that stretch of time, your experience has taken on a character (and not just the property of being a music-hearing experience) that is strongly different from what was present before you tuned in or after you tune out—though some of it, of course, may linger even as you turn to the jangling telephone or the inopportune (even if welcome) television repairman at the door. So it seems important, indeed essential, to introduce a broader concept of the aesthetic in experience, while reserving the term "aesthetic experience," as a count noun, for rather special occasions.

It was such considerations as these that led me . . . to explore the possibility of treating the aesthetic character as a species of hedonic quality, working with the terms "enjoyment," "satisfaction," and "pleasure." Here I believed myself to have a good deal of support from a number of eighteenth-century thinkers, especially in Great Britain. And again, I am still persuaded that there is important truth in this doctrine: I haven't found any serious and cogent refutation, at least, of the proposition that experiences with aesthetic character *are* intrinsically enjoyable (which is not to say they are intrinsically valuable, of course . . .). Examples of unpleasant objects that have been placed in galleries (for example, the famous figures of decaying corpses by Gaetano Zumbo—but choose your own examples; they are not hard to find these days) only go to show that unpleasant objects have been placed in galleries, unless we go on to argue (1) that our experience of them has aesthetic character and (2) that, taken all in all, our experience of them does not involve an enjoyment that encompasses or assimilates the disgust (the small size of Zumbo's figures creates a certain detachment). Still, enjoying is taking pleasure in, and a particular kind of enjoyment must in the end be a function of the kind of thing in which pleasure is taken. There is something threateningly reductionistic about taking the defining feature of aesthetically characterized experiences to be a particular kind of pleasure; and there are theoretical problems that arise in relating such a view to the justification of reasons in art criticism. . . . So I have thought it worthwhile to cast about for a promising alternative.

My present disposition[2] is to work with a set of five *criteria of the aesthetic character of experience.* I suggest that we apply these criteria as a family, with one exception of a necessary condition: an experience has aesthetic character if and only if it has the first of the following features and at least three of the others. (But I am not wedded to a particular formula, rather trying to open up a line of further inquiry; it may be that the list of criteria should be expanded or that the number of features specified for the application of the term "aesthetic character" should be decreased.)

1. *Object directedness.* A willingly accepted guidance over the succession of one's mental states by phenomenally objective properties (qualities and relations) of a perceptual or intentional field on which attention is fixed with a feeling that things are working or have worked themselves out fittingly.

2. *Felt freedom.* A sense of release from the dominance of some antecedent concerns about past and future, a relaxation and sense of harmony with what is presented or semantically invoked by it or implicitly promised by it, so that what comes has the air of having been freely chosen.

3. *Detached affect.* A sense that the objects on which interest is concentrated are set a little at a distance emotionally—a certain detachment of affect, so that even when we are confronted with dark and terrible things, and feel them sharply, they do not oppress but make us aware of our power to rise above them.

4. *Active discovery.* A sense of actively exercising constructive powers of the mind, of being challenged by a variety of potentially conflicting stimuli to try to make them cohere; a keyed-up state amounting to exhilaration in seeing connections between percepts and between meanings, a sense (which may be illusory) of intelligibility.

5. *Wholeness.* A sense of integration as a person, of being restored to wholeness from distracting and disruptive influences (but by inclusive synthesis as well as by exclusion), and a corresponding contentment, even through disturbing feelings, that involves self-acceptance and self-expansion.

Each of these features calls for a little commentary; and the last one takes us back to a continuing controversy that I should like to resume briefly.

The first feature, object directedness, is one on which I believe general agreement can be had. It is, of course, framed to apply quite broadly. I have in mind not only the plain and obvious cases where we are intensely absorbed in the contemplation of a painting or paying close and undivided attention to the course of a musical composition, but also other cases where the object or situation in question is merely intentional: we are concerned with what is happening in the world of a novel, we are thinking intensely and seriously of the symbolic significance of a figure in a painting, or, confronted with an instance of conceptual or "idea" art, we consider a proposition or a theme or a possible state of affairs the artist brings to our attention. When the work embodies instructions for apprehending it in a determinate serial order, we follow the way it works itself out, and this is a process of discovery; but even in the case of a painting or a sculpture there is of course the same process of discovery, of gradual revelation of its nature as we explore it probingly; and thus there can be the same controlling or emerging sense that something is worked out and is accepted for what it is. This willing surrender, limited and actively engaged as it is, has often been noted as characteristic of our experience of artkind instances. And, as I suggested above, it seems to me plainly present even when what we are dealing with is a tragedy of horrors or a poignant and (by itself) painful reminder of real evils about us. If we are repelled and turn away, of course there can be no claim that the experience, even while it lasted, had aesthetic character (we looked because we were forced to, or ordered to, or in some other way involuntarily, not because we willingly accepted the object's control over our mental states). If we choose to continue the experience because we must actually see and feel the working out of what is there, and the rightness of that working out, then our experience satisfies at least the first—and necessary—criterion of aesthetic character.

Felt freedom is perhaps the hardest feature to talk about very definitely. I point to it as a notable ingredient in that experience I alluded to earlier, of turning on the radio and suddenly hearing, say, the first-movement second subject of Mozart's String Quartet in A: that lift of the spirit, sudden dropping away of thoughts and feelings that were problematic, that were obstacles to be overcome or hindrances of some kind—a sense of being on top of things, of having one's real way, even though not having actually chosen it or won it. Much deeper senses of "freedom"—metaphysically and epistemologically speaking—have been invoked in talking about the arts, by Kant and Schiller and others; I am staying with what I take to be phenomenology here, however, without moving to transcendental psychology (of course there is a good deal of valid phenomenology in Kant and Schiller, too). It is, I take it, this felt freedom that has been so feared and condemned by the Puritan—religious or political—as a temptation to dangerous escapism and failure of nerve amid the actual trials of the religious or the revolutionary life. And he is right to be concerned. For it is in respect to this second feature that art has affinities with certain drugs, which can also generate (though of course not through their mere cognition) intense forms of felt freedom. It is in this respect that art can be enervating and antisocial, and many other unfortunate things it has often been accused of. I am convinced that this second feature is real and significant. Nevertheless, I do not want to make it a necessary condition of the aesthetic; in our encounter with artkind instances that are intricate and puzzling and hard to make out, that offer resistances and obstacles to understanding or perception, this felt freedom may be absent or at a low pitch. Yet even such experiences may have the aesthetic character if they meet the other criteria.

The element of detachment in aesthetic experience, under various terms, such as "disinterestedness," "psychical distance," and "will-less contemplation," has very often been remarked, and (at least before the post–World War II avant-garde) has very often been considered central to its nature. I do not wish to formulate this feature so that it becomes enmeshed in the controversies surrounding the terms in which it has been described, or in such a way that it is tied to any particular metaphysical or epistemological or ethical theory. The heart of the matter is that when we view, say, the Gaetano Zumbo sculptures, however strongly or even violently we may respond, it is still true and highly important to add that we do not confuse them with genuine corpses, that we can avoid feeling full emotions as we naturally would do with corpses, that our feelings are therefore somewhat muted, gently screened from direct contact with reality outside the sculptures themselves. In many different typical ways, instances of artkinds are designed to lend some degree of detachment to the affects they produce: giving an air of artifice, of fictionality, of autonomy and reflexiveness, of separation from other things, and so on. But of course this is not always true, and as has also often been pointed out, there is often the attempt at a kind of brinkmanship, coming close to the borders of the seeming-real and risking the disappearance of detachment. Even so, artists generally try not to come as catastrophically close as, say, when the high-wire artist falls to his death, or the realistic life-size imitation of a museum guard is asked for directions to the men's room. Sergei Eisenstein remarks that when he staged Tretiakov's play *Gas Masks* (1923–24), about a gas factory, in an actual gas factory, it was a failure—I take it, from the aesthetic point of view. Now, it might not have been a failure even if the setting proved too realistic to preserve detachment of affect, provided it had something else to offer in the way of aestheticity; so I do not propose to make even this important and extremely common feature of art experience a necessary condition.

It is extraordinarily difficult to capture in words the exact ways in which the practical or technological aspect of an object can and cannot enter into the experience of it if that experience is to have this third feature of detached affect. Even so excellent a phenomenology of aesthetic experience as that presented by M. J. Zenzen—drawing upon Heidegger and Merleau-Ponty—exhibits these difficulties. For example, he remarks that "unlike the case of normal perception where objects are always experienced as systems of instrumentality, in an aesthetic experience the object is stripped of its instrumental 'values.' "[3] It is true that in detached affect there is a lack of concern about the instrumental values, but there need not be a lack of awareness of such values—and in the aesthetic experience of architectural works, for example, such awareness ought to be present. Zenzen also holds that in aesthetic experience of a painting the knowledge "that the work at which I am looking can be taken as canvas and paint . . . must be forgotten and transcended to the painting as art-work. . . . [It] must hide itself in order for the art-work to show itself; but in hiding itself the knowledge must not be lost."[4] Here the paradoxical language, I think, helps to bring us close to a grasp of the subtle difference between the way in which the knowledge is present and the way in which it is absent.

It seems to me that I have always thought of the act of apprehending an artkind instance as basically a cognitive act, though I may have insufficiently stressed this point or failed to grasp its consequences. Certainly I did not adequately understand the importance of this fact until such thinkers as Gombrich, Goodman, and Arnheim taught it to me in recent years. At any rate, I see now more clearly than I ever did before that one of the central components in art experience must be the experience of discovery, of insight into connections and organizations—the elation that comes from the apparent opening up of intelligibility. I call this "active discovery" to draw attention to the excitement of meeting a cognitive challenge, of flexing one's powers to make intelligible—where this combines *making sense of something* with *making something make sense*. In this aspect, experiences with aesthetic character overlap with experiences of empirical scientists and mathematicians; here is the link between them. There is a common thrill—speaking as always phenomenologically, and reminding ourselves that the enjoyment of emerging intelligibility or order or system may be exactly the same, even for the scholar or scientist, whether the order turns out to be empirically real (such as the table of the elements, the taxonomy of animals and plants, and the progression of artistic styles from 1350 to 1650) or an illusion (such as the classification of people according to the signs they were born under, the distinction of autonomous Spenglerian cultures, and the Baconian cypher). In some artkind instances on the minimalist side, the experience is mainly, or at least primarily, one of coming to see how some few things are related, and this by itself doth not an aesthetically characterized experience make. In other artkind instances, the intellectual element is too small to attribute this feature of active discovery, though of course there must always be *something* there to be apprehended, and there is always something going on that can be called, in a broad sense, understanding.[5]

The fifth feature, wholeness, is surely very central to any acceptable account of the aesthetic character—so much so that it may well deserve to be ranked with the first as essential. In trying to clarify this concept for myself as well as others, I have (gratefully) bowed to well-formed criticisms, especially those of George Dickie, and steered away from unity in the dimension of completeness in order to concentrate on unity in the dimension of coherence. And I want to keep in view two levels of this wholeness: the coherence of the elements of the experience itself, of the diverse mental acts and events going on in one mind over a stretch of time; and the coherence of the self, the mind's healing sense (which, again, may be illusory) of being all together and able to encompass its perceptions, feelings, emotions, ideas, in a single integrated personhood. To a large degree this feature of the usual art experience may be a consequence of other features; but it is, I think, distinct. It is found, of course, in many other regions—in commerce with nature, in certain kinds of religious experience, in the exciting climaxes of games, and even in concentrated intellectual activity, though in these latter cases there is a tendency to achieve unification of experience and of self through narrowness of focus and the pushing away of intrusive elements, rather than through the widening and deepening of a pattern or network of relations to take in contrasting elements.

The legitimacy of this concept of the unity of experience (in a phenomenological rather than a Kantian sense) has been a point of contention between George Dickie and myself through a debate that has continued intermittently and happily for many years—part of a genuine dialogue between us that has been one of my most cherished memories. Since Dickie, at the time of this writing, has had the latest word,[6] I think it's my turn to carry the debate into another round, by responding briefly to a few of the interesting new criticisms he has offered.

My concept of experiential coherence is that of the elements of experience having the appearance of belonging together: some parts of the phenomenally objective (perceptual or intentional) field with other parts, some feelings with other feelings, some thoughts with other thoughts—and each of these sorts of mental element with the others. . . .

> The first difficulty with Beardsley's view is that there are many cases regarded by everyone as aesthetic experiences but having no affective content caused by a work of art. . . . I have in mind, for example, the experience of a certain kind of abstract painting which has a good but simple design and which can be taken in, as it were, at a glance.[7]

This comment is to the point, and helps me to clarify my view, as well as to defend it. First, I should like to formulate my fifth criterion of the aesthetic in experience so as to render it immune to this criticism: *if* there are experiences with aesthetic character that are affect-free—that include no feelings at all—then whatever elements they *do* include may still more or less cohere. The criterion can still be applied, only there will be less to apply it to, fewer sorts of element to take into account. But second, and more important, I cannot bring myself to accept the antecedent of the above conditional. If the design of a painting is in fact "taken in at a glance," I agree that there may be no affect, but I don't think there is an aesthetically characterized experience, either—one could do no more than scan and mentally classify, and that doesn't give room for a buildup of the features I have described. If, on the other hand, we stay with the picture—"such paintings frequently repay continued attention," Dickie says[8]—something more could happen, an intensification of interest, an increasingly keen appreciation of the color relationships, a feeling of uneasiness about the violent hard-edge contrasts, a touch of vertigo, or an unanticipated calmness. If Dickie is "inclined to think that many of our aesthetic experiences are without affective content, not just a few ones of abstract paintings,"[9] it may be, as his examples (from Goya and Arthur Miller) of affective works suggest, that he thinks of feelings as like full-fledged emotions, whereas I do not.

Finally, Dickie is still doubtful about the concept of a coherence of emotions, when they vary and succeed each other. Of *Hamlet* he says: "During the course of the play I might have felt fear, anger, distrust, irritation, pity, indignation, excitement, pity, and sadness, not to mention the many other feelings the play might produce in a spectator. How does this sequence of affects constitute a unity?"[10] This is a difficulty, but I think not a fatal one—even if we do not invoke the nonnecessity of my fifth criterion. These emotions directed to the events of the play are indeed, I would say, brought into coherence in the playgoing situation far more than they would be in ordinary life. First, they are all muted by a degree of detachment through the fictionality of their objects, and this helps to keep them from flying off in different directions like "real" emotions. Second, to the extent to which the events of the play are tied together by psychological inevitability (and *Hamlet* is no doubt not the best example of this!), the emotions themselves can be felt to follow naturally upon one another. Third, the emotions, when considered in their specific quality as well as in their intensity (as responses to the developments in the plot), form certain patterns, rhythms of contrast and curves of strength. Fourth, involved in all the different emotions, continuing from one emotional phase to the next, and underlying their differences, there are other important feelings—a gradually growing concern that Hamlet will not extricate himself from his situation without bringing tragedy to himself and others, along with a gradually growing feeling of acceptance of this tragic denouement as a release from torment, and as an inevitable expression both of Hamlet's brilliance and sensitivity and of his fatal limitations. These pervasive feelings give the experience of the play much of the unity that it has.

When we look again at the five criteria, we see, I think—for all their intended tentativeness—that they may well prove to be not unuseful. They are vague, of course; but that is to be expected at this stage, and perhaps to a considerable extent at any stage. They cannot be used in certain convenient ways that would be open if we had a set of necessary and sufficient conditions; but it seems that we must be content with what we can find. They show how, and in what ways, aesthetically characterized experience overlaps with experiences obtained in areas of life quite remote from art; they allow for the evident fact that we even find the aesthetic character in unexpected places. In a recent essay, Joel J. Kupperman has commented on my earlier remarks about aesthetic experience, especially in Essay 5; quoting my characterization of aesthetic experience,[11] he writes: "This definition on one hand appears too broad, since it could apply to a sexual experience as well as an aesthetic experience. On the other hand the requirement of unity appears unwarrantedly to legislate *a priori* that aesthetic experiences have firm boundaries."[12] I am not fully convinced of either of these charges. But if my earlier wording does admit sexual experience, I hope that the new criteria reveal both ways in which aesthetic experience differs from, and some features it may share with, sexual experience. Moreover, if the earlier formula did insist too much on completeness, that insistence has been properly withdrawn.

In any case, the proposed account of aesthetic character does enable us to admit numerous clear-cut cases of artkind instances to the class of things capable of providing experience with this character (it would be absurd if it turned out that a competent hearing of Mozart's A-major string quartet had no aesthetic character after all). And it shows us how to rule out other phenomena that either have some pretensions to provide aesthetic character or may be expected or mistakenly believed to do so. I cite two examples.

Commenting on an exhibition of "color-field optical paintings" by Wojciech Fangor, David L. Shirley writes:

> If Mr. Nangor has masterfully used space and color to create a very special experience, albeit at times unpleasant, the experience is no more than just that. Attempts to dazzle, blind, overwhelm, even in such a spectacular way, are still attempts to dazzle, blind, and overwhelm. Even when the canvasses are generating their own particular environments, they are much closer to artifice than to art.[13]

I make no assumptions, of course, either about the paintings, which I have not seen, or the critic, whom I know little about. But if he is right in his account, the experience of viewing these paintings does seem not to be an aesthetic one, by my criteria. (Whether the paintings are art is another question. . . .)

Somewhat later, commenting on a show by G. E. Moore, the same critic says it contains

> a sustained, sinister threat of imminent destruction. . . . The works that pose a threat to the viewer are a pile of rough-hewn bricks stacked up on a glass plate that leans out toward the viewer, a low glass bench, that, if sat upon, could splinter into painful pieces, a doorway stretched tight with rubber strips that pinch and press when you try to go through them and two sets of blinding hot lights set up on door jambs so as to cause great discomfort when you pass them. . . . There is nothing visually exciting but the conveyor belt

that sweeps through the air with the élan of a trapezist and the bricks that have a kind of power in their potential movement. If the other works happen to threaten us on a physical level, they never challenge us on an esthetic level.[14]

This is the sort of discrimination that critics are called upon to make—distinguishing as clearly as possible between those works that push aesthetic experience into new directions, expanding the range of qualities it can encompass, and those works that renounce their interest in aesthetic experience and abandon it in favor of something else, something quite different. Such an alternative, for example, is also described by Shirley, recalling, in the same review, a "Destruction in Art Symposium" in 1969 at Finch College, in which a live chicken was beheaded with a pair of scissors and "several artists scratched, beat, and punched one another until their clothes were in shreds and their flesh running with blood"—these "realizations" accompanying an exhibition of "dismembered mannequins, slit and gouged canvases, gutted furniture, defaced books, plastic dresses burnt full of holes, and new violins that had been shattered into splinters."

NOTES

1. *Aesthetics: Problems in the Philosophy of Criticism*, 2d ed. (Indianapolis: Hackett, 1981). See "Postscript 1980."

2. First presented in a presidential address to the Eastern Division of the American Philosophical Association, December 1978 ("In Defense of Aesthetic Value"); see *Proceedings and Addresses of the American Philosophical Association* 52 (1979): 723–49. See also Essay 6, sec. 2.

3. M. J. Zenzen, "A Ground for Aesthetic Experience," *Journal of Aesthetics and Art Criticism* 34, no. 4 (Summer 1976): 471.

4. Ibid., p. 477.

5. See "Understanding Music," in *On Criticizing Music: Five Philosophical Perspectives*, ed. Kingsley Price (Baltimore: Johns Hopkins University Press, 1981).

6. In the first chapter of *Art and the Aesthetic: An Institutional Analysis* (Ithaca: Cornell University Press, 1974).

7. Ibid., p. 189.

8. Ibid., p. 190.

9. Ibid., p. 101.

10. Ibid., p. 102.

11. See p. 81 above. [The reference is to Beardsley's "Aesthetic Experience Regained," reprinted in Beardsley's *The Aesthetic Point of View*, ed. Wreen and Callen—Eds.]

12. Joel J. Kupperman, "Art and Aesthetic Experience," *British Journal of Aesthetics* 15, no. 1 (Winter 1975): 34.

13. *New York Times*, 19 December 1970.

14. *New York Times*, 23 January 1971.

MARCIA MUELDER EATON

Interpretation

What was my surprise, then, on taking [the novel] up with a group of students, to discover that not one of them interpreted it as I did. My faith in what seemed to me the obvious way of taking the story would have been shaken, had I not, on explaining it, found the majority of my fellow readers ready to prefer it to their own. And this experience was repeated with later groups. Yet, even after several years, it had not occurred to me that what seemed the natural interpretation of the narrative was not the generally accepted one among critics, however little it might be among students. And then one day I ran on a comment of Mr. Chesterton's on the story. He took it precisely as my students had. I began watching out in my reading for allusions to the story. I looked up several references to it. They all agreed. Evidently my view was heretical. Naturally I asked myself more sharply than ever why I should take the tale as a matter of course in a way that did not seem to occur to other readers. Was it perversity on my part, or profundity?

—H. C. Goddard

The Nature of Interpretation

A Puzzling Case

. . . [A] significant and influential group of theorists believes that we can never interpret completely or correctly what others say or write. If we cannot interpret a work—say what it is—it follows that it is meaningless to try to say whether it is good or bad. Other theorists believe that this is nonsense—that we can and do explain and evaluate (with varying degrees of difficulty) all the time.

Professor Goddard taught English at Swarthmore College for many years [and] . . . was in the business of introducing students to reading, understanding, and appreciating literary works.[1] He chose Henry James's *The Turn of the Screw,* as have hundreds of his English-teaching colleagues, and, he tells us, was continually surprised that his first reading of that novel, one he thought obvious, was not the first reading of his students. It was not just that their interpretations differed over details or generated shades or nuances of meaning. They differed radically.

For those of you not familiar with the short novel in question, I shall provide a summary. This is not easy (and I do not want to spoil your reading), for one's interpretation colors how it is summarized. In its prologue, guests at a Christmas gathering are exchanging ghost stories. One of the guests says that he can top them all— but that he must first send for a manuscript that he says was given to him by his sister's governess. When it arrives, he reads it aloud. (It is taken down by the narrator, and thus we have a three-tiered tale: governess, guest, narrator. This itself has been the focus of much critical discussion.) The governess has been hired by the uncle of two children who live on a country estate. The man lives in London and wants to be freed of all responsibility for the children, so he asks the young woman to take it all upon herself. She is attracted to him and, with great intensity, undertakes to do what he requests. Shortly after arriving at the estate, the young woman comes to believe that it is haunted by two evil ghosts and sets out to protect the children from them. In the process the children become terrified; in the end the little girl flees with a housekeeper, and the little boy dies in the arms of the governess.

As Goddard has, I have used the novel in class, and each time there have been wildly divergent readings. Some students believe that the story is a straightforward ghost story. (This is the initial reading of Goddard's students.) Others believe that the ghosts are the creation of the governess's imagination. Both readings lend themselves to variations. The ghosts are (1) real and (a) are a real danger to the children or (b) are in cahoots with the children, and all four symbolize evil and corruption over which the governess triumphs. Or the ghosts are (2) not real but (a) the result of the governess's sexual frustration, (b) the results of general Victorian repression, or (c) the result of the housekeeper's suggestions.

Goddard's reading is a version of 2a. Although his students when told of his reading were persuaded by it, he found that other critics read it as the students first did—a simple ghost story. He began to wonder if his interpretation were profound or perverse (and, if the latter, one imagines he must have worried about what he was doing to his poor students).

Several questions are raised by this dilemma, and trying to answer them has occupied many philosophers of aesthetics. Is Goddard's reading correct? Or, if not correct, is it nonetheless a better reading? Is it possible for someone to have a good, but incorrect interpretation—one that provides the reader with a great deal of satisfaction but is inconsistent with the way most experts describe a work? Why do Goddard's students change their minds? What must or can be done to settle the question of whether what the governess says is true or false? Is there any objective basis for determining whether the novel is or is not a straightforward ghost story or for deciding whether it is a good or bad novel? James himself said that the story was just a ghost story. Some critics who prefer the other reading try to show that he was intentionally deceptive when he made such statements. But suppose we believe he was telling the truth. Must we then read the novel as a ghost story, even if we believe that it is better if read as a psychological thriller? If an expert's interpretation that is different from mine yields less pleasure for me, why should I ever accept it?

Good and Correct Interpretations

One way to justify an interpretation different from the artist's or the experts' (or even a friend's) is to say that it provides us with more pleasure. We might admit that the writer intended to produce a ghost story, but still insist that reading it as a psychological study of sexual repression is more aesthetically satisfying.

We can, for example, distinguish between *good* and *correct* interpretations and acknowledge that the two sometimes diverge. This will allow us to retain the freedom to look aesthetically at things in our own ways, while acknowledging that others may stick more closely to the artist's intentions or to the work as it is more generally understood. Someone might admit that James meant *The Turn of the Screw* as a ghost story and that the words do constitute a ghost story, but insist that he or she gets more of an aesthetic kick from the text when it is read according to Freudian analysis. We could thus understand someone who said, "I know my interpretation is not the standard one, but it is better for me; mine is good though probably incorrect."

Understanding or getting the meaning of something straight is usually a matter of knowing what the words or other symbols mean. Sometimes, especially when the vocabulary is unfamiliar, we have to go to dictionaries or other sources . . . , hoping that this will help us to determine what the correct interpretation is. Of course, we are free to ignore such facts as the seventeenth-century meaning of a word or a nineteenth-century musical practice, if we believe a better interpretation is obtained by sticking to twentieth-century meanings; "better" here means "yields more pleasure."

Or, if we want a correct interpretation, we may have to know what the artist intended. Then if we think we know what James was doing, we will take his reading seriously. We often want to learn what people we believe are in a position to know have to say about things. Consulting artists' own statements about their work is not just a sign of timidity or intimidation, though it can be this. Usually we consult them because we think that what they have to say will be helpful and will bring a fuller appreciation of a work.

The question of "correct interpretation" has been applied to several contemporary transcriptions of music written in early centuries. The classical performer Andrés Segovia and Leo Kottke have both played Bach's "Jesu, Joy of Man's Desiring" on the guitar, and Walter Carlos's "Switched-On Bach" provides a synthesizer version. Some people believe that Segovia's is most true to Bach's orchestral version and thus better than Kottke's twelve-string rendition or Carlos's electronic production. Fans of Kottke and Carlos often say that "truer" and "better" are not the same. Some who insist on a correct interpretation argue that the original work simply disappears when we can no longer hear human voices reacting and interacting with an orchestra. Others claim that the work is still there and provides much, if different, pleasure when reproduced however one chooses.

If we do not want to limit ourselves to a *correct* account of a work's content, we are free to disregard any information that might determine which of several conflicting interpretations is correct. (Here, "correct" means consistent with the author's intention or an established standard.) If, for example, we want to get as much aesthetic pleasure from a work as possible, and believe we can get it by forgetting what scientific discoveries had been made or what musical instruments were available in a certain period, we can provide our own idiosyncratic interpretations.[2] But are we doing something "wrong" if we do so?

The Lack of Facts

If what we are after is a correct interpretation, we must try to "get the facts" about a work's production to determine what it really means. The problem with many works of art is, of course, that we are often not in a position to determine once and for all whether a claim is true or false. Given his Scandinavian ancestry, we may want to claim that Hamlet had blue eyes. Given the genetic dominance of brown eyes, it may be more reasonable to believe that they were brown. Which view is correct? There is no place in Shakespeare's play *Hamlet* where his eye color is mentioned. There seems then to be no *fact* of the matter.

Philosophers use the word *underdetermined* to describe statements for which there is insufficient evidence. A claim is underdetermined if we cannot say whether it is true or false because there is nothing that will settle the matter. Given the underdetermined nature of *Hamlet* with respect to eye color, it may not be plausible to believe either that Hamlet's eyes were blue or brown. Nothing in the play settles this question. Of course, *if* we come across another portfolio with a revision of *Hamlet* in which Shakespeare has him say, "Oh, that these too, too bright blue eyes would close," that would seem to settle the matter. The newly discovered play would be a more complete version of the same play. Of course, one can object that it does not make any difference what color Hamlet's eyes are. But many underdetermined items are not so inconsequential; they are directly relevant to interpretive puzzles. Nowhere in *The Turn of the Screw* does the governess or any other character explicitly state that she was crazy. If we were to come across a version of the novel in which the governess's reports are no longer underdetermined (she says, for example, "Of course, I was crazy at the time"), it would no longer be the same novel. Even to speak of a "different version" here seems incorrect.

The philosopher Robert J. Matthews believes that we must distinguish between *description* and *interpretation*.[3] Because we often cannot *settle* (or finally determine) the matter with respect to an interpretation, we are less certain about our claims. Our descriptions, however, can be definitely determined because they depend upon things in the work to which we can directly point. We *describe* the governess as a young woman, and *interpret* her as sexually repressed. Description depends upon being able to know if what we say about a work is true or false. Interpretation depends upon being in a position to know whether what we say is plausible, reasonable, or defensible.

The problem, of course, is trying to decide which of several interpretations is plausible. Rarely can we point to one feature of a work to settle the question of which interpretation is the most reasonable. *The Turn of the Screw* is fascinating because the questions it raises cannot be settled easily. Critics make their various cases by pointing to a variety of things: the artist's life, the text, dictionaries, artistic

practices in the period, and psychological theories with which
James might have been familiar. Critics even disagree about which
of these things are reliable sources. . . .

Some theorists have decided that it is useless to try to come up
with either correct or plausible interpretations. They conclude that
interpretations are purely a matter of subjective opinion. Others,
however, reject this and maintain that even in the face of lack of
what we might call "hard facts" some interpretations can be shown
to be more nearly correct than others. It will become apparent later
that I favor this latter view.

The Possibility of Objectivity

John M. Ellis, a literary theorist, believes that saying that interpretation is "underdetermined" is based on a confusion.[4] Of a claim
made by David Frost about the president's Watergate activities, Richard Nixon said, "That's just an interpretation." He meant that
Frost was saying something about which he could not be certain
and could never prove. Ellis thinks critics do not "just interpret" in
this sense.

Ellis believes that some critics have tried to avoid making interpretative and evaluative claims because they have mistakenly
viewed what other critics do as unleashed speculation ("just an interpretation"). The former have instead tried to turn criticism into a
more genuinely empirical activity by restricting themselves to facts
that can be objectively described. For example, in the hope of becoming truly scientific, they count words to determine authorship.
(As with fingerprints, the frequency with which individuals use
particular words can be used for identification.) According to Ellis,
the belief that one can become "scientific" by distinguishing facts
from interpretations and sticking solely to facts is to misunderstand
completely both the nature of criticism and the nature of science.

One lesson of modern science, and of the philosophy of science,
is that observations and theories cannot be neatly separated. Statements of facts embody theories and vice versa. Scientists constantly
move back and forth between theory and fact. Both outside and inside of academic science—that is, in our daily lives as well as in
more sophisticated investigations—we are not neutral observers.
Our theories color our observations.

The philosopher of science Karl Popper writes, "I do not think it
is helpful to express the difference between universal theories and
singular statements by saying that the latter are 'concrete' whereas

theories are *merely* symbolic formulae or symbolic schemata; for exactly the same may be said of even the most 'concrete' statements."[5] Our minds are not blank tablets upon which information is written while we stand passively by. Our minds, to use a Popperian metaphor, are more like searchlights; theories and concepts already formed influence what we actively look for and then discover in the world. There is no hard, fast line that separates facts (what is out there in the world) from theories (what is in here in our minds).

What is true of science is also true of art. . . . E. H. Gombrich (who credits Popper's influence on him) and Nelson Goodman describe looking at art as a kind of reading; habits and theories that we bring with us determine what we see or hear. Describing and interpreting are not separable if what we see or hear involves decoding. Richard Wollheim discusses an interesting example of another sort of interconnectedness. In *Macbeth* some of the title character's speeches are incoherent. Some critics have attributed this to grammatical ignorance, others to deep psychological disorder. The text itself does not settle the dispute; no simple description of what is going on can be given, for how one describes the text will depend upon one's interpretation.[6] One could *repeat* the text—that might be neutral—but then one would not be *describing* it.

When the deep connection between description and interpretation is not understood, Ellis says, "Both parts of the cycle are devalued, and the critic is set free to say whatever he wants to say."[7] I think Ellis is quite right about this. The sort of distortion that has led creationists to puff themselves up by claiming that evolution is "just a theory, too," has too often characterized critical relativism and the view that any old interpretation is as good or bad, just as objective or subjective, as any other.

"An interpretation is a hypothesis about the most general organization and coherence of all the elements that form a literary text," says Ellis.[8] The best interpretation is the most inclusive. Observation and interpretation are carried on (and out) simultaneously. Hypotheses direct attention, which then may come up with things that make us revise our hypotheses. Ellis's view is certainly born out in practice. Students report experiences such as the following with regard to *The Turn of the Screw:* "Suddenly I noticed that no one else saw the ghosts." Readers form new hypotheses as they go along and consequently notice new things—the governess's nervousness, for instance.

Justifying an interpretation is not merely a matter of being able to point to a body of facts to support a claim. The facts must be organized and often supplemented by reasonable hunches. It is impossible to come up with clear (let alone hard and fast) rules about what constitutes the best interpretive strategies. But, says the philosopher David Pole, there aren't *rules* for the best ways of doing science or philosophy either. As Savile does . . . , Pole believes that artworks are public objects with a history and that they invite interpretation. They can be *mis*interpreted, especially if their history is ignored. Often critics act as frustrated artists, "producing variations on a theme—a thing harmless in itself."[9] They read or put more into a work than they read or get out of it. This practice becomes harmful when they confuse what they are doing with giving a correct interpretation.

Two things encountered in art call for an interpretation, according to Pole. First, sentences or features sometimes make no sense, and we want them to. We have no idea what the words mean, or why there is a bagpipe in a painting of a Dutch interior. Consulting a dictionary or an iconologica like Cesare Ripe's may help here. Second (and more typically), objects make sense, but we want to know how special effects are achieved. We are not just interested in whether the governess actually sees ghosts, or if the man with the pipe is doing something evil. We want to know what James does to produce suspense or how Steen conveys the feeling of lively camaraderie. We want to explain why these works are as good as they are. This calls for something quite different from going to reference books.

Many people have claimed that we need to give *reasons* for why a particular work of art affects us, how it is effective. Thus the role and nature of reasons in art criticism has received a great deal of attention. . . . First, we shall examine the differences between interpretation and evaluation.

Separating Interpretation and Criticism

Ellis believes that some contemporary theorists mistakenly believe that they can be scientific by avoiding interpretations and sticking to descriptions. The philosopher Stein Haugon Olsen believes that a similar mistake is made if we think we can separate interpretation and evaluation and stick only to interpretation. The view that value judgments are unempirical, he says, has led many contemporary theorists (Northrop Frye, for example) to try to do without them—to be, instead, empirical and descriptive only. But this separation cannot happen because, as Olsen notes, "Value considerations determine the very nature of interpretive judgments."[10]

People who believe that interpretation and evaluation can be separated usually do so because they think the first is required for the second—interpretation must be carried out (if not completed) before evaluation can begin. We must, to echo Plato . . . know what is being done before we can know if it is being done well; we must know what x *is* before we can say whether it is a *good* x. . . . [S]uch an attitude lies behind Kendall Walton's contextual theory.

The possibility of separating interpretation and evaluation is an important issue. In an article examining reasons given in support of interpretations, Charles L. Stevenson gives the following examples of various reference sources: dictionaries, other works by the same artist, revisions of the work, or simply an acknowledgment that a work is better if interpreted in one way rather than another. The last example, he says, "reminds us that the interpretation and evaluation of a poem are rarely separable steps in criticism. We do not first *interpret* it and then evaluate it, taking each step with finality. Rather we test a tentative interpretation by considering the tentative evaluation of the poem to which it leads, progressively altering works in the light of the other."[11] (Again we see parallels with scientific activity.)

Sometimes when we ask what a work means we want to know what the artist meant. But this is not always or even most often the case. According to Stevenson, a better construal of the question is, "What does it mean to someone or to a particular group?" It is difficult to specify the group; it doesn't mean "the average person" or "the experts." The group can only be described, he believes, in *evaluative* terms: *best, proper, ideal, skillful,* and *sensitive.* What does a poem mean, for instance, to an ideal reader? The kind of criticism that we engage in presumes beliefs we have about what features make a group (or us) "ideal" or "sensitive."

This is why interpretation itself is evaluation—not because it concerns evaluations of particular works but because it concerns how we think we should look at works. We can distinguish giving reasons for an interpretation and giving reasons for giving that sort of reason!

Stevenson believes that we can show that something is a good or a bad standard to use in interpreting artworks, though he admits that evaluations are open-ended. We can give reasons for the relevance of an artist's intentions or our reliance on dictionaries or iconologica. Put simply, it is reasonable in general to refer to intentions when we explain human action and products of that action. It is reasonable to consult dictionaries when we want to explain what something means. Such methods of explanation are usually reliable and people should try to apply them whenever they can. Some methods, on the other hand, are "indicative of habits of mind that no one *ought* to have," as Stevenson says.[12] Distorted perspective or obsessive attention to just one sort of feature is not a characteristic of a well-rounded, reasonable person, let alone a good critic.

NOTES

1. The remarks by Goddard that serve as an epigraph for this essay are from his article "A Pre-Freudian Reading of *The Turn of the Screw*," *Nineteenth-Century Fiction* 12 (1957): 3–4.

2. For more on this topic, see Marcia M. Eaton, "Good and Correct Interpretations of Literature," *Journal of Aesthetics and Art Criticism* 29, no. 2 (Winter 1970): 227–33.

3. Robert J. Matthews, "Describing and Interpreting a Work of Art," *Journal of Aesthetics and Art Criticism* 36, no. 1 (Fall 1977): 5.

4. John M. Ellis, "Critical Interpretation, Stylistic Analysis, and the Logic of Inquiry," *Journal of Aesthetics and Art Criticism* 36, no. 3 (Spring 1978): 253–62.

5. Karl Popper, *The Logic of Scientific Discovery* (New York: Basic Books, 1969), p. 59.

6. Richard Wollheim, *Art and Its Object*, 2d ed. (Cambridge: Cambridge University Press, 1980), p. 88.

7. Ellis, "Critical Interpretation," p. 256.

8. Ibid., p. 258.

9. David Pole, "Presentational Objects and Their Interpretation," *Philosophy and the Arts*, Royal Institute of Philosophy Lecture Series 6, 1971–72 (London: Macmillan, 1973), pp. 150–51.

10. Stein Haugon Olsen, "Value Judgments in Criticism," *Journal of Aesthetics and Art Criticism* 42, no. 2 (Winter 1983): 135.

11. Charles L. Stevenson, "On the Reasons that Can be Given for the Interpretation of a Poem," in *Philosophy Looks at the Arts*, ed. Joseph Margolis (New York: Scribner's, 1962), p. 124.

12. Ibid., p. 135.

HAROLD OSBORNE

Assessment and Stature

Ever since the ancient Greeks instituted dramatic and musical contests on the analogy of the Olympic Games people have looked for foolproof ways of assessing works of art. We want to know what to admire and why, what is more likely than another thing to repay the often strenuous preliminaries to appreciation, what to award a place in our public galleries and museums, what to buy for ourselves at some terrifyingly exorbitant price, where to allot prizes, how to adjudicate public competitions, on hanging committees, and so on. And we are passing through a period when principles of assessment have become confused and submerged as never before. This has been a century of constant changes and rapid experiments until there is nobody left, including the artists themselves, who can confidently tell what is spoof and what is serious. We are presented with creations whose only claim on our attention resides in the conceptual idea—and since artists are not always philosophers this is often childishly elementary, as in the work of Joseph Kosuth in the Museum of Modern Art, New York, which consists of a chair, a photograph of a chair, and a photographic enlargement of a dictionary definition of a chair. Jean Tinguely exhibits functionlessly operating machines somewhat the worse for wear. Marcel Duchamp became notorious by signing and exhibiting a public urinal as a practical demonstration of the absurdity of forming an exhibiting association without a selection committee. It is now solemnly recorded in the history books as a serious aesthetic gesture. Not many decades ago directors of public museums accepted that it was their responsibility to decide on what to spend the public funds in their charge. I myself remember when they opined that Henry Moore would have done well to go down the mine and that their very young children could do it better than Picasso, whom they did not like or understand. Now they have lost heart through the experience of many mistakes. They have thrown in the sponge, renounced the duty of judgment, and claim that it is their business to follow, not lead, public taste. Public taste is now voiced and directed by the critics, who are trained, if at all, as art historians. And we all know that it is the professional failing of art historians that through much detailed study they have lost any ability they ever had to perceive a work of art though they can tell us everything that anyone else ever said about it. All this makes it all the more necessary for us, as aestheticians, to go back to first principles; for when judgment is in chaos, if we are content to accept the guidance of competent authorities, we shall surely be misled.

It is my aim in this paper to illuminate some of the principles which play a leading role in our actual assessments of works of art. If these are revealed to be not entirely coherent but often inconsistent with each other, leading to contradictory judgments, this conclusion is not foreign to the purpose of the paper. It is not part of my purpose to dictate how we ought to judge in these matters, but rather to remove some of the confusion about what it is we are judging when we do judge.

It is of course possible to ascribe value without instituting comparisons. But assessment involves comparison; it is evaluation rather than valuation. When we assess anything at all we either compare it with several other things of roughly the same kind or we compare it with a vaguely formulated average among such things. And by "compare" I mean that we weigh or judge it in respect of some defining property which it possesses in common with those other things, though they possess it in different degrees, or in respect of the effectiveness with which it serves some purpose common to them all. This is what evaluation means and this is how artifacts other than works of art are in fact assessed.

But it is now accepted that works of art have no extraneous defining purpose. Alone among artifacts they have no common function in virtue of which they can be compared, except indeed that which is indicated by the vague formula that they must be suitable for evoking and sustaining aesthetic contemplation. When we confront anything aesthetically, as a work of art, we discount any extraneous purpose it may have and "aspect" it (to borrow Paul Ziff's word) from this point of view. This is what is meant by saying that aesthetic interest is "disinterested."

Works of art can, of course, be compared in respect of specific aesthetic properties. Indeed a prominent part of critical writing on all the arts is aimed at inducing readers to give their attention to this or that aesthetic property of the work in question or to invite comparison between different works in respect of aesthetic properties that they have in common. It is easy to draw up a list of such properties as long as your arm and all of them will be relevant for critical description of this or that work.[1] But the aesthetic properties of works of art differ in an important respect from the other properties of the things with which we have to do in life. As there are no extraneous purposes which all works of art have in common, so there are no particular aesthetic properties that must be possessed by all works of art which we call "good," none whose presence is always an advantage and none which always improve a work if they are present in a greater rather than a lesser degree.[2] My first contention therefore is that enumeration and comparison of particular aesthetic properties cannot determine the assessment of works of art.

On these grounds evaluation in the arts has sometimes been repudiated as an illusion.[3] I do not believe that so drastic a conclusion is necessary. In any case evaluation is there and is there to stay. We do in fact assess works of art overtly and implicitly and there are cogent practical reasons why we shall continue to do so. Nor is it necessary to regard all such assessments as futile. Even in the most matter-of-fact art history which excludes overt judgments of value, evaluation is everywhere implicit in the decisions of the historian (or his predecessors) on what to include and what to exclude, how much space to allot, and so on. Such decisions may indeed be based on sociological or ethnological grounds as well as aesthetic grounds. But we are here concerned with aesthetic assessment and I want first to distinguish two principles which are in fact common to our aesthetic assessments in all the arts.

1. *Artistic Excellence.* As has been said, it is a matter of definition, or a stipulative condition, that whereas other artifacts are valued in accordance to the importance we ascribe to the ends which they are fashioned to serve and with their effectiveness in serving those ends, only works of art have no ulterior defining purpose other than evoking and sustaining aesthetic contemplation. Yet in fact other factors besides function do enter into our assessments of artifacts in general. Although the old theory of Functionalism has long been exploded, it remains true that we value crockery, spectacles, motor cars, smoothing irons, and so on also for the beauty and distinction of their shapes. We also admire—and this is the point of importance—the economy and precision, the elegance and unobtrusiveness, the assurance and directness (sometimes called "honesty" in critical writing), with which an artifact fulfills its intended purpose. And much as we deplore the display of virtuosity for its own sake—as we deplore any other act of exhibitionism—we none-

theless admire and enjoy any concrete manifestation of a deep acquaintance with the natural potentialities of materials and trained
skill in the invention and manipulation of instruments for the fashioning of materials. These qualities involve much more than mere
manual dexterity and we welcome them both in the handicrafts and
in the products of machine craft. Under the name "artistic excellence" we value very similar qualities in the fine arts. For although
art has no single defining purpose, individual works display a wide
variety of different aims and intentions. By "artistic excellence,"
therefore, we do not mean simply virtuosity in the manipulation of
artistic material for the production of this or that group of aesthetic
properties, but rather a capacity for judgment and a sense of appropriateness inherent in skills and accomplishments that are inseparable from mastery of the artistic materials whether they be musical
sounds, pigment colors, or the finer shades of meaning inherent in
the words and traditions of a language, and the successful employment of this mastery to create a work which manifestly achieves its
own particular purpose.

We do indeed evaluate works of art in terms of artistic excellence
so understood. But, as Anthony Savile has rightly emphasized,[4]
evaluations in terms of artistic excellence are very restricted in
scope and their significance rapidly fades if they are attempted between works of different artistic kinds. One can sensibly compare
the draughtsmanship of Picasso with that of Andy Warhol and perhaps venture a judgment that Warhol came closest to any contemporary artist to rivaling Picasso in this respect. But to compare the
draughtsmanship of Picasso with Milton's craftmanship in the use
of words or Warhol's draughtsmanship with the craftsmanship of
Pope is to embark upon a broad sea of incorrigible vagueness. One
can appreciate what Albeniz did to enlarge the expressive sonority
of the piano and perhaps compare it in very general terms with
what Liszt did earlier in the same direction. Or one can appreciate
what Helen Frankenthaler and Morris Louis did to enlarge the expressive and aesthetic potentialities of pure color, perhaps even institute a vague comparison with advances inaugurated by Eugène
Delacroix. But to institute an evaluative comparison between the
contributions of Albeniz and Louis cannot escape from the realms
of fantasy.

2. *Aesthetic Satisfaction.* The second overall principle of assessment
which I want to discuss is the power of a work to support aesthetic
contemplation. For to say that the proper function of the fine arts is
to evoke and sustain aesthetic experience is not, I would suggest, so

vacuous a formulation as it has sometimes been taken to be. To spell out a detailed argument would take me too far from the main theme of this discussion, and I do no more than outline a line of thought which I believe may prove fruitful. It runs like this: In the course of evolution mankind has developed so-called "spiritual" needs supervening on the physical requirements of comfort and survival. It must have happened somewhat as follows. As men in general, or some men in some societies, were gradually and partially liberated from the all-engrossing pressures of physical needs, they were able to divert time and energy to the cultivation for their own sake of faculties which had been evolved in the interest of satisfying physical needs. The faculties were not new. But their partial liberation from practical necessities liberated also impulses to exercise and perfect them for themselves. This is what lies at the root of men's "spiritual" needs and is the source of our social and cultural values, the so-called "higher" values. As the intellect and reasoning powers ceased to be completely preoccupied by practical concerns of living, they were exercised autonomously for their own satisfaction, and philosophy, mathematics, and theoretical science came into being. When curiosity ceased to be orientated solely to the necessity of acquiring familiarity with the immediate environment, as a cat perambulates a new locale before settling down, history and the taxonomic sciences were born. Among these emergent "spiritual" values is a specific aesthetic need, which combines a love of perfection for its own sake with the cultivation and expansion of the faculty for direct apprehension that underlies all our cognitive powers. For vague though the term is, there is general agreement that aesthetic contemplation demands primacy for direct perceptual awareness above theoretical and practical interests. What the fine arts have in common is the basic impulse from which they arise and by which they are nourished: the impulse to foster and expand our capacity for direct apprehension, the faculty of percipience which makes possible all our cognitive contacts with the environment and with other people. It is the provision of artifacts suitable for the stimulation and enhancement of perception itself rather than for any utilitarian motive that lies at the core of the modern conception of fine art. A work of art is thought to be a complex unity for perception with a hierarchy of emergent properties whose apprehension extends perceptual activity to an unusual level of alertness. Therefore it is that our experience of fine art removes us temporarily out of the commonplace world of cause and effect, means and ends, and immerses us in a rarer state of concentrated vision. For this is what

aesthetic attention is when it is successfully directed upon an adequate object. Not passive, hazily directed emotional indulgence, but
hard, active, engrossed awareness.

From Kant and the English eighteenth-century aestheticians onwards many people have observed that successful appreciation of a
work of fine art culminates in increased mental alertness, a sense of
heightened vitality, and in an intensity and clarity of feeling beyond
the ordinary. Kant used the terms *Erlebung* (animation), *Erleichter-
ung* (quickening), and *Erweiterwung* (expansion) to describe this effect. Recently it has become the fashion to talk about such
intensification of perceptual alertness in other contexts than the aesthetic. It is a state of mental being which mystics have sought in
religious revelation, some people from psychedelic drugs, some in
yoga practices and other techniques of meditation. It is significant
that when Imrat Khan first played in Europe the rumor went
around in certain circles that by the music of his sitar he could
"send one on a trip" without the use of drugs. There are people
who enjoy a similar experience in contact with the beauties of wild
nature, when it often combines with a feeling of oneness with the
natural world to create that form of refined animism which trans-
fuses the writings of some literary artists and has inspired some
painters. In a rudimentary way, below the level of deliberate appreciation, it probably enters into much of our varied experience of life.
But it is at its most intense in our contact with the arts, and the
provision of artifacts suitable for sustaining this kind of experience
at a high voltage is the proper aim of the arts as such.

We do undoubtedly evaluate works of art by reference to the
quality and intensity of the aesthetic experience which they evoke.
But as assessments made on the basis of artistic excellence are limited in scope, in evaluations made on the basis of aesthetic experience subjective elements inevitably bulk large and cannot be exactly
measured or eliminated. As different works differ in their capacity
to sustain aesthetic experience, so people differ in their capacity for
it both overall and in relation to the different arts. Natural endowment requires cultivation to become skilled appreciation and few
people are endowed with or develop the skill to appreciate widely
over the whole field of art.[5] Therefore, while there is no good reason to doubt the theoretical objectivity of evaluative judgments
based on aesthetic experience, nowhere is there certainty or assurance in particular assessment and comparisons.

Yet even when this is taken into account it is pretty clear that the
two principles of judgment often lead to evaluations which conflict.

Excellence of artistic craftsmanship and the power to evoke and sustain aesthetic experience do not always, or perhaps often, co-exist in the same work.[6] Admirable aesthetic facture is not of itself sufficient to ensure a work of art capable of sustaining aesthetic experience at a high voltage. But neither is it always necessary. Indeed in certain styles of contemporary visual art a particular point has been made of eschewing, or at any rate concealing, aesthetic craftsmanship. The more extreme ranges of gestural art in Europe, including the *art brut* of Jean Dubuffet, and Action Painting in America are cases in point.

Yet these two principles, variously weighted, determine most of our aesthetic judgments of traditional and ethnic art. There is indeed some contemporary art production to which they do not apply. The functionless machines of Tinguely, for example, do not aspire to finesse of facture and do not invite aesthetic contemplation, appealing rather to a sense of wonder that such things should be made and bewilderment at the reason for their exhibition. In such cases, as with most Conceptual art, there is as yet no recognized principle of assessment or evaluation.

When in works of traditional art artistic excellence and the power to afford aesthetic satisfaction are both present in a high degree, each adequately supporting the other, we tend to speak of a "masterpiece." This is a curiously ill-defined term; but the point I want to make here is the revealing one that although we compare masterpieces descriptively in respect of this or that particular aesthetic quality, it would be odd to assess them on an aesthetic scale. In a sense, each masterpiece represents a peak or culmination. Nevertheless we do speak of "great" masterpieces and "little" masterpieces. And I want now to discuss this quality of greatness, grandeur, or stature, which I believe exercises an important unrecognized influence on our judgments over the whole field of fine art. I shall argue that this is a fully justified principle of assessment; but it is not a specifically aesthetic principle and confusion arises when it is tacitly fused with aesthetic assessments. The prevalent discontent with "Formalism" owes much to an incorrect idea that its effect is to preclude judgments of this sort.

3. *Stature.* In a book I wrote as far back as the 1950s I suggested that our assessments of works of art are made not only in terms of an aesthetic scale but in terms also of a not exclusively aesthetic quality which I called "greatness." I now prefer the term "stature" as being more neutral. What I want here to say in elaboration of this idea has to some extent been anticipated by Anthony Savile in *The*

Test of Time and although I am not able to go all the way with him, the extent of my debt to him will be apparent to all who have read that book.

It is important to be clear that although conscious and unconscious assessments of stature influence and permeate our actual aesthetic evaluations inextricably, stature is not in fact a specifically aesthetic quality. We apply the same criterion to other than aesthetic objects, including human personality. We speak of great or profound, slight or superficial philosophical writings without intending aesthetic implications. In history one might contrast Thucydides with Polybius among the ancients, Gibbon with Trevelyan among the moderns. We speak of great statesmen and great ideas, great preachers, great painters, and great poets. In the realm of the arts stature is dependent upon purpose. Certainly, aesthetic interest is nonutilitarian, not parasitical upon function. And works of art have no common defining purpose other than effectiveness for evoking and sustaining aesthetic experience. But in fact of course works of art have always served a wide variety of other purposes in all cultures ancient and more recent. They have been made and valued for reasons magical, devotional, recreational, religious or ideological indoctrination; for education, persuasion, decoration, commemoration, display, amusement, and so on indefinitely. Our evaluations in terms of stature are related to these subsidiary functions and are in fact composite: provided that any artifact sustains aesthetic experience adequately, we ascribe stature to it in accordance both with the importance we attach to the subsidiary function which it fulfills and in accordance with the effectiveness with which it fulfills that function. Among the functions most emphasized are those of promoting understanding, the presentation of nonverbal thought, and the expression of embodied feeling. These will be discussed briefly. There are others, of course, who look to fine art primarily for religious or sociological propaganda.

As a concept may sometimes be illuminated by looking at its antitheses, so with "stature." In some of their applications "mediocre," "negligible," and perhaps "trivial," "banal," and "superficial," fall within the general concept of "stature." All these terms are derogatory when applied to works of art.[7] But this is not the case with "slight," which is the direct opposite of "great" in this context. A slight work is not necessarily inferior art to a greater work. Slightness does not exclude a high assessment either of artistic excellence or of evocative aesthetic power.[8] It may be useful, therefore, to establish the relations between the nonaesthetic criterion of stature and the aesthetic criteria of artistic excellence—what Anthony Savile calls "executive aesthetic skill"—and the power to "transport" in aesthetic experience.

i. I am fully in agreement with Anthony Savile that there is no necessary connection between artistic excellence and greatness of stature. Few people would dispute that *Hamlet* and *King Lear* have greatness despite their flaws as tragic drama. And while Picasso imparted some smatch of grandeur and dignity even to his slightest productions, Warhol for all the excellence of his draughtsmanship was obsessed with the trivial—fancy ladies' shoes provided the theme with which he felt most at home—and his work is not called "great."

ii. The case is otherwise with aesthetic power. We do not think of any work as great if it lacks the power to sustain some intensity of aesthetic experience. This is why despite their artistic skill and grandiosity of conception Alfred Stevens's *Valour Spurning Cowardice* and *Truth Tearing out the Tongue of Falsehood* on the Wellington Monument in St. Paul's Cathedral fail to achieve greatness. So Blake's "Jerusalem," Browning's "The Ring and the Book," Shelley's "Cenci," and "The Revolt of Islam" have grandness of conception but for want of unified cohesion fail in greatness. The greatness of the "Iliad" and the "Aeneid" does not derive primarily from the conception, which does not notably surpass that of many other heroic epics. Grandeur and nobility of conception are not alone enough to ensure that a work of art be great, though they are a necessary condition of artistic greatness. A corresponding power of aesthetic "transportation" is also demanded.

In conclusion I shall discuss briefly three subsidiary purposes which are given particular prominence in assessments of artistic stature today.

i. *The Promotion of Understanding.* In a recent article David Best wrote that "it is intrinsic to at least most of the arts, by contrast with the aesthetic, that they can give expression to moral and social issues, insights into personal relationships and character development."[9] Bringing the concept of "greatness" into line with Kant's "art of genius," Anthony Savile argues that there are certain aims by which alone the persistence of fine art as an autonomous social institution is guaranteed and prominent among these he places the function of some nonabstract art to supply imaginative models for thinking about aspects of the world—including human nature—which are worked out and tested against the detail of individual cases.[10] It would be ridiculous to dispute that some works, particularly of literary and dramatic art, do provide material for a deeper understanding of the world and human nature, material that is more vivid and more concrete than the generalization to be found in handbooks of sociology and psychology. But to suppose that the promotion of understanding is a main purpose of art or that we go to works of art for the sake of increasing our understanding of the things of which they speak betrays a lamentable misapprehension of the situation. It is in virtue of our existing understanding of human nature or whatever that we are able to recognize and assess the insight, the penetration, and the truth of a work. To use it as a source of data for the sake of understanding is to misuse it as a work of art. We ascribe stature to art objects from alien cultures or the distant past without knowing or worrying about the function they once served for understanding—or influencing—life and the world within the culture and for the people among whom they originated. We admire a Benin bronze head, select one Dogon ancestral figure as great while ascribing only ethnological interest to another, without needing to know what their functions were in their own society or how effective they were believed to be for the fulfillment of those functions. We can only speculate about the meaning and purpose of Palaeolithic cave art. The statues around San Agustín in Colombia impress as magnificent though nobody knows the meaning they once held or the purpose they served and certainly people who are now overwhelmed by them do not pause to ask whether or how they contribute to an understanding of life and the world. We call the Elgin Marbles great, but they certainly function differently in the British Museum for the art institution of our own culture from the meaning they had when affixed to the Parthenon for the Greeks of the fifth century B.C. Greek drama no doubt still holds for us insights into human nature; but we do not maintain it in being in order that we may learn. This conception of art is too intellectualized and does not correspond with usage. Even with the art of our own time we are more interested in experiencing imaginatively what it would be like if people and the world were as they are represented to be than in learning from it how things really are.

ii. *Nonverbal Thought.* We also apply the concept of stature to the abstract arts of music, architecture, nonrepresentational painting and sculpture, kinetic art which exploits the aesthetic qualities of movement, and so on. In this field stature is related to quality—the depth or superficiality—of the nonverbal thought embodied in a work. For there exists nonverbal thinking, thinking in terms of musical sounds, colors and shapes, architectural volumes, bodily movements, etc. Such thoughts can be directly apprehended but cannot be translated into the verbal propositions of discursive understanding.[11] We ascribe depth and profundity to Bach's "Brandenburg Concertos" and to "The Art of the Fugue," to Beethoven's "Diabelli Variations" and to Stravinsky's "Symphony of Psalms." We call the Parthenon, the Taj Mahal, Santa Sophia, and Chichen Itzá great architecture for the thought that is there. We can speak *about* these things, perhaps draw inferences from them about the way of life and thought of the peoples for whom they were made; but we cannot put into words the thought that is in them that contributes to their stature. We might say that the sculpture of David Smith has on the whole greater depth of thought than that of Tony Smith or Robert Bladen, that the abstracts of Morris Louis and Mark Rothko have on the whole greater profundity than those of Josef Albers or Robert Motherwell's *Elegies to the Spanish Republic*. But these are things which must be apprehended directly and cannot be measured with a foot rule. The quality of nonverbal thought is an important factor in ascriptions of stature. And this is true not only of abstract art but—a point which is too easily overlooked—also of the nonverbal thought inherent in the formal or structural aspects of representational art.

iii. *Emotional Quality*. As feeling and emotions are said to be shallow or sublime, tenuous or intense, concentrated or diffuse, so it is commonly held that the quality of feeling embodied in works of art may be superficial or sublime. It is believed that the arts, particularly music, can embody profundities of emotion which extend and expand our capacity for feeling. This too enters into our assessments of stature in both abstract and representational art. Gounod's "Ave Maria," which Hermann Scherchen described as "anything but an ill-constructed melody,"[12] is nevertheless superficial, almost banal, while few would dispute that Schubert's "Ave Maria" has greater profundity. The "Hymn to Joy" theme in Beethoven's Ninth Symphony is by common consent one of the most sublime of all melodies; yet it can be analyzed by the same principles as Rubinstein's "Melody in F." If the fourth note is raised to B instead of the repeated A, the melody becomes banal; yet understanding cannot explain these things. The expressiveness of works of art, their embodied emotional meaning, is an emergent quality which cannot be reduced to rule or analyzed into the emotional quality of elements (e.g., musical intervals) and the relations in which they stand to each other. Like nonverbal thought, emotional expressiveness is a feature which contributes largely to our ascriptions of stature, but which cannot be brought within the range of discursive understanding.

I have argued that we assess works of art in accordance with two aesthetic standards, which often lead to incompatible conclusions. Closely combined with these in actual judgments is a nonaesthetic standard which I have called "stature." The point I am making is that time will be saved, misunderstandings obviated, disputes often avoided, and clarity enhanced if we make clear to ourselves and to others what standard or standards we are using when we judge on any occasion.

NOTES

1. See Karl Aschenbrenner, *The Concepts of Criticism* (Boston: D. Reidel, 1974).

2. In his essay "Of the Standard of Taste" David Hume took it for granted that Addison was a finer writer than Bunyan because he was superior in "elegance." I remember once causing astonishment when I said that elegance is not always a "good" feature in a work of art. We recognize elegance in Gainsborough's *The Blue Boy*, in *Le Chapeau de paille* by Rubens, and in *Madame Moitessier* by Ingres—a different elegance of course in each case. (This is a particularity of aesthetic properties in works of art: even when we can name them with assurance they are distinctive on each occurrence and do not generalize easily.) But it would be wrong to suggest that any of these pictures would be a better work of art if it were more elegant. And it would be on the ridiculous to suggest that Chardin's *Self-Portrait* in the Louvre or Van Gogh's *Self-Portrait* in the Courtauld Galleries, depicting himself after he had cut off an ear, or Fernand Léger's *Three Women* would be improved by a touch of elegance. We praise Raphael's *School of Athens*, Leonardo's *Last Supper*, Rembrandt's *Staal Meesers* for their qualities of composition. But precisely the qualities which we admire in them were repudiated by the *art informal* school of Wols, Gerard Schneider, and the Canadian Jean-Paul Riopelle. So in all the arts. In music the Impressionists Debussy and Ravel cultivated different qualities of excellence from those established in the age of the Baroque and different again from those of Alban Berg and Edgard Varèse.

3. In *A Theory of Art* (1982) Stephen David Ross writes: "How then are works of art judged better than others? Most of the time, I suggest, they are not so comparable except in a particular respect. Some paintings are more balanced, more serene, more harmonious, than others, better perhaps in that respect—but not overall, in all respects. I think it is a fundamental error pervasive throughout the history of art to suppose that artistic value forces a scale of measurement upon us." But we do of course make such judgments and say that an amateur daub is inferior as a work of art to a great painting by a master.

4. Anthony Sarvile, *The Test of Time* (New York: Oxford University Press, 1982), particularly chap. 9.

5. See my *The Art of Appreciation* (New York: Oxford University Press, 1970), chap 1.

6. To illustrate from the art of sculpture, compare the *Moses* of Ivan Mestrovic with the *Moses* of Barlach, *The Kiss* of Reid Dick with *The Kiss* of Rodin, his *Pietà* in the Kitchener Memorial Chapel with Eric Gill's *Stations of the Cross* in Westminster Cathedral, or his *Force Uncontrolled* on Unilever House with Ben Enwonwu's carvings for the *Daily Mirror* building in High Holborn. Compare Sergeant Jagger's *Artillery Memorial* with Epstein's *Day* and *Night* on the London Transport Headquarters Building at St. James's Park, his *Shackleton* at the Royal Geographical Society with Leon Underwood's *The Pursuit of Ideas* commissioned for the Hilgrove Estate. One could go on indefinitely. And so in the other arts.

7. Triviality, mediocrity, banality, etc., may constitute the theme of a work which has greatness, as for example Flaubert's *Madame Bovary*, Goncharov's *Oblomov*, Robert Musil's *The Man without Qualities*, and perhaps the Henkerin in Pavel Kohout's novel of that name. In painting, *The Old Woman Frying Eggs* by Velazquez and *Danseuses ajustant leurs chaussons* by Degas are two examples from many works which have greatness despite trivality of subject. But to apply such terms to the works themselves precludes a high assessment.

8. It is in their stature but not in their quality as art that Browning's "Home-Thoughts from Abroad" differs from "Rabbi Ben Ezra," "Lycidas" from *Paradise Lost*. The difference does not reside simply in length or scope. Lord Herbert of Cherbury's "Sonnet to Black Beauty" and Marvell's poem "To His Coy Mistress" are properly called "slight" while Shakespeare's "The Triumph of Death" and Milton's sonnet "To His Blindness" have grandeur and depth. It would be verging on the absurd to say that Wordsworth's poem "She dwelt among untrodden ways" is inferior as a piece of literary art to Tennyson's "In Memoriam." Lyly's "Cupid and Campaspe play'd" and Herrick's "A Sweet disorder of the dress" are slight poems but claim a permanent place in English literature.

9. David Best, "The Aesthetic and the Artistic," *Philosophy* 57 (1982).

10. Anthony Savile, *Test of Time*, chaps. 5 and 7.

11. It is sometimes said that there cannot be nonverbal thought because the aim and the criterion of thinking is truth, and truth belongs only to propositions or statements. The argument is, of course, circular. It defines thought in terms of a property which belongs only to what is verbal.

12. See Hermann Scherchen, *The Nature of Music*, trans. William Mann (Chicago: H. Regnery, 1950), p. 69.

NELSON GOODMAN

When Is Art?

1.The Pure in Art

If attempts to answer the question "What is art?" characteristically end in frustration and confusion, perhaps—as so often in philosophy—the question is the wrong one. A reconception of the
problem, together with application of some results of a study of the
theory of symbols, may help to clarify such moot matters as the role
of symbolism in art and the status as art of the 'found object' and
so-called 'conceptual art.'

One remarkable view of the relation of symbols to works of art is
illustrated in an incident bitingly reported by Mary McCarthy:[1]

> Seven years ago, when I taught in a progressive college, I had a
> pretty girl student in one of my classes who wanted to be a short-
> story writer. She was not studying with me, but she knew that I
> sometimes wrote short stories, and one day, breathless and glowing,
> she came up to me in the hall, to tell me that she had just written a
> story that her writing teacher, a Mr. Converse, was terribly excited
> about. "He thinks it's wonderful" she said, "and he's going to help
> me fix it up for publication."
>
> I asked what the story was about; the girl was a rather simple being
> who loved clothes and dates. Her answer had a deprecating tone.
> It was about a girl (herself) and some sailors she had met on the
> train. But then her face, which had looked perturbed for a moment,
> gladdened.
>
> "Mr. Converse is going over it with me and we're going to put in
> the symbols."

Today the bright-eyed art student will more likely be told, with
equal subtlety, to keep out the symbols; but the underlying assumption is the same: that symbols, whether enhancements or distrac-
tions, are extrinsic to the work itself. A kindred notion seems to be
reflected in what we take to be symbolic art. We think first of such
works as Bosch's *Garden of Delights* or Goya's *Caprichos* or the Unicorn tapestries or Dali's drooping watches, and then perhaps of re-

ligious paintings, the more mystical the better. What is remarkable here is less the association of the symbolic with the esoteric or unearthly than the classification of works as symbolic upon the basis of their having symbols as their subject matter—that is, upon the basis of their depicting rather than of being symbols. This leaves as nonsymbolic art not only works that depict nothing but also portraits, still-lifes, and landscapes where the subjects are rendered in a straightforward way without arcane allusions and do not themselves stand as symbols.

On the other hand, when we choose works for classification as nonsymbolic, as art without symbols, we confine ourselves to works without subjects; for example, to purely abstract or decorative or formal paintings or buildings or musical compositions. Works that represent anything, no matter what and no matter how prosaically, are excluded; for to represent is surely to refer, to stand for, to symbolize. Every representational work is a symbol; and art without symbols is restricted to art without subject.

That representational works are symbolic according to one usage and nonsymbolic according to another matters little so long as we do not confuse the two usages. What matters very much, though, according to many contemporary artists and critics, is to isolate the work of art as such from whatever it symbolizes or refers to in any way. Let me set forth in quotation marks, since I am offering it for consideration without now expressing any opinion of it, a composite statement of a currently much advocated program or policy or point of view:

"What a picture symbolizes is external to it, and extraneous to the picture as a work of art. Its subject if it has one, its references—subtle or obvious—by means of symbols from some more or less well-recognized vocabulary, have nothing to do with its aesthetic or artistic significance or character. Whatever a picture refers to or stands for in any way, overt or occult, lies outside it. What really counts is not any such relationship to something else, not what the picture symbolizes, but what it is in itself—what its own intrinsic qualities are. Moreover, the more a picture focuses attention on what it symbolizes, the more we are distracted from its own properties. Accordingly, any symbolization by a picture is not only irrelevant but disturbing. Really pure art shuns all symbolization, refers to nothing, and is to be taken for just what it is, for its inherent character, not for anything it is associated with by some such remote relation as symbolization."

Such a manifesto packs punch. The counsel to concentrate on the intrinsic rather than the extrinsic, the insistence that a work of art is

what it is rather than what it symbolizes, and the conclusion that
pure art dispenses with external reference of all kinds have the solid
sound of straight thinking, and promise to extricate art from smoth-
ering thickets of interpretation and commentary.

2. A Dilemma

But a dilemma confronts us here. If we accept this doctrine of the
formalist or purist, we seem to be saying that the content of such
works as the *Garden of Delights* and the *Caprichos* doesn't really matter and might better be left out. If we reject the doctrine, we seem
to be holding that what counts is not just what a work is but lots of
things it isn't. In the one case we seem to be advocating lobotomy
on many great works; in the other we seem to be condoning impu-
rity in art, emphasizing the extraneous.

The best course, I think, is to recognize the purist position as all
right and all wrong. But how can that be? Let's begin by agreeing
that what is extraneous is extraneous. But is what a symbol symbolizes always external to it? Certainly not for symbols of all kinds.
Consider the symbols:

(a) "this string of words," which stands for itself;
(b) "word," which applies to itself among other words;
(c) "short," which applies to itself and some other words and
many other things; and
(d) "having seven syllables," which has seven syllables.

Obviously what some symbols symbolize does not lie entirely outside the symbols. The cases cited are, of course, quite special ones,
and the analogues among pictures—that is, pictures that are pictures of themselves or include themselves in what they depict—can
perhaps be set aside as too rare and idiosyncratic to carry any
weight. Let's agree for the present that what a work represents, except in a few cases like these, is external to it and extraneous.

Does this mean that any work that represents nothing meets the
purist's demands? Not at all. In the first place, some surely symbolic works such as Bosch's paintings of weird monsters, or the tapestry of a unicorn, represent nothing; for there are no such
monsters or demons or unicorns anywhere but in such pictures or
in verbal descriptions. To say that the tapestry 'represents a unicorn' amounts only to saying that it is a unicorn-picture, not that
there is any animal, or anything at all that it portrays.[2] These

works, even though there is nothing they represent, hardly satisfy the purist. Perhaps, though, this is just another philosopher's quibble; and I won't press the point. Let's agree that such pictures, though they represent nothing, are representational in character, hence symbolic and so not 'pure.' All the same, we must note in passing that their being representational involves no representation of anything outside them, so that the purist's objection to them cannot be on that ground. His case will have to be modified in one way or another, with some sacrifice of simplicity and force.

In the second place, not only representational works are symbolic. An abstract painting that represents nothing and is not representational at all may express, and so symbolize, a feeling or other quality, or an emotion or idea.[3] Just because expression is a way of symbolizing something outside the painting—which does not itself sense, feel, or think—the purist rejects abstract expressionist as well as representational works.

For a work to be an instance of 'pure' art, of art without symbols, it must on this view neither represent nor express nor even be representational or expressive. But is that enough? Granted, such a work does not stand for anything outside it; all it has are its own properties. But of course if we put it that way, all the properties any picture or anything else has—even such a property as that of representing a given person—are properties of the picture, not properties outside it.

The predictable response is that the important distinction among the several properties a work may have lies between its internal or intrinsic and its external or extrinsic properties; that while all are indeed its own properties, some of them obviously relate the picture to the other things; and that a nonrepresentational, nonexpressive work has only internal properties.

This plainly doesn't work; for under any even faintly plausible classification of properties into internal and external, any picture or anything else has properties of both kinds. That a picture is in the Metropolitan Museum, that it was painted in Duluth, that it is younger than Methuselah, would hardly be called internal properties. Getting rid of representation and expression does not give us something free of such external or extraneous properties.

Furthermore, the very distinction between internal and external properties is a notoriously muddled one. Presumably the colors and shapes in a picture must be considered internal; but if an external property is one that relates the picture or object to something else, then colors and shapes obviously must be counted as external; for the color or shape of an object not only may be shared by other objects but also relates the object to others having the same or different colors or shapes.

Sometimes the terms "internal" and "intrinsic" are dropped in favor of "formal." But the formal in this context cannot be a matter of shape alone. It must include color, and if color, what else? Texture? Size? Material? Of course, we may at will enumerate properties that are to be called formal; but the "at will" gives the case away. The rationale, the justification, evaporates. The properties left out as nonformal can no longer be characterized as all and only those that relate the picture to something outside it. So we are still faced with the question what if any *principle* is involved—the question how the properties that matter in a nonrepresentational, nonexpressive painting are distinguished from the rest.

I think there is an answer to the question; but to approach it, we'll have to drop all this high-sounding talk of art and philosophy, and come down to earth with a thud.

3. Samples

Consider again an ordinary swatch of textile in a tailor's or upholsterer's sample book. It is unlikely to be a work of art or to picture or express anything. It's simply a sample—a simple sample. But what is it a sample of? Texture, color, weave, thickness, fiber content. . . ; the whole point of this sample, we are tempted to say, is that it was cut from a bolt and has all the same properties as the rest of the material. But that would be too hasty.

Let me tell you two stories—or one story with two parts. Mrs. Mary Tricias studied such a sample book, made her selection, and ordered from her favorite textile shop enough material for her overstuffed chair and sofa—insisting that it be exactly like the sample. When the bundle came she opened it eagerly and was dismayed when several hundred 2" × 3" pieces with zigzag edges exactly like the sample fluttered to the floor. When she called the shop, protesting loudly, the proprietor replied, injured and weary, "But Mrs. Tricias, you said the material must be exactly like the sample. When it arrived from the factory yesterday, I kept my assistants here half the night cutting it up to match the sample."

This incident was nearly forgotten some months later, when Mrs. Tricias, having sewed the pieces together and covered her furniture, decided to have a party. She went to the local bakery, selected a chocolate cupcake from those on display and ordered enough for fifty guests, to be delivered two weeks later. Just as the guests were beginning at arrive, a truck drove up with a single huge cake. The lady running the bakeshop was utterly discouraged by the complaint. "But Mrs. Tricias, you have no idea how much trouble we went to. My husband runs the textile shop and he warned me that your order would have to be in one piece."

The moral of this story is not simply that you can't win, but that a sample is a sample of some of its properties but not others. The swatch is a sample of texture, color, etc., but not of size or shape. The cupcake is a sample of color, texture, size, and shape, but still not of all its properties. Mrs. Tricias would have complained even more loudly if what was delivered to her was like the sample in having been baked on that same day two weeks earlier.

Now in general which of its properties is a sample a sample of? Not all its properties; for then the sample would be a sample of nothing but itself. And not its 'formal' or 'internal' or, indeed, any one specifiable set of properties. The kind of property sampled differs from case to case: the cupcake but not the swatch is a sample of size and shape; a specimen of ore may be a sample of what was mined at a given time and place. Moreover, the sampled properties vary widely with context and circumstance. Although the swatch is normally a sample of its texture, etc., but not of its shape or size, if I show it to you in answer to the question "What is an upholsterer's sample?" it then functions not as a sample of the material but as a sample of an upholsterer's sample, so that its size and shape are not among the properties it is a sample of.

In sum, the point is that a sample is a sample of—or *exemplifies*—only some of its properties, and that the properties to which it bears this relationship of exemplification[4] vary with circumstances and can only be distinguished as those properties that it serves, under the given circumstances, as a sample of. Being a sample of or exemplifying is a relationship something like that of being a friend; my friends are not distinguished by any single identifiable property or cluster of properties, but only by standing, for a period of time, in the relationship of friendship with me.

The implications for our problem concerning works of art may now be apparent. The properties that count in a purist painting are those that the picture makes manifest, selects, focuses upon, exhibits, heightens in our consciousness—those that it shows forth—in short, those properties that it does not merely possess but *exemplifies*, stands as a sample of.

If I am right about this, then even the purist's purest painting symbolizes. It exemplifies certain of its properties. But to exemplify is surely to symbolize—exemplification no less than representation or expression is a form of reference. A work of art, however free of representation and expression, is still a symbol even though what it symbolizes be not things or people or feelings but certain patterns of shape, color, texture that it shows forth.

What, then, of the purist's initial pronouncement that I said facetiously is all right and all wrong? It is all right in saying that what is extraneous is extraneous, in pointing out that what a picture represents often matters very little, in arguing that neither representation nor expression is required of a work, and in stressing the importance of so-called intrinsic or internal or 'formal' properties. But the statement is all wrong in assuming that representation and expression are the only symbolic functions that paintings may perform, in supposing that what a symbol symbolizes is always outside it, and in insisting that what counts in a painting is the mere possession rather than the exemplification of certain properties.

Whoever looks for art without symbols, then, will find none—if all the ways that works symbolize are taken into account. Art without representation or expression or exemplification—yes; art without all three—*no*.

To point out that purist art consists simply in the avoidance of certain kinds of symbolization is not to condemn it but only to uncover the fallacy in the usual manifestos advocating purist art to the exclusion of all other kinds. I am not debating the relative virtues of different schools or types or ways of painting. What seems to me more important is that recognition of the symbolic function of even purist painting gives us a clue to the perennial problem of when we do and when we don't have a work of art.

The literature of aesthetics is littered with desperate attempts to answer the question "What is art?" This question, often hopelessly confused with the question "What is good art?," is acute in the case of found art—the stone picked out of the driveway and exhibited in a museum—and is further aggravated by the promotion of so-called environmental and conceptual art. Is a smashed automobile fender in an art gallery a work of art? What of something that is not even an object, and not exhibited in any gallery or museum—for example, the digging and filling-in of a hole in Central Park as prescribed by Oldenburg? If these are works of art, then are all stones in the driveway and all objects and occurrences works of art? If not, what distinguishes what is from what is not a work of art? That an artist calls it a work of art? That it is exhibited in a museum or gallery? No such answer carries any conviction.

As I remarked at the outset, part of the trouble lies in asking the wrong question—in failing to recognize that a thing may function as a work of art at some times and not at others. In crucial cases, the real question is not "What objects are (permanently) works of art?" but "When is an object a work of art?"—or more briefly, as in my title, "When is art?"

My answer is that just as an object may be a symbol—for instance, a sample—at certain times and under certain circumstances and not at others, so an object may be a work of art at some times and not at others. Indeed, just by virtue of functioning as a symbol in a certain way does an object become, while so functioning, a work of art. The stone is normally no work of art while in the driveway, but may be so when on display in an art museum. In the driveway, it usually performs no symbolic function. In the art museum, it exemplifies certain of its properties—e.g., properties of shape, color, texture. The hole-digging and filling functions is a work insofar as our attention is directed to it as an exemplifying symbol. On the other hand, a Rembrandt painting may cease to function as a work of art when used to replace a broken window or as a blanket.

Now, of course, to function as a symbol in some way or other is not in itself to function as a work of art. Our swatch, when serving as a sample, does not then and thereby become a work of art. Things function as works of art only when their symbolic functioning has certain characteristics. Our stone in a museum of geology takes on symbolic functions as a sample of the stones of a given period, origin, or composition, but it is not then functioning as a work of art.

The question just what characteristics distinguish or are indicative of the symbolizing that constitutes functioning as a work of art calls for careful study in the light of a general theory of symbols. That is more than I can undertake here, but I venture the tentative thought that there are five symptoms of the aesthetic:[5] (1) syntactic density, where the finest differences in certain respects constitute a difference between symbols—for example, an ungraduated mercury thermometer as contrasted with an electronic digital-read-out instrument; (2) semantic density, where symbols are provided for things distinguished by the finest differences in certain respects— for example, not only the ungraduated thermometer again but also ordinary English, though it is not syntactically dense; (3) relative repleteness, where comparatively many aspects of a symbol are significant—for example, a single-line drawing of a mountain by Hokusai where every feature of shape, line, thickness, etc., counts, in contrast with perhaps the same line as a chart of daily stockmarket averages, where all that counts is the height of the line above the base; (4) exemplification, where a symbol, whether or not it denotes, symbolizes by serving as a sample of properties it literally or metaphorically possesses; and finally (5) multiple and complex reference, where a symbol performs several integrated and interacting referential functions,[6] some direct and some mediated through other symbols.

These symptoms provide no definition, much less a full-blooded description or a celebration. Presence or absence of one or more of them does not qualify or disqualify anything as aesthetic; nor does the extent to which these features are present measure the extent to which an object or experience is aesthetic.[7] Symptoms, after all, are but clues; the patient may have the symptoms without the disease, or the disease without the symptoms. And even for these five symptoms to come somewhere near being disjunctively necessary and conjunctively (as a syndrome) sufficient might well call for some redrawing of the vague and vagrant borderlines of the aesthetic. Still, notice that these properties tend to focus attention on the symbol rather than, or at least along with, what it refers to. Where we can never determine precisely just which symbol of a system we have or whether we have the same one on a second occasion, where the referent is so elusive that properly fitting a symbol to it requires endless care, where more rather than fewer features of the symbol count, where the symbol is an instance of properties it symbolizes and may perform many interrelated simple and complex referential functions, we cannot merely look through the symbol to what it refers to as we do in obeying traffic lights or reading scientific texts, but must attend constantly to the symbol itself as in seeing paintings or reading poetry. This emphasis upon the nontransparency of a work of art, upon the primacy of the work over what it refers to, far from involving denial or disregard of symbolic functions, derives from certain characteristics of a work as a symbol.[8]

Quite apart from specifying the particular characteristics differentiating aesthetic from other symbolization, the answer to the question "When is art?" thus seems to me clearly to be in terms of symbolic function. Perhaps to say that an object is art when and only when it so functions is to overstate the case or to speak elliptically. The Rembrandt painting remains a work of art, as it remains a painting, while functioning only as a blanket; and the stone from the driveway may not strictly become art by functioning as art.[9] Similarly, a chair remains a chair even if never sat on, and a packing case remains a packing case if never used except for sitting on. To say what art does is not to say what art is; but I submit that the former is the matter of primary and peculiar concern. The further question of defining stable property in terms of ephemeral function—the what in terms of the when—is not confined to the arts but is quite general, and is the same for defining chairs as for defining objects of art. The parade of instant and inadequate answers is also much the same: that whether an object is art—or a chair—depends upon intent or upon whether it sometimes or usually or always or exclusively functions as such. Because all this tends to obscure more special and significant questions concerning art, I have turned my attention from what art is to what art does.

A salient feature of symbolization, I have urged, is that it may come and go. An object may symbolize different things at different times, and nothing at other times. An inert or purely utilitarian object may come to function as art, and a work of art may come to function as an inert or purely utilitarian object. Perhaps, rather than art being long and life short, both are transient.

NOTES

Editors' Note: In the notes below, *LA* refers to *Languages of Art*, 2nd ed. (Indianapolis: Hackett, 1976; first published 1968); *PP* to *Problems and Projects* (Indianapolis: Hackett, 1972).

1. "Settling the Colonel's Hash," *Harper's Magazine*, 1954; reprinted in *On the Contrary* (Farrar, Straus, and Cudahy, 1961), p. 225.

2. See further "On Likeness of Meaning" (1949) and "On Some Differences about Meaning" (1953), *PP*, pp. 221–38; also *LA*, pp. 21–26.

3. Motion, for instance, as well as emotion may be expressed in a black and white picture. . . . Also see the discussion of expression in *LA*, pp. 85–95.

4. For further discussion of exemplification, see *LA*, pp. 52–67.

5. See *LA*, pp. 252–55 and the earlier passages alluded to there. The fifth symptom has been added above as the result of conversations with professors Paul Hernadi and Alan Nagel of the University of Iowa.

6. This excludes ordinary ambiguity, where a term has two or more quite independent denotations at quite different times and in quite different contexts.

7. That poetry, for example, which is not syntactically dense, is less art or less likely to be art than painting that exhibits all four symptoms thus

does not at all follow. Some aesthetic symbols may have fewer of the symptoms than some nonaesthetic symbols. This is sometimes misunderstood.

8. This is another version of the dictum that the purist is all right and all wrong.

9. Just as what is not red may look or be said to be red at certain times, so what is not art may function as or be said to be art at certain times. That an object functions as art at a given time, that it has the status of art at that time, and that it is art at that time may all be taken as saying the same thing—so long as we take none of these ascribing to the object any stable status.

PART THREE

_Purposes of
Aesthetic Education_

Introduction

In "The Arts as Basic Education" Harry S. Broudy addresses the justification question by asking in what sense we may think of art as a basic subject. His approach distinguishes not only the instrumental and foundational senses of the term "basic," but also the arts of expression and impression, popular and serious art, presentational and referential symbols, and an impoverished and a cultivated imagination. Arts education is basic in an instrumental sense when it develops in the young a capacity to perceive works of art somewhat after the manner of artists, thus enabling them to apprehend the peculiar value import of artistic images. Arts education is basic in a foundational sense when its images influence the perception and understanding of life's various roles, rituals, and ideal possibilities. Although it is doubtlessly true, writes Broudy, that our era is not generating compelling images which function as a strong, cohesive force, a cultivated imagination may be required to recognize them when they do appear. Broudy's brief for aesthetic education then is for the cultivation of the imagination, in behalf of which he has argued many times over a distinguished career.

To speak of aesthetics as a discipline or to discuss some of the typical concerns of philosophers of art is one thing; it is something else to indicate the relevance of aesthetics to the goals and purposes of aesthetic education. This is the task Ralph A. Smith sets in his "Philosophy and Theory of Aesthetic Education." Following Israel Scheffler, Smith first distinguishes scientific from practical activities, in the instance at hand the practical activities of aesthetic education. He then indicates how aesthetics can inform a curriculum for the secondary years of schooling. Assuming that aesthetic literacy implies a disposition to appreciate works of art for the worthwhile experience they are capable of providing, Smith indicates how one kind of worthwhile experience, aesthetic experience, contributes to the realization of educational goals and objectives. Aesthetic experience not only intensifies and clarifies human experience, it also provides a special kind of enjoyment or gratification and strengthens a

sense of human freedom. Smith further points out that the development of an appreciation of the intrinsic values of art is not incompatible with a sense of social responsibility, so that aesthetic
education need not pursue distinctively ideological or political goals
and is in danger of going astray if it does.

Broudy cautions that metaphors such as "the language of the
arts" and "artistic literacy" twist the meaning of "language" almost
beyond recognition but are acceptable so long as they are not taken
too literally. With this in mind, Maxine Greene in "Aesthetic Literacy" understands aesthetic competence as the capacity to experience things from an aesthetic point of view. The purpose of
aesthetic perception is to make aesthetic sense of things, and this in
turn presupposes an educated eye and imagination. No single definition of art's meaning or function will suffice for this task; yet aesthetics, or philosophy of art, is a valuable resource that provides
helpful accounts of the aesthetic complex (artist, object, and audience) and the aesthetic transaction itself.

Why, asks Greene, should we cultivate aesthetic literacy? What
are its special benefits? Nothing less than the enhancement of life
and consciousness and the feeling of being more alive and free:
more alive because one discovers and establishes rapport with the
qualitative immediacy of life and freer because one has acquired a
new power that makes one less dependent on stereotyped ways of
seeing, thinking, and acting. While the capacity for aesthetic perception is innate and unfolds naturally to a certain extent, its full
reach cannot be realized without instruction. Ultimately, says
Greene, the justification of aesthetic education lies in its opening up
a new world of meaning to the young, a fresh orientation to life that
makes them more open-minded and adventuresome.

E. F. Kaelin's remarks emphasize the social or institutional aspects of art and aesthetic education. His interest exemplifies yet another of the typical kinds of questions asked by aesthetics. After a
brief review of the phases through which attempts to define art
have passed, Kaelin fastens on the third phase, the attempt to define art institutionally, and extends it for purposes of justifying aesthetic education.

Taking his lead from George Herbert Mead's theory of social interactionism and its view of human relationship and learning, Kaelin, a principal exponent of Continental aesthetic ideas, believes that
the arts are good mainly for the aesthetic experiences they provide.
An aesthetic experience is worthwhile, says Kaelin, because it stimulates intense feelings at the same time that it cultivates sensibility

and enlarges imagination. The control and discipline exercised during aesthetic experience, moreover, are functions of demands that arise in the aesthetic situation. Kaelin thinks that an understanding of these demands is central to a freely functioning aesthetic institution whose primary concern is with the creation of aesthetic value. Given this organizing assumption, aesthetic education can be said to imitate the aesthetic institution of society by featuring its basic components and operations, namely, artistic creation, art criticism, art history, and philosophy of art or aesthetics. Teachers of art must understand such arts-related disciplines if they are to teach students to play their proper roles in the art world.

The benefits of aesthetic education, however, extend beyond the having of aesthetic experiences and their effects on feeling and imagination. The ultimate social product of the aesthetic institution, says Kaelin, is the defanaticized individual who knows how to appreciate works of art with the proper critical attitude. It is clear that Kaelin is remarking the kinds of constraints on creative and cultural activities experienced by members of totalitarian societies.

The theme of the usefulness of ostensibly nonutilitarian activities such as art and aesthetic experience is also stressed by Alan Simpson. When examined carefully, says Simpson, the term "aesthetic education" has a number of potential uses that can alert us to the distinctiveness of arts education, especially if we take a unified view of aesthetic learning. In such a view the young would be inducted into an autonomous realm of study, the arts, where the creation and appreciation of art would feature modes of perception and judgment that would be worthwhile not only for their own sakes but also for what they contribute to human freedom. What is more, by including aesthetic contemplation and reflection among basic human needs, aesthetic education fills out the picture of human potentiality; it balances the scales of human interest with a concern for the meaning and quality of life that only the arts can provide.

Simpson's unified view of aesthetic education emphasizes a type of judgment that, among other things, is contemplative, critical, and dispassionate. Yet such judgments are often considered to be incorrigibly subjective. David Best, a British philosopher who in numerous articles and books has clarified a number of misconceptions that mislead us in thinking about art and arts education, gives the lie to the claimed subjectivism of aesthetic value judgments. In his discussion of reasons and judgments in artistic and scientific fields, Best concludes that just like those of science, value judgments of artistic merit are rationally supportable so long as they derive from a proper understanding of the subject in question and its criteria or standards of merit. That there are important differences in our scientific, moral, and aesthetic deliberations does not rule out the possibility of our giving reasons in support of aesthetic judgments. Learning to make rational aesthetic judgments should, Best thinks, be one of the major objectives of aesthetic education, especially in light of the power we attribute to art to shape thought and feeling.

While there is considerable overlap among the interests of the writers just summarized, it may be helpful to compose their ideas and accents into a comprehensive statement: The purpose of aesthetic education is seen as the development of aesthetic literacy (Greene) through an autonomous, unified field of study (Simpson) in which emphasis is placed on cultivating the imagination (Broudy), the essential capacities of which are those required for aesthetic experience (Smith) and critical judgment (Best), all of which contribute toward the efficacious functioning of the social institution of art (Kaelin).

HARRY S. BROUDY

The Arts as Basic Education

Aristotle and other wise ancients counseled moderation in all things. We Americans seem to avoid moderation in anything and most assuredly in launching educational bandwagons. To attract attention an idea, a personality, or a product has to be blown up and sold as a media event. Exaggeration is a good way of doing it. Once the innovation becomes a media event, its promoters have to claim spectacular successes to preserve a place on the talk shows.

The drive for academic excellence for the elite of the early sixties, the surge of compassion for minorities in the late sixties, and the current rage for the basics for everybody gained attention, publicity, and funds, i.e., they became media events, by exaggerating one important ingredient of the educative process to the point of absurdity. There is a saying to the effect that anyone standing still long enough will in time be leading the parade. In the matter of educational bandwagons, one does not have to wait very long; the most publicized educational trends of the last fifteen years have lasted about five years. Educational entrepreneurs who want to cash in on these trends have to move fast. There is no reason to believe that the passion for the basics will be longer lived than its immediate predecessors. What is important and true about excellence, compassion, and the basics has been with us and will remain with us for a long time; only ignorance of history makes them seem novel. It is their show biz, public relation aspects that sensible people must patiently endure and, if possible, ignore.

Yet it is not safe to ignore the clamor, the editorials, the viewing of schools with alarm. They have a way of inciting legislators to produce mandates and energetic publishing houses and testmakers to turn out marketable packages. So at least once every decade it becomes necessary to restore perspective, to cool off those who perspire too easily, and to remind ourselves that education perhaps more than any other institution is concerned with *all* aspects of human life, not only as it exists, but as it might and ought to be. The omnirelevance of education overflows all attempts to reduce it to any one of its components.

The basics boom threatens other components of the public school curriculum because it preempts shrinking budgets. Among the early victims is arts education, but it will not be the only one. Every school activity that is not one of the three R's or a very close relative is endangered. The arts, however, are especially vulnerable because they have never been regarded as the bread and butter of schooling any more than of life itself. At best, they have been classed with the niceties of life and schooling, not the necessities; at worst, as beguiling frills. If the arts can justify a place at the curricular table, it is because they are necessary as well as nice. Only then can they claim to be basic education.

Foundational and Instrumental Basics

In what sense then can arts education be regarded as basic? One meaning of "basic" is that of a base, a foundation on which something is erected and presumably indispensable to hold up the building. Or "basic" can refer to such skills as bricklaying, carpentry, welding, etc., that are indispensable to the construction of buildings. On the foundational meaning, basic education refers to a body of knowledge that is presupposed by other bodies of knowledge, e.g., mechanics presupposes a knowledge of physics. On the second meaning, basic education refers to reading, writing, and computing—symbolic skills—that are used to encode information in all forms of knowledge. When it is asked whether the arts can be considered as basic education, one may have either or both meanings in mind, viz., that the arts are skills that, once mastered, function as tools or instruments in a wide variety of situations or that, as works of art, they are avenues to other resources of the culture.

On either meaning it is well to remember that skills can be mastered and concepts learned without being used for further learning or for the enrichment of life, just as many a saw or hammer or screwdriver is rusting in many a garage or cellar and many a foundation remains without a superstructure. It has been the bane of pedagogy in all ages that to teach something one has to isolate and methodize it, but, once isolated, there is no guarantee that it will be used for anything else.

All formal instruction, consequently, runs the risk of becoming separated from use or application, and the basics, whether foundational or in the form of instrumental skills, are no exception. However, there is an important difference between a foundational basic and the skill kind. It lies in the fact that whether deliberately applied or not, foundational studies such as history, mathematics (not computation as such), and science can and often do function tacitly even when they cannot be reinstated explicitly as learned.[1] They function by supplying contexts for meaning as skills do not. Accordingly, if a school study provides necessary and distinctive contexts, it can claim to be basic in the foundational sense. Does art education supply contexts that other studies do not? And are certain artistic skills needed to carry out the context-building function? If so, they are basic in the instrumental sense. Are there such skills?

Artistic Skills of Expression and Impression

There have been attempts to argue that art is a fourth R, a claim made more plausible by such metaphors as "the language of the arts" and "artistic literacy." But this argument twists the meaning of language almost beyond recognition. Indeed, the strength of the arts lies in their claim that they are *not* abstract cognitive symbolic systems; that they are "presentational" symbols, not referential ones; that they convey images of human import directly and are not the result of decoding and translation. D-O-G does not smell, sound, or look like man's best friend—a picture can display the friendliness as well as the dogginess unmistakably—sometimes sickeningly so.

Attempts to construct arts alphabets are not very convincing. Colors, sounds, textures, gestures, lines, and shapes can be thought of as elements out of which aesthetic images are assembled, but the resulting images cannot be looked up in a standard dictionary for definitions. Conversely, these individual lines, shapes, and colors often have an expressive power that letters of the ordinary linguistic alphabet almost never have.

Does the arts program improve performance in the three R's? There is little evidence that instruction in the arts or the lack of it affects reading, arithmetic, and writing scores. However, even if it were demonstrable that arts instruction increases these scores, it would still be a very roundabout way of doing so. A crash program using techniques of behavior modification and electronic technology could do the job more efficiently, albeit not so pleasantly.

Some arts educators claim that arts education improves general liking for school and in doing so also motivates study of the basics. At least one teacher in a ghetto school in the inner city reports that the rate of absenteeism drops dramatically when an art lesson is scheduled. Clearly this is a tribute to the interest potential of the arts lesson, but what does it indicate with regard to its relation to the basics? First of all, it does not seem to lower the rate of absenteeism for the nonart lessons. Second, it gives credence to the belief one would like to displace, viz., that the arts programs are forms of pleasant entertainment or hobbies—a relief from the so-called basics rather than a part of them.

To qualify as a fourth R (reading, writing, 'rithmetic, and 'rt) in the instrumental skill sense, the arts program need only demonstrate that there are skills that function as instruments for impression and expression in the aesthetic domain of experience with somewhat the same generality as do the symbolic skills in the cognitive domain. And one can do this with some plausibility if the metaphor of the language of the arts and artistic literacy is not taken too literally.

That there are skills of expression is witnessed by schools of music, painting, dance, theater, and creative writing. Arts programs in the schools for a very long time have concentrated on developing expressive skills, chiefly in music and the graphic arts. Unfortunately, the skills of expression, i.e., of the making of images that express human import of one sort or another, tend to become less functional for more and more people as linguistic forms are developed. Beyond the age of seven or eight, ordinary language takes the place of imagery as forms of expression for all but a tiny minority of individuals, artists.

Much has been made of the fact that persons, especially children, who have difficulty with linguistic skills often develop artistic ones as means of expression. An extreme case is that of an autistic girl who displayed an extraordinary talent in drawing at a very early age. Yet when after much difficulty the child acquired a very rudimentary ability to communicate in words, the amount and quality of the drawing dropped off sharply.[2]

Anyone who in a foreign country has been reduced to using drawings instead of words realizes—unless one is a pretty good artist—how cumbersome a means of communication it is. Yet in the hands of a competent artist how much more immediate and expressive is the drawing than the words of any particular language! How many words, for example, would it take to convey the information expressed by one caricature?

When it is said that the arts are means of expression, it is not ordinary communication of information that is meant. Rather it is the expression of subjective experience, usually of an emotive sort—the sort that adolescents want to express in poetry and many others express to their psychiatrist or marriage counselor. For this purpose the arts are preeminently suited, and one would like to think of a citizenry that could express itself in poetry, paint, clay, dance, and drama. The hitch is that once naive childhood, in which one's drawing or song or rhyme serves as a means of expression even if it does not meet the technical demands of adults, is gone, we are not satisfied with our art products unless we have the technique to make them really expressive rather than a gesture of expression. In plain language, unless we have some talent and a willingness to work hard and long enough to master technique, we do not use artistic skills as a means of expression. To try to justify a more central place in the curriculum for arts education on these grounds, therefore, is neither credible nor advisable. So long as arts education programs restrict themselves to the skills of expression—image making—they will retain their status as pleasant accomplishments but not really necessary for anyone save prospective artists.

The situation is quite different with respect to the skills of impression. In the first place, all of us are consumers of images even if most of us do not deliberately contrive them. In the second place, there is a difference between a response to serious art that creates images of human import in a very special way and our response to the images we encounter in everyday life and in the popular arts. Whether or not a formal program of arts instruction is justified in the public schools depends a great deal on this difference.

For example, in ordinary life we react to aesthetic clues (the appearance of things, persons, and places) with fairly uniform and stereotyped responses.

The sky is threatening; let's postpone the picnic.

Here comes one of those long-haired hippies; probably strung out on drugs.

That building doesn't look like a bank, and the president doesn't look like a banker. Let's put our money elsewhere.

I've got a piece of the rock!

These are examples of the hundreds of inferences about fact that we draw from aesthetic clues that may or may not be mistaken. We rarely investigate their accuracy. Similarly in daily life, the popular arts pour out steady streams of images that evoke ready-made responses and interpretations. Madison Avenue is an image-making industry. Television shows us the proper image of feeling about soap and love, war and peace, life and death; so does popular music. We do not realize and perhaps do not want to know how much of our "real" selves is fashioned after the images provided by the popular arts. The point to be made is that for the appropriation of the popular arts and the interpretations of the standard images of our daily life, no formal instruction is needed; we do not need to develop skills of impression. But there is no such automatic response to serious art, and if consumers do respond with the stereotypes of ordinary aesthetic experience, they may be puzzled, irritated, and in any event out of tune with the artist.

Ordinary life rarely sounds like a Mozart symphony or looks like a Pollock painting or a Moore sculpture or a Martha Graham dance. Serious art in any of the media uses sensory materials and shapes them by many formal devices into shapes that mysteriously express something of interest to human beings. These apparitions of feeling, emotion, and attitude are not scientific messages of fact but rather a struggle to objectify significance, possibility, and inspiration.

Serious art, like serious science, transforms our expectations and standards, and the skills of aesthetic impression enable us to take the first steps toward connoisseurship. Thereafter the images of the mass media and of popular art find less automatic interpretation and acceptance. The massive force of mass cult, for that individual at least, is no longer so overpowering.

The challenge to the schools is to produce a curriculum for skills of aesthetic impression that can be taught to the total school population. Elsewhere I have argued that such skills of aesthetic perception can be taught as a method of artistic scanning in any medium. Moreover, they can be taught to persons without special artistic talents for creating aesthetic objects.[3] The skills of aesthetic perception qualify as instrumental skills.

Arts Education as Foundational

Yet the argument for the artistic skills fails to convey the fundamental and distinctive role of images and of imagination in life and learning. The role of cognition by contrast is clear and compelling. It provides reliable knowledge. Indeed, part of its job is to correct the vagaries of images and the imagination that produces them. Scientists, especially social scientists, are forever exploding myths. Imagination, except for the artist and inventor, has had a bad press through the ages. It connotes the wild, the bizarre, the eccentric, the unreal, the dangerous. Fantasy is akin to imbalance and neurosis. Only in recent times has its importance for science and indeed for every form of cognition been recognized.

However, only a few of us will be artists, scientists, or innovators of any kind. Can the rest of us dispense with the work of the imagination after childhood has had its fill of make-believe? If arts education is basic in the foundational sense, images and imagination pervade all thought and discourse and their impoverishment is a root disease, not merely the withering of transient blossoms. To qualify as a foundational basic education, arts programs have to show—or at least promise—that they provide indispensable, distinctive resources for the kind of cultivation commonly called education.

Just how foundational images are becomes clear only when we consider how discourse becomes intelligible. Given a dictionary, one can decode virtually every word in a language. The fundamental syntax of a language, especially spoken language, is either innate or learned very early in the game. Meaning, however, is more than finding linguistic equivalents of words in sentences. Meaning always emerges out of a context that the reader or listener has to supply and which the communicator assumes will be supplied. For example, without an appropriate context, the following sentence remains indeterminate in meaning. "I am not my father's son." It might mean that "I" refers to a woman or that my father has characteristics that I do not have, or that my legal father is not my biological father. Dictionaries do not supply these contexts; our store of concepts has to do so. "Father, son, and the Holy Ghost" is wholly opaque outside the context of Christian theology. Idiomatic use of language, so important in discourse, is unintelligible without certain images as context: "We worked around the clock"; "She worked her fingers to the bone"; "Salvation comes by faith not works." Discourse is incurably metaphorical. When one reads materials within a discipline, the concepts of that discipline, its facts and relations either supply the context or it remains just a series of words, even though pronounced correctly and lexically understood.

On almost any theory of aesthetics, the work of art reveals the human import in an image. It does so directly and immediately as if our primordial understanding of the world is reinstated. For our original interpretation of the world must have in the first instances appeared not only as a shape or sound or texture, but as a useful, friendly, or hostile shape, sound, or texture. Supernatural forces revealed themselves as animals, stones, trees, stars, and planets that "looked" especially significant—sacred. The artist keeps the fountain of the imagination flowing with ever new images of ever new possibilities of human feeling. To cut oneself off from this source is to lose access to the raw materials of all our thought and judgment. The impoverishment of the imagination is more often the cause of difficulty in school learning than failure to master the mechanics of the three R's or the factual content of textbooks. It is in this context-building sense that the arts contribute to the learning of the three R's.

But there are other reasons for the arts to be regarded as foundationally necessary. They touch on the role of art and the artist in society. One of these is the role of art as a value marker. Whatever a society regards as of major importance it underscores by using art. Crucial episodes in its history, critical events—birth, marriage, war, death—are stylized by ritual and ceremony so that all members of the community perceive their import through a standardized image. Rituals create a powerful and reliable community of attitude. A society that cannot bind to itself the loyalty of its members with the bonds of its images is fragile and brittle—not long for this world. A society that keeps its people chained to stereotyped images may also be dying. Imagination delights in being captured but not in remaining a captive.

Furthermore, society relies upon the images of art to define the social roles of the family, government, religion, and the status of the individuals in these institutions. The appropriate behavior of a man, a father, a husband, a worker, or a soldier is made clear and vivid by the portrayals of art in the various media. Popular arts in the mass media provide the standard image; serious art creates more sophisticated and complex images for these roles. It is to the arts that we look for the model of our national heroes, military and moral, as well as of the good life. More character training was accomplished by the Horatio Alger stories than by any school program of character education. We grasp the problems of industrial England through the works of Dickens more vividly than through scholarly history. The Statue of Liberty has brought catches to the throats of more Americans than all the tracts of political science.

NOTES

1. I am here referring to the work of Michael Polanyi on tacit knowing and to my own attempts to translate this into the associative and interpretive uses of knowledge. Cf. Polanyi's *The Tacit Dimension* (Garden City, N.Y.: Doubleday Anchor, 1967), and my "Tacit Knowing and Aesthetic Educa-

tion" in *Aesthetic Concepts and Education,* ed. Ralph A. Smith (Urbana: University of Illinois Press, 1970)

2. Review of Lorna Selfe's *Nadia: A Case of Extraordinary Drawing Ability in an Autistic Child* (New York: Academic Press, 1978) by Nigel Dennis in *The New York Review of Books,* 4 May 1978.

3. The sensory, formal, technical, and expressive properties of a work of art, or, indeed, any perceptible object, can be perceived more fully and with more discrimination by such scanning. In other words, the pupil begins to approximate the modes of *perception* of the artist. Cf. my *Enlightened Cherishing* (Urbana: University of Illinois Press, 1972).

Ralph A. Smith

Philosophy and Theory of Aesthetic Education

In addressing the question of the relations between philosophy and the theory of aesthetic education, I accept both Harold Osborne's belief that philosophers should examine aesthetic problems with the advancement and progress of humanity in mind[1] and Eugene F. Kaelin's that aesthetic education constitutes a proper concern of aesthetics.[2] With rare exception, however, modern aesthetics does not reflect Osborne's belief, and "the phrase 'aesthetic education,'" writes Francis Sparshott, "plays little part in aesthetics generally."[3] The attitude of aesthetics toward education is, of course, consistent with its bias toward philosophical analysis for its own sake. On the other hand, one of the principal contributions of philosophical aesthetics to a theory of aesthetic education lies in its clarification of a number of aesthetic concepts that figure not only in specifically philosophical analysis but also in the language of teaching art. A practical theory of aesthetic education thus has much to learn from philosophical aesthetics. What do we mean when we speak of a practical theory of aesthetic education?

In *Of Human Potential*, a volume indirectly relevant to justifying aesthetic education, Israel Scheffler[4] distinguishes a scientific from a practical theory by saying that in their drive to give truthful representations of the phenomena studied, scientists attempt to formulate systems of lawlike statements in the terminology of a given discipline that are judged by the criteria of logical coherence, explanatory power, and heuristic efficacy. In the search for more general understanding, theories become increasingly systematic, abstract, and autonomous and thus more and more remote from the terms of ordinary language and practical experience. Conversely, the propositions of a practical theory are organized for the purpose of guiding some kind of practical endeavor, for example, the activities of education. Since no single discipline is adequate for purposes of describing and explaining the complex activities of education, practical theories of education must in comparison with scientific theories be necessarily composite and inelegant. We may say then that a practical theory of aesthetic education applies the insights of a range of disciplines to the problems of teaching an understanding and appreciation of works of art. I will show the relevance of philosophical aesthetics to a theory of aesthetic education by indicating how an analysis of the idea of aesthetic experience can significantly contribute to an understanding of our responses to works of art. For perspectives on the nature of aesthetic experience, I draw on the writings of Monroe C. Beardsley, Harold Osborne, Nelson Goodman, and Eugene F. Kaelin.[5]

Monroe C. Beardsley: Aesthetic Experience as Essentially Gratifying

The late Monroe C. Beardsley's *Aesthetics: Problems in the Philosophy of Criticism*, first published in 1958 and updated in 1981,[6] has been one of the most widely read works in American philosophical aesthetics since John Dewey's *Art as Experience. Aesthetics* is a systematic examination of a wide range of aesthetic topics, but it is particularly concerned with the analysis of the presuppositions of art criticism Beardsley detected in a large number of critical statements made by art, music, and literary critics. However, one cannot determine the relevance of reasons and judgments without a theory of relevance, and thus Beardsley also provides an instrumental theory of aesthetic value that both influences his analysis of concepts and reveals a serious concern with the role of art in human life. This latter concern makes Beardsley's writings one of the rare instances in modern aesthetics in which the human significance and relevance of art are kept constantly in mind. This is also what gives Beardsley's writings inherent educational significance.

In view of the above it is not surprising that the conceptual problem Beardsley wrestled with more than any other is whether there is a kind of human experience we may appropriately call aesthetic that is not only sufficiently distinct from other kinds of experience but also important enough to warrant society's efforts to cultivate it. He was particularly interested in the possibility that works of art may be ideally suited to occasion such experience even though other things might also possess aesthetic capacity in varying degrees. Beardsley never took his success in answering these questions for granted and he usually expressed some dissatisfaction with his own analytical efforts. Although he modified details of his theory over the years, he held to the belief that the aesthetic value of art—its artistic goodness in contrast to its cognitive or moral value—consists of its capacity to induce in a well-qualified observer a high degree of aesthetic experience. Such experience is valuable for a number of its features but mainly for the special feelings of pleasure, enjoyment, satisfaction, or gratification it provides, the range of terms suggesting the difficulty of saying precisely just what sort of hedonic effect characterizes our commerce with art, although Beardsley came to prefer gratification.[7]

To say all this is to classify Beardsley's theory as a hedonistic one, but not in any simple sense. Aesthetic gratification is neither a general state of feeling well nor the kind of enjoyment that attends the informal congeniality of friendly conversation, partisan cheering at sports events, or participation in political activities. It is the kind of gratification derived from sensitively and knowledgeably experiencing outstanding works of art—a painting by Raphael, a piano sonata by Beethoven, a sonnet by Shakespeare.

What was perhaps Beardsley's last essay on aesthetic experience is contained in his *The Aesthetic Point of View*, published in 1982,[8] a collection of essays edited by two of his students. In this essay Beardsley asks us to consider a characterization of aesthetic experience having as many (or as few) as five features, although not all five must be present for aesthetic experience to happen. This is to say that aesthetic experience does not consist of a single pervasive quality, feeling, sensation, or emotion, but rather a cluster of features. It is this clustering that makes aesthetic experience both compound and disjunctive.

A compressed paraphrase of Beardsley's characterization of aesthetic experience could run as follows. In our aesthetic experience of an outstanding work of art attention is fixed on an object of notable presence whose elements, formal relations, aesthetic qualities, and semantic aspects are freely entertained. One indication of the presence of aesthetic character is the feeling that things are working themselves out in appropriate and fitting ways. Another indication of aesthetic character is a diminished concern about the past and future in favor of an intense engagement with what is immediately presented or invoked by the object. Aesthetic involvement further consists of a certain emotional distancing of the object that enables persons to rise above rather than to be overwhelmed by any tragic import it might have. The effect of detached engagement does not, however, deny the possibility of feeling exhilarated by the success of one's efforts to make conflicting stimuli cohere into formal patterns that are imbued with expressive qualities and human import. An experience that is notable for its feelings of object directedness, free participation, detached involvement, and active discovery may also result in feelings of personal integration and a greater acceptance and expansion of the self.

Beardsley acknowledges that aesthetic experience might well contain more or fewer features than his account of it indicates; the intention of his essay is to open up rather than close off a line of thought. But for all that may be experienced, felt, or learned through aesthetic experience, Beardsley believes that its unique value consists in the quality of gratification it provides. Rare, he says, are those stretches of time during which the elements of human experience combine in just these ways; when they do the state of being they constitute is one of gratified well-being. And we can only agree. When in the course of a typical day do we experience the stimulation, the sense of freedom, the controlled emotional involvement, the feeling of genuine discovery, the self-fulfillment that we tend to feel during the experience of a great work of art? Such a state of mind is a distinctive form of human well-being and therefore a part of a good or worthwhile life. It constitutes a significant realization of human value. It is by virtue of aesthetic experience, then, that Beardsley thinks works of art "realize their potentialities and serve as well in their fashion."

Harold Osborne: Aesthetic Experience as Intrinsically Valuable Perception

"To realize their potentialities and serve well in their fashion"— the words are Beardsley's but they could be those of Harold Osborne who believes that works of art serve us well by stimulating and expanding the powers of percipience.

What is percipience? In *The Art of Appreciation*, published in 1970,[9] Osborne assimilates percipience to aesthetic appreciation and experience. He understands the aesthetic experience of a work of art to involve the direction of attention over a limited sensory field during which the field's qualities are brought into focus according to their own inherent intensity, their similarities and contrast, and their peculiar groupings. Such perception is full and complete and proceeds without the kind of editing that characterizes our practical concerns and activities. The mental attitude assumed during aesthetic experience is further unlike that required for conceptual analysis or for the historian's rooting out of causes and effects; instead, aesthetic experience involves the exercise of integrative or synoptic vision. Identifying the representational contents of Picasso's *Guernica*, for example, is not the same thing as perceiving its fusion of subject, form, and expression in an act of integrative perception.

The kind of rapt attention that marks aesthetic interest also lends aesthetic experience a characteristic emotional color; its mood, Osborne thinks, approximates serenity even when the object being perceived has a dynamic character. It is further important to realize that because of our perceptual absorption in the object during aesthetic experience, our interest involves less a consciousness of our own feelings than an awareness of the object's qualities and properties. It is as if we live in the object itself. The demands of perceptual awareness and the obligation to see the object in its full complexity also tend to discourage mere idle musings and associations. Aesthetic experience thus has a characteristic rigor; imagination is required to comprehend a work's qualities but imagination is also held in check. Another feature of aesthetic experience is the priority of appearance over material existence. The fact that an object is a material thing existing in the world is of less interest than the imagery the material thing presents. Such imagery is suited to sustaining awareness in the aesthetic mode because it takes us out of ourselves into new worlds. Ego consciousness, however, never completely disappears; otherwise we would risk losing contact with the work's qualities and meanings.

Osborne reminds us that aesthetic percipience is exercised in many areas of human life, but he thinks that works of fine art and their counterparts in nature are capable of expanding it to its fullest. To repeat, at their best, works of art can extend the perceptive faculties and demand ever-increasing mental finesse to contain them. Central then to Osborne's theory is the heightened awareness of things felt during aesthetic experience. Such awareness not only makes persons feel more vital, awake, and alert than usual, it also allows the mind to work with a greater sense of freedom and effectiveness. And new discoveries are its constant reward.

In his argument for deliberately cultivating percipience for its own sake Osborne emphasizes that such cultivation has always been the motive for the expression of spiritual needs and aspirations. Whatever the ideology, liberation from life's material constraints for the purpose of realizing more fully and more freely one's humanity is a near-universal yearning and guiding ideal. The British art historian Kenneth Clark also believed that even in a predominantly secular society the majority of people still long to experience moments of pure, nonmaterial satisfaction and that such satisfaction can be obtained more reliably through works of art than through any other means.[10] This suggests that when we talk about the uses of art we must do so in a very special sense. Reason too, says Osborne, should be cultivated for its own sake, but reason characteristically finds its fullest outlet and expansion in philosophy, logic, mathematics, and the theoretical sciences.

Nelson Goodman: Aesthetic Experience as Understanding

In addressing the work of Nelson Goodman we confront ideas that originated in modern developments in the theory of understanding and the logic of symbolic systems. It is generally agreed that Goodman's perspective is not only novel but also has radical implications for understanding art. Regarding the importance of Goodman's work, Francis Sparshott likened the appearance of Goodman's *Languages of Art* to a shadow cast by a giant rock upon a dreary field, while Howard Gardner expressed the opinion that overnight Goodman single-handedly transformed aesthetics into a serious and rigorous field of study. Beardsley likewise acknowledged the enormous value of Goodman's aesthetic writings. Such encomia certify Goodman's stature, and there is no question that his major thesis—that art is essentially cognitive—has encouraged educational theorists to use his ideas to ground more firmly a justification of aesthetic education.

The central proposition of Goodman's *Languages of Art*[11] is that art is a symbolic system of human understanding and shares with other forms of inquiry, including the sciences, the human quest for enlightenment. Condensed accounts of Beardsley's and Osborne's ideas of aesthetic experience having been provided, here is how Goodman describes our engagement with art. "Aesthetic experience," he writes, "is dynamic rather than static. It involves making delicate discriminations and discerning subtle relationships, identifying symbol systems and characters within these systems and what these characters denote and exemplify, interpreting works and reorganizing the world in terms of works and works in terms of the world. Much of our experience and many of our skills are brought to bear and may be transformed by the encounter. The aesthetic 'attitude' is restless, searching, testing—is less attitude than action: creation and re-creation."[12]

In these words we detect what is shared with and what is different from the accounts of aesthetic experience given by Beardsley and Osborne. All three—Beardsley, Osborne, and Goodman—acknowledge that perception is dynamic, discriminating, and interpretive and that a person's view of the world may be transformed by aesthetic encounters. Goodman's account is distinguished by what he does and does not emphasize. Identifying symbol systems and characters within these systems has a technical meaning in Goodman's theory; it involves understanding the ways in which the characters of works of art denote and exemplify. Goodman's account of aesthetic experience does not feature any specific quality of gratification; he does not think that the criterion of the aesthetic is to be found in a superior quality or quantity of satisfaction. And though he emphasizes that in art the primary purpose is cognition in and for itself, he does not stress cognition for its own sake the way Osborne does. It is sufficient for Osborne that the cognition of art animate and strengthen the faculty of percipience. Goodman goes beyond this to stress the role of cognition in the shaping and reshaping of worlds, in short, in providing understanding. Goodman thus plays down the state of well-being and peculiar energizing of mind emphasized by Beardsley and Osborne. Instead, he places emphasis on the symbolic functioning of artworks and the enlightenment they yield. This is what constitutes the pedagogical relevance of his theory for aesthetic education.

In saying that works of art provide understanding, Goodman has in mind their capacity to make us see, hear, and read differently and to make new connections between things. And with this said some of the differences among Beardsley, Osborne, and Goodman begin to fade, although others still remain. We should also realize that Goodman's theory of art, although he uses the term "aesthetic experience," is less a detailed account of the nature of perceiving and appreciating works of art than an explanation of art's cognitive status. What Goodman calls the symptoms of the aesthetic—syntactical and semantic density, relative repleteness, exemplification, and multiple and complex reference[13]—are not aesthetic qualities but technical terms that refer to the functions of characters in a work of art construed as a symbol system. They explain how works of art, even nonrepresentational or strictly formal ones, denote and refer.

Eugene F. Kaelin:
Aesthetic Experience as Institutional Efficacy

The aesthetic ideas of Eugene F. Kaelin, presented mainly in articles, a monograph, and *Art and Existence* (1970),[14] constitute yet another philosophical perspective on the arts and aesthetic experience. Although Kaelin writes from a Continental existential-phenomenological point of view influenced by Sartre, Merleau-Ponty, Husserl, and Heidegger, the benefits of aesthetic experience he describes are similar to those described by Beardsley, Osborne, and Goodman. Works of art are good for the aesthetic experiences they provide, which in turn are good for the aesthetic communication that occurs and the intensification and clarification of human experience that take place. The satisfaction felt in successfully fusing the system of counters of a work of art (that is, a work's surface and depth features) constitutes the hedonic aspect of aesthetic experience, and in this respect Kaelin's resembles Beardsley's theory. Art's capacity to intensify and clarify human experience also accommodates Osborne's belief regarding an artwork's capacity to stimulate the powers of percipience for their own sakes. Although Kaelin's philosophical orientation is antithetical to Goodman's, Kaelin stresses precisely what Goodman does insofar as both writers value art's ability to present fresh perceptions of things. Indeed, an interesting result of the comparison and contrast of aesthetic theories is the discovery that ontological and epistemological differences do not necessarily affect the kinds of benefits derivable from the arts.

Noteworthy in Kaelin's aesthetics so far as this discussion is concerned is the value he places on human freedom and the ways in which the cultivation of the capacity for aesthetic experience through schooling is consistent with the free functioning of the institution of art. Aesthetic experience, in other words, has both personal and social value. A theory of aesthetic education thus helps to define the kind of individual any free society would wish to produce; such an individual is one who exemplifies the human values of tolerance, communication, judgment, and freedom in contrast to the disvalues of intolerance, dogmatism, conformity, and suppression. How, according to Kaelin, does aesthetic experience exemplify such values? The answer lies in understanding the ways in which aesthetic experience originates, unfolds, and achieves closure.

Kaelin describes how percipients when confronting works of art bracket out irrelevant considerations and create contexts of significance whose intrinsic values provide the material for immediate aesthetic experience. Attention to the presentational qualities of works of art involves perception of what is variously termed matter and form, subject and treatment, and local and regional qualities all of which are aspects of a work's surface and depth relations. Successful perceptual fusion of a work's system of counters results in

acts of expressive response that constitute the consummatory value
of aesthetic experience. In Kaelin's terminology "felt expressiveness" implies a sense of fittingness or appropriateness between surface and depth counters. A case in point is his description of the
counters of Picasso's *Guernica*. After indicating and interpreting the
work's various features, Kaelin writes that "so interpreted, our experience of *Guernica* deepens and comes to closure in a single act of
expressive response in which we perceive the fittingness of this surface—all broken planes and jagged edges in the stark contrast of
black and white—to represent this depth, the equally stark contrast
of the living and the dead."[15] What Kaelin calls a single act of expressive response is what Osborne calls an instance of synoptic or
integrative vision.

Once more the point of looking at notable works of art consists of
the worthwhile aesthetic experiences they afford, where worthwhileness consists of the value of aesthetic communication and the
exercise of perceptual skills and aesthetic judgment. All of this occurs in a context of significance governed by the intrinsic values of a
system of counters. Kaelin in effect offers his own version of Erwin
Panofsky's belief that a work of art is essentially a man-made object
that demands to be experienced aesthetically.[16] Works of art "come
to exist," writes Kaelin, "only in the experience of persons who
have opened themselves to the expressiveness of a sensuous surface
and allowed their understandings and imagination to be guided by
controlled responses set up therein."[17] Everything that we value in
the traditional ideal of liberal education is present in Kaelin's account of aesthetic experience, especially the notion that disciplined
encounters with excellence test, strengthen, and expand basic human powers.

One further aspect of Kaelin's idea of aesthetic experience deserves mentioning. A willingness to be guided by a work's context
of significance means that a work's value cannot be predetermined
or assessed on the basis of conformance to rule or ideology. The
method of phenomenological analysis takes its cues from the immediate givens of a work of art and assumes that value emanates from
a work's unique context of significance and not from the superim-
position of official and interpretive frameworks insensitive to intrinsic values. There is no knowing in advance what a work of art will
feature or what it might say of our relations to reality and to each
other. Aesthetic communication is thus essentially free communication. Through acts of artistic creation and appreciation, persons

choose their futures—in the first instance by creating new worlds of aesthetic value, and in the second by opening themselves to new possibilities of experience. Art thus serves Being by helping to realize human powers and potentialities that benefit both the individual and society.

Some Concluding Observations

I once more recall Osborne's belief that philosophers should address aesthetic questions with the advance and progress of humanity in mind. Not only Osborne but also Beardsley, Goodman, and Kaelin do this and hence provide material for a justification of aesthetic education.

Beardsley contributes to humanistic objectives and a solution to the justification problem by telling us how to distinguish superior from less excellent works; we do so by assessing their capacity to afford high degrees of aesthetic experience. By supplying criteria of aesthetic value, he helps us to discern those works that vitalize rather than anesthetize the mind.

Osborne contributes to humanistic objectives and the justification of aesthetic education by describing the quality of experience excellent art is capable of engendering, which he then contrasts to the impoverished experience afforded by amusement art. He further discriminates among styles of vanguard art and prefers styles that present significant new ways of viewing reality. He thinks that the art of Monet, Cézanne, Matisse, and Picasso, for example, is far more likely to endure than the work, say, of latter-day conceptual artists.

Goodman's powerful case for art's cognitive character has the effect of diminishing the distance between the two cultures of scientific and artistic understanding. This helps to establish the seriousness of aesthetic studies in a way that should make justifying aesthetic education less difficult. As Goodman puts it, in art (as in science) "the drive is curiosity and the end enlightenment"; the primary purpose "is cognition in and for itself; the practicality, pleasure, compulsion, and communicative utility all depend on this."[18] Under the direction of Howard Gardner and David Perkins, a research unit founded by Goodman at Harvard University in 1967 has been investigating the dynamics of artistic cognition in the creation and appreciation of art.[19]

Kaelin contributes to humanistic objectives and the progress of humanity by stressing the important role that art plays in establishing aesthetic communication among a free people. Artistic and aesthetic encounters exemplify the human values of openness, relevance, autonomy, and freedom, all vital to the efficacious functioning of the institution of art. Only a highly educated and aesthetically literate society can ensure that conditions of aesthetic freedom and communication will prevail and not be controlled by extra-aesthetic considerations.

One upshot of this discussion is a realization that it is not necessary for a theory of aesthetic education to decide one way or the other the question that Sparshott thinks is the only one that keeps aesthetics alive—the question of art's cognitive status. It is sufficient to appreciate the fact that in addition to providing occasions for aesthetic gratification, the stimulation of direct perception, and the intensification of expression, art also makes possible new perspectives on the world and self that constitute understanding of a sort. In comparing the accounts of aesthetic experience by the four theorists in question, I found little disagreement regarding the important values to be derived from contemplating works of art: works of art at their best afford a fresh outlook on the world that enables us to see the familiar in an unfamiliar light and to perceive new connections among things in light of which we organize and reorganize our experience of reality. Their individual philosophical orientations, methodological assumptions, and categories of description and explanation notwithstanding, all writers concur on art's capacity for human renewal.

We should not, of course, confuse the proximate and prospective values of art. Proximate values are the immediately felt qualities of aesthetic experience. Examples of prospective values are general percipience, imagination, and sympathetic understanding which it is reasonable to suppose a disposition to regard artworks aesthetically can strengthen. A goal of aesthetic education research is to understand better the connections between proximate and prospective benefits. What I call proximate and prospective values Beardsley calls intrinsic and inherent values, Osborne principal and subsidiary functions of art, and Kaelin aesthetic and nonaesthetic considerations. But a firm linkage between different kinds of values is not crucial to a justification of aesthetic education. One can argue convincingly that aesthetic experience is a special form of human awareness that serves individuals in ways other forms of awareness do not and that it accordingly contributes to the actualization of worthwhile human potential. A life bereft of aesthetic capacity is only partially fulfilled and it is a serious indictment of societies and their educational systems if they permit the young to pass through schooling without helping them to realize a significant part of their humanity.

All four theorists discussed in this article—Beardsley, Osborne, Goodman, and Kaelin—contribute to a theory of aesthetic education by virtue of their persuasive articulation of a number of art's functions. Such articulation is certainly one fundamental way in which philosophical aesthetics becomes relevant to a theory of aesthetic education. Indeed, Sparshott goes so far as to say that the principal reason for formulating theories of art is to help organize instruction,[20] but obviously numerous motives influence theorizing.

A few final words: Although a theory of aesthetic education may be influenced by several different perspectives on the nature and function of art, the ideas and theories chosen will be a function of individual temperament and current social conditions. Some educational theorists prefer a Goodman-like justification because it seems to bolster the case for arts education in the schools. Anything that promises understanding reinforces the educator's argument. However, a too exclusively cognitive interpretation of art's function risks overintellectualizing aesthetic education and underplaying the importance of personal participation so crucial to aesthetic experience. In words that perhaps cannot be repeated too often, Frank Sibly has emphasized that one always needs to see and feel things for oneself.[21]

The four theorists I've discussed are further important because they stress art's inherent nature and characteristic accomplishments. They all appreciate the peculiar energies of art and understand the ways works typically realize their potentialities. This is important at a time when so much theoretical writing overemphasizes the social and political uses of art. But when art and aesthetic education are interpreted principally in ideological terms the central business of art is undervalued. Virgil C. Aldrich has written "that the greatest art is formally expressive at once of materials on the one hand and of subject matter on the other, doing justice to both in a reciprocal transfiguration, each inspiring the other in the context of the composition."[22] Necessary qualifications and elaborations notwithstanding, especially in the case of works in which subject matter plays no part, this is the fundamentally aesthetic business and achievement of art. The more the subtle and precarious balance

among the relations of medium, form, and content is upset—as it is
with the inordinate intrusion of ideological concerns—the less like-
lihood a work has of achieving its full potential for expressive statement and aesthetic response.

It is not, I should add, that no connections at all are possible
between the appreciation of the intrinsic values of art and social
change or reform. Persons of cultivated aesthetic dispositions
should be ill-disposed toward tolerating assaults on human sensibility and the environment and inclined to strive to bring about a
higher level of culture and quality of life. Developing aesthetic sensitivity is not incompatible with acquiring a sense of social responsibility. But a single-minded concern with ideology and the political
uses of art corrupts the aesthetic imagination. In this respect, we do
well to recall the words of the historian Richard Hofstadter: "If
there is anything more dangerous to the life of the mind than having no independent commitment to ideas, it is having an excess of
commitment to some special and constricting idea." The intellectual
function, he said, and I would add the aesthetic function, "can be
overwhelmed by an excess of piety expended within too contracted
a frame of reference."[23] Partly for this reason I have accommodated
not one but four perspectives on the nature of art and its characteristic functions. To be sure, aesthetic theorists are correct to continue
the search for the essence of art, to distinguish art's primary and
secondary functions, and to express concern over hazy speculation.
I hardly underestimate the value of rigorous philosophical analysis.
Nonetheless there is an important truth in the words of Morris
Weitz, who says that it behooves us to entertain a range of aesthetic
theories because "their debates over the reasons for excellence in
art converge on the perennial problem of what makes a work of art
good."[24] I understand the theories of Beardsley, Osborne, Goodman, and Kaelin in this spirit, as contributions to the critical dialogue about excellence in art and aesthetic education.

NOTES

1. Harold Osborne, "The Twofold Significance of 'Aesthetic Value,' "
Philosophica 36, no. 2 (1985).

2. Eugene F. Kaelin, "Aesthetic Education: A Role for Aesthetics
Proper," *Journal of Aesthetic Education* 2, no. 2 (April 1968).

3. Francis Sparshott, *The Theory of the Arts* (Princeton: Princeton University Press, 1982), p. 484.

4. Israel Scheffler, *Of Human Potential* (Boston: Routledge and Kegan Paul, 1985), p. 5.

5. The discussions of Beardsley, Osborne, and Goodman draw substantially on my essay *Aesthetic Education in Modern Perspective* (Provo: College of Fine Arts and Communication, Brigham Young University, 1986).

6. Monroe C. Beardsley, *Aesthetics: Problems in the Philosophy of Criticism*, 2nd ed. (Indianapolis: Hackett, 1981). First edition published 1958 by Harcourt, Brace and World.

7. I have traced this shifting terminology in my "The Aesthetics of Monroe C. Beardsley: Recent Work," *Studies in Art Education* 25, no. 3 (Spring, 1984).

8. Beardsley, "Aesthetic Experience," in *The Aesthetic Point of View: Selected Essays of Monroe C. Beardsley*, ed. M. J. Wreen and D. M. Callen (Ithaca: Cornell University Press, 1982).

9. Harold Osborne, *The Art of Appreciation* (New York: Oxford University Press, 1970), esp. chap. 2.

10. Kenneth Clark, "Art and Society," in his *Moments of Vision* (London: John Murray, 1981), p. 79.

11. Nelson Goodman, *Languages of Art*, 2nd ed. (Indianapolis: Hackett, 1976).

12. Ibid., pp. 241–42.

13. Multiple and complex reference as a symptom was added by Goodman after *The Languages of Art* was published. See his note in *Ways of Worldmaking* (Indianapolis: Hackett, 1978), p. 67.

14. In discussing Kaelin, I draw on the following works: *Art and Existence: A Phenomenological Aesthetics* (Lewisburg, Pa.: Bucknell University Press, 1970); *An Existential-Phenomenological Account of Aesthetic Education*, Penn State Papers in Art Education No. 4 (University Park: Pennsylvania State University, 1968); "Aesthetic Education: A Role for Aesthetics Proper"; and "Why Teach Art in the Public Schools?" *Journal of Aesthetic Education* 20, no. 4 (Winter 1986).

15. Kaelin, "Aesthetic Education: A Role for Aesthetics Proper," p. 154; reprinted in R. A. Smith, ed., *Aesthetics and Problems of Education* (Urbana: University of Illinois Press, 1970).

16. Erwin Panofsky, "The History of Art as a Humanistic Discipline," in his *Meaning in the Visual Arts* (Chicago: University of Chicago Press, 1982; first published 1955), p. 11.

17. Kaelin, "Aesthetic Education: A Role for Aesthetics Proper," p. 155.

18. Goodman, *Languages of Art*, p. 258.

19. See Goodman's *Of Mind and Other Matters* (Cambridge, Mass.: Harvard University Press, 1984), chap. 5.

20. Sparshott, "On the Possibility of Saying What Literature Is," in *What Is Literature?*, ed. Paul Hernandi (Bloomington: Indiana University Press, 1978), p. 14.

21. Frank Sibley, "Aesthetic and Nonaesthetic," *The Philosophic Review* 74, no. 2 (April 1965): 135–37.

22. Virgil C. Aldrich, *Philosophy of Art* (Englewood Cliffs, N.J.: Prentice-

23. Richard Hofstadter, *Anti-intellectualism in American Life* (New York: Alfred A. Knopf, 1963), p. 29.

24. Morris Weitz, "The Role of Theory in Aesthetics," in his anthology *Problems in Aesthetics*, 2nd ed. (New York: Macmillan, 1970), p. 180.

MAXINE GREENE

Aesthetic Literacy

There is considerable doubt . . . whether "art" can ever be finally or conclusively defined. Every day new forms appear: minimal art; aleatory art; plotless stories; constructivist sculpture; pieces intended to shock and to surprise. None of the existing theories can account for such phenomena, although people continue to devise theories of art, even as they work out theories of beauty, harmony, organic unity. Certain theories in the past have focused on the relation of works of art of the universe or the forms of nature; others have explained art forms by their relation to particular artists, who have been thought to embody their personal feelings or perceptions of reality in poetry, painting, song.

Oedipus Rex, Hamlet, and Michelangelo's *David,* for example, have been partly accounted for by the ways in which they "imitate" or represent cosmic rhythms, forces, patterns, forms. Men and women have always been moved or ennobled or instructed by them, it is said, because they bring living beings in touch with something ultimate, with the "really real." Lyric poems, according to the expressive theories, exemplify something quite different: they bring readers in touch with the artist's emotions (recollected or present); they communicate in the dimension of sentiency. Expressiveness, in whatever form, is presumed to impart efficacy and power to the aesthetic experience. Directly or indirectly, percipients are brought in touch with artist' emotive lives; or they come to understand "the form of feeling"[1] by attending to their works.

There are other theories as well, alternative definitions: those that explain art in terms of the responses it evokes; those that center on the self-enclosed poem or painting or piece of music, upon its autonomy, its "significant form."[2] Still others direct attention to the hidden meaning in each work of art, something to be uncovered by a grasping consciousness; still others, to the ways in which a work presents itself to perception and is brought into existence as a work of art. There is today, however, a general agreement that no one of the theories mentioned can do more than disclose certain dimensions of or perspectives on the artistic-aesthetic. They function to draw attention to aspects of what is involved.[3]

The philosopher of criticism, Morris Weitz, believes that none of the theories succeeds in defining "art" once and for all, especially in the face of the fact that new forms are constantly challenging what we have "known" and taken for granted about aesthetic phenomena. He proposes, therefore, that "art" be treated as an "open concept" and that we think about *how* the concept should be used rather than expecting an answer to the question, "What, finally, is art?" And, indeed, there would seem to be a value in consideration of aesthetic theories, because they teach us "what to look for and how to look at it in art." Weitz goes on to say: "To understand the role of aesthetic theory is not to conceive it as definition, logically doomed to failure, but to read it as summaries of seriously made recommendations to attend in certain ways to certain features of art."[4] This is how teachers ought to read it—not for the sake of becoming aestheticians but for the sake of discovering the modes of attending they can associate with aesthetic literacy.

Most philosophers of art agree that one perspective is not enough. They presume that understanding is enriched when various, overlapping perspectives are used for examining the artistic-aesthetic domain. This does not exclude the necessity for locating specific modes of awareness in the artistic-aesthetic province of meaning. Nor does it diminish the importance of urging persons "to attend in certain ways" so as to bring aesthetic objects into existence as works of art. There is little question but that such attending enables people to see more, to take more into account. Art, as Herbert Marcuse has said, "breaks open a dimension inaccessible to other experience."[5] Doing so, it provides a vantage point on other experience, a standpoint from which to attend to patterns and nuances, to see what is ordinarily obscured. Joseph Conrad was exemplary when he wrote: "My task which I am trying to achieve is by the power of the written word to make you hear, to make you feel—it is, before all, to make you see. That—and no more, and it is everything."[6] Writing about Paul Cézanne, Maurice Merleau-Ponty said: "Cézanne, in his own words, 'wrote in painting what had never yet been painted, and turned it into painting once and for all.' . . . The painter recaptures and converts into visible objects what would, without him, remain walled up in the separate life of each consciousness."[7] He, too, makes the world visible; he, too, enables human beings to see. Meyer Schapiro, discussing modern painting, speaks of multiple new orders being created before our eyes, permitting us, if we are perceptive enough and free enough, to see forms we have never imagined before. And he goes on: "Only a mind opened to the qualities of things, with a habit of discrimination, sensitized by experience, and responsive to new forms and ideas, will be prepared for enjoyment of this art."[8]

"Will be prepared," says Schapiro. It appears to be the obligation of the classroom teacher to open minds in the way Schapiro describes, to empower young persons to discriminate and to respond. The point is that none of the arts makes itself naturally available for understanding and enjoyment. The visions so many critics describe, the dimension the artistic-aesthetic promises to "break open," can only be made accessible through some mode of aesthetic education, some stimulation of aesthetic literacy.

Teachers and students require a minimal cognitive familiarity with the symbol systems and with the cognitive style involved. Such familiarity may feed into the reflectiveness that deepens and extends experiences with art forms. Also, it enables persons to encounter works of art in their own spaces, on their own aesthetic terms. A painting is more likely to be enjoyed for what it enacts upon the canvas rather than as a representation of something outside in the world—a bather, say, or a viaduct, or a cafe scene; and it will not be seen as a mere illustration of something that can be better said in words. Understanding of this kind may enable persons to distinguish between the text of a poem and the notation required if a musical work is to be performed and therefore heard. Perceptual and imaginative awareness must be deliberately cultivated against the background of this understanding if Melville's "Bartleby the Scrivener" is to emerge as a fiction rather than as a case history, if Othello's passion is to be responded to in *Othello*'s dramatic space.

Such concepts as the concept of psychic distance or disinterestedness[9] ought to become familiar to those who come to witness a play like *Othello*, an opera like *Tosca*, or even *A Chorus Line*, so that audiences will become able to watch the enactments on the stage as enactments taking place, not in the ordinary, commonplace world, but in an alternate world, an aesthetic space. Without some acquaintance with the notion of "uncoupling" from the familiar and the inescapably personal, spectators cannot establish themselves in the special psychic relationship required for the achievement of *Othello*, *Tosca*, or any other enacted work as a work of art. Those who come to see a classical ballet or to hear a symphonic poem must know enough to break with ordinary expectations and affairs if the dance piece or the music is to enter their consciousness as art. This is not to be taken to mean that spectators must take an impersonal or detached view, that they must not be present as persons with a history. It simply means that mundane and practical interests ought not to be allowed to overcome the imaginative engagement with the works at hand. A memory of a jealous relative or a prejudice against Moors ought to be set aside if *Othello* is to be realized; so ought a resentment of kings and princes, or of aggressive women, be set aside if *Tosca* is to exist for the spectator as a work of art.

No one can be "trained" into this sort of awareness or what we are calling aesthetic literacy. It is not the kind of attainment that can be separated out into discrete "competencies." A kind of aesthetic education must be invented, therefore, that provides certain fundamental insights, certain ways of proceeding; but its emphasis must be on releasing learners to attend in such a fashion that they are moved to go further on their own initiative, to begin teaching themselves as they uncover (through repeated readings, viewings, hearing) particular works, and as they move more and more deeply into the province of the arts.

Aesthetic Educating

A teacher who attempts to educate with such ends in view ought to be perceptually and imaginatively involved with several of the arts and have experience with shaping the raw materials of at least one into something approximating an expressive form. It would help to experiment with writing short poems or paragraphs of imaginative prose, to experiment with the sounds emitted by a recorder. It would certainly help if teachers were familiar enough with their own physical beings to experience some degree of body response when attending to a ballet they wish to make accessible to students. To say all this, however, is equivalent to saying that all practicing teachers ought to feel alive and in the world, excited about their subject matter, even in love with some of it. To say this is equivalent to saying that teachers need to keep their own questions open, continually to break with "created structures," striving to move beyond.[10]

What, then, can such a teacher do to enhance students' opportunities to achieve aesthetic literacy? It is important, first of all, to realize that the domain of the aesthetic is more far-reaching than the world in which works of art exist. Everyone has some memory of sunsets, moon-flecked woods, snowy streets, children's hands. An awareness of certain aesthetic concepts (distancing, let us say, shape, timbre, form) may move an individual teacher to uncouple certain phenomena from the context of ordinariness and to perceive them aesthetically: a black tree shape on a winter day; the texture of a flower petal; the wind moving the leaves. In the effort to enhance perceptual acuity among students, the teacher might urge attending to the appearances of things around them in unaccustomed ways. If teachers can enable the students to detach what they see and hear from its use value for a time, from its mundane significance, the students may be brought in touch with shapes, masses, shadings, tonalities of which they are hardly likely to have been aware.

The weight of the flagstones making up a wall, the deepening green on the playing field, the wail of a railway whistle: these are the kinds of qualities a teacher might bring into the field of attention. They are attributes of actual objects and events that may be made to appear intrinsically interesting and expressive when heeded in a certain way. Not only may this provoke certain persons to heightened attentiveness. It may introduce them to the idea of the qualitative, an idea focal to aesthetic literacy. It may, in some cases, permit a return to some original landscape, what William James called "the world of living realities" that he identified with "that sense of our own life which we at every moment possess." He said that the world (that landscape) is "the hook from which the rest dangles, the absolute support."[11] It is the world in which human beings are aware of the qualities that underlie and ground the logical properties they devise, the scientific judgments they make. They come in touch with these, it well may be, when certain suggestive notions direct their retinal viewing, when they are enabled to uncover their qualitative worlds.

This mode of attending, of qualitative perceiving, is fundamental to aesthetic literacy. No matter how the concept "art" is understood, the notion of perception always has a central role to play. For a long time, it was believed that perceiving entailed a passive taking in of images and shapes and sounds that later would be conceptually ordered into a pattern. According to this view, a person might see a dancer's body flashing through space, circles of light, the curve of an arm, the lift of a leg. Then one would work mentally to organize the disparate sense data in order to give them meaning, to interpret what had been sensed as dance. Or, contemplating an oil painting, a beholder might single out a red apple, a fold of drapery, a china vase, and only later pattern the disparate parts into an organized whole. It is now known that perceiving must be understood as an active mode of grasping the structures of the world of appearances, or what is otherwise called the "phenomenal" world.

We grasp the painting or the dance as a whole, fused with whatever meaning is imparted to it, depending upon our past experiences and the expectations those experiences have raised. It is our "subsidiary awareness," writes Michael Polanyi, that endows an object or an event with meaning.[12] In the case of an oil painting, we have a subsidiary, almost an unconscious awareness of colors, lines, contours to use as visual clues. We attend *from* those clues *to* the forms of apples, folds of drapery, wallpaper patterns that make up the picture before us, the painting of which we are focally aware. We would be unable to endow it with meaning as a painting were it not for our tacit awareness of colors, lines, contours, and the rest.

More is required, however, if we are to perceive the painting as a work of art. It might be said that the painting as a work of art was created for precisely the kind of perceiving described above: the perceiving of the qualitative, of the appearances of things. In that respect the work (like all other works of art) is what we have called a privileged object when compared to the flagstone wall or the green playing field or the whistle of a train. It is an object or event that can be brought into being as a work of art if those who attend to it are capable of a special sort of noticing, of apprehending, of personal grasping. The object or event is a selection from the world as perceived, the shaped and colored and sounding world in which we live our lives. It is the kind of selection that must be located in what we have called aesthetic space, in part created by the intensity of the qualities of the medium involved.

The painting may, of course, be examined for its chemical composition, its weight in pounds, its worth in dollars, the history of its ownership. If it is to be achieved as a work of art, however, it must be treated as an object made for a certain *kind* of perceiving. Unlike the chalkboard or the office wallpaper or the flagstone wall, it offers itself in a distinctive way to the body and mind of the person who is interested in it sufficiently to make it the object of his or her own perspective. Also, unlike the chalkboard and the wallpaper and the flagstone wall, the painting is likely to disclose more and more of its qualities or its perceptual attributes the more often and more attentively it is viewed. The range of visual clues may be extended; the teacher (or the students) may point out colors, contours that were not visible at the beginning, that cannot be seen from a single perspective. The more clues, the richer the subsidiary awareness; and the more opportunities exist for attending from visual details to forms, folds, patterns, nuances, shadows, glimmers of light.

Even if one chooses to apprehend a painting or a dance piece as an emotional communication through the medium of color and movement, or as an imitation of something large and representative in the surrounding world, one is still required consciously to attend if the painting or the dance or the poem is to be realized as a work of art, no matter how "art" is defined. Dewey has written about the "work to be done on the part of the percipient" with respect to all aesthetic forms. "The one who is too lazy, idle, or indurated in convention to perform this work will not see or hear. His 'appreciation' will be a mixture of scraps of learning with conformity to norms of conventional admiration and with a confused, even if genuine emotional excitation."[13] Like many other students of aesthetic experience, Dewey was suggesting that an appropriate stance must be taken and that persons must live up to certain norms of perceiving if works are to exist for them as aesthetic objects.

Ernst Gombrich has also laid stress upon the mind's constitutive acts and upon the importance of "mental sets."[14] For him, there can be no such phenomenon as the "innocent eye," either on the part of the artist or a person who succeeds in realizing an object as a work of art. All art, he writes, must be understood as illusion; it always involves image making and transformation. The transformation takes place through the use of certain "cryptograms," largely to be understood in terms of other symbols used in other works. We come to works of art, he writes, "with our receiver already attuned. We expect to be presented with a certain notation . . . and make ready to cope with it."[15] Our expectations are set up by previous experiences or by acquaintance with certain styles; and there are occasions when we are prevented from either seeing or interpreting because our expectations interfere.

The implications for aesthetic education are considerable. Not only ought young persons (in association with their teachers) be provided a range of experiences in perceiving and noticing. They ought to have opportunities, in every classroom, to pay heed to color and glimmer and sound, to attend to the appearances of things from an aesthetic point of view. If not, they are unlikely to be in a position to be challenged by what they see or hear; and one of the great powers associated with the arts is the power to challenge expectations, to break stereotypes, to change the ways in which persons apprehend the world. George Steiner has written that "Rembrandt altered the Western perception of shadow spaces and the weight of darkness. Since Van Gogh we notice the twist of flame in a poplar."[16] We can say the same about alterations in our vision due to the work of writers ranging from Shakespeare to Sartre, alterations in our hearing due to composers from Bach to Schoenberg and John Cage. The point is that such perspectives do not open up spontaneously. The capacity to perceive, to attend, must be learned.

There is also the capacity to imagine. There is the whole matter of imaginative awareness, an awareness that is also required if works of art are to be achieved. Imagination has long been conceived as a mode of effecting relationships, bringing (as Virginia Woolf once put it) "several parts together,"[17] making metaphors, creating new integrations and unities. Perceiving affects the patterns, the configurations of what we see; but imagination transforms what is perceived. Gombrich gives an example of the work of imagination in one of his discussions of impressionist painting when he explains how "the beholder must mobilize his memory of the visible world and project it into the mosaic of strokes and dabs on the canvas" when he sees a Monet painting. And he points out that "the willing beholder responds to the artist's suggestion because he enjoys the transformation that occurs in front of his eyes."[18] Without imagination, there could be no image creation on the part of the beholder; nor could there be the transformations that any art form allows.

The same thing happens when imagination goes to work on the language of poetry: on Robert Frost's "woods on a snowy evening," T. S. Eliot's "dry brain in a dry season." There is Melville's white whale to conjure up; there are the derelicts in Beckett's *Waiting for Godot*, Willy Loman in *Death of a Salesman*, Blanche DuBois in *A Streetcar Named Desire*. Any of these ought to evoke the capacity to transform, to build imaginary worlds in the course of doing so, worlds alternative to the worlds of everyday. Doing so, we may recognize the sense in which we all stand against a world of possible forms. It is imagination that puts us in relation to such possibilities, when imagination is stimulated by engagement with the arts. Dorothy Walsh has said that works of art, confronting us as physical things and as cultural products, are at the same time "imaginative vistas out of the actual." She went on: "To enter into the contemplation of a work of art is to pass through the context of the actual to the appreciation of a unique, discontinuous possibility."[19] The poet

Wallace Stevens has made all this dramatically clear in his poetry: in, for example, "Thirteen Ways of Looking at a Blackbird" and "The Latest Freed Man." In the latter poem, he writes of a man who is wearied of familiar and old descriptions of the world and who suddenly finds a banal landscape becoming meaningful to him because he sees it so differently when it is imaginatively described.

> It was how he was free. It was how his
>   freedom came.
> It was being without description, being an ox.
> It was the importance of the trees outdoors,
> The freshness of the oak-leaves, as the way
>   they looked.
> It was everything being more real, himself
> At the center of reality, seeing it—
> It was everything bulging and blazing and big
>   in itself.[20]

Not only does the poem illuminate the transformations of reality provoked by imaginative activity. It makes clear the idea that aesthetic perception is a mode of viewing that can only be *personally* undertaken, by an individual present to himself or herself. To be "at the center of reality, seeing it" is to grasp what surrounds from one's own center and, in so grasping, to be conscious of one's consciousness. It is in this sense that the artistic-aesthetic domain brings us in touch with our authentic visions, allows us—as unique individuals—to be.

Again, this can only happen if a person is interested in an aesthetic object or event, if one can become absorbed in its qualities for a time for their own sakes. Melvin Rader, discussing the transforming effect of imagination, has made the point that one phase of the imaginative mode of awareness is "attentional." He meant that imagination (in one of its phases) permits us to focus disinterestedly on an object, to distance it, and, by distancing, to grasp the painting or the poem or the sonata "in its full qualitative richness and imaginative fecundity."[21] In another phase, the "elaborative" phase, we elaborate the experience made possible by our focusing. This elaboration is a "moody and imaginative mode of vision for the enrichment of the intrinsic perceptual value of the object."[22] It is at this point that the object or event is in some fashion incarnated. But there would be no such significant personal experience if it were not for the capacity to focus, to attend; and we have made the point that that capacity can be learned.

There is among certain educators the view that children are naturally imaginative, and that oppressive social structures serve to tramp down and frustrate their creative energies. Recent research indicates that young children tend to be literalists, and that young adolescents show themselves to be even less imaginative than when they were in the early grades.[23] Persons are clearly born with the capacity to see and hear, taste and feel; but they do not, simply through maturation, develop the ability to use such capacities. Whether this is because our culture discourages this development, or because the kinds of social conditioning provided results in its deflection, the fact is that attention needs to be paid in all kinds of classrooms if children are to effect the connections and make the transformations associated with imagining. Situations must be devised to make possible the recognition and invention of metaphors. Storytelling, the writing and reading of poetry must be encouraged, even as young students are learning how to look and how to see. The ability to categorize in various ways and to transfer schemata between realms is as relevant to scientific thinking as it is to the appreciation of art.[24] Artworks and art activities, it appears, may be useful and illuminating in many kinds of learning.

The artistic-aesthetic cannot, therefore, be identified only with the emotive or the intuitive. There is no question but that informed engagement with the several arts enables persons to explore experiential possibilities they never imagined before. To perceive, to imagine new possibilities of being and action is to enlarge the scope of freedom for the individual; and, when people work to open new perspectives together, they may even discover ways of transforming their lived worlds. Students may become increasingly familiar with the symbolic characteristics of the several arts without finding the arts wholly reduced to the cognitive. They may be freed to apprehend works of art through their feelings without finding them reduced to noncognitive forms. Emotion may be a means of discovering the properties and qualities of many kinds of art; but, without some acquaintance with their languages, people may become incapable of interpretation, of making sense of art *qua* art. Moreover, it might be difficult for them to make appropriate distinctions among the arts. To identify a painting with a written text and to attempt to "read" the painting as if it were a poem would be to falsify. But once students and their teachers are enabled to recognize the languages of both painting and poetry, once they understand that Rembrandt's or Rothko's cryptograms cannot be translated into Baudelaire's or Debussy's or Beckett's, they must bracket out or put aside certain of their formal understandings. Only then can they respond to the summons of particular works, narrow their attention, permit them to inhabit their consciousness. Only then are they likely to value them as created realities made for their appreciation and to hear, to disclose, to see.

Herbert Marcuse, exploring such experiences, writes that the languages and images found in works of art make perceptible, visible, and audible that which is no longer or not yet "perceived, said, and heard in everyday life. Art makes the petrified world speak, sing, perhaps dance."[25] To be petrified is to be granite-like, susceptible neither to learning nor to change. If the artistic-aesthetic can open up the petrified world, provide new standpoints on what is taken for granted, those who are empowered by their teachers to engage with the arts may find themselves posing questions from their own locations in the world and in the light of what they themselves are living, what they themselves are discovering to be warranted, to be true. This is because engagements with works of art—aware, informed engagements—make individuals present to what is given to them, personally present, no longer lulled by the natural attitude. And it is those who can ask their own questions, ask them in person, who are the ones most ready to learn how to learn.

The classroom teacher and the general educator are challenged to open up a new province of meaning for those they teach, a province that may be opened to them through the doing of philosophy with respect to the several arts. They are asked to make possible the enlargement of experience that can only derive from informed engagements. At a technological moment, when so many forces are working to thrust persons into passivity and stereotyped thinking, the open-mindedness and the sense of exploration fostered by aesthetic involvements may well move diverse individuals to break with "the cotton wool of daily life."[26] To break with ordinariness and stock response is, at any age, to achieve a new readiness, a new ripeness. Not only will there be an awareness of things in their particularity, of beauty and variety and form. There will be a fresh orientation to the search for meaning in the many spheres of life. And this, fundamentally, is the point of aesthetic literacy. People may be brought to watch and to listen with increasing wide-awakeness, attentiveness, and care. And they may be brought to discover multiple ways of looking at blackbirds and whales and riverbanks and city streets, looking at things as if they might be otherwise than they are. If this occurs, they will have learned how to move into the artistic-aesthetic domain; and they may have come closer to discovering how to be free.

NOTES

1. Susanne K. Langer, *Problems of Art* (New York: Scribner's, 1957), p. 88.

2. Clive Bell, *Art* (London: Chatto and Windus, 1914).

3. Morris H. Abrams, *The Mirror and the Lamp* (New York: Norton, 1958), pp. 3–8.

4. Morris Weitz, "The Role of Theory in Aesthetics," in *Problems in Aesthetics*, ed. Morris Weitz (New York: Macmillan, 1959), p. 155.

5. Herbert Marcuse, *The Aesthetic Dimension* (Boston: Beacon Press, 1978), p. 72.

6. Joseph Conrad, Preface to "The Nigger of the 'Narcissus,' "in *Three Great Tales* (New York: Modern Library Paperbacks, n.d.), p. ix.

7. Maurice Merleau-Ponty, "Cézanne's Doubt," in Maurice Merleau-Ponty, *Sense and Non-sense*, trans. Hubert L. Dreyfus and Patricia A. Dreyfus (Evanston, Ill.: Northwestern University Press, 1964), pp. 17–18.

8. Meyer Schapiro, *Modern Art: 19th and 20th Centuries* (New York: George Braziller, 1978), p. 232.

9. See Edward Bullough, "Psychical Distance as a Factor in Art and an Aesthetic Principle," in *The Problems of Aesthetics*, ed. Eliseo Vivas and Murray Krieger (New York: Holt, Rinehart, and Winston, 1965), pp. 393–405.

10. Maurice Merleau-Ponty, *The Structure of Behavior* (Boston: Beacon Press, 1967), pp. 160–66.

11. William James, *The Principles of Psychology*, vol. 2 (New York: Dover, 1950), p. 207.

12. Michael Polanyi, "Sense-Giving and Sense-Reading," in *Knowing and Being*, ed. Marjorie Greene (Chicago: University of Chicago Press, 1969), p. 184.

13. Dewey, *Art as Experience*, p. 54.

14. E. H. Gombrich, *Art and Illusion* (New York: Pantheon, 1965), p. 60.

15. Ibid., pp. 39–41.

16. George Steiner, "The Kingdom of Appearances," *New Yorker*, 4 April 1977, p. 132.

17. Virginia Woolf, *Moments of Being*, ed. Jeanne Schulkind (New York: Harcourt Brace Jovanovich, 1972), p. 72.

18. Gombrich, *Art and Illusion*, p. 202.

19. Dorothy Walsh, "The Cognitive Content of Art," in *Contemporary Studies in Aesthetics*, ed. Francis J. Coleman (New York: McGraw-Hill, 1967), p. 297.

20. Wallace Stevens, "The Latest Freed Man," *The Collected Poems* (New York: Alfred A. Knopf, 1964), p. 204. © Alfred A. Knopf. Reprinted with permission.

21. Melvin Rader, "The Imaginative Mode of Awareness," *Journal of Aesthetics and Art Criticism* 33 (Winter 1974): 136.

22. Ibid.

23. See Howard Gardner, "Promising Paths towards Artistic Knowledge: A Report from Harvard Project Zero," *Journal of Aesthetic Education* 10, nos. 3–4 (July-October 1976): 201–7.

24. Howard Gardner, "Sifting the Special from the Shared: Notes toward an Agenda for Research in Arts Education," in *Arts and Aesthetics: An Agenda for the Future,* ed. Stanley S. Madeja (St. Louis, Mo.: CEMREL, 1977), pp. 267–78.

25. Marcuse, *The Aesthetic Dimension,* p. 73.

26. Woolf, *Moments of Being,* p. 70.

E. F. KAELIN

Why Teach Art in the Public Schools?

When it comes to answering questions, art educators have always been better at their staples, such as What should we teach? To whom? and In what sequence? than at finding some kind of answer to the question superintendents of schools find still more basic, Why teach art at all? In the grips of any imaginable budget crunch no one charged with making the decision would continue to face his or her constituency with no better answer to this one than the supposition that artworks and the arts are nice to have, like flowers on madame's Easter bonnet or the lights on a Christmas tree. We think we know why, in every move back to the basics of education, we strengthen our instruction in reading, writing, and basic mathematics. These core studies are necessary for entrance into the study of the sciences, where the knowledge produced has that rare capacity of exhibiting on its face the very social utility it is the business of public education to promulgate. Why couldn't we argue that teaching art in the public schools is good for enhancing our society's culture? Indeed, we might, but we couldn't let it go at that. For either we are engaging in tautologies, which give us no information, or we continue to assume that culture is some kind of good in itself, concerning which it is bootless to pose the question of utility.

Do we mean by "culture" only the making and appreciating of works of art in the various media? If so, we have the tautology. If culture is a good in itself, questioning its utility deserves the same kind of response Louis Armstrong is reported to have given the aficionado when asked, "What is jazz?" "If you have to ask, you will never know." Puritans ask, because they fear the "immorality" of art; so do Philistines, who find it useless in an economy of personal power; as do our proletarian common folk, who see in it only a personal luxury, good only for the idle rich.[1]

In what follows, I shall argue the paradoxical case, that what is good about the arts is the aesthetic experiences they provide—the case of art for the sake of art—in an attempt to show that society stands to gain most by allowing its institutions to function freely, as they are designed to function, for the purpose of liberating the human impulse to masterful self-expression.

Perhaps a little bit more quickly than it should have been, my hand has been played. Art does have a function, and more than one at that; just as sex has a function, and more than one at that. If George Bernard Shaw could refer to marriage as the most licentious of our institutions, he had in mind the power of the institution to liberate the libidinal energies of the people who enter into it by contract for that specific purpose; and no one who understands the arrangements permitted by the contract is shocked by the comedian's insinuations. His barb is comic only because it states an ultimate truth concerning our society and the place of individuals seeking fulfillment within its institutions, that these have been established for the purpose of permitting the achievement of deeply felt personal values—sexual gratification in this case—at the same time society stands to gain for the regulation of behavior that, outside of the institutionally permitted framework, may have disastrous effects for that society, such as an increasing teen-age pregnancy rate and the corresponding increase in abortions, foundlings in need of homes, or young women tied as single parents to the nurture of their offspring.

These consequences, like some others mostly medical, such as the increase in uncontrollable sexually transmitted diseases, call for social control in other institutions: in the courts, where women's rights to control their own bodies may someday be settled; in the procedures for adoption; in improved day-care centers; and, finally, in the profession of medicine in all its functions: in the healing and prevention of disease and in the basic research which makes the other two possible.

Can there be an "institutional definition of art"? And what would be its consequences for art education? For the second time in this essay, I shall cite the aesthetics of DeWitt H. Parker: "Since . . . art is a social phenomenon, we shall have to draw upon our knowledge of social psychology to illumine our analysis of the individual's [aesthetic] experience."[2] The question comes down ultimately to the relations between an individual's impulse to action (of a certain type) and the set of institutions within our society that give form to this impulse.

It may come as a surprise to some students of aesthetics to be reminded that Parker's suggestion was made as early as 1920, the year of the first edition of his *Principles of Aesthetics*. He, of course, was intent upon describing the necessary psychological component within the study of aesthetics and sensed that the "mental facts" of the aesthetic discipline were influenced by the habits and customs of groups to respond in correlatively similar ways to apparently similar stimuli. I mention the fact almost in passing; for the irony of the matter is that it fell to a student of Parker, the late Morris Weitz, to produce the impetus for the current drive toward an "institutional definition of art."

The move was curious in that Parker's initial essentialism was reflected in Weitz's early *The Philosophy of the Arts*,[3] in which the author argued for an "organic theory of aesthetic expression." In spite of the success of that treatise, Weitz fell under the influence of Wittgenstein, following a tour to England, and published the essay that was to determine a new direction of aesthetic inquiry in American letters. He argued, in "The Role of Theory in Aesthetics,"[4] that art was an open concept and hence could not be defined by a set of necessary and sufficient conditions that would govern its use in a theoretical context; consequently, all attempts at aesthetic theorizing, including his own prior attempt, should be interpreted as so many suggestions of what might be found in our cursory examinations of works of art, which, like "games," would exhibit a nest of characteristics possessing "family resemblances" between one another, but never an essential characteristic shared by everything so called.

It was Maurice Mandelbaum, responding in general to the Wittgensteinian confusion of "exhibited" and merely "relational" characteristics of works of art, who examined the various forms the notion of the open concept of art had taken in recent analytic aesthetics. He criticized the work of Paul Ziff, imputing to him an implicit theory of art in his identification of Poussin's *Rape of the Sabine Women* as an obviously good work of art; of Weitz, for confusing the issue of defining works of art with foreclosure on the use of a concept; and of P. O. Kristeller, for his confusion of the issue of a possible classification of the arts with the possibility of a variable aesthetic theory.[5] Of all these criticisms, it was the distinction between "exhibited" and "nonexhibited" or relational characteristics that produced the theoretical consequences of note.

Two primary examples of these consequences are so similar that they have become interpreted as a single theory. I am referring, of course, to the so-called "Danto-Dickie institutional theory" of art.

Danto had appealed to the "relational" characteristics of artworks as differentiating between impostures and fakes on the one hand and copies on the other, and between both of these and original works of art. He reasoned that if there were no necessary and sufficient conditions for the correct employment of an aesthetic concept, there seemed to be at least two "defeasible conditions" for attributing (or ascribing) the condition of art to certain artifacts. For example, if the artifact is a fake painting, it is essentially not a work of art; it does not deserve the name, since "it makes no artistic statement." Likewise, if the artifact is not the product of an artist but of a child, a chimpanzee, or a copyist, it should not be considered a work of art. What makes art of an artifact is its entrance into the "artworld," the institutional complex within which bona-fide works of art receive the ascription of art much in the same way as a child becomes a "Christian" at baptism. That an artifact be considered a work of art, even in the classificatory sense of the term, means only that someone has conferred upon it by the outward sign of entry into the artworld that inner state of grace that stems from the work's making an artistic statement.[6]

Accepting the fact that the status of being a work of art may be conferred by the relational properties of certain artifacts to enter into socially determined relationships, George Dickie propounded his own "institutional definition" of a work of art.[7] Although he at first thought that even artifactuality could be conferred upon a work of art, since some *objets trouvés* were admitted by the artworld to be authentic works of art without having been specifically fashioned into the form in which they were exhibited as such, Dickie later insisted that the classificatory genus of artworks was indeed their artifactuality (since any change in the context within which such works are exhibited changes the very nature of the object viewed in the newer context), and in consequence that only the special status attributed to some artifacts by members of the artworld has been socially conferred upon works of art—just as the baptized infant changes from a state of original sin to a state of acquired grace for the passage of the cleansing waters. The point here, as at the baptismal font, is only that someone authorized to make the conferral has indeed conferred the proper status upon the subject or object in question. For artifacts, what is conferred is the status of being a "candidate for appreciation." The two additional characteristics of aesthetic objects beyond their generic artifactuality are: conferral of the status by someone speaking in the name of the artworld, and the candidacy of the artifact as worthy of appreciation. Together, they constitute the specific difference needed to complete the canonic form for an Aristotelian definition.

I do not wish to confute the claims made by the Danto-Dickie theory of art, nor to question why our theoretical definitions need take an Aristotelian form. I merely wish to point out that no one has yet attempted, to my knowledge, to reap the full benefits of an institutional account of artworks. The new approach, as indicated above, grew out of the frustrations felt by aestheticians to come up with a viable definition of any sort for works of art. What Dickie found in Danto was, as he called it, the beginning of the third phase of the problem of defining art, a change from the "dreary and superficial definitions" of the pre-Wittgensteinian aesthetic theorizing (phase I) through the absolute denial of the possibility of a theoretical definition, as in Ziff and Weitz (phase II). The gambit which opened phase III had already been set up by Mandelbaum's criticism of phase II of this historical development within traditional aesthetic theory.

Perhaps Dickie's greatest obstacle was the opposition of his colleagues to accept the term "institution" in the way he insisted it should be employed, i.e., as an established practice, law, or custom. If he is right, what makes works of art works of art is the network of behavioral patterns by which they are made (their artifactuality) and by which their status as artworks has been conferred upon them, beginning with criticism and (sometimes) ending in exhibition in a public place, where an audience may repair to appreciate them, even to judge whether a mistake had been made by the initial conferral of status. But such a judgment is obviously only another example of artistic criticism, as informed or uninformed as it may be.

We may generalize on Dickie's definition, it seems to me, by postulating the existence of an aesthetic institution, whether we call it "the artworld" or not, that is similar in structure to religious, educational, legal, medical, and like institutions, which have as their purpose both to permit and to regulate the behavioral patterns constituting the formal practices of producing, criticizing, exhibiting, and appreciating works of art. In this way, the work of art is viewed as the vehicle by which the aesthetic motivations of individuals come to be expressed in a social context. Making the work of art constitutes a gesture (of establishing its artifactuality); responding to one gives it its aesthetic significance, as recorded in the conferral of its status. When, moreover, the person making the gesture and the person perceiving it respond in similar ways, we may say that communication has taken place.

Danto, we recall, thought it was necessary for a work of art "to make a statement"; his analysis of the "artworld" indicates that making an artistic statement is no simple matter, but requires a series of roles, each defining the other in their relationship, which allow individuals to enter into the social fabric of human institutions where their behavior becomes mutually communicative and significant. Indeed, what we call a "society" is from one point of view—the social interactionist—a nexus of such institutions making overlapping and sometimes conflicting claims on the behavior of individuals pursuing the values embodied within the practices permitted by the institutions. George Bernard Shaw may have been right, but we had already learned all the theoretical background to his jibe by reading G. H. Mead's *Mind, Self and Society from the Standpoint of a Social Behaviorist.*[8]

It is at this point that art educators may pick up the thread. In one sense, of course, we must educate both teachers and students of the arts to perform according to their various roles in the schools, themselves institutions of our society. What I am proposing is that we allow the students to play the role of artists, to make something of interest to them that may be of interest to someone else. The aesthetic institution exists for the purpose of creating the maximum of aesthetic value. But "making an artistic statement" or making a gesture that is to become a candidate for aesthetic appreciation necessitates the complementary role of critic. That is the role proper to the teacher, whose appreciation must be informed with a set of workable aesthetic categories, not only out of fairness to the student artist, but also as a guarantee for the effectiveness of his or her own participation in the communicative process.

By way of illustration, consider the range one might find in student works. It is certainly to be expected that this range will already have been exhibited in the history of the art under consideration—from totally nonobjective works exhibiting only the Gestalt properties of sensuous elements; to superrealistic works that attempt to represent natural objects such as they appear to our natural perception; to "abstract" works, in which natural objects are represented in such a way as to emphasize the sensuous values of the medium used to make the representations. All these may be "candidates for our aesthetic appreciation," but it seems nothing but fair, on the part of our teachers, that they be able to explain the categories they have used to make their critical judgments. Aesthetics, as the criticism of criticism, and art history make their formal entry into the aesthetic education process at this point.

For those readers already familiar with the movement, it should be clear that my institutional account gives some credence to the new "discipline-based art education" program now being developed by the Getty Center for Education in the Arts. That program considers four arts-related disciplines to constitute the domain of art education: art production, art history, aesthetics, and criticism. A "discipline" is given the contextual definition as being constituted by three component elements: (i) a corps of expert practitioners, (ii) a body of knowledge and concepts, and (iii) a formalizable set of principles for making an inquiry into the domain of art.

But it seems clear upon reflection that the four disciplines mentioned above exemplify these three components in uneven and different ways. We can avoid the charge of making art production look too much like the other "arts-related" disciplines—especially with respect to their rule-governed behavior—if we merely agree to take the institutional point of view according to which the producers of art participate in the aesthetic institution by playing a distinctive role, and that this role finds its complement in the roles of critic, aesthetician, and historian.

One simple change is being requested—that we stop envisaging ourselves as "experts," whose educational practice is to teach a subject discipline. What we actually do is to teach students, either children or adults, with the aid of a complementary set of knowledge bases, each of which has been established by a history of codifiable behavioral practices. That is what makes it possible for them to become functioning roles within the aesthetic institution.

What then would be the purpose of promulgating the aims of the aesthetic institution in the public schools?

If social interactionism may be introduced as the theory by which our educational practices are to be justified, the answer now seems clearer, if not totally perspicuous. Promoting the conditions for the creation and appreciation of novel significances within the aesthetic institution will have educational benefits no other "discipline" can provide so well. Let us only agree that we learn by doing something, and that doing something in repeated patterns produces a habit. We conclude that the good of aesthetic education is the habits it inculcates. And what are these?

Consider only two further characteristics of the process.

First, that aesthetic activity engages our sensibility, not for its own sake, but for its connection with the vague feelings controlled by the subtle tonal differences perceptible by our senses; that it engages our imaginations to view objects and ideas under the guise of the manner in which they have been represented in successful works of art, and so to control our depth feelings associated with the objects of our natural environment. But, whether the artwork be nonobjective, representational, or to some degree "abstract," the value of experiencing such objects is the enjoyment of feelings, either of a vague or depth nature, only as these feelings are controlled by the vehicle of perception.

There is a whole theory of aesthetics embedded in these assertions, without a doubt. But what that theory allows us to perceive is that the ultimate social product of the aesthetic institution is not more works of art, even as candidates for our appreciation, but the type of person capable of appreciating works of art with the appropriate critical attitude. For want of a better term, I call such persons "defanaticized." The value of a defanaticized consciousness to the general society, when that society is democratic, seems as patent to me as that of the research scientist whose work allows us to solve the problems of our everyday living by making clear what results can be expected to follow upon sets of given conditions.

My second consideration is merely to point out that pursuing art for art's sake is the same as to allow the free function of the aesthetic institution within our society. Like all other institutions, it is both permissive and regulatory: it permits the maximal pursuit of novel significance, and it regulates the way in which such significance comes to be appreciated, through informed criticism.

At this stage I hope I have made my case that teaching art in the public school makes perfectly good sense, if only we view it as an institution by which complementary social roles guide individual conduct. The habits promulgated within this institution are nowhere else so readily attainable, so that to exclude the arts from the curricula of our schools is to deprive ourselves of an obvious social good—a wider range of citizens capable of whatever kind of behavior is permitted by heightened sensitivity, imagination, and the depths of feeling experienced under conditions of perceptual control. Why Plato should have wished to make philosophers kings after having banished the poets from his ideal society I could never understand. Was it a bad theory of art, as representation of real objects? A bad theory of criticism? Or merely a bad theory of justice? In my estimation, it was a little bit of all three.

Since I have already gone on too long, I can hope to do no more in the space remaining to me than to indicate that an institutional view of aesthetic behavior not only gives an answer to the question why we should promote it in our public schools, but likewise goes a long way to show the best way for how this is to be done.

In a word, we shall have to begin—and to end by—teaching our students how to play the aesthetic education game, how to enter into their roles, and what expectation it is rational to bring to their performances. We must stop teaching the subject matters of our disciplines and start teaching students to behave in the ways prescribed by the aesthetic institution with the matters of our disciplines, be they art history, art criticism, or aesthetics. The creative process itself is a discipline only in the sense that its limits are prescribed by both subjective and objective conditions: by the force of an artist's imagination, and by the qualities of some medium of art to be transformed by the artist's skill to present a novel significance to our critical appreciation.

NOTES

1. See DeWitt H. Parker, *The Principles of Aesthetics*, 2nd ed. (New York: F. S. Crofts, 1947), pp. 271ff.

2. Ibid., p. 7.

3. Morris Weitz, *The Philosophy of the Arts* (Cambridge, Mass.: Harvard University Press, 1950).

4. Morris Weitz, "The Role of Theory in Aesthetics," *Journal of Aesthetics and Art Criticism* 15, no. 1 (September 1956): 27–35.

5. See Maurice Mandelbaum, "Family Resemblances and Generalization Concerning the Arts," *American Philosophical Quarterly* 2, no. 3 (July 1965): 219–28.

6. The simile is suggested by George Dickie in "What Is Art?: An Institutional Analysis," reprinted in *A Modern Book of Esthetics*, 5th ed., ed. Melvin Rader (New York: Holt, Rinehart and Winston, 1979), pp. 459–72. For two accounts of Arthur C. Danto's theory, see his "The Art World," *Journal of Philosophy* 61, no. 19 (October 1964): 571–84; and "Artworks and Real Things," *Theoria* 39 (1973): 1–17.

7. In the above-mentioned "What is Art?: An Institutional Analysis," by George Dickie; and, more recently, in his *The Art Circle: A Theory of Art* (New York: Haven Publications, 1984).

8. G. H. Mead, *Mind, Self and Society from the Standpoint of a Social Behaviorist*, ed. Charles Morris (Chicago: University of Chicago Press, 1934).

ALAN SIMPSON

The Usefulness of *"Aesthetic Education"*

This essay derives from two things; first my long-held interest in the idea of "aesthetic education" and secondly, my impression that the term (or similar terms such as "aesthetic subjects" or "aesthetic development") is being used with increasing frequency in this country but without the benefit of much serious examination.[1] There are some exceptions, such as Elliott's article . . . in which he discusses the dangers of "aestheticism,"[2] but in other instances there is considerable confusion. To some extent the term "aesthetic" has, in sociological jargon, been "legitimized" by its use in [Department of Education and Science] publications,[3] but in some cases it carries positive connotations and in others negative ones. I believe that the conception "aesthetic education" merits consideration and is worth more than cavalier and vague application which merely renders it vulnerable to "takeover."[4] It should not be assumed from these remarks that I am going to set matters straight by producing a strict definition of the term; I wish simply to examine some of its applications and connotations and the extent to which the concept may be useful. Thus, for example, "intelligence," "initiation," "child-centered education," and "liberal education" have been *useful* in a variety of ways and in various degrees; in focusing critical attention on standard assumptions of such things as educational purpose, learning, methodology, in bringing fresh impetus to research,[5] and in functioning as regulative ideas for education.[6] This last use seems to me to be particularly important. Regulative ideas or principles inform, control, and modify our practices which, to that extent, are theory-laden, whether such principles are explicitly formulated, undisclosed, or even covert assumptions of which we are unaware. Some conceptions are especially fascinating in that they are at one and the same time both cautionary and inspirational in character. On "creativity" Elliott writes as follows:

In reflecting upon it we relate the ideas of freedom, founding, innovation, progress and autonomy to education. It reminds us that education is concerned with the development of energies which will
transform the material and moral environments, yet it suggests also
that education is for the sake of the individual soul—that it is not
in the students' interest for them merely to gain the world. It proclaims the strength of the spirit against necessity. If we allow it
to become associated with narrow, unimaginative aims and with
achievements which are too exclusively materialistic it has the power
to call us back from our error. Its chief value lies in its inspirational
force and its capacity to make us reflect on the connection between
the nature of education and the meaning of life. Despite its "unfinished" character it functions as a regulative idea for education. Such a
concept can have "usefulness" that goes beyond mere precise, practical applicability.[7]

My purpose is to consider whether "aesthetic education" may claim
to have similar usefulness.

First, it must be acknowledged that "aesthetic" is often an ambiguous and elusive term. The narrow version confines its use to the
contemplation of form, rather as Roger Fry attempted to discuss the
formal properties of paintings separately from what he called their
"literary" aspects.[8] But the broader version, although it demands
disinterestedness, i.e., an attention free from prejudice and fixed
ideas,[9] does not insist that the only appropriate object of attention
is form; representation, expression, narrative, social comment, psychological insight, technique are all subsumed or "embodied"[10]
within a holistic approach which, crucially, remains attention to the
object for its own sake. When "aesthetic" is joined with "education" the ambiguities are compounded: we have immediate uncertainty as to whether "aesthetic education" is concerned only with
the arts (and we need to specify what we include in the "arts"), or
whether it is to have a wider application across the curriculum.
Therefore I shall look very briefly at some accounts of "aesthetic
education" and without claiming to exhaust the possibilities, categorize them crudely as follows.

(1) The "comprehensive" view which sees an aesthetic element
or dimension not only in the arts but in every domain of human
life, and so sees "aesthetic education" as a fundamental part of *all*
education.

(2) The "unitary" view which sees the aesthetic as that which
gives the arts their distinctive character as *arts*, while not denying
the individuality of each particular art form.

(3) The "kaleidoscopic" view which does not see the aesthetic as singularly essential but as one of a number of equally important focuses that may be brought to or developed within the arts.

(4) The "peripheral" view which awards the aesthetic only minor significance, subordinate to other aspects of the arts in education.

The last category need not detain us long as, by definition, it allows limited usefulness to the aesthetic. On this view, attitudes and practices in the teaching of the arts are dominated by other emphases, e.g., development of practical skills and technical accomplishment, self-expression, social awareness, or therapeutic experience. It is not uncommon to find the aesthetic conflated with the historical, and its claims supposedly met by a small proportion of the available time being allocated to some sort of historical survey.

Perhaps the preeminent example of the "comprehensive" view of "aesthetic education" is that of Herbert Read, who challenges the style and form of education in general.[11] He rejects the traditional disciplines or subjects in favor of a curriculum deriving from concepts of "mind" and "organic development" which rely heavily on the psychology of "types."[12] Read suggests four broad headings (drama, design, dance, and craft) under which all, or most, of the various aspects of conventional subjects are subsumed and integrated in all manner of "creative activities." Thus education is seen as a process analogous to that of art, or of play. It is not that children must constantly be painting pictures, but that all their activities must have a broadly aesthetic form or character. Read sees this as the most natural, balanced mode of education, free from arbitrary and restrictive systems that, in his view, inhibit development of the individual as a whole. There is a strong moral tenor throughout Read's work which insists that the fullest development of each individual is vital in a truly democratic society. Art or art-type activities not only ensure the psychological balance of the individual, but are also *aesthetic* education in that they are interest-free in the sense of being apolitical or free from dogma.

We may sympathize with Read to the extent of recognizing that there are aesthetic elements such as economy and elegance in all subjects and that appreciation of these qualities is highly desirable; but this does not mean that the subjects should be taught *like* art, or by means of art. Secondly, there seem no obvious reasons why aesthetic aspects should be given overriding importance in subjects other than the arts. Thirdly, Read is in danger of applying "aesthetic" so extensively as to render the term vacuous. Finally, to give it such exaggerated importance that it dominates the whole of education does not seem justified.

In the "unitary" version, the arts are fundamental to "aesthetic education," the central examples being drama, dance, music, literature, and the visual arts. This position is unequivocally stated by Harry Broudy, who considers the aesthetic to be one of a number of value domains,[13] each having intrinsic qualities and extrinsic, instrumental roles in relation to the other value domains; both the intrinsic and the extrinsic features of the arts are the proper concern of "aesthetic education."[14] Like Read, Broudy regards the aesthetic as an inherently basic feature of human life but does not share his faith in a "natural" aesthetic insight; on the contrary, Broudy maintains that without deliberate teaching, the capacity for aesthetic experience will remain dormant or even regress to the lowest, commonplace level, and will be subject to the conformist, manipulative pressures of the "media," "popular taste," and commercial exploitation.[15]

The basic aim of aesthetic education is to initiate children into the serious arts in order to enable them to operate within the "languages" of the several art forms. His emphasis in programs for the arts in general education (i.e., within a common curriculum) is on the development of perceptual skills and critical awareness, rather than on artistic performance or "art appreciation." He states, "The goal of aesthetic education is to prevent stereotyped perception and judgment. . . . If a predetermined response to the work of art is insisted upon, there can be no aesthetic education, for there can be no aesthetic experience."[16] Although he thus stresses the importance of direct experience and individual decision-making, nevertheless his approach represents a "classical" view, i.e., one which emphasizes criticism, culture, and standards, all of which are contained in his notion of "connoisseurship." His view is open to attack from the "romantic" standpoint, with its counteremphases on self-expression, plurality, and subcultures.[17] Typical charges made against the classical view from this perspective are those of "elitism," denial of "community" arts, whether indigenous or ethnic, and of supporting the bourgeois establishment and therefore being inimical to the creative expression of "the people."[18] It is not my purpose to enter this ideological battleground. The point about the "unitary" view of aesthetic education is that it attempts to provide an overarching conception for the arts in education which, unlike some other justificational positions, does not rely on the claim that the arts arouse or express emotion.

The most recent attempt, in Britain, to establish the case for the arts as a coherent group within the curriculum is that of the Gulbenkian Report, *The Arts in Schools*.[19] It is founded on the classic cultural-epistemic proposition "that human rationality comprises a number of different *forms* or *modes* of understanding and communication through which we interpret and make sense of ourselves, of others and of the world itself."[20] The authors seem to equate these modes (or "intelligences and feelings") with traditional areas of the curriculum and state that "the aesthetic and creative . . . is exemplified by the arts."[21] However, "the aesthetic and creative" had already been identified in a DES paper as one of the "areas of experience" that should form an "essential" part of a curriculum for all pupils.[22] In making out a case for *all* the arts the authors were clearly trying to forestall such threatening assumptions as the "taster" notion that *one* of the art forms would suffice to provide the requisite experience.[23] The Gulbenkian Report, as per its brief, attempts to give a comprehensive overview of the arts in schools, but in endeavoring to take account of the multivariate nature of the arts (and of society) it becomes the prime candidate for our "kaleidoscopic" category.[24] Thus the aesthetic is one aspect among many such as the moral, cultural, creative, psychological, and recreational. There is strong general argument for the arts but no especial advocacy of "aesthetic education" as a unifying conception. Although "aesthetic and creative" are claimed to be fundamentally important, a whole chapter is devoted to the latter but considerably less attention is paid to the former.

I have already rejected the "comprehensive" version of aesthetic education as being too catholic to be genuinely useful. In the "kaleidoscopic" view, its use is, I suspect, too uncertain and vague to be considered secure as a regulative principle. The "unitary" view remains as that which sees "aesthetic education" as the conception that should give the arts their distinctive character, and this is the view I shall try to support. I should stress that I am not concerned here with methodology, nor do I suggest that an account such as Broudy's is the definitive one, but perhaps before proceeding further I should consider one or two counterarguments.

One of the most serious of these arises in the DES assessment of a performance discussion document which was published in 1983 and entitled, somewhat ironically, *Aesthetic Development*. Whilst this brief document is concerned with the possibilities of national assessment monitoring, nevertheless its authors justify their decision to concentrate on the arts by pointing to the distinction between "artistic" and "aesthetic," and in particular to a broad cross-curricular application of "aesthetic" which would be unmanageable in assessment terms. Such pragmatism is not unreasonable, but unfortunately the authors insist on imbuing "artistic" with great import and reducing "aesthetic" to trivia. It is stated that

> Artistic experience is not simply a matter of pleasure or entertainment, from which there is nothing to be learned. This indicates a crucial difference between the aesthetic and the artistic, and is one of the most important educational reasons for the Group's decision to concentrate centrally on the arts. (There is a very common misunderstanding which often underlies the prevalent and serious undervaluing of the contribution of the arts to society generally.) Involvement in the arts can extend and deepen the capacity to learn about oneself; it can give increasing perceptiveness and insight about almost every aspect of life and the world around us. (p. 3 para. 3.2)

The imputation of mere "pleasure and entertainment" misrepresents the "aesthetic"; and to elevate the "artistic" to such an exalted plane as the authors do is unwarranted. Experience of any kind, religious, scientific, moral, aesthetic, or artistic, *may* be slight and of little significance even to ourselves, but may equally be profound and enrich our personal insights and sharpen our perceptions of the world in general. None has a special prerogative here. The instrumentalist justifications for the arts are not without substance; they can, and do, lead to "good" outcomes. But there is an embarrassingly large amount of evidence to support an entirely opposite view.

A more casual objection to the "unitary" notion of "aesthetic education" is to point out that the Gulbenkian approach, for example, is not greatly dissimilar and has the advantages of being more flexible and less ambiguous. Why therefore insist upon "aesthetic education" rather than the expression "the arts in education"? But "arts" and "arts subjects" are by no means unambiguous terms;[25] "art" can simply mean a highly developed skill, and, in academic circles, "arts subjects" still means English, History, Philosophy, etc.—those subjects deriving from the seven "liberal arts." The difficulties are demonstrated at a practical, administrative level in schools by the number of titles one finds for very similar groupings of subjects in "faculties" such as "creative and technical subjects," "expressive and performing arts," or simply "design." Similar uncertainties come to mind in other groupings under headings such as "liberal studies" and even "European studies." It does not seem unreasonable to argue that "aesthetic education" identifies subjects at least as clearly as "the arts in education" or "artistic education," and, further, it gives a particular characteristic emphasis. "The arts in education," with its stress on doing, favors the conception of the arts as productive skills, and so of Literature as "creative writing." However, criticism is taught through Literature more than through any other subject, and "aesthetic education," while it includes artistic production, *attaches no less importance* to reflection and to the development of critical skills. From a practical, pedagogical point of view, the usefulness of "aesthetic" lies in its very openness. It may function in the narrow sense if we wish to concentrate attention on formal properties, for example, or more broadly if we wish to consider wider aspects of a work. Music and Literature are obvious though perhaps misleading examples here, for we *choose* the narrow or wide application of the term according to its appropriateness to the particular work, rather than by reference to the art form to which the work belongs: aesthetic attention is singular, not generalizable, and cannot be delineated within a precise boundary.[26]

It may not be a wholly popular move to assert the value of "aesthetic education" because it emphasizes appreciation as an autonomous discipline. Attitudes to the whole battery of responses, criticism, analysis, and insights that go to make up appreciation are ambivalent and uneven. It is still commonplace in such areas as the visual arts and drama to find a commitment to self-expression to which any notion of critical appreciation is anathema. And there is the complaint that English studies are dominated by "lit-crit" at the expense of creative writing. Whatever sort of balance teachers work out, it is fruitless and misconceived to prescribe some arbitrary proportioning of these aspects. The force of "aesthetic education" is that the appreciative and the creative are crucially interrelated. However loose or Romantic the conception of what it is to be highly creative, ranging from the insistence on a thoroughly cognitive process to that of the outpouring of feelings, there is the built-in assumption of a penetrative critical awareness. As his work progresses, the artist is constantly making critical decisions, making adjustments, discarding some ideas and developing others; and although he may be unwilling or unable to articulate such judgments—indeed it may be strongly argued that attempts to do so are inevitably counterproductive—nevertheless he actively *appreciates* the effects of what he is doing. The popular stereotypes of the scientist crying "Eureka!" and of the artist working furiously in his garret rely on their ability to recognize the flash of insight or moment of inspiration when it occurs. But there is plenty of evidence of the critical rigor of acclaimed creative artists in their preparatory studies: many Beethoven manuscripts, for example, Picasso's sketches for *Guernica* or, say, Dylan Thomas's very many drafts for *Fern Hill*. These provide graphic illustrations of the demandingly critical nature of the artist's creative activity. The other side of the coin of the appreciative-creative relation is the positive view that sees appreciation as a dynamic, creative, or re-creative act of perceptual awareness by the observer. Thus appreciation is not just static acceptance, or unquestioning adulation; neither is it merely destructive criticism based on prescriptive criteria, but imaginative, critical involvement with the work and, as such, it is a *skill* that we learn.[27]

Immediacy of involvement with the work is essential, for second-hand aesthetic experience is a contradiction in terms. Although appreciation may involve a great deal being said, the experience of the work cannot be entirely superseded by talk. Sensitive and well-informed commentary is very helpful in preparing us for a work, like program notes at a concert, but no description, whether scrupulously factual or imaginatively interpretative, can take the place of the experience of the work; no matter how good the description may be, there remains an ineffable residue. This dimension of "silence" is what Denis Donoghue called the "mystery" of art.[28] As Wittgenstein said, "There are indeed things that cannot be put into words. They make themselves manifest."[29]

An immediate objection might be to ask how any teacher can hope to penetrate the "silence" of the work of art. But our acknowledgment of art's mystery does not mean that we must therefore abandon the notion of "aesthetic education," for what cannot be said can be shown. A great deal of the armory of teaching is employed to enable pupils to *see* things for themselves. In drawing attention, in pointing to qualities and relationships, we use demonstration, comparison, explanation, and also gesture and other less formal means, to show pupils what is there in the object. To recall the analogy with "creativity," acceptance of the notion of creativity neither commits us to any particular kind of teaching nor guarantees that every industrious student will achieve creativeness, but this does not diminish the concept's usefulness. Aesthetic experience and sensitivity are similar to creativity in these respects. Nevertheless, "aesthetic education" carries with it the idea that the capacity for aesthetic experience, and aesthetic sensitivity, can be developed.

Two related and currently dominant views in the philosophy of the curriculum concern "value" and "knowledge" in that (i) certain pursuits are seen as being inherently worthwhile in themselves and (ii) they constitute ways of knowing or modes of experience that are available by no other means.[30] If it is incumbent that the arts be justified primarily for their intrinsic value, then "aesthetic education" ought to be the regulative principle underlying their teaching in educational institutions. Without the notion of aesthetic experience and the correlative notions of aesthetic qualities and values, the idea of the autonomy of art, and with it that of distinctive artistic standards, are very difficult to sustain. If such things as expression, historical accuracy, moral or religious import, psychological insight are given priority, then art is made instrumental to these external ends. Although many works have such features, the standing of any object as a *work of art* is reliant on its aesthetic qualities and on our unconditional, unprejudiced attention to the work for its own sake. Similarly, unless the aesthetic is central to the arts in education then, inevitably, their chief functions will be to serve as vehicles for other ends.

My final point arises from the peculiar nature of aesthetic judgment which distinguishes it from practical, moral, or any other kind of judgment. Aesthetic judgment is preeminently a *free* judgment: it is made directly and independently by the individual without any indulgence or conscious striving on his part either for mere sensuous gratification or for the conceptual categorization which is entailed in our normal, everyday articulation of experience.[31] Strictly speaking, it is purposeless, free not only of prospects of utility, whether relevance for job training or moral improvement, but also from exploitation of the "Admass" kind which preys on such things as vanity, envy, and the desire for social status. Of course, such a conception is vulnerable in numerous ways. It may be subject to "takeover," as in the current moves to make art education "relevant" by converting it to "design education." Secondly, it may be objected that "freedom" may become mere license, as in the anarchy that has typified much of twentieth-century arts.[32] Thirdly, it may be argued that the notion of "aesthetic disinterestedness" is too tainted with the élitism of a social structure in which the rich upper class enjoyed their leisured freedom at the expense of the working class. Nevertheless, to assert the value of aesthetic perception and judgment is to cherish a mode of perception and awareness not enslaved by expediency or obligation and is a celebration of the freedom to enjoy and value something for its own sake. In Donoghue's words: "In one way the arts are quite useless: they won't cure a toothache. But in another way they are really momentous, because they provide for spaces in which we live in total freedom."[33] The aesthetic lawfulness against which this freedom operates does not carry the same necessity as logical judgments, nor does it carry the aura of sanction that surrounds moral judgments.[34] A person committing an immoral act is likely to feel guilt or at least will want to keep his action secret, whereas a person is hardly likely to suffer similar qualms because of a lapse in taste. It is not surprising that common attitudes to the arts are often ambiguous or even antipathetic, nor that the "serious" subjects dominate at their expense. But their "playfulness" is, paradoxically, their strength as well as their weakness: individual freedom is crucial to aesthetic judgment and it is this, and the sense of it, which must underpin any notion of aesthetic education.

Summary

In this essay I have tried to examine the idea of "aesthetic education" and to consider its usefulness. There are many questions I have ignored, such as what distinguishes someone who is aesthetically educated, and I have not attempted to give anything like a phenomenological account of aesthetic education. Instead I have looked very briefly at some conceptions of "aesthetic education," rejecting all save that which makes it the central, regulative principle of the arts in education. Although, as I have argued, the idea does have pedagogical usefulness, its value "goes beyond mere precise, practical applicability."[35]

The analogy with "creativity" is nevertheless limited; although "aesthetic" may be widely applied, it is not so useful across the whole curriculum as "creativity" is.

"Aesthetic education," however, does have usefulness for the arts in education, for three main reasons.

(i) It emphasizes contemplative, critical reflection and articulate, dispassionate judgment as well as the importance of direct acquaintance. It does not reject creativity, but it brings a balance which is lacking when the arts are thought of as solely "creative activities"— where in practice it is common to find an uncritical passion for doing, with teachers engaged in an increasingly frenetic search for novelty in materials and ideas, and for yet more new "activities."

(ii) It provides a justification for the arts as autonomous and worthwhile pursuits within the curriculum.

(iii) It values a mode of perception and judgment that is free of utilitarian needs and which, along with the capacity for rational thought and moral action, goes to distinguish human beings. Indeed, in their very "uselessness" the arts celebrate man's freedom.

Such reasons patently overlap with reasons for the place of aesthetic education within education as a whole. It is also important to recognize that the notion is open to abuse and to dangers such as a retreat into "aestheticism." But to endorse "aesthetic education" does not mean that other, more clearly instrumental aspects of the arts must be decried or eschewed. I would argue that they need to be remembered if the concept is to achieve its full educational credibility; and, perhaps above all, "aesthetic education" is useful insofar as it makes us reflect on the relationship of education both to the meaning and the quality of life. As Schiller reminded us, scales balance when they are full as when they are empty.

NOTES

1. "Aesthetic education" is well established in the U.S.A. where the idea has been more thoroughly examined than in [Great Britain], thanks largely to the work of Ralph A. Smith, founder-editor of the *Journal of Aesthetic Education*, at the University of Illinois.

2. R. K. Elliott, "Aestheticism, Imagination and Schooling: A Reply to Ruby Meager," *Journal of Philosophy of Education* 15 (1981): 33–42. The pejorative connotations of "aestheticism" are also picked up by M. S. Lindauer, "Aesthetic Experience: A Neglected Topic in the Psychology of the Arts," in D. O'Hare, ed., *Psychology and the Arts* (Sussex: Harvester Press, 1981). At the outset of his paper Lindauer clearly wishes to separate "aesthetic" from "aestheticism."

3. E.g., DES (1980) *A View of the Curriculum* (London: HMSO); DES (APU) *Aesthetic Development*, 1983.

4. R. K. Elliott, "Versions of Creativity," *Proceedings of the Philosophy of Education Society of Great Britain* 5, no. 2 (1971).

5. This point is made by J. Freeman, H. J. Butcher, T. Christie, *Creativity: A Selective Review of Research* (Society for Research into Higher Education, 1968).

6. Elliott, "Versions of Creativity."

7. Ibid.

8. R. Fry, *Vision and Design* (Harmondsworth: Penguin, 1937).

9. I have borrowed here from Hume's point about prejudice in his essay on taste and, of course, from Kant's "determinant concepts" in the *Critique of Judgment*.

10. L. Arnaud Reid, *Meanings in the Arts* (London: Allen and Unwin, 1969).

11. H. Read, *Education Through Art* (London: Faber, 1943).

12. It is remarkable how many psychologists Read refers to or quotes directly, and many of them, e.g., Kretschmer, Sheldon, Galton, put forward theories of personality in terms of "types."

13. H. S. Broudy, *Building a Philosophy of Education* (Englewood Cliffs, N.J.: Prentice Hall, 1954).

14. H. S. Broudy, *Report on the Aesthetic Education Project* (Spencer Foundation, 1982).

15. A similar point is made with some force by P. Abbs, *Reclamations* (London: Heinemann, 1979).

16. H. S. Broudy, "Tacit Knowing and Aesthetic Education," in R. A. Smith, ed., *Aesthetic Concepts and Education* (Urbana: University of Illinois Press, 1971).

17. I am indebted here to D. Jenkins, "Romantic and Classic in the Curriculum Landscape," in *Curriculum Philosophy and Design* (Milton Keynes: Open University Press, 1972.

18. There are several examples of this or similar views, e.g., S. Braden, *Artists and People* (Henley: Routledge and Kegan Paul, 1978), and R. L. Taylor, *Art, an Enemy of the People* (Sussex: Harvester Press, 1978).

19. Calouste Gulbenkian Foundation, *The Arts in Schools*, 1982.

20. Ibid., p. 19.

21. Ibid., p. 20.

22. DES (1977, 1979), *Curriculum 11–16* (London: HMSO).

23. A tightly argued version of this assumption is implicit in Hirst's advocacy of the use of paradigm cases; see "Liberal Education and the Nature of Knowledge," in R. D. Archambault, ed., *Philosophical Analysis and Education* (London: Routledge and Kegan Paul, 1965).

24. This categorization is somewhat similar to Lanier's "mosaicist" view; see V. Lanier, "The Five Faces of Art Education," *Studies in Art Education* (USA), 18, no. 3 (1977).

25. In *The Fontana Dictionary of Modern Thought* (London: Fontana/Collins, 1977), the editors, A. Bullock and O. Stallybras, bring under "arts," "A variety of pursuits whose definition has been for centuries a stumbling block to aestheticians and encyclopaedists alike."

26. This point is made convincingly by R. Wollheim in *Art and Its Objects* (London: Harper and Row, 1968), see especially section 39.

27. H. Osborne, *The Art of Appreciation* (London: Oxford University Press), chap. 1, "Appreciation as a skill."

28. D. Donoghue, "The Arts without Mystery," BBC Reith Lectures 1982, reprinted in *The Listener*, 11 November–16 December 1982.

29. L. Wittgenstein, *Tractatus Logico-philosophicus*, 6.522, trans. D. F. Pears and B. F. McGuiness, 2nd ed., 1971.

30. See, e.g., R. S. Peters, *Ethics and Education* (London: Allen and Unwin, 1966); P. H. Hirst, "Liberal Education"; Gulbenkian Report.

31. I am indebted to Harold Osborne for this point.

32. See, e.g., J. Barzun, *The Use and Abuse of Art* (Princeton: Princeton University Press, 1974); B. Martin, *A Sociology of Contemporary Culture Change* (Oxford: Blackwell, 1981).

33. D. Donoghue, "Arts without Mystery," lecture 6.

34. This point is made by R. Scruton, *Art and Imagination* (London: Methuen, 1974), chap. 16.

35. Elliott, "Versions of Creativity."

DAVID BEST

Questions

Value

[A]rtistic appreciation is a fully rational activity in that the judgments involved are supportable by reasons. The objection is sometimes raised that even though judgments of meaning and interpretation may be open to rational discussion, these are irrelevant to the central issue, since the *real* problem of artistic appreciation is that of value judgments.

It is clearly implausible to contend that interpretation is irrelevant to evaluation since it is impossible to evaluate a work unless one understands it. For instance, one's evaluation may change if one comes to recognize that it has ironic or other subtleties which one had previously failed to appreciate. Moreover, some evaluative judgments are obviously incompatible with certain interpretations.

More important . . . evaluative judgments cannot be differentiated in this respect since they are also open to rational justification. It should be noticed that the nonrational responses or attitudes which underlie reasoning involve evaluations. Responses of wonder, delight, excitement, and disappointment, for instance, are clearly evaluations of their objects, and these responses and evaluations may change on reflection, or as a result of recognizing the cogency of reasons for a different point of view. Thus arts education, for instance, is inevitably concerned with the education of value judgments; with what counts as good within the particular art form. Surprisingly often one encounters scepticism about the rationality of a certain area of discourse or activity on the grounds that values are involved in it. Yet to be inducted into *any* subject, discipline, or area of knowledge *is* to learn to grasp its criteria of value. One has, for instance, to learn what counts as good, better, or worse reasoning or evidence, and clearly to judge evidence as good and reasoning as weak *is* to evaluate. Thus one could not be said to understand a subject unless one had learned to evaluate by its criteria. Moreover, as Holland puts it:

Those for example who profess enthusiasm for everything in music
from Bach to boogie must actually be indifferent to music or interested in it solely as a diversion, otherwise it would matter to them
what kind of music they heard. . . . How much a person cares about
a pursuit, whether it means much or little to him is attested by the
liveliness of his appreciation of the distinction between the superior
and the inferior in that *genre*, between the genuine and the faked, the
impeccable and the slipshod.[1]

Discussing the long history of philosophers, especially of the empiricist tradition, who have persistently misconstrued value-judgments as mere subjectivist feelings or intuitions, in sharp contrast
to those areas of knowledge which supposedly deal in value-aseptic
logic and facts, Bambrough writes:

Value, far from being contrasted with fact and logic as swamp with
firm ground, or little sister with big twin brothers, is more fundamental than either. . . . Neither logic nor history nor physics nor
philosophy nor any other sphere in which this is *preferred* to that,
where one view may and must be compared in *soundness* with another, where reasons may be adjudged good or bad, strong or weak,
can be a point of vantage from which a philosopher may look down
on the concept of value, unless we talk of looking down to mark the
necessary but rare recognition that here if anywhere is the bedrock in
search of which so many philosophers have scanned the sky.[2]

It is surprising how persistent is the assumption that evaluation
is purely subjective. For instance, people sometimes say: "Oh, that's
just a value-judgment," as if nothing more can be said since, it is
assumed, value-judgments are unsupportably subjective. Yet of course
one can and frequently does offer reasons in support of one's value
judgments, and not only in the arts. One may be mistaken, there
may be disagreements, but such possibilities presuppose rationality.

This assumption is part of the prevalent notion that artistic appreciation is, or is primarily, an expression of personal likes and
dislikes. One is reminded of the "Boo-Hurrah" theory of ethics, that
is, the notion that moral judgments amount merely to nonrational
boos or hurrahs of approval or disapproval.

Despite the prevalence of this assumption, it is difficult to give
any sense to the notion that evaluative judgments are, or can be
reduced to, mere personal preferences, or subjective likes and
dislikes. . . . For example, a consequence would be that it would be impossible to distinguish between evaluative judgments and likes and
dislikes, whereas this is a distinction which obviously can be made.
On such a view, the sentence "He is a superb operatic tenor, but I
dislike operatic tenors" would be self-contradictory, or it would

have to be denied that "superb" is an evaluative term, which is implausible. Similarly, we can and often do distinguish between liking and artistically evaluating films and television programs. Someone might like *Dallas*, while recognizing that it has no artistic value whatsoever. Conversely, someone may recognize that Shakespeare's plays are great art, while not particularly liking them.

A largely contributory factor to this misconception is the assumption that when reasoning is appropriate it is always possible to reach definitive conclusions. Yet . . . that assumption is equally mistaken in other disciplines, such as the sciences. That reasons can be adduced in support of evaluative judgments does not imply that where there are disagreements it is necessarily the case that they can be resolved by rational argument.

It should be emphasized again that there could be no place in education for artistic appreciation if it consisted merely in statements expressing nonrational personal preferences.

This point should not be misunderstood. It clearly is an important aim of arts education to encourage a genuine love of the arts, a desire to engage in them, and a recognition of how much is to be gained from involvement with them. It is an aim of education to encourage students' likes and dislikes to coincide as far as possible with their evaluative judgments.

Beauty

It is frequently assumed that artistic appreciation is centrally or even exclusively concerned with questions of beauty. Thus it is sometimes objected that although reasons are important for interpretation, it is not clear how they can apply to such explicitly evaluative judgments as "This is a beautiful painting."

The question of value has been considered above. There are two further issues here. First, it seems to me equally strange to claim that reasons cannot be given for one's judgment that something is beautiful. Even in the case of natural phenomena such as sunsets and landscapes, one could give reasons to support one's judgment. That someone may not accept them, or may fail to recognize their point, tells as little against the possibility of rational support in this area as it does, for instance, in the sciences. . . . [R]easons may be given which may allow someone to see a situation or a work of art under a different aspect, so that he sees beauty where he did not see it previously.

Secondly, this assumption may to some extent reflect the conflation of the aesthetic and the artistic. . . . Moreover, although it is true that judgments of beauty have traditionally been assumed to be central to artistic appreciation, and thus have been central to philosophical debate, this assumption seems to me obviously mistaken, and it is surprising that it continues to be so prevalent. Terms such as "beauty" appear very little in informed discussion of the arts, for instance, by knowledgeable critics. If someone were to express his opinion of music, concerts, plays, paintings, dance performances, and literary works such as poems and, say, the novels of Dostoevsky and George Eliot in terms of "They are (or are not) beautiful," or some similar comment, and if these were the only kinds of comment he made, that would be a good ground for denying, or at least entertaining grave scepticism about, his capacity for artistic appreciation.

In my view it is doubtful whether there are any terms which are typical or characteristic of artistic appreciation. . . . However, I would suggest that terms such as "sensitive," "imaginative," "carefully observed," "lively" and "perceptive insights" are far more often used.

Art and Science

To repeat, since the issue is important and has been misunderstood, I am certainly not arguing that scientific methods are parallel to, or can be used in, the support given to artistic judgments, but that judgments in the two areas are open to rational justification. The difficulty of grasping the point may stem from the common assumption that the scientific is the paradigm, the standard, by which other claims to rationality are assessed. Yet what this amounts to is a confusion of standards. As an illustration, consider the contention, from the recent history of philosophy, that not even scientific propositions for which there is the soundest possible empirical evidence can be regarded as certain since they do not have the infallibility of the deductive knowledge of, say, mathematics. Thus, for instance, on this view, although the sun may have risen every morning of recorded history, this cannot justify my claim to know that it will rise tomorrow, since it is *logically* possible that it will not. But questions of logical possibility are irrelevant. My claim is justified by the fact that there is sound *empirical evidence*—that is what justification amounts to in this context. It would be a similar confusion to deny that I can know that a window will break if I hit it hard with a hammer, on the grounds that there is no logical contradiction involved in asserting that it will not break. I know for certain that it will break, because windows always do break in such circumstances, and logical possibilities are irrelevant.

It is a confusion of standards to regard the deductive as *the* paradigm to which any scientific claim must attain if it is to be regarded as knowledge. It is equally a confusion of standards to regard the scientific as the paradigm to which moral, religious, and artistic judgments must attain if they are to be genuinely rational.

To say that scientific judgments cannot be certain because they do not have the deductive certainty of mathematics and the syllogism is merely to say that induction is not deduction—or that science is not mathematics. Similarly to say that artistic judgments are not rationally supportable because they are not scientifically supportable is merely to say that the arts are not science. That is a truism. What is important is to recognize that there are kinds of rational justification *other* than the scientific.

Nevertheless, since I do argue that judgments in both spheres are rationally justifiable, it is incumbent upon me to show the relevant similarities between them. Doubts are sometimes expressed about whether there is such a parallel. For example, if we compare the possibility of proof in the two areas, it may seem that there is a significant difference. Consider the following:

(a) Philip believes that Rembrandt's portraits have no artistic merit.
(b) Philip believes that water freezes at 100° C.

There may seem to be a contrast between the two cases in that whereas in (b) a proof of the mistaken belief can be achieved by a simple empirical test of observation, there is no parallel in the case of (a). Yet (b) is not the straightforward case of an empirically verifiable proposition which it initially appears to be, for it would make no sense to say that Philip *understands* the Centigrade system and still needs empirical evidence to convince him that water does not freeze at 100° C. The very *sense* of the Centigrade scale is given by 0° freezing and 100° boiling. Philip's mistake is conceptual, not empirical—rather as it would be if he wanted to measure a foot to confirm that it was twelve inches long. He does not understand the Centigrade system.

Similarly, it would make no sense to say that Philip understands Western art and yet can seriously assert that Rembrandt's portraits have no artistic merit. Whether or not he dislikes them, if he is unable to recognize in them *any* artistic merit, even of technique, for instance, that would be a good ground for saying, analogously, that he simply has no understanding of what *constitutes* good painting.

The cases are parallel, in that in both Philip's failure is one of conceptual grasp, and the proof in each case will consist in helping him to grasp the concept.

It has also been objected that whereas no one could deny that $2 + 2 = 4$, this contrasts with the differences of opinion which so often arise about the meaning and value of a work of art. This marks a significant distinction between the two cases, the objection continues, with respect to the possibility of giving reasons in justification. But the example fails to provide a parity of cases, since a simple case from one area is compared with a complex case from the other. A legitimate comparison with "$2 + 2 = 4$" might be "*King Lear* is a tragedy." No one could understand the play, and the concepts of tragedy and comedy, and still believe that *King Lear* might be a comedy, any more than he could understand numbers and believe that $2 + 2 = 5$. Parity of cases reveals parity of answerability to rational justification.

The cases cited above are those in which disagreement immediately reveals a failure of understanding. Most cases in science and art are not like this. In science the more usual cases are those in which someone understands the relevant concepts and can be offered empirical proof. Similarly, in the arts someone who understands the relevant concepts could, for example, be shown, where he had previously failed to recognize it, that certain passages in Chaucer or Jane Austen are ironic; or he could be given reasons for recognizing the underlying melancholy in a Shakespearian comedy such as *Twelfth Night*.

Truth

Another serious misconception is expressed in the objection that a significant difference between them is that the sciences are concerned with the truth, whereas the arts are much more a matter of imagination.

It may already be clear from what has been said about interpretation that the objection implies a naïve and ultimately incoherent or at least irrelevant notion of truth, since scientific truth is given by theoretical interpretation, an understanding of which requires imagination. Scientific discovery, the search for truth, . . is not simply a matter of accurate sensory perception but also requires imagination.

It is a fallacy to assume that truth and imagination are distinct and perhaps incompatible notions since it may require imagination, in any sphere, to reach the truth.

There are two principal points to be made with respect to the arts. (*a*) Even if the value of the arts were to lie not in the truths they express but rather in presenting imaginary situations, there are criteria for the effectiveness with which they succeed in achieving this, and these criteria can be adduced as reasons in support of judgments. (*b*) More important, it is often a mark of the greatness of a work of art precisely that it *does* reveal profound truths about the human condition. To take a clear case, an allegorical work such as St-Exupéry's *Le Petit Prince* reveals truths about humanity through wholly imaginary situations.

Reading Meanings In

Another persistent misconception is that, unlike the sciences, any values and meanings attributed to the arts are merely read in. This is simply another version of the misconception inherent in the notion that beauty is in the eye of the beholder, that is, that the characteristics cited as reasons for artistic judgments are mere subjective projections of the spectator. Again, a consequence of such an assumption would be that the notions of valid interpretation, and thus of artistic meaning, would make no sense. Yet, on the contrary, it is precisely the mark of a valid interpretation that it is not read in, but is supported by features of the work. To the extent that it is read in it is invalid. To be valid, a judgment has, for instance, to be supported by the text. Thus there is an exact parallel with the sciences where a valid conclusion has to be supported by the evidence.

Of course, such reading in occurs, in both disciplines, perhaps as a consequence of trying to fit recalcitrant evidence to a theory in the sciences, or of approaching a work of art with certain predispositions. Yet this is equally distorting in, and contrary to the character of, both disciplines, and in both it is important to learn to avoid any such tendency. Education in artistic appreciation consists in learning to recognize and eradicate readings in, and in developing the ability to discern increasingly perceptive interpretations and evaluations of, the works of art themselves.

The same misapprehension often arises over the notion of feeling in the arts. For example, Reid writes of the feelings expressed in art that they ". . . belong, analytically and abstractly regarded, to the side of the subject and not the object."[3] It may immediately strike some as undeniable that at least with respect to feelings subjectivity has to be conceded, since a painting, for instance, cannot feel sad. . . . [S]uch a reaction ignores a central problem of aesthetics which is parallel to some of the issues discussed above. There is an important distinction which tends to be overlooked. The feelings expressed in Picasso's *Guernica*, in the poetry of Gerard Manley Hopkins, in Beethoven's Ninth Symphony, and numerous other works, are *qualities of the works*. These qualities may not coincide with how one may happen to feel in response to them. One may recognize that a work expresses sadness while having a quite different response to it. It is important to distinguish between what one may just happen to feel in response to a work of art, and the feelings which are expressed in it.

While it is, of course, true that only animate beings can *have* feelings, it is equally true that a work of art can *be* sad, or can express sadness, and the quality of sadness is as much a quality of the work as it is a quality of a person when he is sad.

A further very important factor here is the frequent conflation of two senses in which feelings can be said to be subjective. As a consequence, a point about feelings which is trivially true is conflated with a point about feelings which is radically mistaken, and thus the *latter* is assumed to be obviously true. (a) In the first sense, to say that a feeling is subjective is to say that it is felt by someone, and it is, of course, trivially true that only people (and animals) can have feelings. (b) In the second sense, to say that something is subjective is to deny that there can be any limits, and thus to say that feelings are subjective is to deny that there can be any sense in the notion of *appropriateness* of feelings. While (a) is obviously true, (b) is radically mistaken, for there are as obviously appropriate feelings in response to a work of art as there are to situations in life. For example, in normal circumstances, we should be at a loss what to make of someone who, when offered an ordinary toasted crumpet, responded with extreme fear. Such a response would be so inappropriate as to raise questions about his mental state. However, the important point I want to bring out is the danger of sliding between, or conflating, (a) and (b), so that a platitude is confused with a falsehood. This conflation of two senses of "subjective" partly explains how one of the most fundamentally damaging misconceptions about artistic judgments, namely, that because they may be partly expressions of feeling the notion of appropriateness and answerability to reason is out of place, can appear to be obviously true.

Artistic judgments are often partly an expression of one's feeling about a work, but one can give reasons for the feeling by reference to features of the work.

Judgment

A similar confusion can arise from taking human judgments to be necessarily subjective. A prominent figure in educational drama, when asked whether he had really meant that all judgments by drama teachers were subjective, expressed surprise and replied: "What other kind of judgments could there be?" To which the obvious reply was: "Objective judgments."

Of course, like the parallel case of "feeling" discussed above, he may have been using "subjective" to be entailed by "judgment." That is unexceptionable except that it may tend to obscure an important distinction between those judgments which are unduly influenced, for instance, by prejudice or predisposition, and those which are based on the evidence, or on qualities of the object or situation. An example will illustrate the confusion which can arise. I once heard a young teacher, in support of his contention that all human judgment is subjective, cite the assessment of trainees on teaching practice in school, which, he said, is always "disgracefully subjective." The use of the pejorative, of course, reveals the confusion since it clearly implies that such judgments should, and therefore could, be objective.

We do not always know which kind of judgment we are making. One might, for instance, make what one fully believed to be an objective appraisal of music, drama, or dance only to realize later that one had been unduly influenced by a mood, prejudice, or other misleading predisposition. Such a possibility does not in the least, as we have seen before, invalidate the distinction. Indeed, we should be keenly and increasingly aware of it if we wish to extend our capacity for artistic appreciation. The reasons given in support of judgments should be based on the qualities of the work.

Sometimes what underlies the tendency to insist that all judgments must be subjective is the notion that judgments are made by human beings, and thus they depend upon our constitution and cannot be guaranteed infallible. . . . There seems to be, underlying it, a craving for an unintelligible ideal of knowledge as beyond human conception. It should be recognized that according to this usage scientific and mathematical judgments are equally subjective.

There are, of course, important differences between mathematical or scientific judgments and artistic judgments. One important difference is that personal involvement is implied in the arts, whereas in the sciences it is more normal to accept conclusions reached by others. In relation to cars and electrical appliances, for instance, we just use conclusions without knowing how they were reached. In the arts, by contrast, it is doubtful whether one can be said even to *understand* a judgment which one has not reasoned through for oneself. Also by contrast, an artistic judgment commits one much more personally, in that the making of it implies one's own firsthand experience of the work. If I were to say "George Eliot's *Middlemarch* is a fine novel, but I have never read it," there is an oddity about my remark which is not present if I were to say "A Rolls Royce is a fine motor car, but I have never driven one." One could, with propriety, say "I am told that it is a fine novel," but that is not the same thing, and concedes my point. This characteristic, that artistic judgments cannot be made at secondhand, misleads some into assuming that they are subjective in the sense that *all* that is expressed in them is a personal commitment or attitude. It is true that an artistic judgment may partly express the feeling or attitude of the speaker, but the subjectivist exaggerates this to the point of *equating* an artistic judgment with an attitude or feeling, which is usually construed as a mere personal preference. But this is to ignore the equally important *content* of that judgment, namely, the question of its truth or falsity, or whether it can be rationally supported. That is, while an artistic judgment expresses a personal attitude to a personal experience, there are *reasons* for it. The subjectivist does not so much put the cart before the horse as ignore the horse altogether. For he ignores that on which the personal attitude or commitment is based.

That artistic judgments may be partly expressions of feeling, involving personal commitment, does not, then, imply that artistic appreciation is a matter of personal preference, prejudice, or predilection. The judgment expressing the feeling and commitment is answerable to reason, in the sense that one could give reasons for it, and it could in principle be changed by more cogent reasons or reflection. In spheres such as morality and the arts, where feeling and personal involvement are so central, it is if anything even more important than in other spheres, though possibly more difficult, to make judgments which are rationally supportable. Moreover, it is of the first importance that education in the arts and morality should extend students' capacity for making and recognizing the validity of such judgments. Only in that way can one escape the restrictions of predispositions, and enlarge one's horizons.

Reason and Individuality

A related tendency is to assume that the individuality which is such an important characteristic of involvement with the arts commits one to subjectivism and is thus incompatible with the answerability to reason of artistic judgments. Yet so far from there being any incompatibility between the two notions, the possibility of artistic individuality presupposes the shared criteria of an art form which allows for the adducing of reasons. This issue . . . is worth mentioning now because it is so often assumed that individuality implies subjectivism.

For clarity, it is worth discussing the question in terms of the parallel, if not equivalent, issue of objectivity. In relation to moral judgments Bambrough writes:

> To suggest that there is a *right* answer to a moral problem is at once to be accused of or credited with a belief in moral absolutes. But it is no more necessary to believe in moral absolutes in order to believe in moral objectivity than it is to believe in the existence of absolute space or absolute time in order to believe in the objectivity of temporal and spatial relations and of judgments about them. . . . The fact that a tailor needs to make a different suit for each of us, and that no nontrivial specification of what a suit has to be like in order to fit its wearer will be without exceptions, does not mean that there are no rights and wrongs about the question whether your suit or mine is a good fit. On the contrary: it is precisely because he seeks to provide for each of us a suit that will have the *right* fit that the tailor must take account of our individualities of build. In pursuit of the objectively correct solution of his practical problem he must be decisively influenced by the relativity of the fit of clothes to wearer.
>
> Similar examples may be indefinitely multiplied. Children of different ages require different amounts and kinds of food; different patients in different conditions need different drugs and operations; the farmer does not treat all his cows or all his fields alike. Circumstances objectively alter cases.[4]

The same consideration applies to the arts. For example, the good teacher, at any level, will be concerned with what is right for each student and with the development of each student's individual abilities. Yet, so far from there being any incompatibility between them, the possibility of individual expression and interpretation requires a grasp of the criteria of an art form which gives sense to the notion of reasons given within it. Again, in principle, the situation is the same in other disciplines. Scientific progress, for instance, requires individual freedom for innovation, but that is possible and makes sense only by reference to the canons of what counts as sound and unsound evidence.

The anxiety sometimes arises that the notion of answerability to reason in the arts implies artistic authoritarianism. For example, doubts of this kind are sometimes expressed in questions such as: "If the creation and appreciation of the arts are answerable to reason, that implies that there is a correct interpretation or evaluation of, and a correct way to create, a work of art, in which case who decides what is correct?" There are two important misconceptions in the first part of the question. Enough has been said to dispel the fallacy that rationality implies a single correct interpretation or evaluation. Answerability to reason does not mean definitive answers of that kind. Changes of conception have occurred even in the most soundly established scientific theories. Moreover, secondly, the notion of a difference of opinion, so far from supporting subjectivism, is unintelligible on a subjectivist basis. If you and I disagree, there is a position which one of us asserts and the other denies, and an implicit *agreement* between us about what objectively counts as a reason of the kind which would settle the issue, or at least offer support to one or the other. Without such a background of agreed grounds of rationality no sense could be made of the notion of disagreement. On a subjectivist basis a "disagreement" would amount merely to personal likes and dislikes passing each other by. Disagreements are characteristic of the sciences not despite but because of their being rational disciplines. The objective criteria of the subject gives sense to what counts as support for the contending positions, and therefore to the notion of disagreement.

The second part of the question, "Who decides what is correct?," reveals a common misconception, which can be exposed by asking the parallel question, "Who decides that $2 + 2 = 4$?" In this case that incoherence of the question is obvious. We do not accept the latter because of some authoritarian edict, and no one *compels* scientists to accept a particular conclusion for which there is overwhelming evidence. To decline to accept such a conclusion, at least provisionally and in the absence of sound countervailing reasons or evidence, is a manifestation not of individuality but of a failure to have understood the scientific discipline. Similarly, to decline to accept an interpretation of a novel or play for which the textual evidence is overwhelming and in the absence of countervailing reasons is a manifestation not of unfettered individuality but of a failure to understand the work and the relevant concept of art. The question of obeying or disobeying an authority does not come into it.

In fact, so far from conducing to authoritarianism, a genuine commitment to rationality precludes it, *because* a judgment has to be answerable not to edict but to reasons. Moreover, one's judgment may have to be modified or rejected in the light of sound reasons for a better interpretation or evaluation. Thus a commitment to rationality implies the repudiation of dogmatism, and any attempt to impose interpretation or evaluation by the exercise of authority. If anything, the danger of authoritarianism is greater from the subjectivist, since there is no way in which he can be shown to be wrong.

It may now be apparent that, in this sense, subjectivism is self-defeating. It arises largely as a result of a commendable and correct emphasis on individuality expressed in the possibility of differences of opinion. Yet differences of opinion are possible only if there can be an exchange of reasons for one's judgments, if there is agreement about what counts as a valid reason and if there is agreement about the issue which is in dispute.

Artistic appreciation is certainly an individual matter, in that fully to appreciate a work of art one must have experienced and thought about it for oneself. But so far from implying, that precludes subjectivism. What can thought here amount to if it is not thought *about* the work? The response is not simply a subjective experience, it does not depend solely upon the constitution or attitude of the spectator. The point becomes particularly clear, perhaps, when one considers not discussion with others, but working out one's own interpretations and evaluations of art. To focus on the formulation of one's own opinion underlines the fact that the work is independent of the spectator, and his response is given by his understanding of it. Although there can and should be individual responses, and perhaps differences of interpretation, such differences and individuality are possibilities which have and arise from limits. Beyond certain limits . . . one's response would not be an expression of individuality, but of lack of understanding. Not anything can count as a response to a work of art, just as not anything can count as a reason for artistic appreciation.

NOTES

1. R. F. Holland, *Against Empiricism* (Oxford: Blackwell, 1980), p. 24.
2. J. R. Bambrough, *Moral Skepticism and Moral Knowledge* (London: Routledge and Kegan Paul, 1979), p. 106.
3. L. A. Reid, *A Study in Aesthetics* (New York: Macmillan, 1931), p. 79.
4. Bambrough, *Moral Skepticism and Moral Knowledge*, pp. 32–33.

PART FOUR

_____

Curriculum
Design and Evaluation

Introduction

In "An Excellence Curriculum for Art Education," Ralph Smith accents the importance of quality in arts education and discusses four propositions contained in a monograph written on behalf of the National Art Education Association. A commitment to excellence, says Smith, implies a commitment to common, general education of which the study of the arts should be a basic component. Students would strive to attain the capacity to appreciate quality in art in a number of contexts which presuppose on the part of the teacher of art substantive training in the humanities, especially aesthetics and the history of art. Smith also dissolves the elitism versus populism controversy by arguing that the pursuit of excellence is not incompatible with democratic values.

Smith's overarching goal for aesthetic education—the development of a capacity to appreciate excellence in art for the sake of the worthwhile experience that art at its best is capable of affording—indicates how the visual arts in particular can be enlisted in the service of such a goal. In "Justifying Music Education," David N. Aspin addresses the curriculum question with music in mind. Aspin recommends the study of music's historical, cultural, interpersonal, and international aspects, as well as its cognitive, moral, and specifically aesthetic dimensions, the latter consisting of the special modes of perception, awareness, and understanding required by music. In terms reminiscent of Nelson Goodman, Aspin emphasizes how the meanings embodied in music contribute to human understanding by enabling individuals to achieve fresh perspectives and reorganize perceptions of reality in light of them (Goodman's worldmaking). So far as music's moral aspects are concerned, they pertain to music's capacity to contribute greater width, diversity, and autonomy to human experience. The assumption is that a human life that possesses such values is better than one that does not. Regarding the specific nature of the skills of musical perception and understanding, Aspin recommends close cooperation between music specialists and educators in order to identify such skills and to design curricula to teach them.

Some of the goals and objectives mentioned by Smith and Aspin are also assumed by Albert William Levi in his "Literature as a Humanity," an essay that, though not cast in the language of aesthetic education, contains a set of comprehensive questions that can give direction to the design of units and episodes not only in literature but in all of the arts. Levi's contribution to the theory of aesthetic education consists of his redefinition of the traditional liberal arts. Such redefinition becomes necessary in light of our increasing awareness of the humanities of non-Western civilizations, Chinese, Hindu, African. With their contents thus expanded the humanities must now be understood not only as subject matters to be mastered but also as arts to be acquired, specifically the arts of communication (or languages and literature), the arts of continuity (or history), and the arts of criticism (or philosophy). Levi regards such arts as civilizing skills, or ways of organizing and interpreting experience. Levi then explains how the study of literature in particular can exemplify his redefined sense of the humanities, that is, how it addresses the nature of our humanity and the conditions of social life. That Levi's redefinition of the traditional humanities does not reduce itself to mere method or a set of skills is evident in his discussion of Shakespeare, the study of whom exemplifies Levi's tripartite division of arts. What is important to realize is that any art, and not only literature, can be studied in terms of its historical continuity, its peculiar language or way of communicating, and its manner of criticizing.

Deciding what a discipline is and determining its relevance to teaching art would seem to be a relatively straightforward matter; in truth, it is far from simple. One approach to understanding the relevance of a range of disciplines, for example, the disciplines of aesthetics, art history, art criticism, and artistic creation, is found in "Discipline-based Art Education: Becoming Students of Art" by Gilbert A. Clark, Michael D. Day, and W. Dwaine Greer. The authors explain what they mean by the term "discipline" and how their conceptions of teaching and learning differ from earlier ideas; specifically, they distinguish their approach from that favored by proponents of creative self-expression. The aim of Clark, Day, and Greer is to establish the study of art as a substantive subject in the curriculum of general education, successful mastery of which would enable students upon graduation to engage and judge works of art commensurate with the level of knowledge and sensitivity typical of a nonspecialist. Especially notable is the importance the authors attach to the discipline of philosophical aesthetics and the aesthetic experience of works of art. The brief excerpt reprinted here, like several of the other selections in this volume, is merely an invitation for further reading; the authors' essay must be read in its entirety to afford a full understanding of their intent and arguments.

In "Defining the Aesthetic Field," Peter Abbs, a British author who has written extensively about the aesthetic dimensions of English language education, asks how the idea of an aesthetic field can help formulate a unified concept of aesthetic education for the schools. Construing "the aesthetic" as a distinct mode or category of understanding, Abbs first recalls some meanings and uses of the term before defining "aesthetic field" as an intricate web of energy that animates the acts of making, presenting, responding to, and evaluating works of visual, literary, and performing art. The sequencing of instruction, Abbs points out, will be a function of where one breaks into the aesthetic field.

Alan Simpson's "Language, Literature, and Art" endorses the educational potential of interrelated arts programs and indicates some fruitful ways to link literature and visual art. Having remarked the apparent paradox of aesthetic description—that our words often fail to capture what is most important about art even though language is the principal means we have for sharing our sense of artworks with others—Simpson goes on to explain different methods for connecting literature and visual art. Such connections may be made through an examination of common and analogous concepts, attitudes, and worldviews, through a knowledge of common sources, and through the inseparable integration of the arts in a single work.

After remarking that aesthetic encounters contribute to an imaginative understanding of our thoughts and feelings, H. Betty Redfern, a British theorist who has written extensively on the aesthetics of dance, asks how we might detect the presence of aesthetic understanding and its development. In "Developing and Checking Aesthetic Understanding," she emphasizes the importance of observing the growth in students' comprehension over a period of time. We infer progress in understanding by the character of their artistic performance, capacity for making aesthetic appraisals, and increased tendency to critical reflection. While not insensitive to the qualities of children's art, she is also well aware of the limitations of their artistic products and remarks that "to deny young people firsthand acquaintance with great art, exposing them only to the products and performances of their peers, is clearly to leave them imprisoned within the straitjacket of their own necessarily limited experience."

One wants to add that such a view should be acknowledged more often than it is.

This collection indicates the various ways in which aesthetics, understood here as the philosophy of art, is relevant to the problem areas of arts education. Not too much has been said, however, about the ways in which aesthetics can affect research studies. In "Toward More Effective Arts Education," Howard Gardner describes how the work of Harvard Project Zero has been influenced not only by philosophical but also by psychological and practical considerations. Inspired largely by Goodman's theory of symbolic systems and the insights of cognitive science, the work of project members has been governed by the conviction that central to aesthetic learning and understanding "must be the capacity to handle, to use, to transform different artistic symbol systems—to *think with and in* the materials of an artistic medium." Such abilities can be fostered, writes Gardner, "only if artistic creation remains the cornerstone of all pedagogical efforts." Gardner then describes studies which at the time of this writing were investigating the interaction of productive, perceptual, and reflective capacities within an essentially creative framework. The work of Project Zero is important not only for its insights into the nature of aesthetic understanding and human development, but also for its having restored credibility to talk about creativity in art education, a topic that had lost its appeal for a number of writers since mid-century. Still, the question of what the "cornerstone" of aesthetic learning should be is perennially controversial. Many of the essays in this collection, for example, while not ruling out the importance of creative activities in learning how to understand and appreciate art, would make the cornerstone percipient awareness of works of fine art.

Drawing together the themes of this section we may say that curriculum design and assessment in aesthetic education should increasingly stress the pursuit of excellence (Smith) in a program of unified aesthetic studies (Simpson, and Abbs) that is a distinct and separate area of learning intended for nonspecialists. Aesthetic education is also understood as having a range of worthwhile outcomes, cognitive and moral as well as aesthetic (Aspin). Approaches to curriculum design may be comprehensive in the questions it asks of a work of art (Levi) and involve a range of disciplines in which its content and procedures are grounded (Clark, Day, and Greer). Finally, increasing attention is being given to ways of detecting and assessing aesthetic learning and development (Redfern, and Gardner).

RALPH A. SMITH

An Excellence Curriculum
for Arts Education

The theme excellence in education is one that has been with us since the days of ancient Greece and is likely to be a continuing one in the future. Indeed, it was in the nineteenth century that that extraordinary cultural critic, poet, and school inspector, Matthew Arnold, cautioned that modern democracies would find it difficult to maintain high standards and ideals and thereby implied that a concern for quality must constantly be on a democracy's agenda. In art education we can do this by keeping in mind a number of propositions stated in my *Excellence in Art Education*,[1] four of which I briefly discuss here.

The first proposition asserts that a commitment to excellence in art education is part of a commitment to general and common education from kindergarten through the twelfth grade. Education is general when it consists of learning appropriate for nonspecialists and common when students learn the same concepts and skills and take similar units of work, with, to be sure, some opportunity to pursue personal interests. Although the *Excellence* essay follows the lead of current reports and stresses the secondary years, a commitment to excellence at the secondary level is meaningless unless a concern for quality animates the entire curriculum and school setting. In other words, in talking about excellence in art education we are talking not only about the qualities and meanings of outstanding works of art and the worthwhile experiences they are capable of providing, but also about an attitude toward accomplishment in general. As Moses Hadas, the distinguished classical scholar, reminds us in *The Greek Ideal and Its Survival*, this attitude has a long and venerable history: "What the world has admired in the Greeks is the remarkably high level of their originality and achievements, and this high level premises a deeply held conviction of the importance of individual attainment. The goal of excellence, the means of

achieving it, and (a very important matter) the approbation it is to
receive are all determined by human judgment."[2]

In saying that a commitment to excellence implies a commitment
to common, general education, I am not saying that art is merely
part and parcel of all school subjects and settings; rather I am emphasizing that art deserves study as a subject in its own right, as a
field that has distinctive purposes, concepts, and skills. As one of
the supreme achievements of humankind whose power for affecting
thought and action has been remarked since antiquity and whose
potency is especially attested by totalitarian societies in their determination to control it, art demands its own curriculum time and
space.

This view is consistent not only with a number of reports, studies, and manifestos currently under discussion—e.g., Mortimer
Adler's *The Paideia Program*, John Goodlad's *A Place Called School*, Ernest Boyer's *High School*, and Theodore Sizer's *Horace's Compro-
mise*[3]—but also with a substantial literature of educational theory
that has appeared since the early sixties. In this respect, the interest
in excellence is but a rerun of yesteryear. What is different about the
situation today is that studies and reports about educational reform
are receiving unprecedented publicity that is fueling discussion
and debate.

What is significant about the literature in question from the vantage point of professional arts education associations is that it no
longer considers the study of the arts marginal to schooling; rather
art is understood as a basic subject of the curriculum. Typical are
Ernest Boyer's remarks in the Carnegie report titled *High School*; he
writes that "the arts are an essential part of the human experience.
They are not a frill. We recommend that all students study the arts
to discover how human beings use nonverbal symbols and communicate not only with words but through music, dance, and the visual arts."[4] It is imperative, therefore, that we seize the moment to
reassert our beliefs about the importance of art and the special role
it plays in human life.

It does little good, however, to say that art should be studied as a
subject in a program of general education and be committed to excellence without saying more specifically what this means. The *Excellence* essay states that the general goal of art education is the
development of a disposition to appreciate excellence in art, where
excellence implies two things: the capacity of works of art at their
best to intensify and enlarge the scope of human awareness and
experience and the peculiar qualities of artworks whence such a ca-

pacity derives. More briefly, the goal of art education is to develop in young people the disposition to appreciate works of art for the sake of the worthwhile experience that artworks at their best are capable of providing. The *Excellence* essay accordingly devotes a chapter to explaining the nature of aesthetic excellence in art and acknowledges that excellence can be found in all eras and cultures; but it emphasizes that any curriculum that gives short shrift to the Western cultural heritage would be seriously remiss.

There is not space to elaborate the criteria of excellence in art, but we may gain a general sense of what they are in Lord Kenneth Clark's essay *What Is a Masterpiece?*[5] Clark talks about the inspired virtuosity, supreme compositional power, intensity of feeling, masterful design, uncompromising artistic integrity, imaginative power, originality of vision, and profound sense of human values found in such works as Giotto's *Lamentation over the Dead Christ*, Raphael's *School of Athens*, Rubens's *Descent from the Cross*, Rembrandt's *Night Watch*, Courbet's *Funeral at Ornans*, and Picasso's *Guernica*.

The second proposition of an excellence curriculum states that striving to appreciate quality in art means striving in contexts in which students learn to perceive art, to understand it historically, to appreciate it aesthetically, to make it, and to reflect about it critically. Such contexts imply a range of teaching methods which include the direct imparting of information, the guiding of problem solving, and the coaching of perceptual and critical skills. The ideas and skills we teach in these various contexts constitute the structure of knowledge in art education.

Contexts, however, must not be casually juggled. An excellence curriculum is committed to cumulative, progressive learning. Neither can an excellence curriculum be indifferent to the fact that the other major arts—especially music and literature—make legitimate claims on the curriculum. This means that attention must be given to designing an arts education curriculum in which the visual arts find a place along with the other major arts.

The *Excellence* essay suggests that learning in the major arts should follow similar sequences of studies consisting of introductory units, historical units, appreciation units, studio and performing units, seminar units, and, when feasible, cultural service units—in all, eleven units distributed over six years, grades seven through twelve. If all the arts currently taught at the secondary level could be reorganized and put in the service of developing a disposition to appreciate excellence in art, then such a recommendation is not unrealistic. Nor, once again, is it novel; it simply recalls a number of philosophies of secondary education published over the past three decades.

The *Excellence* essay argues that progressive, cumulative learning is crucial because of the need to build systematically a sense of art[6] with which one thinks and feels when experiencing works of art. Such a sense is developed first from a preliminary idea of art and then from the historical study of art, appreciation in depth of selected classics and masterpieces, studio and performing exercises which refine the feel for the qualities and powers of works of art, critical analyses of puzzling topics and issues, and work in cultural organizations which conveys a sense of the artworld's institutional realities.[7] Having undergone such a sequence of studies, students upon leaving school should be prepared to engage art with a degree of independent awareness.

The reasons for stressing sequential learning now being apparent, perhaps one example of what the *Excellence* essay means by it will be sufficient. In explaining the qualities of masterpieces, Kenneth Clark points out that of all the marks of aesthetic excellence two are especially important: he speaks of "a confluence of memories and emotions forming a single idea, and a power of recreating traditional forms so that they become expressive of the artist's own epoch and yet keep a relationship with the past."[8] What he is underlining, of course, is the significance artistic genius assigns to both continuity and change. Thus one cannot fully appreciate a masterpiece unless one sees how elements of the old and the new are transmuted in the creation of a compelling image. This is no less true of a good film or work of architecture than of a painting or work of sculpture. Once more, studying art sequentially in the contexts mentioned serves the objectives of historical awareness, aesthetic appreciation, and critical judgment—the three major dispositions called into play when encountering works of art. Creative activities help refine and strengthen these dispositions.

It should be noted that such goals and objectives—historical understanding, aesthetic appreciation, and critical thinking—reflect the thought of some of the best writers in the field of art education. In this respect the *Excellence* essay simply takes its lead from the literature of art education. Such goals are further congruent with the aims of the National Art Education Association and of a number of public and private agencies.

Once the goals of an excellence curriculum are apparent, curriculum evaluation falls into place. Questions of assessment center on whether or not proper objectives have been set and things are moving along in the right direction, in the proper sequence as it were, and whether or not evidence is available that relevant dispositions are being developed. This is how the *Excellence* essay addresses the curriculum questions of what, when, how, and how well.

A third proposition of an excellence curriculum for art education states that the preparation of art teachers must devote more time to substantive work in the humanities, in particular to historical, philosophical, and critical studies of art.

In taking seriously the more academic interest in art that is representative of current writing about art education, the *Excellence* essay raises for discussion and debate the question whether secondary teachers of art are being adequately prepared to handle academic responsibilities and, if not, whether we need new patterns of teacher preparation. For example, should the training of secondary teachers of the arts adopt the pattern of English, history, mathematics, and foreign language departments in which prospective teachers of these subjects acquire mastery of subject matter in schools of humanities and colleges of liberal arts and sciences? Might not newly designed fine arts education units be created in such schools and colleges that would be responsible for coordinating study in the humanities and other liberal subjects with colleges of education? Colleges of education should, of course, continue to provide work in educational theory and assist in the supervision of student teaching. I do not recommend the dismantling of colleges of education.

But if we are talking about excellence in art and art education, if we are stipulating historical, appreciative, and critical objectives, if we are construing the study of art more academically, if we are thinking about a fundamentally different conception of instruction at the secondary level, then the idea that we should prepare teachers in a different atmosphere seems to follow. If art education departments can transform themselves and develop good working relations with schools and departments of humanities, then of course new settings and mailing addresses might not be necessary. It is not obvious, for example, that humanities departments want additional responsibilities, especially educational ones. Yet they have accepted such responsibilities in the areas of English, history, math, and foreign language instruction.

The suggestion to move toward a more humanities-like conception of art education at the secondary level and to prepare what would in effect be secondary humanities teachers of the arts in new settings may prove to be one of the more controversial aspects of

the *Excellence* essay. The suggestion, however, is not stated dogmat-
ically; it is intended to open up a line of discussion. And surely it is
not remiss to suggest that a profession should occasionally reexam-
ine its ideas about teacher education. The major consideration in
entertaining these suggestions is whether new patterns of teacher
preparation will ultimately result in improved learning about art in
the schools and attract well-qualified young people to the field.

Another question that the *Excellence* essay asks is whether not
only current patterns of visual art education are in need of reexam-
ination but also those of arts education. The current excellence-in-
education literature makes the point that excessive bureaucracy and
cumbersome routine often get in the way of effective teaching and
learning. The *Excellence* essay likewise asks whether the splintering
of arts instruction does not similarly inhibit effective learning in the
arts. Talk about cooperation notwithstanding, arts education associations tend to go their own way and are intent on protecting interests developed over a long period. Yet the result is a condition of
aesthetic learning in the schools that is difficult to sanction from a
substantive point of view. Granted that there are numerous good
teachers of the arts and sound programs of art in the schools today—presumably the Rockefeller Brothers Fund and the Getty Center found some of them—we cannot discount what John Goodlad
found in his impressive study of schooling. Goodlad discovered a
general state of disarray in the teaching of the arts in which there is
far too much emphasis on merely "playing, polishing, and
performing"[9] and far too little on the study of art as a cultural object. Not only that; while students tend to enjoy art classes, they
think such classes are easy and unimportant. Now, Goodlad, a frequent and welcome contributor to the conferences and literature of
arts education, has too much credibility to be dismissed. And so the
Excellence essay asks that we take stock of the disarray Goodlad
found. One fact we cannot overlook is that young people today are
finding other professional fields more attractive to enter than education, and this includes arts education. To say that the survival of the
field depends on changing is doubtless to put too ominous an interpretation on the current situation, but neither should we pretend
there is nothing to worry about.

A fourth proposition of an excellence curriculum states that a
commitment to excellence implies an acknowledgment of the claims
of both traditional and modern art and that a sense of the former is
preconditional to understanding the latter. It is held that an intelligent transaction with a work of art presupposes a rich apperceptive

mass made up of numerous items, but most of all of a richly developed sense of art and art history. This in itself would seem to justify
the development of historical understanding. Even artists who self-
consciously repudiate history do so with a strong sense of what they
are rejecting. But there are comparatively few such artists. The majority of artists tell us that traditional art is important by virtue of
their constantly returning to it for ideas, inspiration, and models. We
think of Cézanne in the nineteenth century recalling Poussin of the
seventeenth, and Picasso in the twentieth recalling practically all
previous eras, not least the classical period. And today, in such tendencies as neo-romanticism, neo-realism, and neo-expressionism,
we are experiencing varieties of interpretations of the recent past.

We nonetheless continue to read that the study of the past is irrelevant and that it is even elitist to acquaint the young with the
finest achievements of the human spirit, in part because of what
Kenneth Clark himself acknowledges—that traditional art was in
large part commissioned by the dominant groups in the society for
the purpose of celebrating the values of such groups, whether sacred or secular.[10] But it is not only by reason of this fact that traditional works of art are believed irrelevant; they are also said to be
inaccessible to members of working-class culture and ethnic groups
who purportedly resonate to different beliefs and values. In short, it
is occasionally said that the pursuit of excellence and democratic
values are incompatible, even that the current excellence-
in-education movement is a trumped-up strategy to oppress minorities and stamp out student creativity. And to say this is to say that
the pursuit of excellence implies acts of political oppression. In contrast, people should be free to choose the kind of culture they
want.[11]

There is yet another belief that the study of the best that has been
created is elitist because it presupposes disciplined understanding
and cultivated sensibilities to appreciate, and no one, it is said, should
be required to expend their energies on something in which they
have no immediate interest. For all of these reasons something had
to be said in the *Excellence* essay about the charge of elitism in the
pejorative sense of this term. The response went something like this.

In reply to the belief that the art of the past is irrelevant to the
present because it was created by an elite of artists to celebrate the
values of the dominant groups in the society, we may say that yes it
was often so created, but also point out, as Kenneth Clark has, that
records clearly reveal that such art was often enormously enjoyed
by the large majority. We can read, for example, of how the citizens

of Siena in the early fourteenth century rejoiced in the completion of Duccio's great altarpiece the *Maestà* and how upon the occasion of its completion there was great festivity and processions through the city streets. If we want a contemporary example of such cultural and civic pride being expressed by the majority in works of high accomplishment from the past, we can find it in the reaction of the residents of Reggio di Calabria in the south of Italy on the occasion of the discovery in its offshore waters of classical sculpted figures, the so-called Warriors of Riace.[12] Had these figures been merely third- or fourth-rate, less attention would have been paid to them and probably no competition with Florence would have occurred for their permanent display, with Reggio di Calabria winning out. Stuart Hampshire also points out that high cultural achievement is a continuing source of pride to any city, nation, or civilization.[13] We also do well to recall some words of Hannah Arendt[14] in her study of the human condition; works of art gloriously transcend both the periods and the eras in which they were created and the functions they were originally intended to serve.

As one example of the power of art to transcend its time and purpose, the *Excellence* essay cites the case of Nelson Edmonson who asked why he, an agnostic, could appreciate not only the formal qualities but also the expressive meaning of many works of traditional religious art. Taking the Byzantine icon called *Vladimir Mother of God* as a case in point, which depicts Mary and the Christ Child, he recalls the role that icons perform for the faithful; they relate to the goal of receiving grace and the fulfillment of God's prophetic vision. But whatever its religious meaning and function, Edmonson remarks that for him the icon "manifests mankind's remarkable creative ability to focus in one potent image, and thereby raise to a shared consciousness, the common human condition of suffering alleviated by love." He goes on to say that persons of all beliefs or of no belief can thus experience "a sense of being an integral factor in a larger human drama, of having, as it were, an extended historical companionship."[15] This is one way in which works of art transcend religious doctrine and their own time. What we respond to in such works is the sense of a shared humanity. This example, merely one among many that could be recalled, clearly establishes the significance of much traditional art and helps us to appreciate why William Arrowsmith (a classical scholar who also happens to write about film) thinks that the cultural heritage simply trembles with relevance.

Given such considerations it is difficult to accept the belief that efforts to acquaint the young with the best that has been created in the cultural heritage are politically oppressive. Of course, the choice of terms prejudices matters. If instead of speaking of imposition with its associations of the forcible and illegitimate we spoke of providing access, if instead of fearing the suppression of individual interests we emphasized liberating young minds from nature for culture, and if instead of denouncing the wielding of state power we spoke of enfranchising the young in matters of understanding and appreciation, then the language of political oppression would assume a strained quality. To place within the reach of the young that which has the capacity not only to intensify their experience but also to enlarge the scope of human awareness is neither snobbish, authoritarian, nor elitist. On the contrary, it is to wish for the large majority what up to now has been the privilege of the minority.

As for the belief that persons should be given the kind of culture they want, persons, especially young people, are often uncertain about their interests and hence need to know something about the range of what it is possible to enjoy and admire before they can intelligently decide things for themselves. Certainly it is presumptuous to assume that given the opportunity to cultivate a taste for the best, persons will turn their backs on it. There is too much evidence to the contrary. Stuart Hampshire has even gone so far as to say that to treat people as if they already know what they like, or ought to, is to treat them as less than human.

The *Excellence* essay suggests that we might well be instructed in such matters by the British, who have wrestled with these issues for a long time. According to Richard Hoggart, a respected member of the political Left in Great Britain, who himself has working-class origins and has written sympathetically about the values of the working class, the problem of culture in Great Britain turns on the relative virtues of transmitting the cultural heritage and the stressing of communitarian values, the latter being favored by the far Left. However, the problem with communitarians, says Hoggart, is that they confuse good intentions and human and social concern with artistic merit. He furthermore points out that there is a working-class tradition of learning in Great Britain that transcends communitarian interests. "Among its many great qualities," he writes, is "the belief that people should be able to stand up and reach for the best and the most demanding" and that given opportunities to stretch their capacities ordinary people will reveal "far more abilities than either a closed elitism or an ill-thought-through communitarianism had realized. So they have a right to the best, no less."[16]

One is reminded of the dream immigrant parents in America had for their children. Such parents knew there was something of value beyond their immediate and often confining environments and those who managed to escape such confines were often envied. This does not necessarily mean that those who escaped then turned their backs on their origins; it is that they and their parents had an intuitive sense that one achieved genuine selfhood through transcendence.[17] One also thinks of Marva Collins's school for minority children in Chicago which conjoins the building of identity with respect for the best in the tradition.

But then in America as well as in Britain there is a tradition of democratic egalitarianism that honors excellence. Charles Frankel, who was a philosophical liberal in the best sense of the word, wrote that this tradition realizes the inevitability of variable talents and believes strongly in "the need in every society to give public recognition to things noble and excellent lest everything in the society's culture be regarded as disposable."[18] Frankel's remarks reveal the concerns of liberalism to be not only political and economic, but, as Arthur Schlesinger, Jr., has pointed out, moral and cultural as well, as much associated with Whitman, Emerson, Thoreau, and Melville as with Jefferson and Jackson, or "with all those who insisted on holding America (and themselves) up to stringent standards."[19]

To say all these things is to recall those famous words of Arnold, who said that the true apostles of equality are those "who have had a passion for diffusing, for making prevail, for carrying from one end of society to another, the best knowledge, the best ideas of their time; who have labored to divest knowledge of all that was harsh, uncouth, difficult, abstract, professional, exclusive; to humanize it, to make it efficient outside the clique of the cultivated and learned, yet still remaining the *best* knowledge and thought of the time. . . ."[20] There is, I think, no better ideal for democratic education. Lawrence A. Cremin,[21] the preeminent historian of American education, believes that a commitment to the humanization of knowledge in the Arnoldian sense in fact defines the genius of American education. In short, sentiments regarding things "noble and excellent," "access to excellence," "stringent standards," and "the *best* knowledge and thought of the time" all find a place of honor in the *Excellence* essay.

Were there space, it would be worth summarizing Robert Penn Warren's 1974 Jefferson Lecture, *Democracy and Poetry*, in which he states that the values of democracy and poetry, and by poetry he means art in general, are indeed compatible. His eloquent argument concludes by saying that an outstanding work of art is valuable not only as a vital affirmation and image of the organized self, but also as "a permanent possibility of experience" that "provides the freshness and immediacy of experience that returns us to ourselves."[22] Warren was subsequently appointed America's first poet laureate.

The idea of excellent art as a permanent source of worthwhile experience provides a convenient conclusion to my remarks. Everything the *Excellence* essay says on the matter of quality underscores the realization that while democracies value the common man, they do not ultimately value what Ortega y Gasset[23] called the commonplace mind, a mind, he said, that not only knows itself to be commonplace but also proclaims the right to impose its commonplaces whenever possible. Arnold also realized that with the coming of mass democracy the freedom and energy of large numbers of people would be dissipated if not employed in the service of an ideal higher than that of the ordinary self, that is to say, unless they were employed in the service of the best possible self.[24] It is then the potentiality for transcending our ordinary selves and for becoming uncommon that is important. Art at its best is one of those things of the world that is a perpetual reminder of the possibility of transcending the ordinary; excellent art constantly calls us away from a pedestrian existence. Art education should do no less.

NOTES

1. Ralph A. Smith, *Excellence in Art Education*, updated version (Reston, Va.: National Art Education Association, 1987).

2. Moses Hadas, *The Greek Ideal and Its Survival* (New York: Harper Colophon Books, 1966), p. 13.

3. For a discussion of this literature, see R. Smith, *Excellence in Art Education*, chap. 5.

4. Ernest Boyer, *High School: A Report on Secondary Education in America* (New York: Harper and Row, 1983), p. 98.

5. Kenneth Clark, *What Is a Masterpiece?* (New York: Thames and London, 1979).

6. The notion of a sense of art was suggested by Arthur Danto's *The Transfiguration of the Commonplace* (Cambridge, Mass.: Harvard University Press, 1981).

7. The idea of a service unit is borrowed from Boyer's report *High School*, chap. 12.

8. Clark, *What Is a Masterpiece?*, pp. 10–11.

9. John I. Goodlad, *A Place Called School* (New York: McGraw-Hill, 1984), pp. 218–20.

10. Kenneth Clark, "Art and Society," in his *Moments of Vision* (London: John Murray, 1981).

11. This is the position of Herbert S. Gans in *Popular Culture and High Culture* (New York: Basic Books, 1974).

12. For a description of such festivities, see John Canaday, *Lives of the Painters*, vol. 1 (New York: Norton, 1969), pp. 15–16. A report on the reactions of the residents of Reggio di Calabria to the discovery of the classical figures in question may be found in the *New York Times*, 12 July 1981.

13. See, e.g., Stuart Hampshire's remarks in "Private Pleasures and the Public Purse," a review of Janet Minahan's *The Nationalization of Culture* (New York: New York University Press, 1977), in the *Times Literary Supplement*, 13 May 1977.

14. Hannah Arendt, *The Human Condition* (Chicago: University of Chicago Press, 1958), p. 167.

15. Nelson Edmonson, "An Agnostic Response to Christian Art," *Journal of Aesthetic Education* 15, no. 4 (October 1981): 34.

16. Richard Hoggart, *An English Temper* (New York: Oxford University Press, 1982), p. 160.

17. For some interesting ideas along these lines, see Walter Kaufmann, *The Future of the Humanities* (New York: Thomas Y. Crowell, 1977); and John Wilson, "Art, Culture, and Identity," *Journal of Aesthetic Education* 18, no. 2 (Summer 1984).

18. Charles Frankel, "The New Egalitarianism and the Old," *Commentary* 56, no. 3 (September 1973):61.

19. Arthur Schlesinger, Jr., "The Challenge to Liberalism," in *An Outline of Man's Knowledge of the Modern World*, ed. Lyman Bryson (New York: McGraw-Hill, 1960), p. 473.

20. Matthew Arnold, *Culture and Anarchy* (1869) (New York: Cambridge University Press, 1960), p. 70.

21. Lawrence A. Cremin, *The Genius of American Education* (New York: Random Vintage Books, 1966).

22. Robert Penn Warren, *Democracy and Poetry* (Cambridge, Mass.: Harvard University Press, 1975), p. 72.

23. Ortega y Gasset, *The Revolt of the Masses* (New York: Norton, 1932), p. 18.

24. For a discussion of Arnold's notion of the best self, see G. H. Bantock, *Studies in the History of Educational Theory*, vol. 2: *The Minds and the Masses, 1760–1980* (Boston: George Allen and Unwin, 1984), chap. 9.

DAVID N. ASPIN

Justifying Music Education

What . . . are the justificatory arguments that can be deployed in the case of music? I believe they are summed up under the following headings: historical background; cultural heritage; understanding of the world; personal enrichment; and the furtherance of interpersonal and indeed international understanding. And on these bases I believe an argument can be developed that supports the retention of music as an indispensable element in the curricula of all educating institutions for the future generations of our community.

1. The first argument for the inclusion of music on the curricula of our educating institutions may be one drawn from history. It is commonly argued that no proper understanding of the world in which we live and of the culture of which our society is a part and a manifestation is possible without the constituent members of it having at least some minimal grasp of the roots of that culture and society, an awareness of the springs and origins of the institutions and traditions in which their community is now embodied and which are its chief constitutive elements and components. Our culture and society stand on the shoulders of all that has gone before; we can only fully understand the meaning of the present and grasp the potentialities of the future by means of and as a result of our appreciation of the past. Thus in science, for example, the achievement of Einstein has to be seen against the background and in the tradition of earlier systems of physics, in particular the Newtonian. So it is with music. It is a matter of cultural history and quite beyond dispute that one of the most potent forces to have influenced the shaping and development of our cultural heritage and whole intellectual tradition has been music. This is as true of the times of the Greeks, their festivals and hymns; of medieval times with their courtly lays and ballads; and of the more recent cultural history in Europe, as it is indeed of whole political movements fundamental to the fabric of our civilization in all its multifariousness. Not to take account of the musical traditions and creations of our past would in a quite decided way be to fail to take account of at least some of the

forces that have shaped it and attempted to add an increment of richness and quality to the brute fact of human beings' naked existence. In the concept of the development of "civilization" it cannot be doubted that musical creation and communication have played a crucially determinative part. To have some grasp of the growth of our civilization, therefore, it is necessary that we have some awareness and understanding of one of the principal forms of communication in which that development can be most clearly and sharply discerned—the world of music.

But this does not mean doing the "history" of music—for that would be to teach *history*; it means actually endeavoring to get pupils on the inside of those modes of musical expression and creation—at least, that is, so far as one is able to (cf. the difficulties notoriously surrounding the understanding and interpretation of the music of classical Greece)—in order that they should have some appreciation and comprehension, from within the tradition, of the contribution made by that form of communication to the life of its times and to the mainstream of culture generally. And this can and probably will create enormous burdens for the teacher of music, not all of whose experience and training have involved contact with past traditions. But that it *must* (logically) be done seems to me quite clear for any developed concept of the part played by music in the emergence of our civilization and its cultural elements.

2. A stronger form of this argument may be found in the case for music in the curriculum not only on the grounds of its place as a manifestation of our cultural tradition, but also on the grounds of its having provided some of the finest achievements and artifacts that make up our cultural heritage. If education's endeavors may be aimed *inter alia* at giving the pupil a "knowledge of all that is finest and noblest done, thought or said in the world," then clearly music and music teaching will have a part to play in this task. For among the finest creations of the mind and hand of man are those pieces of music that have been seen to be of enduring value and to provide paradigms of the highest class of what counts as noble, uplifting, and elevated in the world of human artistic creation and performance. Nothing is necessarily being said here about "classical music" or *a fortiori* about "high" or "low" culture. The idea of "excellence" in performance or achievement does not entail that it be associated with any particular version of what counts as excellent: acceptance of the idea of a paradigm does not carry with it the application that musically educated people must have a preference for any *particular* paradigm. The same qualification will also attach to

the often postulated correlation between certain types and classes of musical creation and certain classes and subcultures in society: it simply does not follow. Similarly, there is nothing necessary in the idea of excellence that roots music and its cultural heritage firmly in the past, for although certain achievements that are widely regarded as excellent stem from the past, music and its language are dynamic modes of communication, and this means that its literature is being added to all the time. So, there will be quite as many excellences in today's musical compositions as there were in the times of two hundred years ago. To think otherwise is to betray a predilection for certain forms and/or periods of musical creation only rather than a commitment to the idea and value of excellence *per se*. And I take it that that is what musicians are committed to *ex hypothesi*. As R. G. Collingwood remarked[1] all art will be good art, of its kind and *qua* art, for it will be seen as being good in so far as it meets the canons or criteria of correctness, validity, and relevance that function as normative determinants of admissibility in the whole world of musical meaning at any one time and over all time. Access to and knowledge and appreciation of these "excellences" in any field of the arts, however, will then act so as to add considerably to the quality of a person's life, in terms of the pattern of preferred life options he will work out for himself, having regard to his respect for and pursuit of what constitutes excellence of him, in as narrow or as wide a spectrum of choices and activities as he wishes. But one focus for such worthwhile activities and pursuits will be found in the world of musical performance and creation. (Cf. also the evaluative point under argument 4.)

3. Perhaps one of the most crucial arguments for the inclusion of music in the curriculum, however, is that based on the idea of people's gradually coming to organize, structure, and make meaningful their perceptions of reality. For only on the basis of such structures and categories of meanings can they have some understanding of the world in which they live and thus be able to plan for and direct their lives, not merely on the basis of the minimum exigencies necessary for survival, but also so that their world can be illuminated and made intelligible by the ways in which their senses and cognitions of their world are transformed in the highly complex codes of meaning communication in which mankind has defined, characterized, and given significance to the world and the communications of its constituents. In order for people to have the minimal ability to come to terms with the world's various and highly heterogeneous and complicated structures of meanings, to have some minimal un-

derstanding of them and some minimal competence at compre-
hending and communicating within them, they have to be initiated
into the various modes of perception and awareness and appraisal
through which their world becomes intelligible to them. One such
code is that of mathematics, in which structure of the world is perceived in terms of its numerical relationships and the ways in which
reality may be numerically cognized. Another is that of the natural
sciences, in which such concepts as temperature, mass, and volume
function so as to give particular intelligibility to one of our explanations of the ways in which the world may be perceived. Another
such language will be the language of the visual arts, in which various concepts relating to color, shape, and texture fix a man's appraisals of his reality in his visual perceptions of it and the ways in
which these can be organized and made intelligible. Lastly, in our
case—music—the same may be said with respect to the development of a capacity to perceive and discriminate in the world of
sound—both natural and artificial—as a prelude to our being able
to give sense and intelligibility to our aural awareness and to our
powers of communicating our prehension of meanings in this mode
of awareness to our fellows. The world of organized sound and our
entrance into it is one of the fundamental bases of any autonomy in
the world. For without acute aural awareness and powers of discrimination, judgment, and conclusion, our lives would remain not
merely significantly impoverished, but also actually bereft of a constituent part of our individual and social being and reality. The sorts
of difficulties arising from the absence of the power of "music" for
those persons who become or are born deaf are eloquent testimony
to the importance of this mode of awareness to our lives. Sometimes
our very lives, and certainly our regulation of our social intercourse,
depend crucially upon it.

Thus, as Pythagoras insightfully observed,[2] our discerning of the
patterns and structures of sounds and their organization—what we
may call "music"—are actually also, in a sense, discernments of
the structure and pattern of the universe. For the structured organization of sound constitutes one of the key modes of intelligibility in
our appraisals of the world, not only of natural sound (such as the
thunder of a dangerous waterfall), but also of man-made sound—
such as the rattle of trains over points, the ticking of a clock, the
creaking of a door, or the siren of an ambulance or fire engine. To
live in our society, we simply have to be on the inside of the language of such sounds; not to be is, in a quite significant sense, to
live cut off from the most normal social conventions and institutions.

But there is a further point about the world of organized sound: man possesses the capacity to make patterns and structures of sound of his own, for purposes other than mere survival and social convention. Man has found it possible to put together such patterns and structures in novel ways that have no strict utility but can rather be used to create and furnish new insights into the world. In this respect making, performing, or listening to music, as here defined, are exemplifications of some of the key features of the "aesthetic" mode of discourse and appraisal within which it is centrally located. For in the factitious and innovative organization of sound meanings it is possible to follow what is perhaps one of the key features of the logic of all the arts: the bringing together, in new creations and conjunctions, of what have been previously and are otherwise normal categories of a strictly conventional kind in a way that creates new kinds and levels of meaning. In music it is possible to conceive of alternative worlds, and it is in this sort of "unhitching" of normal category divisions and boundaries and in this crossing of category boundaries to form new categorical combinations and even new categories that musical *imagination* is best exemplified.[3] Such new kinds and patterns of meaning function so as to give us insight into and access to a whole range of alternative possible structures worth looking at both in and for themselves, but also for the potentialities of the new illumination of the universe of human existence that such new patterns of meaning exhibit and promote. The visual arts do this through the medium of perceived objects of a certain color, texture, and shape; music does it through the tentative erection of new concatenations of sounds of a certain pitch, frequency, and rhythm. It is in such tentative explorations of the world through the medium of sound patterns and structures that new meanings consist and can be made intelligible. But to have access to these new potentialities for the illumination of artistic "truth," one has to be inducted into the cultural community in which such meanings are instantiated and deployed.

Another crucial characteristic of the logic of this form of discourse is what Anton Ehrenzweig called its function of "dedifferentiation":[4] that is to say, in one work of art there will be whole layers of meaning that are not only encapsulated but also inextricably entwined. The meaning of *Guernica*, like the meaning of Blake's "The Sick Rose" and of Britten's setting of that poem, can only be perceived by attending to the *totality of* the work. In this respect music, as all the arts, acts as a powerful agent, not only of cutting across traditional categorizations of the world, but also of "integration," in the very real sense that wide ranges of meaning and communication are presented for appraisal in one manifestation—one *Gesamtkunstwerk*. So far as I can think, this characteristic is to be found in no other mode of discourse, where the general tendency—in some, the whole emphasis—is on analysis and dissection rather than synthesis and *unification*—that feature of the arts in the objects, creations, and performances of which alone, to use L. Arnaud Reid's terms, meanings are *embodied*[5] and presented for cognition in their own particular form.

4. Of course human beings erect such novel structures and conceptions of alternative possible worlds of meaning (in this case, in sound) not only for purposes of minimally coping with the world, but also so that human beings may elaborate and then enjoy lives of a degree of quality and of value. Value is placed on the idea of rich increments to be added to our ordinary worlds by producing artifacts that can not only decorate and enrich the cultural milieu in which we live, but also add new insight and illuminations to it and thus act so as to transform the world and make it "better." And it will be made better for the individual in the ways in which his access to this form of creativity and understanding will give him access to great sources of personal satisfaction and enrichment that have the potentiality of transforming the quality of that individual's life and thus the way in which he views the world, a world in which the valued pursuits and objects on which he considers it worthwhile spending time will be given over to aesthetic values (among other such analogous but dissimilar forms of normative discourse as the moral, the political, and the economic). Here the principal preoccupation will be with beautifying and adding dignity and richness to his world; for, as W. D. Hudson has remarked,[6] "Someone who had no conception of beauty would surely be, to that extent, subhuman." An appreciation of the world of beauty is one of the universes of discourse and meaning that constitute and define a life of any tolerable quality.

This is true *a fortiori* for the societies in which the artist works, for it will be his function to communicate to the cultural community that sense of glory and grandeur, beauty and sublimity with which mankind broadens its horizons and elevates its vision beyond a concern for the trivial, the commonplace, and the everyday to conceptions and speculations about the nature of reality, the environment, and the human conditions that make it possible to see these in a totally different and transformed light and give him a "golden vision" of it and of its potentialities. Introducing our young into worlds where such values are prized and made preeminent is to introduce them to sources of enrichment and fulfillment that will form part of their pattern of preferred life options; and one of these sources is the world of music—in all its forms.

To think in terms of providing in our educational institutions access to sources of and avenues to personal enrichment and transformation for all persons implies that we give them access to all the multifarious forms and modes of which that particular cultural community is constituted and on which it lays value. The implications of this for music teaching are obvious: we have to give our pupils access to and entrée into the most catholic, heterogeneous, and diverse subcultures in which musical meaning is capable of being transmitted, in the expectation that in one or more of them there will be satisfaction for one or more of our pupils and future enjoyers. The utilitarian principle of value here entails that the music syllabuses of our schools cover and exemplify the widest possible range of interpretations of what can constitute significance and meaningfulness in the world of organized sound—from the Pink Floyd to Bach, from the Rondo to Reggae. For all are species of beauty and aesthetic value, in their own way and according to the terms of their own sublogics.

5. This also implies a moral value judgment. The argument advanced so far has been conceptual, relating to the competences held to be needed by individuals seeking to achieve competence in rendering the world intelligible to themselves within all the various forms of communication and comprehensibility that have been progressively developed and separated out to give structure and sense to man's perception of his experiences of it. But that an individual should have access to great sources of satisfaction and enrichment that could so work as to transform the quality of his life clearly presupposes a moral stance: the notion that individuals should be so enriched, should have greater sources and modes of achievement, creation, performance, and communication in which their personal autonomy can be developed and extended, clearly places a moral value upon the concepts of width, diversity, and autonomy—of which the aesthetic enrichments and enmeshments of the arts in general and of music in particular are certainly, or are certainly regarded as being, among the most profound. Thus to seek to *educate* the individual in the arts and into music is to engage in an enterprise of a moral kind. For the outcome aimed at is nothing less than what we see as being the welfare of the individual and the promotion of his autonomy so that he can, of his own free will and

on his own informed judgment, make a decision as to what the good life for him shall consist in and be taken up with.

There is more to it than this, however. For if the values of music and the arts are being urged in terms of their potential for transforming not only the lives of individuals, but also of the overall culture in which such individuals find themselves by beautifying and dignifying that culture with its artifacts, achievements, and performances, then clearly the moral judgment is conceived in terms of the welfare of the whole of society—the good life for all. And this differs from individual moral value in this respect: insofar as we are exposing and introducing our young to all the pursuits and activities that individuals might find worthwhile as forming the basis for their own patterns of preferred life options, we are also tacitly presupposing that there will be enough respect for other persons and consideration of their interests, mutual tolerance, and fraternal regard for us all to accord greatest importance to the principle of mutual benevolence and impartiality, in which the value preferences and choices, judgments and pursuits of each individual will be of equal acceptability and standing. There is thus in music education conceived in this way a stress of values of a highly moral, not to say democratic, kind in the bases and outcomes aimed at by us in our introducing our young to as many forms of musical worthwhileness as we do. In each person's subsequent choices the principles of impartiality and universalizability of an informed version of a choosable and chosen good life will be promoted, exemplified, and safeguarded.

In this sense and in this way music education will not be a species of language education and aesthetic education; it will also be most decidedly a form of moral education. And it will be moral in more than one way: for, like science, mathematics, poetry, philosophy, history, and art, music is one of those worthwhile activities that are worthy of serious engagement and commitment, not only for the outcomes they promote and make possible, but also in and for themselves—being pursuits whose final value is that intrinsic to the activity.[7] Indeed, music is one of those fields of human activity that may be regarded as being absolutely worthwhile, in the sense that (a) they do not, like games, sports, and pastimes, need to be confined to particular times, seasons, places, physical states, and emotional moods but are such that they can be practiced anywhere and at any time; and that (b), unlike military or physical prowess, material possessions, and commercial undertakings, their nature is such that they are not subject to greed, envy, or competition (though that is not to say that competitiveness in them may not often—though contingently—arise). *All* can have access to the greatness and sublimities—moral and aesthetic— of the worlds of music and the arts; they are in no one's particular possession but are, as Pericles remarked in the Funeral Oration,[8] a "possession for all and for all time." And in that their large-scale moral virtue also resides: not only does music make possible expansions of the good life for the individual, it also promotes it for all men. Music is, in other words, a powerful vehicle and potent force for good in the interpersonal and international understanding that it can and indeed does promote.

Any of the arguments here rehearsed has a weight and, to my mind, persuasiveness that buttresses claims as to the intrinsic worthwhileness of music on the curriculum. Taken altogether, however, I believe, their effect is cumulative and powerful; for we have a case that bases its claims to persuasiveness on conceptual, practical, aesthetic, and moral grounds and on ends arising out of these. In sum, it would seem, to have music on the curriculum of our educating institutions is a matter of ineluctable conceptual necessity and of the highest aesthetic and moral desirability. For music is part of the very fabric of our culture, of our whole civilization and *modus vivendi*. Failure to come to terms with and make provision for this would mean that one would, in a quite significant sense, be not only culturally impoverished—though that would be bad enough in terms of the value our society places on plurality and diversity—but also discernibly and distinctively what Hudson tellingly terms a "subhuman" participant in the goods of human society and its various institutions in which those values are instantiated and given meaning.

This brings us round full circle, however. For, apart from the general argument from the philosophy of language and the metaphysics of interpersonal communication, we have still not delineated what might be meant by the concept of intelligibility in music. In what, we now have to go on to ask, does the musical awareness or understanding, so often spoken of by so many music teachers for whom it is *the* desirable curriculum goal, or one of the chief of them, consist? How is it to be recognized? How is it defined? What are its characteristic forms and *modi operandi*? What are the criteria of achievement and communicative competence which we wish to see our music pupils attain and become adept in? At this point the inquiry has to be pressed further, into the philosophy of music. It is at this point that musicians and philosophers have to sit down together "with their coats off," so to speak, and engage in some intense, rigorous, and highly theoretical analyses and "unpackings" of the concepts of music, musical expression and communication and understanding. For the ontological questions about the nature of music and the epistemological questions as to the character of musical experience have still to be answered. And it will not do to try to evade this issue by talking in terms of the "expression of emotion" or "creativity" or "understanding and awareness"—though these are all admirable aims. The point is that such generic labels can refer to outcomes in any subject, whether it be artistic or scientific, analytical or empirical. It is at this stage that teachers of this particular subject have to be prepared to get down to the hard work of spelling out precisely what musical understanding consists in: what are the precise skills of comprehension, communication, and appreciation at which they are aiming; the particular concepts and networks of conceptual relationships that will constitute significance, meaningfulness, and validity in their field? And in the case of music and the arts this will be particularly difficult, for we are here requiring such articulation and elaboration of a form of creation and communication whose logic is essentially of a nondiscursive kind.

That is no excuse, of course, for not making the attempt. Indeed the concept of public accountability incumbent on those in the education service requires that it be attempted. Perhaps one of the most valuable and important places to start such an attempt would be to point out to our teachers that this particular form of human being and communication is not amenable to the kinds of demands being made in certain other areas—for example, the demand for "productivity," "economy," "relevance," and other such fashionable shibboleths. For to make such a demand betrays a profound misunderstanding of the nature of what it is that music is and what it is that its teachers are seeking to bring about—a misunderstanding that is nothing more or less than a category mistake. Music has to be judged by other criteria and other concepts of value; and what some of those concepts and values are has been tentatively set out in this essay. But the more difficult question of the ontological and epistemological kind still remain to be tackled, and that clearly merits separate and extended treatment.

NOTES

1. R. G. Collingwood, *The Principles of Art* (Oxford: Oxford University Press, 1938).

2. Cf. G. S. Kirk and J. E. Raven, *The Presocratic Philosophers* (Cambridge: Cambridge University Press, 1957), pp. 228ff.

3. On "imagination," see Mary Warnock, *Imagination* (London: Faber, 1976), and also her *School of Thought* (London: Faber, 1977), pp. 151ff. Roger Scruton, *Art and Imagination* (London: Methuen, 1974), chaps. 7 and 8. Also J. Ollington, "Kierkegaard, Imagination, and Education," *Journal of Philosophy of Education* (1979); M. A. B. Degenhardt, "Sartre, Imagination, and Education," *Proceedings of the Philosophy of Education Society of Great Britain* 9 (1975). Also Aaron Copland, *Music and Imagination* (Cambridge, Mass.: Harvard University Press, 1952); and Nicholas Rescher, *A Theory of Possibility* (Oxford: Basil Blackwell, 1975).

4. For this idea, cf. Anton Ehrenzweig, *The Hidden Order of Art: A Study in the Psychology of Artistic Imagination* (Berkeley: University of California Press, 1976). Also Sonia Greger, "Aesthetic Meaning," *Proceedings of the Philosophy of Education Society of Great Britain* 6 (July 1972).

5. L. A. Reid, *Meaning in the Arts* (London: Allen and Unwin, 1969).

6. W. D. Hudson, "Is Religious Education Possible?," in *New Essays in Philosophy of Education*, ed. Glenn Langford and D. J. O'Connor (London: Routledge and Kegan Paul, 1973).

7. Cf. R. S. Peters, "Worthwhile Activities," in his *Ethics and Education* (London: Allen and Unwin, 1966), chap. 5, from which much of the following argument is derived.

8. Thucydides, *Histories*, II.43.

ALBERT WILLIAM LEVI

Literature as a Humanity

For reasons which are partly logical, but which also reflect a whole series of historical accidents, those studies which we think of today as "the classical humanistic disciplines" are usually identified as the numerous *languages and literatures, history,* and *philosophy.* The term "humanities" or "humane letters" was coined by the Romans to refer to the literature, rhetoric, philosophy, and history of their mentors—the Greeks. It expressed their enormous admiration for a civilization which they recognized as superior to their own, and these Greek works—the humanities—became for them the content of their preferred and prescribed education and the source through which a man might become educated, learned, cultivated, and wise.

But the notion of "the classics" is of Renaissance coinage. It represents a sophisticated sense of "periodization" in the cultural history of the West and above all a distinct consciousness of "looking back," of "rediscovering," of "recovery." For history is now seen as continuous, although the continuity was thought to have been seriously compromised by "the dark ages," and the ties with Greece and Rome in need not simply of discernment but of reconstitution. For above all the continuity was literary—expressed in "works"— and the rehabilitation of Plato and Sextus Empiricus or of Livy, Cicero, and Tacitus became a matter of searching the monasteries, the libraries, and the few remaining private collections for the manuscripts in whose ink and parchment their wisdom was embedded. This was a historical accident, but one with serious psychological consequences. For it caused *tradition* to be seen finally less as habits of procedure, of ways of doing, feeling, thinking, and valuing, than as the transmission of literary *artifacts.* Literary culture became a matter of bibliography and the things of the spirit assumed a mysterious substantiality. The consequences of this Renaissance accident persist today: in Hutchins and Adler's concept of "the great books" and in T. S. Eliot's doctrine of the changing *body* of tradition in which this body is composed of "works of art" and of "existing monuments." And it is also, I think, largely responsible for our post-Renaissance penchant for viewing the humanities not as arts, skills, or cultivated methods of educational procedure, but as subject matters.

The fate of the humanities since Roman times is a long and complicated story. To the Greek classics the Renaissance added the Roman and to these in turn we have added the important books in history, philosophy, and literature of each of the important nations of the Western world since the Renaissance. So that today the "works" which comprise the humanities have multiplied like flies. Also, the provincialism and narrowness which once caused educators to believe that only those works in the rich stream which flows from ancient Athens to modern London, Paris, and New York were truly "humane," has been broadened and enlightened so that we today include in our humanities the literary, historical, and philosophic products of India, Africa, and the Far East. This is surely a tribute to changing requirements of contemporary emphasis and practice. From the days of Thomas More to the time of John Locke, the Greek and Latin classics were taught at Oxford and Cambridge to humanize the law and to provide a more magnanimous foundation for the national civil service. In the nineteenth century there was at the University of Berlin a renaissance of the study of ancient history to provide the metaphors and the examples for Prussian unification. And toward the end of that century there was a resurgence of philology at the University of Vienna to produce those linguistic skills necessary for the administration of a polyglot Habsburg empire. But today . . . it is natural to turn to the arsenal which includes the Chinese novel, the Hindu erotic story, the Arabic Hadith, and the African folktale. But for all the richness of these additions, the tendency still persists to treat these humanistic works as contents, that is to say component parts of subject matters. So our course offerings become swollen and almost unmanageable as we add to our curriculum in the humanities such subjects as "African Literature," "Chinese History," and "Hindu Philosophy."

But there is another way to view the humanities—one which is suggested by an educational tradition just as old, and perhaps even more important than that which has given us the term "humanities" itself. This is the way of viewing learning which has caused us to put a division of "Arts and Sciences" in every modern university and has given us our chief institution of undergraduate instruction—the "College of Liberal Arts." Originating in the ancient world, but coming to flower in the Middle Ages, the idea of the liberal arts rested not upon a content to be mastered, but a technique to be acquired. Grammar, rhetoric, and dialectic—the stock-in-trade of the early cathedral schools of Chartres, Orleans, and Paris—meant skill in reading, skill in speaking, skill in understanding and in rational argument and, therefore, not knowledge to be added to an intellectual storehouse, but habits to be learned so as to constitute elements of character and perhaps even qualities of personality. This transformed the center of learning from the substantive to the procedural!

Perhaps the simplest of all distinctions within the field of learning is that between the arts and the sciences. And just as science can be subdivided into the *natural sciences* and the *social sciences*, so the arts can be subdivided into the *fine arts* and the *liberal arts*. The fine arts are those which *produce* novels, paintings, poems, sculpture, architecture, and musical compositions; the liberal arts are those which *study* the fine arts as well as language, history, and philosophy.

When in this matter one follows the Middle Ages rather than the Renaissance, and thinks not in terms of the substantive but of the procedural, it becomes clear that the "humanities" are exactly the same as the "liberal arts" and that these arts are three: *the arts of communication* (the languages and literatures), *the arts of continuity* (history), and *the arts of criticism* (philosophy). And this carries with it one great advantage: it permits us to view the humanities less as rigid subject matters than as civilizing skills; less as mere types of information than as *ways* of organizing and interpreting experience.

I do not wish to imply that the passage from "subject matters" to "arts" requires recourse to the technological at the expense of the humane. For these "techniques" are not separated from the requirements of our human nature but are rather *defined by them*. The liberal arts of communication, continuity, and criticism are based upon the employment of methods and the acquisition of skills, but it is clear that they are much more than that. For they are grounded in the very nature of our humanity and the conditions of our social life. The problems which they seek to solve are rooted in the deepest needs and perplexities of the human person as he searches for his own identity, faces the challenges of communal existence, and seeks to ground meaning and value in a cosmos wider than the limits of the merely human horizon.

The arts of communication in particular are founded upon the clear intuition that language can never be merely private, that our forms of speech are clues to our evaluations of "things" and "persons," and that a language in all its nuances of statement and implication constitutes, as Wittgenstein said, "a form of life." The identity of the individual, the realities of social life, and our perceptions of the cosmos as a whole are reflected in language. The expressiveness of our mother tongue sets the limits of our intellectual and emotional perceptions. The dialect in which we speak (racy or subdued, provincial or "knowing," as the case may be) is an attribute of our character. And the modalities of our forms of expression, elevated or slangy, pictorial or precise, popular or ceremonial, give us our dramatic resonance and our "style." The arts of communication are, therefore, deeply rooted in the human quest for expression and response—in our determination *to be* and in our passion *to share experience*. The entire repertory of our meaningful sounds, our sociable noises, even that arsenal of those purely vocal exercises which have little more for motivation than the prevention of silence—who can deny that behind them something is at work which we call Will or Mind or the Soul of Man?

As the arts of communication are founded upon *the need for human expression*, so the arts of continuity are founded upon our perception of the reality of "time" and *our search for roots*. They are closely related. Everything in our present experience has, as Dewey said, "conditions" and "consequences." They stem from something prior and they will lead to something later. And this *ongoing stream of time* which gave us ancestors and will leave us descendants provides the details in which we may find our own well-defined and significant *place*. The provision of these details, and the description of the great stream of time in which all human events are located, are precisely the tasks of *history*. But history as a humanity (as contrasted with history as a social science) is never simply the description of an impersonal sequence of causes and effects. It is this sequence viewed from the perspective of *the human standpoint* and described not "impersonally," but with constant reference to notions of human "relevance" and human "importance." One relevant and important human need is to search for and to find roots with which one may identify—to establish or discover a "tradition" into which one falls. All of the common and very natural concerns about the past of "my family," "my country," or "my religion" are clearly expressions of this need. The arts of continuity are, therefore, the instrument for our understanding about human "time," the tools we use for the establishment of tradition, the methods we employ in our continuous search for roots.

As the arts of communication are founded upon the need for human expression, and the arts of continuity are founded upon the human need for orientation in time, so the arts of criticism (philosophy) are founded upon the *human search for reasonableness*. Reflection, thought, criticism are the activities through which we are able to clarify our meanings, identify our values, and so, to modify (for the better, we hope) the conditions of our existence. Whether conservative or radical, all social theories are predicated upon a supposed perception of value, and it is the act of criticism through which standards are supplied, modified, and replaced in the ongoing processes of life. For the nature of human existence is such that within it norms come constantly into question. Ideally, logic attempts to provide the critical standards for how we ought to think and reason. Ideally, ethics provides the critical standards for how we ought to act and judge the behavior of others. Ideally, aesthetics attempts to provide the critical standards for how we ought to appreciate and enjoy. And in this way the arts of criticism, like their sister humanities, the arts of communication and the arts of continuity, take their rightful place in the spectrum of liberal education.

. . . I hope that the wholistic, unificatory aim of my strategy is now clear. It is simply to assert that for any literary work to be taught as a humanity is to bring to bear upon it the arts of communication, of continuity, and of criticism—that is to say, to attempt its *simultaneous illumination* as an example of *linguistic expressiveness*, of *temporal situation*, and of *rational reflection*. Every literary work, we shall have to say, is less an absolutely frozen and encapsulated text than a variable with a range of values. Most immediately it can be taught (in my tripartite format) as language, as history, and as philosophy. Any critical methodology which does not employ the full range of this humanistic spectrum is seriously flawed through atomism and partiality.

As language, every literary work is written in a particular vernacular, has a definite literary structure, and is written in a particular literary style. These three: *language, structure, style*, interrelated and mutually referential, as they necessarily must be, are the categories or dimensions of *literature as communication*.

Anyone who has worked long or intensively upon the Shakespearean canon will find himself deeply indebted to Henry Bradley, G. S. Gordon, and G. H. McKnight on *"Shakespeare's English,"* to A. C. Bradley's *Shakespearean Tragedy*, R. G. Moulton's *Shakespeare as a Dramatic Artist*, and to the numerous "Prefaces" of H. Granville-Barker on the *structure* of the plays, and to such original and imaginative treatments of Shakespeare's *style* as are to be found in

George Wyndham's *The Poems of Shakespeare,* Caroline Spurgeon's *Shakespeare's Iterative Imagery,* and in G. Wilson Knight's *The Wheel of Fire.* It would hardly occur to anyone to found an exclusive critical method upon Gordon or Moulton or Spurgeon. It is difficult to hold that the interpretative possibilities of Shakespearean drama are exhausted either through a careful examination of the vocabulary, grammatical forms, and idioms occurring in the Shakespearean writings or of the statics and dynamics of the development of the five-act Elizabethan plot, or in the curious way in which specific images illustrate the major themes of Shakespeare's poetic imagination. But it is also to be noted that just these works of Gordon, Moulton, and Spurgeon would be viewed with extreme favor by Wellek and Warren and by Cleanth Brooks. Their concerns with language, structure, and style were what The New Criticism was all about; what they, in fact, meant by the "intrinsic" study of literature. And they would look with considerably less enthusiasm upon the next of our three humanistic concerns.

For every literary work is also a human creation, produced in time, and taking its place within a larger context of tradition. It therefore not only has a date, but was written at a certain place by a certain person in a particular social situation and probably for a certain set of people. These three, *date, situation, audience,* interrelated and mutually referential as they must be, are the categories or dimensions of *literature as continuity.*

When in 1916 the editors of the great two-volume *Shakespeare's England* composed their preface, they began as follows: "The purpose of this book is to describe the habits of the English people during Shakespeare's lifetime. The attempt would be worth making even if Shakespeare had never lived. It has been made in the belief that an understanding of the world he lived in is a step to the understanding of Shakespeare. Language is, no doubt, a great preservative, and Shakespeare speaks directly every day to many people who never trouble themselves with the changes that have come over England since he was buried at Stratford. Nevertheless, they would understand him better if they knew more of his surroundings and of the audience that he addressed. Half the errors and fantasies of popular Shakespeare criticism find their opportunity in indifference to these matters, or in ignorance of them." Much Shakespearean scholarship has been directed to the man and his time, "his surroundings and the audience he addressed." E. K. Chambers's biography *William Shakespeare* and his four-volume *The Elizabethan Stage* reflect a lifetime spent with the dramatist and his environment, as do W. W.

Greg's studies of Henslowe's diaries and other dramatic documents of the Elizabethan playhouses. A whole host of scholars headed by G. B. Harrison have concerned themselves with Elizabethan history and the national background, for this adds enormous insight, particularly with respect to the history plays and their major themes.

Shakespeare's fifteen great years between *Henry VI* and *Coriolanus* (1592-1607) were haunted by the ghost of the Spanish Armada, by the threat to Calais from the Spanish in the Low Countries, by rebellion in Ireland and riots in London, and by ever-present anxiety lest the question of the succession should lead to civil war. It is not to be forgotten that *Richard II* was produced during a year of rioting in London, *Henry V* and *Julius Caesar* in the year of Essex's expedition to Ireland and his disgrace, *Coriolanus* in a year of further troubles in Ireland and riots over the threat of enclosures. And it is noteworthy that although kingship, its duties and responsibilities as well as the problem of loyalty to the sovereign, were constant Shakespearean themes, they do not recur in serious fashion in any play written after the death of Queen Elizabeth in 1603.

Even the tone and characterization in Shakespeare's histories are responsive to the temper of the times. In 1592, when military expeditions to the continent were still popular in England, Shakespeare's portrayal of the heroic patriotism of Talbot in Part I of *Henry VI* became a mirror of general feeling, but eighteen months later, with the fiasco of the Island's Voyage, military glory began to be regarded with cynical eyes and Falstaff's parody of Hotspur's commitment to honor in Part II of *Henry IV* found popular response. Falstaff's acceptance of bribes to excuse the best recruits for the army was the mirror of a common public scandal, although a year later the fanfare of the departure of the Earl of Essex for Ireland revived a latent patriotism which was to find direct expression in the chorus which preceded Act V of *Henry V* and throughout that heroic play.

The plays of Shakespeare are better understood when one comprehends the point in time in which they were composed, the contemporary Elizabethan situation, the Elizabethan stage, and, insofar as possible, the events in the life of the dramatist. But the question For whom were the plays written? also has its relevance for understanding and appreciation. A. H. Thorndike and J. Q. Adams, as well as E. K. Chambers have devoted attention to this question. And Alfred Harbage has written a little book specifically entitled *Shakespeare's Audience*. And in his conclusion he wrote: "I should guess that the audience as a whole understood and appreciated what it bought and approved. Its approval could not have been easy to win. Unlike some other audiences existing in and near his time, Shakespeare's audience was literally popular, ascending through each gradation from potboy to prince. It was the one to which he had been conditioned early and for which he never ceased to write. It thrived for a time, it passed quickly, and its like has never existed since. It must be given much of the credit for the greatness of Shakespeare's plays . . . a glimpse into the collective mind of the audience: perhaps that is what a glimpse into Shakespeare's would be. His plays were not wholly dissociated from other phenomena. The tendency to consider them so has encouraged the tendency to view their author as a ghost." However The New Criticism would like to consider them so, the plays of Shakespeare cannot be "wholly dissociated from other phenomena." And it is precisely the consideration of literature in terms of the arts of continuity (frowned upon by The New Critics, but which Traill, Parrington, and Boynton would have approved) which prevents the great masterpieces of literature as well as their authors from becoming abstract ghosts.

Every work of literature is a human creation produced in time, but it is also the product of a philosophy of life and is therefore implicitly or explicitly a work of criticism. It expresses perforce certain attitudes of acceptance or alienation; it asserts and denies certain constellations of value; it contains either implicitly or explicitly some critical message. These three, *attitude, values, message*, interrelated and mutually referential as they must be, are the categories or dimensions of *literature as criticism*.

Anyone who reads Shakespeare's history plays attentively can discern the natural traces of a conservative politics. Shakespeare's politics expresses the search for order just as unambiguously as two hundred years later Schiller's politics was to express the search for freedom. "Form" and "fixity" were for Elizabethans generally the guide posts of a rational politics and civil wars the worst that can befall a state. Just this is the political moral of Shakespeare's early Yorkist tetralogy (the three parts of *Henry VI* and *Richard III*), which reveals the same fear of civil strife and faith in strong centralized monarchical authority asserted by Hobbes in the *Leviathan* sixty years later. Thomas Heywood in his *Apology for Actors* (1612) wrote of the dramatic histories of his time: "Plays are written with this aim . . . to teach the subjects obedience to their King, to show the people the untimely ends of such as have moved tumults, commotions, and insurrections, and to present them with the flourishing estate of such as live in obedience, exhorting them to allegiance, discouraging them from all traitorous and fellonous stratagems." If this is so, Shakespeare's great series *Richard II, Henry IV, Henry V, Henry VI, Richard III* states a political attitude, expresses political values, and constitutes a political message. It begins with the downfall of Richard II and ends with Richmond's triumph. It registers the valuational convulsions that brought England from the medieval epoch to the Tudor Age.

The type of criticism to which this type of Shakespearean analysis is particularly congenial is Marxist, and something of its spirit has been expressed by Jan Kott, Polish Marxist and professor of literature, in *Shakespeare Our Contemporary*. Kott too sees the history plays not as great works of art which have an autonomous existence, but as registers of "the great mechanism" of political ambition, murder, and usurpation in which violence is regarded as a historical necessity, as something "natural" to political life. In Shakespeare's world he sees a contradiction between the order of action and the moral order which is the human fate, but he admits that we interpret Shakespeare in the light of our own contemporary experience of war, violence, and Fascist cruelty. Also portions of Shakespeare remind him of the insights of Marx and Bertold Brecht. We are here in the atmosphere of the same school of literary interpretation as that of Lukács and Goldmann, but with a very different individual slant. Yet what is important is that all three read literature in much the same fashion. For Goldmann the writer always expresses an *attitude*—a *vision du monde*. For Lukács European realism is significant for the *values* it proclaims. For Kott Shakespeare's history plays contain a political *message*. It is obviously not the Marxist ideology which I find worthy of note here but rather the method of reading literature as criticism. Theodore Spencer in his *Shakespeare and the Nature of Man* also reads Shakespeare in much the same manner, but with a totally different outcome. He finds in Shakespeare the attitudes, the values, and the message of Renaissance Humanism.

For my treatment of literature as a humanity, as illuminated respectively by means of the arts of communication, the arts of continuity, and the arts of criticism, I have taken all of my examples from Shakespeare. This is not because the subject is unique—Dante or Sophocles or Molière or Goethe could alternatively have been selected—but because for any truly great figure of world literature the body of criticism is so broad as to include almost every possible approach. And my purpose has indeed been Hegelian—to establish that inclusive totality which the critical and the teaching enterprise demands.

We have always unconsciously recognized the Procrustian character of literature—the multiple subject and subject matter functions which it serves. Now we can insist that any piece of literature whatsoever, from the standpoint of the humanities, should be considered in terms of the nine categories of *language, structure, style, date, situation, audience, attitude, values, message;* and these categories, converted into questions, become the teaching strategy for courses in literature, whatever works are chosen for content, and from whatever global area they may come.

(1) What is its language?
(2) What is its structure?
(3) What is its style?
(4) When was it written?
(5) Why was it written?
(6) For whom was it written?
(7) What attitudes does it express?
(8) What values does it assert or deny?
(9) What message (if any) does it convey?

These categories become the universal questions relevantly asked through the liberal arts of any work of literature whatsoever.

In putting it this way, I have sought a universal critical matrix to substitute for the partiality so frequently illustrated by the variant schools of critical practice. For it has become clear that The New Criticism was really an appeal to the arts of communication; the sociologism of Parrington was really an appeal to the arts of continuity; while the Marxism of Lukács and Goldmann was in fact an appeal to the arts of criticism. We can no longer afford exclusive dependence upon any one of these critical resources. All are required conjointly if we are to make the study of literature a supremely valuable experience.

GILBERT A. CLARK, MICHAEL D. DAY & W. DWAINE GREER

Discipline-based Art Education: Becoming Students of Art

Introduction: Art as a Subject for Study

This essay is about teaching art in schools and deals with a major shift in theory and practice in the field of art education that had its beginnings a quarter century ago. It is about a contemporary orientation to art education that presents a broad view of art and emphasizes art in the general education of all students from kindergarten through high school. This approach integrates content from four art disciplines, namely, aesthetics, art criticism, art history, and art production,[1] through a focus on works of art. The term *discipline* in this context refers to fields of study that are marked by recognized communities of scholars or practitioners, established conceptual structures, and accepted methods of inquiry. Decisions with respect to topics such as curriculum, instruction, learning, and evaluation are based upon the belief that art should be an integral part of general education. Art is viewed as a subject with content that can be taught and learned in ways that resemble how other subjects are taught in schools. Teachers are expected to teach their students by using written, sequentially organized curricula, and student progress is verified through use of appropriate evaluation methods. Goals, procedures, and evaluation are specific to the content of art but are consistent and compatible with those of general education. This approach has become known as *discipline-based art education* (DBAE).[2]

Theories in any field are built upon work of the past, and the theoretical construct presented here is no exception. This paper refers to scholarly contributions from the past two decades and recognizes the inclusion of many ideas from the professional literature of education. . . . The explication of this theory and its identification by a recognizable and descriptive name are steps toward a general shift in the curricula and practices of art education.

This shift began during a time of general curriculum reform in the 1960s and was influenced by prominent ideas of that time. DBAE might be viewed by some as a belated application of old ideas, some of which subsequently have been discredited. The curriculum reform movement of the sixties emphasized the structure of academic disciplines in education in order to improve the nation's scientific, technological, and military capabilities. Contemporary critics of the curricula of that era have pointed out serious problems with content-centered, or discipline-centered, approaches that might conceivably be applied to the current discipline-based orientation in art education. The discipline-based art approach has taken twenty-five years to develop, however, and differs from the earlier movement in a number of significant ways. Clear distinctions can be made, therefore, between the content-centered approaches of the sixties and DBAE as outlined in this paper.

The content- or discipline-centered movement of the sixties was a comprehensive curriculum reform movement supported by the federal government and intended to influence the entire school curriculum. In contrast, DBAE has been generated from the field, funded by public and private agencies, and related particularly to art education. The sixties movement cast university scholars from the disciplines as curriculum developers and experts in matters of content to be taught.[3] Within DBAE, art curriculum specialists are recognized as experts in selection of art content appropriate for various age groups and in curriculum development. Figure 1 outlines major differences between the discipline-centered curriculum reform movement and the discipline-based art education orientation.

Figure 1. Comparison of the Discipline-centered Reform Movement and Discipline-based Art Education.

Sixties Discipline-centered Reform	Discipline-based Art Education
A general curriculum reform movement.	A specific effort to reform curriculum in art education.
Scholar-specialists as curriculum developers.	Art curriculum specialists as curriculum developers concerned with schools/communities.
Attempted to make "teacherproof" curricula.	Recognizes essential roles of teachers and administrators in curriculum implementation.

Focused on math, science, and foreign language.	Focuses on art in general education.
Implementation directed by federal funds granted to individual teachers for in-service training.	Implementation with public and private funds in cooperation with local school districts in local contexts.
Focused on structure of disciplines as content source.	Focuses on dynamic view of art disciplines including concepts, methods of inquiry, and communities of scholars.
Focused on purity and abstraction of disciplined knowledge.	Focuses on integrated understandings of aesthetics, art criticism, art history, and art production.
Model of learner as a discipline specialist.	Model of learner as a person with a well-rounded education.

These differences are significant because they mark a shift in theoretical foundations for art education, and although the current effort has adapted ideas from the earlier curriculum reform work, development of the DBAE orientation has been marked by determined efforts to avoid misjudgments made in the 1960s. Within the discipline-centered reform movement, for instance, changing practice was a matter of installing "teacher-proof" programs. In contrast, DBAE uses a district-wide team effort by school board members, superintendents, principals, and teachers to bring about changes.

As a contemporary configuration of ideas, the DBAE orientation also differs significantly from the creative self-expression approach to art education that has dominated the field for forty years.[4] Within the creative self-expression rationale, art is seen as an instrument for developing what is assumed to be each child's inherent creativity and expressive abilities. In the early 1960s, at the height of the popularity of creative self-expression, several conferences were held in which art educators questioned fundamental assertions of the creative self-expression approach and suggested alternatives.[5] Since then, theorists, scholars, and researchers have developed a body of literature that has moved the field consistently away from the creative self-expression approach.[6] It was not until the mid-1980s, however, that these early questions and suggestions, reinforced by twenty years of constructive criticism and scholarly writings, resulted in an alternative approach to art education.

The creative self-expression approach places great emphasis on art activities; DBAE, in contrast, requires a balanced art curriculum that emphasizes content from the four art disciplines. These differences reveal shifts in practice and curricula that distinguish the two approaches. Figure 2 compares differing conceptions about essential education topics held within each of the two approaches.

Figure 2. Comparison of Creative Self-expression and Discipline-based Art Education.[7]

Creative Self-expression	Discipline-based Art Education
Goals	
Development of creativity; self-expression; personality integration; focus on child.	Development of understanding of art; art essential for a well-rounded education; focus upon art as a subject for study.
Content	
Art making as self-expression; variety of art materials and methods.	Aesthetics, art criticism, art history, and art production; art from world's cultures and eras.
Curriculum	
Developed by individual teacher; nonsequential, nonarticulated implementation.	Written curriculum with sequential cumulative, articulated, district-wide implementation.
Conception of Learner	
Learners are innately creative and expressive; need nurture rather than instruction; exposure to adult art images inhibits learners' natural creative development.	Learners are students of art; need instruction to develop understandings of art. Exposure to adult art images enhances learners' creative development.
Conception of Teacher	
Provides motivation, support; does not impose adult concepts or images; care not to inhibit child's self-expression.	Provides motivation, support; helps child understand valid art concepts at child's level; uses culturally valued adult art images; encourages child's creative expression.
Creativity	
Innate in child; develops naturally with encouragement and opportu-	Creativity as unconventional behavior that can occur as conventional

nity; lack of development is usually result of adult intervention.

art understandings are attained; untutored childhood expression is not regarded as necessarily creative.

Implementation
Can be achieved on a single-classroom basis; coordination among classrooms and schools not essential.

Requires district-wide participation for full effect of sequence and articulation.

Works of Art
Adult works are not studied; adult images might negatively influence child's self-expression and creative development.

Adult works are central to the study of art; adult images serve as focus for integrating learning from the four art disciplines.

Evaluation
Based on child's growth and process of art making; evaluation of student achievement generally discouraged.

Based on educational goals; focuses on learning; essential for confirming student progress and program effectiveness.

A creative self-expression program, even with the addition of some art history and criticism for enrichment or motivation, still differs from DBAE because of fundamentally different philosophical foundations and different psychological orientations. . . . The ideas that describe and define DBAE . . . are organized around the defining characteristics of a DBAE program (see figure 3).

Figure 3.

Defining Characteristics of a DBAE Program

A. Rationale
  1. The goal of discipline-based art education is to develop students' abilities to understand and appreciate art. This involves a knowledge of the theories and contexts of art and abilities to respond to as well as to create art.
  2. Art is taught as an essential component of general education and as a foundation for specialized art study.

B. Content
  3. Content for instruction is derived primarily from the disciplines of aesthetics, art criticism, art history, and art production. These disci-

plines deal with: (1) conceptions of the nature of art, (2) bases for valuing and judging art, (3) contexts in which art has been created, and (4) processes and techniques for creating art.

4. Content for study is derived from a broad range of the visual arts, including folk, applied, and fine arts from Western and non-Western cultures and from ancient to contemporary times.

C. Curricula

5. Curricula are written with sequentially organized and articulated content at all grade levels.

6. Works of art are central to the organization of curricula and to integration of content from the disciplines.

7. Curricula are structured to reflect comparable concern and respect for each of the four art disciplines.

8. Curricula are organized to increase student learning and understanding. This involves a recognition of appropriate developmental levels.

D. Context

9. Full implementation is marked by systematic, regular art instruction on a district-wide basis, art education expertise, administrative support, and adequate resources.

10. Student achievement and program effectiveness are confirmed by appropriate evaluation criteria and procedures.

Conclusion: A Paradigm Shift in Art Education

In real-life experiences with art, those who have completed a discipline-based program should be able to respond comfortably and intelligently as they confront original works of art in galleries, museums, or other settings. They should possess the means to discuss and evaluate art as informed adults and should be able to understand unfamiliar or unusual works of art, including contemporary art or art from other cultures.

Because of their newly acquired aesthetic sensitivities, students' lives will be enriched as they experience works of art, the built environment, and the phenomena of nature. Educated adults will be able to discriminate between simplistic or insincere manifestations of the visual arts and those that are credited with high standards, pursuit of perfection, and lasting value. High standards among those who admire and purchase art as consumers should result in higher standards of artistic production.[8]

For some who have completed a discipline-based program, production of their personal art will hold a special place in their lives. Through artistic expression it will be possible for them to give form to their feelings and express their ideas with concrete visual materials. For others, the attraction of creative expression in visual media or the production of art criticism, art history, or aesthetics may result in the pursuit of an art discipline as a career. For many others, art will continue to be a meaningful and satisfying avocation. For perhaps the largest portion of high school graduates, knowledge of making art and understanding art will enhance their abilities to create art and to view the work of others with empathy and enjoyment. They are the ones who will support art education and art in society in the future.

This essay—which emphasizes the values of an art education that opens avenues of aesthetic experience, stimulates the mind, and provides students with a lens of the arts through which they can gain additional meanings from the world—acknowledges also that certain more practical values should be recognized. We live in a world in which the appearance of our clothing, the places where we reside, and the environments we create convey aesthetic attitudes and meanings. In our daily lives, we are virtually bombarded with influential messages conveyed through the arts. No other subject in school provides students with instruction in visual aesthetic discrimination and decision making. No other subject provides students with knowledge about the purposes and traditions of the visual arts that are necessary for informed choices. In the words of John Dewey, "Possession of this understanding broadens and refines the background without which judgment is blind and arbitrary."[9]

In a discipline-based art program, content of the art disciplines and the educational outcomes are emphasized to enrich the lives of individuals and benefit society. One need only imagine how our immediate environments might appear if all decision makers in our society had achieved the goals of DBAE or how the lives of so many might be enriched if they had developed the lens that would allow them to experience the world of the visual arts.

NOTES

1. Throughout this essay, these disciplines are referred to alphabetically.

2. W. Dwaine Greer, "Discipline-based Art Education: Approaching Art as a Subject of Study," *Studies in Art Education* 25, no. 4 (Summer 1984): 212–18; Getty Center for Education in the Arts, *Beyond Creating: The Place for Art in America's Schools* (Los Angeles: J. Paul Getty Trust, 1985).

3. In their complete and cogent discussion of the discipline-centered curriculum movement initiated in the late 1950s and marked by the spending

of hundreds of millions of dollars through the National Defense Education Act of 1958 and the National Science Foundation, Daniel and Laurel Tanner [*Curriculum's Development: Theory into Practice,* 2nd ed. (New York, Macmillan, 1980] list five realizations gained from successes and failures of the movement. These were that curriculum development requires consideration of (1) the nature and interests of the learner, (2) the problems of society, (3) the interdependence of knowledge, (4) the continuity between theoretical and applied knowledge, (5) the authentic function of general education as compared with that of specialized education, and (6) involvement of the whole school community, and not merely the scholar-specialist (p. 561).

4. Viktor Lowenfeld, *The Nature of Creative Activity* (London: Kegan Paul, Trench, Truber, 1939); idem, *Your Child and His Art* (New York: Macmillan, 1954); idem, *Creative and Mental Growth* (1947; reprint, New York: Macmillan, 1957); Victor Lowenfeld and W. Lambert Brittain, *Creative and Mental Growth* (1964; reprint, New York: Macmillan, 1982); Herbert Read, *Education through Art* (1945; reprint, New York: Pantheon, 1958); Victor E. D'Amico, *Creative Teaching in Art* (1942; reprint, Scranton, Pa.: International Textbook, 1966); Natalie R. Cole, *The Arts in the Classroom* (New York: John Day, 1940); idem, *Children's Art from Deep Down Inside* (New York: John Day, 1966); Henry Schaefer-Simmern, *The Unfolding of Artistic Activity* (Berkeley: University of California Press, 1948); Manuel Barkan, *A Foundation for Art Education* (New York: Ronald Press, 1955).

5. Edward L. Mattil, ed., *A Seminar in Art Education for Research and Curriculum Development* (University Park: Pennsylvania State University, 1966); Howard Conant, ed., *Seminar on Elementary and Secondary School: Education in the Visual Arts* (New York: New York University, 1965); Harlan E. Hoffa, *An Analysis of Recent Research Conferences in Art Education* (Bloomington: Indiana University Foundation, 1974).

6. Manuel Barkan, "Transition in Art Education: Changing Conceptions of Curriculum and Teaching." *Art Education* 15, no. 7 (October 1962): 12–18; Elliott W. Eisner and Dave W. Ecker, eds., *Readings in Art Education* (Waltham, Mass.: Blaisdell, 1966); Michael D. Day, "The Compatibility of Art History and Studio Art Activity in the Junior High School Program: A Comparison of Two Methods of Teaching Art History," *Studies in Art Education* 10, no. 2 (Winter 1969): 57–65; Edmund B. Feldman, *Varieties of Visual Experience* (Englewood Cliffs, N. J.: Prentice-Hall, 1971); Ralph A. Smith, ed., *Aesthetics and Problems of Education* (Urbana: University of Illinois Press, 1971); June McFee, *Preparation for Art* (1961), 2nd ed. (Belmont, Calif.: Wadsworth, 1971); Elliott W. Eisner, *Teaching Art to the Young: A Curriculum Development Project on Art Education* (Stanford, Calif.: Stanford University School of Education, 1969); idem, *Educating Artistic Vision* (New York: Macmillan, 1972); Vincent Lanier, "A Plague on All Your Houses: The Tragedy of Art Education," *Art Education* 27, no. 3 (March 1974): 12–15; Arthur Efland, "The School Art Style: A Functional Analysis," *Studies in Art Education* 17, no. 2 (1976): 37–44; Francis Hine, Gilbert A. Clark, W. Dwaine Greer, and Ronald Silverman, *The Aesthetic Eye Project: Final Report* (Los Angeles: Office

of the Los Angeles County Superintendent of Schools, 1976); Laura Chapman, *Approaches to Art in Education* (New York: Harcourt Brace Jovanovich, 1978); Gilbert A. Clark and Enid Zimmerman, "A Walk in the Right Direction: A Model for Visual Arts Education," *Studies in Art Education* 19, no. 2 (1978): 34–39; idem, "Toward a Discipline of Art Education," *Phi Delta Kappan*, 63, no. 1 (September 1981): 53–55.

7. This comparison contrasts two extreme theoretical positions for purposes of clarification. In practice, there are few school art education programs that completely exemplify either position. Many programs can be found that fall between the two positions on any of the topics of comparison.

8. Monroe C. Beardsley, "Critical Evaluation," in *Aesthetics and Criticism in Art Education*, ed. Ralph A. Smith (Chicago: Rand McNally, 1966), pp. 315–31.

9. John Dewey, *Art as Experience* (New York: Capricorn Books, G. Putnam's Sons, 1934), p. 312.

PETER ABBS

Defining the Aesthetic Field

Defining the Aesthetic Field

What then do we mean by aesthetic field? And how can such a notion provide a conceptual matrix for the organization of the arts in the curriculum?

The word "aesthetic" has never been a particularly easy one in our language. Coleridge, who was largely responsible for bringing the word into English under the influence of Kant, wrote in 1821: "I wish I could find a more familiar word than aesthetic for works of taste and criticism." And as late as 1842 the status of the word remained uncertain for in his *Encylopaedia of Architecture* Gwilt had called the word "a silly pedantic term" and "one of the useless additions to nomenclature in the arts." Yet the word, instead of folding up and instantly dying, was to become shortly after Gwilt's peremptory dismissal the acclaimed word of a controversial artistic movement. The aesthetes were to congregate together holding to Walter Pater's conception of "love of art for art's sake" as it was eloquently propounded in the last chapter of *The Renaissance*. Aestheticism, for them, meant a refined hedonistic grasping of beautiful experience and of beautiful objects. Yet the word was to survive its temporary annexation and again broaden out to mean a specific mode of responding, making, and knowing which was both autonomous and autotelic. In this broad sense, broadened beyond, but including the category of beauty, it retained its essentially Kantian sense of sensuous perception. Thus in the Gulbenkian Report, *The Arts in Schools*, it is stated quite unapologetically that: "one of those distinct categories of understanding and achievement—the aesthetic and creative—is exemplified by the arts: music, drama, literature, poetry, dance, sculpture and the graphic arts.[1] Aesthetic refers here to a distinct category of understanding. Throughout this essay this is our concept of the word as well.

Aesthetic denotes a mode of sensuous knowing essential for the life and development of consciousness; aesthetic response is inevitably, through its sensory and physical operations, cognitive in nature. Through aesthetic activity we half-apprehend and half-create a world of understanding, of heightened perception, of heightened meaning. Art, we might say, exists for the meaning's sake but that meaning cannot be grasped outside of the form in which it finds expression. Thus we want to say that the aesthetic mode is one distinctive mode for the creation of meaning, of significance, of truth. We have moved a considerable distance from the progressives' talk of "self-expression" and "emotional release," a long way, also, from talk of "art for the sake of art" and the cultivation of "the exquisite" or, even, "the sublime and beautiful." Our essay is, in part, an attempt to reclaim and reanimate the word "aesthetic" and to put it to new purposes in our educational practice.

But what characterizes the aesthetic mode? How does it work in practice? What are its distinctive features? The etymology of the word gives a vital clue. Aesthetic derives from the Greek word *aisthetika*, meaning "things perceptible through the senses," with the verb stem *aisthe*, meaning "to feel, to apprehend through the senses." Here in this small cluster of words—perception, sensing, apprehending, feeling—we begin to discern the nature of the aesthetic mode. We can see how the various meanings that the word has been given in our culture cohere: from "good taste" (the first use of the word) to "the a priori principles of sensuous knowledge" (Kant's understanding) to the appreciation of the Beautiful and Sublime (the general Romantic conception). The unity of these diverse meanings lies in the essential perceptual nature of the activity.

It is important that *the sensing* is observed here. In its root meaning the word "taste" includes the meaning "to feel, to handle, and *to touch*," while the word "touch" itself refers both to sensing an object or texture (through touching) and to being emotionally moved ("it was a touching moment"). The word "feel" can, likewise, denote an affective disposition or the act of touching an object. By a similar inner logic the Latin word for feeling (*tactare*) has given the English language both the notion of tact (having feeling for other people's feelings) and of tactile (where sensory touch is indicated). According to the *Oxford English Dictionary* the word "anaesthesia," first used in 1721, decades before "aesthetic" came into the language, denotes "loss of feeling or sensation: insensibility." The aesthetic, then, must be concerned with all that works through and on feeling, sensation, and sensibility. . . . *Touch, taste, feel, tact:* these are the words, suggesting in their uses the intimate relationship between sensation and feeling, which best bring out the nature of the aesthetic mode. However high art may aspire it is yet always rooted in bodily response and primitive engagement. Of the characteristics of the poet, Coleridge wrote: ". . . a great Poet must be implicité if not explicité, a profound Metaphysician. He may not have it in logical coherence, in his Brain & Tongue; but he must have it by *Tact*/ for all sounds & forms of human nature he must have the *ear* of a wild Arab listening in the silent Desart, *the eye* of a North American Indian tracing the footsteps of an Enemy upon the Leaves that strew the Forest—; the *Touch* of a Blind Man feeling the face of a darling Child."[2] Clearly, this is an aesthetic notion of poetry and, by analogy, of all art which does not lead to aestheticism but, as Edwin Webb also insists in his essay on English, to *cognition and understanding.* Coleridge elsewhere refers to a thinking that takes place when "a succession of perceptions" is "accompanied by a sense of *nisus* and purpose." Thus, inherent in the perception is the whole complex intentionality of the person—feeling, willing, remembering, judging, thinking. It is all but never simply a matter of sensation, for sensation is only the manifest and mediating shaft of the whole mentality, the whole person. Robert Frost describing somewhere the genesis of artwork offers a simple description of the process: "A poem begins as a lump in the throat, a homesickness, a lovesickness. It finds the thought and the thought finds the words." Through sensation into meaning, into understanding, into, literally, *meta*-physics. As we have implied in our defense of tradition and culture, Robert Frost's account is far too simple a concept of art-making; however, what we are keen to establish here is, firstly, the nature of the perceptual mode through which we create and engage with art and, secondly, to show that the perceptual mode is inherently cognitive in its action. All aesthetic activity as it is developed through the manifold forms of the arts is simultaneously perceptive, ·affective, and cognitive; it can offer an education, therefore, of the highest order not through the analytical intellect but through the engaged sensibility.

What then of aesthetic *field?* I have taken the word "field" from quantum mechanics to act not as a precise analogue—the arts have no need of any analogue outside of their own activity—but merely as a suggestive metaphor. I want to suggest that art should not refer to a series of discrete artifacts or what some critics call "art objects" but to a highly complex web of energy linking the artist to the audience, and both artist and audience to all inherited culture as now an active, now a latent shaping force. Ideally, art requires for its understanding a dynamic language of participles and verbs, not of inert nouns referring to discrete objects. Just as in the study of sub-atomic particles so in the field of art our terms should be those of motion, of interaction, of transformation. Just as the nature of matter cannot be separated from its activity, so the artwork should not be conceptually separated from the complex field in which it operates. Just as in quantum physics the field gives birth to a variety of forms, which it sustains, then takes back, then recreates, so the aesthetic field may throw up endless combinations which are, in turn, dissolved and recast again, culture after culture, work after work, symbol after symbol; the "simultaneous order."

"Field," then, in our context, implies an intricate web of energy where the parts are seen in relationship, in a state of reciprocal flow between tradition and innovation, between form and impulse, between the society and the individual, between the four phases of *making, presenting, responding, and evaluating* which mark the four essential elements of the aesthetic field. The concept of an aesthetic field in which all art moves and has its being can be diagrammatically portrayed as follows:

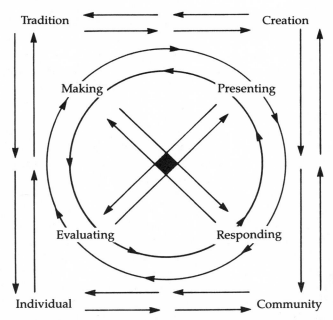

Figure 1. Diagrammatic Representation of the Aesthetic Field

The arts teacher can break into the aesthetic field at any point and be led by an invisible pattern of relationships into the whole circuit—for the parts are not self-contained but gain their meaning through connection with all the other parts. All points, therefore, can be starting-points *and there can be no one way of sequencing the teaching of the arts*. What is important for the teacher is to discern *the whole complex interaction of the field and to use that knowledge in the organizing and planning of work*.

For our own purposes we will break into the aesthetic field at the point of making (M), move to presenting (P), continue by considering responding (R), and close with evaluating (E). What matters, though, is not the establishment of one of the parts but the vivid realization of the whole field. . . . [We] are often still very far from achieving this in the teaching of the arts, and in some arts, as with film, the aesthetic field hardly exists at all.

Making

Igor Stravinsky describing his own method of composition wrote: "All creation presupposes as its origin a sort of appetite that is brought on by a foretaste of knowledge."[3] That seems an eloquent definition of the origins of art-making: *appetite moved by the foretaste of knowledge*. The appetite—the impulse to expression—animates the specific medium of the art-maker (in the case of Stravinsky the "twelve sounds in each octave and all possible rhythmic varieties"), and in the encounter between appetite and medium the artwork begins to take shape. Soon after naming "appetite," Stravinsky goes on to stress the importance of technique in the process of making: "This foretaste of the creative act accompanies the intuitive grasp of an unknown entity already possessed but not yet intelligible, an entity that will not take definite shape except by the action of a constantly vigilant technique.[4] Appetite-knowledge: creative art-technique. Here are the essential reciprocal forces at work in the process of composing the artwork.

The medium, it is worth observing, is not a neutral space through which the creative act passes; it is rather the tangible material which makes the act possible and, as tangible material, it has its own character, inviting certain movements of the art-maker, resisting or confounding others. The material also carries with it a history, a repertoire of previous uses, of working conventions, of established connections and meanings, both convert and hidden. In engaging with the material, the art-maker thus engages both consciously and unconsciously with tradition, with the forms already used and the modes and the techniques those forms have employed and passed on. Indeed, sometimes, the art-maker in the process of composition will actively study other artists' work. And so, art does not come solely out of appetite but also out of other art. Each work of art in its making manifests the whole field.

In his account Stravinsky compares the activity of the composer to that of an animal grubbing about, using his senses and his body to instinctively locate what he needs. This is an evocative image for *the perceptual mode*. And, again, Stravinsky is emphatic about the importance of *working*, the absolute value of the exploratory and cumulative action, the meandering through progressive revision to embodied vision: "The idea of work to be done is for me so closely bound up with the idea of the arranging of material and of the pleasure that the actual doing of the work affords us that, should the impossible happen and my work suddenly be given to me in a perfectly completed form, I should be embarrassed and nonplussed by it, as by hoax."[5] In the movement from expressive impulse to engagement with the medium to the realization of symbolic form, one notices also a movement in the art-maker from a passionate identification with the material—being, as it were, lost in it—to a more distant stance as the work takes form and the art-maker senses that he has, perhaps, found himself or, at least, his *conception of feeling* within it. Toward the end of the process, the art-maker thus feels ready to release the art into the world, to let it have its own independent existence. Indeed, a sense of an audience has been, invariably, a shaping influence, at least in the latter stages of the art-making process. The completion of the art is deceptive, then, for its apparent completion merely sets into motion further aesthetic actions, another set of related interactions and developments still in the perceptual mode.

Presenting

John Dewey observed that the completed artifact is not *in itself* an aesthetic object but an object that invites aesthetic response from others: "The product of art is not the work of art. The work takes place when a human being cooperates with the product so that the outcome is an experience that is enjoyed because of its liberating and orderly properties."[6] If there was no one to view a Cézanne the painting would be devoid of aesthetic meaning, for aesthetic meaning can only reside in the dynamic interaction between the work and the person looking. Here again, we locate a field concept of aesthetic activity. *The work exists in its action on the senses and imagination of the audience.* No audience—no aesthetic. Merely as "an art object," to be classified by historians or sociologists or archaeologists, the work exists on the other side of the aesthetic field, devoid of its artistic life. In practical terms, this means that the work needs to be shown to a responsive audience. It requires presentation in a specific context which draws out its essential aesthetic import, its liberating and ordered properties. To use Caldwell Cook's formulation, it needs "performance with all due ceremony." Thus our account turns away from static "art objects" to further aesthetic interaction.

In the various arts, presentation takes various forms. In drama, dance, mime, and music—often known as "the performing arts"— the recreation of the dance, score, play, or the narrative demands fresh and exacting acts of creative indwelling and expressive projection which closely parallel the making process already outlined. In some cases, as in jazz and certain forms of drama, dance, and mime, the performing act is itself the primary act of creation with no fixed form prior to its expression. In such cases the art-making and the art-performing exist simultaneously in the achieved moments of continuous improvisation. In the other arts presentation may be overtly less dramatic but, nevertheless, it remains essential—a key element in the aesthetic field. The finished paintings and sculpture are *exhibited* and *displayed;* the novels, stories, poems are *published* or *broadcast;* the films are *shown.* The actual size of the audience may not matter. A small responsive group can form a better audience than an anonymous crowd. What really matters is the drawing of the work into the community, into the imagination and sensibility of human experience. The audience needs the art-maker as much as the art-maker needs the audience—though in aesthetic education the students move constantly from one position to the other, now making, now responding, now performing, now evaluating.

Under the virtual tyranny of the discursive and ideological mode, the performing element in the teaching of literature has been neglected, particularly so with poetry. It has been argued by certain poets[7] that the poem exists aesthetically only at two moments: the moment of its *composition* and the moment of its *performance.* In this view, the poem is conceived as a kind of potential sound-event which rather like scripted drama or the musical score needs for its full aesthetic realization to be rendered to an audience. Each poem has its own voice or, like *The Waste Land,* a polyphony of voices—and the poem lives in the auditory imagination only when the voice or voices are spoken out, given dramatic utterance. From this perspective—a perspective which accords well with the aesthetic-field model—our present teaching of poetry (the *"looking at* meaning" approach) works at a considerable remove from its aesthetic nature. Once again, the discursive method of teaching bypasses and negates the presentational.

Responding

Aesthetic presentation invites aesthetic response. Such response is initially preconceptual—when it is impulsively formulated it is often expressed in such phrases as "Great!," "Terrific!," I want to hear it again!," "I like it!," "I want to touch it!," "Deeply moving!," or, when the response is negative: "Dreadful!," "A right mess!," "Simply awful!" Sometimes the immediate response is to the whole work and represents a kind of intuitive assent (or dissent); at other times it is more a response to a part, some compelling fragment, which we attend to and which like Ariadne's thread takes us down into the labyrinthine complexity of the actual work; or we may be drawn to the work but yet somehow confounded by it and wish to submit ourselves to it further so that it may slowly release the power it appears to have, and yet, on first response, withholds. All these responses—and many more of their kind—are not logical but *intuitive apprehensions working through our senses and our feelings,* through our sensibility.

Responses to art, *as art,* are sensuous, physical, dramatic, bodily, preverbal. For this reason the often-heard casual remark "Well, what's it *do* for you?" is aesthetically much sounder than the intellectual question "What is it *saying?*" or "What did the artist *intend?*" Premature answers to these latter questions take us quickly out of the aesthetic realm into the documentary or discursive. Too much theory, too much knowledge, in isolation from aesthetic experience, can block and impede the immediate bodily response, the imaginative indwelling of mind in the pattern of sensation.

The point and purpose of the art lies in the field of its action. Often in educational contexts the desire to explicate needs to be explicitly suppressed. What needs to be nurtured is trust in the authority of the aesthetic form: trust in the power of the story, the narrative, the nondiscursive symbol; trust in the organs of imagination and sensibility through which they posses their power of meaning. We need, in brief, to cultivate the aesthetic response before works of art; not the political or historical or conceptual.

Yet it is neither possible nor desirable to leave the aesthetic field with these three elements. For we *do* wish to judge aesthetic work and we *do* wish to understand the media it so magically transforms into living symbols, and, at many crucial moments in responding to art, we *do* require information (historical, technical, cultural) to make sense of what we see. To respond fully to many Renaissance paintings, for example, one needs to know the Bible narrative, Greek myths as well as certain emblematic codes. It is this need for understanding and for evaluation which brings us to the last element of the aesthetic field.

Evaluating

"Well, what did you make of it?" is a natural response after any performance or presentation. In the evaluation of art we struggle conceptually to *draw out the value* it has for us.

Evaluating is, then, in large part, an attempt to organize the complex elements of our aesthetic response—to state intellectually our relationship to the work of art, to formulate the aesthetic response (as near as we can get to it) conceptually. In part, this is the attempt both to organize and analyze—which will lead us to a consideration of the *form* of the piece itself, and to that matrix of associations and traditions in which it operates. Discriminating, for example, how the associative network of images in a poem combines to produce its effect, heightens and, in some way, justifies the value of the work's effect upon us. This can come close to an intellectual pleasure in itself—the pleasure we derive from seeing how something works, how it has been made. The symmetries, the flow of movement in the lines of a visual presentation, the modified nuance of a theme repeated in music, the pace and placing of cuts in film, the organization of space in theater production—these and many other characteristics of art-products may be identifiable elements of the total.

To some extent such judging of the work tests out our knowing of the work in the immediacy of our responding to it—for such evaluation is essentially reflective. It is post-event. We put some sort of psychic distance between the event of the art and our formulation of judgment. It is a critical act, but one which—in extreme practices—can become wholly detached, pure cerebration, an intellectualization alone. The fact of established critical vocabulary can here actually promote this disengagement. In the best evaluation, however, there is actually a further engagement: the intellectual and the

PETER ABBS

aesthetic combine *to make sense* of the sensuous. Evaluation makes *intelligible* (and communicable) the aesthetic response.

Here, at its most productive, our knowledge of traditions, our awareness of history and culture, our understanding of the craft, will develop and deepen our aesthetic judgments. The essential elements of reference may be schematically indicated as follows:

(i) An awareness of conventions and of techniques.
(ii) An awareness of the historic development of the art tradition including an understanding of historic background.
(iii) An awareness of some of the best critical and interpretive literature.

In some arts these three areas are well developed—while in others, dance and drama for example, they hardly exist. Yet a discursive understanding of these elements makes discourse possible, gives the means of clarifying and defending aesthetic judgments. Of themselves, of course, they do not constitute aesthetic response, and, therefore, they can very easily miss the point. Thus we can know that Mozart is considered a musical genius, but if we do not *hear* it in the auditory imagination the proposition is void of aesthetic meaning.

What is important, then, is that the intellectual knowledge is turned back into the aesthetic field and continuously linked to the primary elements of making, presenting, and responding. It is merely a part of a greater whole and its meaning derives not from itself alone but from its intrinsic relationship to that totality. On our own cyclical journey through the field, the evaluative habit dissolves and constitutes itself once more as the art-making process, a process enriched by the stages it has traveled through. As in any field of energy there is no final stopping place, so criticism and discourse move on and art, as that awesome activity of creating, begins again.[8]

NOTES

1. Gulbenkian Report, *The Arts in Schools* (London: Calouste Gulbenkian Foundation, 1982), p. 20.

2. Coleridge, quoted in G. Whalley, *Poetic Process* (London: Greenwood Press, 1953).

3. I. Stravinsky, "Artistic Invention," in M. Lipman, ed., *Contemporary Aesthetics* (Boston: Allyn and Bacon, 1973), pp. 373-79.

4. Ibid.

5. Ibid.

6. John Dewey, *Art as Experience* (New York: Minton Balch, 1934).

7. See, for example, P. Valéry, *Aesthetics*, volume 13 of the *Collected Works of Paul Valéry* (New York: Bollingen Foundation, 1964).

8. I am indebted to Edwin Webb for part of the formulation of the above account of the evaluating element in the aesthetic field.

ALAN SIMPSON

Language, Literature, and Art

This essay will briefly examine first, the general relationship between the arts and language; second, the particular interrelationships between visual art and literature; and third, the educational potential of interrelated studies in the arts.

To begin, the arts are cultural phenomena; in Joseph Margolis's terms, they are "culturally emergent."[1] All human societies engage in some form of activity that may be called *artistic*. All human societies have language; no matter how basic it may be, language is fundamental to the most primitive human social group. But it is doubtful that all human societies can be said to have possessed the *concept* of art, and even today there may still remain certain isolated societies that do not have "art" in any conscious sense. For the concept of art seems to be peculiar to highly developed civilizations and to have meaning only in the context of social traditions, practices, language, and values. Still, some would contend that all products of artistic activities—prehistoric cave paintings, Eskimo antler engravings, Dogon masks, or the body adornments of the tribes of the Amazon forests—are *art*, whether the people who made them know it or not, whether the concept of art would be meaningful to them or not. This may perhaps be challenged,[2] for our perceptions of others are largely dependent on our conceptions, and we may be certain these people would not "see" their work in the same way we do. (Of course, members of societies from the Arctic to Africa have been westernized into producing "art," but they may be doing so solely to meet economic demands and not from any aesthetic motives.)

The concept of art is not some universal truth that inhabits a world of superreality. It has evolved and become engrained in language as part of the cultural tradition of which we are the heirs. As such writers as Harold Osborne have shown,[3] our modern conception has been taking shape over the last three or four hundred years and, quite obviously, is not fixed or static today.[4] There are no grounds for believing that the Greeks of the fifth century B.C. were conscious of the aesthetic values that we attribute to their work,[5] nor that a medieval craftsman could have made any sense of the notion of the autonomy of art. The concept and activity have meaning only within the language, conventions, and values of a culture, in other words, within a "form of life."[6]

The dominant means of communication and understanding in any form of life is language. Our whole conception of art as having meaning is language governed; we cannot *share* our experiences of Leonardo's *Last Supper,* or Shakespeare's *Hamlet,* or Bartók's string quartets, without language. Yet it is perfectly feasible to argue that the meanings that inhere in works of art are not entirely accessible to language. To a large extent, we can only attempt to explain the meaning of a work of art by employing such devices as metaphor and analogy; by describing our response to and our interpretation of the work's formal structure, its emotional impact, its social or other symbolism, its significant features; by stating what we infer from the work as its intention or perhaps, if they are known to us, by referring to the artist's intentions. And over and above all these things we might assert that the work has a meaning of its own which must be grasped intuitively. Always we must attend to the work directly. There is the apparent paradox that (i) the arts rely on language for their meaning insofar as we can only share whatever may be communicated through the arts by means of language, but (ii) language is a limited and incomplete means of description and cannot fully explain or replace the work of art. Language can only go so far; no matter how good the description of the work— whether it be painting, dance, drama, music, or even a poem—there remains an ineffable residue, a dimension of "silence."[7]

It is from the dimension of art that may be said to be beyond or outside language that the notion of the autonomy of art has grown. Our conception of "art" or "the arts" has become so complex and sophisticated that the arts are seen as forms with intrinsic meaning and value, whatever additional utilitarian, social, or political values they may have.[8] It is commonplace to hear the arts described as "languages" through which we express and discover meanings that are otherwise unavailable. Similarly, several educational philosophers have espoused theories that the arts provide distinct, even unique, "realms of meaning" or "forms of knowledge."[9] Paul Hirst argues that there are seven unique forms of knowledge, each with its own characteristic concepts, logic, and criteria, and one such form is encompassed by "Literature and the Fine Arts."[10] In a report in England which promotes the case for the arts in schools,[11] the argument relies heavily on acceptance of a generalized version of the view that the arts provide distinctive modes of understand ing. Thus the arts are seen as being *logically related;* they are not regarded as just a loose cluster of activities linked merely by social habits and convention. However, it is fruitless to try to impose necessary and sufficient conditions; the history of art and aethetics is littered with misplaced attempts to confine them within a prescriptive definition. As the great Polish historian of aesthetics W. Tatarkiewicz wrote, "The history of ideas is mostly a history of *corrections,* of alterations. This touches aesthetic concepts no less and no more than it does others." And later, "The history of theories is not a history of corrections so much as it is a history of successive *new attempts.*"[12]

In spite of the notorious instability of the arts, there nevertheless are many instances when features overlap and concepts are shared; indeed, certain motifs and theories—e.g., of imitation and beauty as form—have proved immensely durable. Among the arts, it is interesting to note how the technical vocabulary of such words as color, line, texture, or rhythm is used, and of course, as Kant pointed out,[13] how aesthetic and ethical terms overlap in evaluative appraisals. The more the arts have come to be regarded as *autonomous means of expression,* the more fascinating such relationships have become. It follows from this commonality that interrelated studies in the arts are a rich area for both intellectual and practical exploration. These studies do not deny the integrity of each art form, but they enrich and amplify its meaning and help to relate the arts to their cultural, historical context. In the remainder of this article I shall discuss briefly some aspects of interrelated study that might offer possibly fruitful areas of exploration in the links between literature and art.

The connections between literature and painting have a long history in my own country; in the eighteenth century there was a common belief that a natural alliance existed between them. Galleries were founded upon this assumption,[14] comparisons between them were a matter of course, and pictures of all kinds—not just narrative paintings—were given titles in the form of long extracts of poetry. It is only in this century that literature and painting have become almost completely divorced. Yet even in this age of such determinedly isolated "pure" forms as abstract painting, we still find occasional examples of works that connect the visually and verbally poetic, the illustrative and the narrative, and so on. There are many ways and many levels at which the links between these two art forms may be studied; the following are three short examples.

1. First, what we might call the critical and appreciative category is one that includes studies seeking to identify and examine common and analogous concepts, attitudes, and worldviews. An outstanding period for such study is that of Romanticism. The early emotional tenor was captured in the concept of the "Gothick" (e.g., the novels of H. Walpole and W. Beckford)—partly fantasy, touched with nostalgia, and with a fascination for the unknown and irrational.[15] In painting, the landscapes of Cozens remind us of the sense of awe and wonder associated with one of the dominant themes of Romanticism—*Nature*. It is too broad and complex a notion to do anything other than touch on here; among obvious examples are paintings of Constable and Turner and the poetry of Wordsworth. The word "nature" was often used in terms of a contrast to something else, usually something less wholesome and unsullied. What was natural was inherently good, and what was synthetic or manufactured was mistrusted. These nuances still hold good today; we are overwhelmed in television advertisements with the "natural goodness" of foods prepared the "old-fashioned way" or, better still, "nature's way." These items are presented against a background of idyllic rustic well-being that often deliberately apes the paintings of the great landscape artists of the Romantic period. At that time both painters and poets gloried in nature. Constable spoke of there being two ways, "in Art as in Literature," of seeking to achieve mastery of one's art: by studying masterpieces of others and by studying "perfection at its primitive source, nature."[16] Wordsworth echoed these sentiments exactly, and his writing is full of the revelation of being "at one" with nature. This passage from *Tintern Abbey* sums up his view:

> Therefore am I still
> A lover of the meadows and the woods,
> And mountains; and of all that we behold
> From this green earth; of all the mighty world
> Of eye and ear, both what we half-create,
> And what perceive; well pleased to recognise
> In nature and the language of the sense,
> The anchor of my purest thoughts, the nurse,
> The guide, the guardian of my heart, and soul
> Of all my mortal being.

2. A second category of study in literature and art is that of sources, and especially the way in which each form may have been a source of inspiration for the other.[17] Indeed, in works of this type it may be questioned how far we can be said to appreciate a work if

its sources and subject matter are unknown to us. Of course, we can and do respond to works about which we know nothing, but this may be at a very primitive level, restricted by our habitual expectations and attitudes. I am sceptical of the arguments that (i) amount to an advocacy of ignorance on the grounds that knowledge is said to "get in the way" of direct communion with the work, and (ii) restrict aesthetic perception *solely* to the work's formal properties. I suggest that to be aesthetically educated involves much more than being confined to a particularly essentialist view of a single art form.[18]

Many writers in English literature have been a rich source for artists; an outstanding example is John Milton.[19] The reverence for Milton's genius was enormous. In 1774, the minor painter Thomas Jones tells of a journey into Buckinghamshire with his friend and patron in order to paint a view of the house "whither, according to tradition the Poet Milton retired during the plague in London and where he wrote his 'L'Allegro' and 'Il Penseroso.'"[20] The Swiss-born painter Fuseli drew so extensively on Milton that he founded a highly successful Milton Gallery. Through the eighteenth and nineteenth centuries, from the legion of illustrators of *Paradise Lost* to the supreme work of Turner, on the epic scale of John Martin or in the more intimate, gentle vision of Samuel Palmer, Milton's writing was a rich source of inspiration. The two greatest influences on Palmer "from his earliest youth" were Claude Lorraine and John Milton. Although Milton is an outstanding example in the rich vein of English literature that has been a major source for many visual artists, he is by no means the only one.[21]

3. The few foregoing examples remind us that another aspect of such study might be that of the changes in interpretation between generations—what one generation finds of interest may be less important to another. Then there are those artists who somehow transcend their source and develop and extend their interpretation so strongly that it stands as a uniquely creative work in its own right; the work of the aptly named "visionary" artist-poet William Blake is an obvious example. Thus our third category of study might concentrate on examples in which the integration of the verbal and the visual is so complete that it is impossible and, in fact, meaningless to separate them. The work of Blake comes into this category; but perhaps it is in order to turn to a more recent example. The work known in modern terminology as "concrete poetry" relies on appearance and literal surface meaning *and* on ambiguity which invites imaginative interpretation; we "read into" the work for both

its visual and verbal nuances and associations. The work of the contemporary poet-artist Ian Hamilton Finlay is particularly fascinating in this respect. The typography and layout of his poems are crucial to their meaning, and his use of nonverbal symbols is essentially literary and narrative in character. Although this briefest example must suffice, there are many others, for not only has this field of study a long history—as, say, the recollection of Apollinaire's "Calligrammes" reminds us—it also is international in scope.

Finally, the study of interrelationships in the arts, as the above examples perhaps suggest, can be educationally important in several ways. First, such study does not deny but reinforces the particular identity of each art form, for it should serve to deepen understanding and illuminate appreciation. It is an important antidote against the danger of narrow esoteric specialism that can, at worst, serve to isolate an art form and render it inaccessible to all but a tiny number of initiates; there are many instances of such extremes in which artworks are so occult or so private that they are devoid of public meaning. The arts do not exist (not for long, at least) in a hermetically sealed enclave, not even an aesthetic one.

Second, the history of art is not merely a chronology of artworks, styles, and techniques, but it also refers to the sociocultural context in which the works were produced. Indeed, studies structured according to a strictly chronological sequence model may not be the most fruitful approach in general education. In a stimulating paper Anthony Dyson[22] suggests some six categories in which techniques of comparison may be used, and some of these would be quite compatible with the types of study I have suggested. Among the implications for teachers are the preparation for and the purposes of study in museums, and in parallel there are also the implications for colleagues in museums to consider the educational facilities they provide.[23]

Third, the interrelationships among the arts are a rich source of study at any level of education; they may be examined at the highest academic level and also be a fundamental part of the experience of young children, where it is nonsense for the arts to be rigidly compartmentalized. The notion of "creative activities" in English primary schools may, in some instances, have been overindulged in haphazard free expression, but in many others it is used very positively, especially as a *method* in which language development is a crucial element. This aspect has also been brought out in David Ecker's work on developing critical skills in "aesthetic inquiry" with children and also with graduate students.[24]

A last important factor is that interrelated studies in the arts must inevitably relate them to their cultural context. And in this respect it is important to point out that aesthetic education has, as it were, its internal and external functions. On the one hand it emphasizes the centrality of aesthetic experience and judgment *in* the arts; but it does not, nor should it, stop there, for on the other hand it reminds us that the aesthetic reaches beyond the arts to the quality of life in general. It is in their development from and their enrichment of culture that the values of the arts lie.

NOTES

This essay has been adapted from a paper originally presented at an international symposium, "Integration in General Education with Special Regard to Aesthetic Education," Vesprém, Hungary, May 1984.

1. Joseph Margolis, *Art and Philosophy* (Sussex: Harvester Press, 1980).

2. For example, ethnographic collections are now generally referred to as "primitive art." This term, of course, is not always apt but is useful in its classificatory function.

3. See, e.g., Harold Osborne, "Primitive Art and Society," *British Journal of Aesthetics* 14, no. 4 (1974); also Raymond Williams, *Keywords* (Glasgow: Fontana, 1976).

4. W. Tatarkiewicz in his book *A History of Six Ideas* (The Hague: Martinus Nijhoff, 1980) states in reference to our modern age that "people want change and believe themselves called upon to bring it about. In all things and not least in concepts; in all concepts, and not least in aesthetic concepts" (p. 340).

5. In one of his richly ironic fictions, "Pierre Menard, Author of the *Quixote*," Jorge Luis Borges tells of Menard, his twentieth-century writer who, coincidentially and without reference to the original, rewrites Cervantes's novel *word for word*. And Borges writes: "The text of Cervantes and that of Menard are verbally identical, but the second is almost infinitely richer." In other words, the *Quixote* we read is no more that of Cervantes that are the Greek sculptures we see those of Praxiteles. From within our cultural milieu each of us involuntarily "rewrites" or "re-sees" in his own way the masterpieces of past centuries. J. L. Borges, *Labyrinths: Selected Stories and Other Writings*, ed. Donald A. Yates and James E. Irby (New York: New Directions, 1964), pp. 62-71.

6. Ludwig Wittgenstein, *Philosophical Investigations*, trans. G. E. M. Anscombe (Oxford: Blackwell, 1953).

7. I am indebted to R. K. Elliott for this point.

8. For a discussion of the autonomist vs. instrumentalist argument, see T. J. Diffey, "Aesthetic Instrumentalism." *British Journal of Aesthetics* 22, no. 4 (Autumn 1982).

9. For example, P. H. Phenix, *Realms of Meaning* (New York: McGraw-Hill, 1964); P. H. Hirst, "Liberal Education and the Nature of Knowledge," in *Philosophical Analysis of Education*, ed. R. D. Archambault (London: Routledge and Kegan Paul, 1965).

10. P. H. Hirst, "Literature and the Fine Arts as a Unique Form of Knowledge," in *Knowledge and the Curriculum* (London: Routledge and Kegan Paul, 1974).

11. Gulbenkian Report, *The Arts in Schools* (London: Calouste Gulbenkian Foundation, 1982).

12. Tatarkiewicz, *A History of Six Ideas*, p. 341.

13. I. Kant, *The Critique of Judgment*, trans. J. H. Bernard (1790; New York: Hafner Press, 1951).

14. For example, Thomas Macklin's "Poets' Gallery" in Fleet Street, London, opened in 1788.

15. These points derive from Stephen Prickett, ed., *The Romantics* (London: Methuen, 1981).

16. John Constable, "Various Subjects of Landscape, Characteristics of English Scenery" (1833), in *John Constable's Discourse*, ed. R. B. Beckett (Ipswich: Suffolk Records Society, 1970).

17. See, e.g., Jeffrey Meyers, *Painting and the Novel* (Manchester: Manchester University Press; New York: Harper and Row, 1975).

18. For an interesting paper on this, see Noël Carroll, "The Specificity of Media in the Arts," *Journal of Aesthetic Education* 19, no. 4 (Winter 1985).

19. For a scholarly and fascinating account, see Marcia Pointon, *Milton and English Art* (Manchester: Manchester University Press, 1970).

20. Quoted in ibid., pp. 65-66.

21. See, e.g., George Rodetis, "Delacroix and Shakespeare: A Struggle between Form and the Imagination," *Journal of Aesthetic Education* 20, no. 1 (Spring 1986).

22. Anthony Dyson, "Art History in Schools: A Comprehensive Strategy," *Journal of Art and Design Education* 1, no. 1 (1982).

23. See the *Journal of Aesthetic Education*, Special Issue, "Art Museums and Education," 19, no. 2 (Summer 1985).

24. David W. Ecker, "The Critical Act in Aesthetic Inquiry," in *The Arts, Human Development, and Education*, ed. Elliot W. Eisner (Berkeley, Calif.: McCutchan, 1978).

H. Betty Redfern

Developing and Checking
Aesthetic Understanding

How . . . can another person—a teacher, for instance—know whether or not an individual has gained . . . understanding in the case of art? How is he to know what someone evidently engrossed in a book, a film, a piece of music, etc., is "making" of it, *how* he is responding? To some extent "evidence" may vary as between one art form and another. In the performing arts and in literature, for example, a pupil might be able to indicate something of his response in his performance of the work. Wittgenstein asks, "Isn't understanding shown in the expression with which someone reads the poem, sings the tune?," and answers confidently: "Certainly."[1] But lack of adequate skill is an obvious drawback here; nor can an individual be expected to demonstrate in this way his understanding of *every* role in a play or a dance, *every* vocal or instrumental line of a composition, etc. On the other hand, a technically accurate performance is not incompatible with a certain lack of feeling— though the absence or presence of warmth and sincerity do seem detectable by experienced observers and listeners (a panel of "assessors," rather than a single individual, however, would seem to be the ideal).

Again, the choices that pupils make if they compile their own anthologies, collect reproductions and photographs, bring along favorite records, and so forth, are—provided that they are genuine choices—likely to be revealing. As Casey points out, "finding—or for that matter, writing—a maudlin poem to express one's grief cannot be considered just an accident, a quirk of behavior . . . the choice is governed by a conception of the object."[2] To take account of a range of cases over a period, then, can help to build up a picture of an individual's appreciative capabilities and of his aesthetic development. Perhaps from time to time—as, indeed, even among people we might justifiably call "aesthetically educated"—there may be lapses of taste (using that term in the sense of having to do with discrimination and judgment, not merely personal preference). Yet a lapse does presuppose some level of consistency. In any case, as far as aesthetic education in the arts is concerned, there is often a useful place for the relatively inconsequential in order for young people to get going at all. The educator has to move, as L. Arnaud Reid says, *"from* where the pupil is, *towards* something more discriminating, finer, richer, fuller, more complex."[3]

It might, for example, be helpful in the early stages, as Wilson[4] suggests, to encourage comparisons between good and bad instances of well-known and well-liked inventions that have a recognizable *form*—jokes, riddles, graffiti, and the like—so that children are brought to see that the "same" thing can be done well or badly. What, for instance, makes this limerick sloppy or neat, this Western tedious or dramatic, this line of a song predictable or sentimental while that one has an unexpected twist or in some other way departs from the sterotype?

Nevertheless, Saw is right to question whether "the plain man" really does always know what he likes.[5] Certainly he can only like or dislike what he knows; and it is clearly the job of education to extend children's horizons so that they have at least a glimpse of what lies beyond the presently fashionable, the hackneyed, the trivial and the obvious—beyond that which lacks subtlety and complexity, where there are always happy endings, clear-cut "goodies" that always triumph over clear-cut "baddies," or conversely, where only sordid caricatures of men and women are presented.[6] For there is nothing, as Michael Oakeshott points out, to encourage us to believe that "what has captured current fancy is the most valuable part of our inheritance";[7] and the releasing of pupils from servitude to the current dominant feelings, emotions, images, ideas, etc., of which both he and Hepburn speak seems especially necessary in the case of much (though not all) popular art.

Sometimes, anyway, it may be a good deal more effective for a teacher who is himself fired with enthusiasm for a particular work of a kind unfamiliar to his pupils to plunge them in at the deep end and try to carry them along with him before subjecting the piece *and* his responses to critical scrutiny, rather than first attempt to get them to examine with similar rigor items of the sort with which they are familiar, and on whose behalf they may tend to take up defensive attitudes. Comparisons and contrasts between works (and jokes, etc.) of quality can, however, play a vital role: put Ted Hughes's

Fish beside Yeats's *Byzantium*, for example, and the brisk, urgent and
and erratic movement of the one may point up even more vividly
the grand, spacious sweep of the other.

Whatever a teacher's strategies, it is essential that children are encouraged from an early age to talk about pieces both that they themselves make or choose and that are presented to them. Collinson (who
provides a somewhat exaggeratedly purist account of the aesthetic
such that she herself is aware might give an impression of "an altogether too glaring and blinkered attitude,"[8] characterizes the aesthetically educated person in terms of an individual who stands in
rapt contemplation in front of, say, a painting but who may or may
not be able to "talk about, describe or *comment* on certain objects
and situations in a certain way."[9] She is, of course, right that com-
ments dealing exclusively with technical details are not a sufficient
criterion of aesthetic involvement; but for the purposes of *educating*,
discussion (which might include reference to technical aspects) is
vital both to the fostering of such experience and to attempts to
check, as far as this is possible, whether it has been achieved.

There may, of course, be occasions when a piece is left to make its
own impact, with little said either by way of introduction or follow-
up (as also with children's own pieces): a teacher's silences, like his
stillnesses, can be as eloquent as—and sometimes more eloquent
than—his words and gestures. It is also important to remember that
one needs time to *live* in "the aesthetic moment" and to develop
acquaintance with a work, rather than always move on to something
else or make a verbal response to it or attend to someone else's. Pursuing the analogy with getting to know a person, Collinson insists
that this is spoiled if a third party stands alongside delivering information about that person.[10] Yet it is often helpful if he is *introduced*,
and while on some occasions there might be an immediate *rap-
prochement*, on others one may feel strange and at a loss to know
how to proceed. Here the analogy breaks down, for in contrast to a
person a work can only "stand" there, so to speak, awaiting a further effort on the part of the other. Moreover, delivering information is not all of, and not even chiefly, what is required in arousing
and furthering aesthetic involvement, though it may have an important place by way of preparation for and later study of a piece. The
situation is typically unlike that mentioned by Harry Broudy in respect of Eliot, for whom the ideal critic was one who put before him
something thing that he had never before encountered and then left
him alone with it, relying on his own sensibility, intelligence, and
capacity for wisdom. "That's fine for T. S. Eliot, who already had

well-developed sensibility, intelligence, and capacity for wisdom,"
remarks Broudy, "precisely that which the pupil does not yet
have."[11]

Now at first what children say about a story, a song, a piece of
sculpture, etc., may be little more than "Fantastic!," "It's very
pretty," "I liked that part where . . ." (or, alternatively, "It's bor-
ing," "It left me cold"), and so on. But at least it is appropriate that
a personal response is elicited and expressed—so long as, that is,
this is neither a piece of self-deception (as, for example, when what
one enjoys or dislikes is, rather, some association aroused by the
piece), nor insincere in being calculated merely to please or impress
or conform to expectations, or, by contrast, to shock or annoy teachers and (or) peers: a problem, however, that is not peculiar to the
aesthetic situation, but has much wider implications (social, psychological, etc).

Nevertheless, in order that progress be achieved toward more differentiated responses, more acutely discriminating perceptions, together with consideration of whether those responses are, or are
not, justifiable *in terms of the object*, it is essential that a suitable vocabulary is built up. For without some means of reference both to
ordinarily observable details and to aesthetic qualities not only is
understanding restricted as regards how others respond, and why,
but also one's own powers of perception are limited: that for which
we have no adequate terminology is likely to be missed. Hence the
need for pupils to become familiar with certain technical terms, and
perhaps in music and dance, notational symbols (in both cases there
are simplified forms for learning crucial concepts), as well as with
that imaginative use of words that is characteristic of aesthetic discussion. (All this applies too, of course, in connection with art-
making and performance.)

There would seem to be an especially important need for a technical vocabulary in respect of architecture and sculpture, for ordinary language is somewhat impoverished in names for shapes and
spatial configurations—a factor that may contribute to the difficulty
many people appear to find in appreciating the three-dimensional
arts other than as regards any representational interest they may
have.[12] Similarly in the case of dance, which is still apt to be ap-
proached largely as a musical or a dramatic art.[13]

The use of language in aesthetic appraisals as such is, of course,
often far less exact. Yet it would be wrong to suppose that language
that is suggestive rather than precise, or rich in emotive power and

association, is inappropriate for the purpose.[14] On the contrary, the use of imagery, simile and metaphor (for example, chunky harmonies, swirling arpeggios, flinty rhythms), of expressions which have their natural home in talk about human attributes and mental states (for example, a despairing or triumphant chord, the nervous or resolute lines of a drawing, a gauche or poised literary piece), of words and phrases that might seem to stop short at a concern with craftsmanship and skill (for example, a roughly hewn sonata movement, a finely wrought plot) is the *sort* of linguistic device which serves to guide ear and eye, to reveal and open up fresh perceptions, to communicate both subtle nuances or defects and the overall flavor of a piece. And it is some indication of aesthetic development when pupils become able to employ language in this manner, making more sparing and more judicious use of, for instance, "lovely," "horrible," "nice," "ghastly," and applying a greater variety of terms to music and dance in particular than those old war-horses "jolly" and "sad." The possibility of their picking up clichés and or parroting what others say, or merely making what they take to be the "right noises" has, clearly, to be borne in mind. On the other hand, children's sincerity and the nature of their responses are often manifest in what to the adult may seem unexpected ascriptions or in those of their own invention (for example, "a wiggly, scarifying tune").

To move back and forth between the more straightforwardly descriptive and the more evaluative uses of language is, as we have already seen, a characteristic feature of discussion which involves the attempted justification of aesthetic appraisals. And here the educator faces a most challenging task. For by their very nature aesthetic appraisals are always subject to revision, and, in the case of the arts, further knowledge about works from the past, together with changing social and cultural values, may make for the significance of now this aspect of a work, now that, being highlighted in such a way that it might seem as if in this realm everyone's view is as good as the next one's. The teacher, then, has to try to create the sort of atmosphere and conditions which favor what Collinson calls a "respectful, welcoming attitude" toward an art work (or a child's piece). Yet, while it is desirable to extend "patience and favor" (in Elliott's phrase) to each one, there are limits. "To suspend judgment may be a virtue," remarks Eva Schaper (commenting on Elliott), "to suspend it indefinitely may often be not to say what one thinks."[15] Thus pupils have to be helped, on the one hand, to "give" themselves to a work without, however, allowing it simply to "wash over" them; on the other, to maintain a certain distance from it yet without making a clinical or slick assessment.

The aim within a general education is not, of course, to produce professional critics any more than it is to produce professional artists or performers. Nevertheless, there has to be a commitment (I would claim) to the developing of individuals who are prepared to entertain new ideas and feelings and at the same time are capable of independent judgment. It may, however, be far from easy to get them beyond the stage of merely disagreeing with others. Stock responses among older pupils such as "That's middle-class," "decadent," "out of date," "not relevant," etc., may all too readily be forthcoming without any further attempt on the speaker's part either to say exactly what he means or to support his opinions by means of comparisons or contrasts, references to observable features of the work, and so forth. ("That's a value judgment!" seems often to be trotted out, once the term is acquired, as a label for that about which nothing more can be said—as if it *precluded* rather than *made way* for rational discussion, and with little inkling, it need hardly be said, of the problematic nature of the fact/value distinction.)

Without critical reflection, however, there can be no such thing as aesthetic education: it is part of that larger task which the educator in a liberal/democratic tradition cannot shirk—the task of fostering the give-and-take of informed discussion, which involves not only confidence and skill in expressing and defending one's own views but also a readiness to listen to those of others and to be prepared to reconsider and perhaps change one's initial stance. It is precisely his concern for (and what should be his expertise in dealing with) this aspect of arts education that will make any educator pause before handing over his job to professional artists, no matter how skilled they be in their sphere (as proposed, for instance, in the Gulbenkian *Report on Dance Education*). Moreover, critical appreciation may be linked in practical ways with pupils' own artistic activities—providing verbal introductions, planning catalogues, writing program notes, résumés, reviews, and the like.

Given the nature of the critical enterprise, however, and also the assumptions and traditions that have prevailed for so long in many schools, as well as in teacher-education, it might seem easier and more enjoyable for some, teachers and learners alike, if "creative" work takes precedence over "appreciation." But it does not follow that *as arts education* it is ultimately as important. There is probably a case for young children having the opportunity to participate in "making and doing" with a variety of arts materials, though such a case may well rest on considerations other than those to do with art; and the time often spent in sheer organization before and after lessons might well give pause for reflection as to their precise aims and values. Attempts at art-making might also prove refreshing and profitable with pupils who suffer from programs in, say, music and literature that are geared to examination requirements in such a way that many merely reproduce received opinion or ways of approaching particular works (though bad teaching of this kind may well extend to endeavors to promote creative activity). Yet while pupils' own efforts may be interesting, original, and exciting, they may also be repetitive, cliché-ridden, and dull; and they can hardly be expected to be—nor, typically, are they—profound or disturbing, capable of transporting others, of jolting them out of established patterns of thought and feeling, of illuminating and extending an understanding of the human condition. To deny young people firsthand acquaintance with great art, exposing them only to the products and performances of their peers, is clearly to leave them imprisoned within the straitjacket of their own necessarily limited experience.

Moreover, the capacity to respond to mature works and performances usually far outruns the capacity to create and perform mature works: most individuals whose own efforts are obviously not of the calibre of acknowledged masterpieces are nevertheless often able, particularly with the help of someone more knowledgeable and experienced, to appreciate at least some aspects of those masterpieces. Martha Graham, for example, tells of how a boy of eight once wrote to her saying how much he liked her dance *Lamentation*, but added that he thought it too short. On thinking it over however, he said, he supposed you could not feel such sorrow for any length of time. Here, then, we have a child capable not only of responding to a work that might not have been thought especially suitable for that age but of reflecting on it, as well as on his experience of it, albeit at the level simply of liking.

The loss on the part of many older pupils, so often deplored by teachers, of their earlier freshness, enthusiasm, and general readiness to "have a go" at making and doing in the arts might, indeed, be better regarded as a potential gain—a gain in terms of greater powers of self-criticism, more realistic self-assessment, and increasing awareness of standards. What seems to be dissatisfaction with an activity is frequently, in fact, dissatisfaction with themselves, their own amateurish and perhaps rather pedestrian achievements, as their horizons expand and change. It may also result, as Reid points out, from some teachers, obsessed with ideas about expression, freedom, and the fear of "imposing" anything on pupils, falling into the trap of imposing of another kind—the imposition on adolescents of methods suitable only for young children.[16]

Similarly as regards performing in music and dance. And here the length of time required for the acquisition of skill and for sustained practice within even one branch or style of dance and with most instruments is such that within a general educational program relatively little progress is likely to be achieved without other arts being neglected. Yet, lacking an introduction to a *range* of arts and genres, pupils can build up only a limited, perhaps even distorted, concept of art or even of one particular art form. And to be restricted to those which have traditionally featured most prominently in "creative activities" has meant that many children have grown up with little, if any, critical appreciation of, for example, architecture and those twentieth-century arts of cinema, radio, and television which so powerfully surround them everywhere. Further, since each art form, indeed each work, has a unique contribution to make to the education of feeling, there would seem to be grounds in the case of a compulsory curriculum for a certain width of experience, as contrasted with optional courses in which pupils could pursue those activities in which they have a particular interest or ability to a greater depth.

It would certainly be mistaken to suppose that aesthetic discrimination in one art form automatically carries over to another, or that certain concepts apply, as it were, across the board. The idea that a developed sense of rhythm, phrasing, or other features of music, for example, inevitably makes for awareness of comparable features of dance or poetry is just not borne out in practice: there are many lovers of music who seem to have little "feeling" for either poetry or dance, while there are dancers who lack not only an ear for poetry (let alone a ready appreciation of its other aspects) but also musical discrimination—as witness how some choreographers use pieces of music. And any suggestion that appreciation of, say, the balance and unity of *The Winter's Tale* guarantees immediate appreciation of the balance and unity of Beethoven's Third Piano Concerto or Constable's *The Hay Wain* is quite implausible. To insist once again, aesthetic concepts (that is, concepts functioning aesthetically) are not grasped intellectually and then applied over a variety of instances: appreciation of works even within the same art form requires judgment (in that sense which involves perception and thought in felt experience) *in each particular case.*

Nevertheless, this is often assisted by knowledge of a range of works of art and other objects of aesthetic interest. Moreover, rather as one may come to appreciate the singularity of a person as a result of acquaintance with several, and at the same time develop a richer concept of "person" through knowing individuals, so in becoming familiar with individual art works and increasingly aware of similarities and differences between them one both deepens understanding of the particular work and goes on building up one's concept of art.

NOTES

1. Ludwig Wittgenstein, *Zettel*, trans. G. E. M. Anscombe, ed. G. E. M. Anscombe and G. H. von Wright (Oxford: Blackwell, 1967), para. 171.

2. John Casey, "The Autonomy of Art," *Philosophy and the Arts*, Royal Institute of Philosophy Lectures, vol. 6 (London: Macmillan, 1973), p. 75.

3. L. A. Reid, "Knowledge, Aesthetic Insight, and Education," *Proceedings of the Philosophy of Education Society of Great Britain* 7, no. 1 (1973), p. 1.

4. John Wilson, "Education and Appreciation," in *Growing Up with Philosophy*, ed. Matthew Lipman and A. M. Sharp (Philadelphia: Temple University Press, 1978).

5. Ruth Saw, *Aesthetics: An Introduction* (London: Macmillan, 1972), p. 23.

6. R. W. Hepburn, "The Arts and the Education of Feeling," in *Education and the Development of Reason*, ed. R. F. Dearden, P. H. Hirst, and R. S. Peters (London: Routledge and Kegan Paul, 1972).

7. Michael Oakshott, "Learning and Teaching," in *The Concept of Education*, ed. R. S. Peters (London: Routledge and Kegan Paul, 1967), p. 161.

8. Diané Collinson, "Aesthetic Education," in *New Essays in the Philosophy of Education*, ed. G. Langford and D. J. O'Connor (London: Routledge and Kegan Paul, 1973), p. 207.

9. Ibid., p. 197.

10. Ibid., p. 210.

11. Harry S. Broudy, *Enlightened Cherishing: An Essay in Aesthetic Education* (Urbana: University of Illinois Press, 1972), p. 105.

12. L. R. Rogers, "Sculptural Thinking," in *Aesthetics in the Modern World*, ed. Harold Osborne (London: Thames and Hudson, 1968); idem, *Sculpture* (London: Oxford University Press, 1969).

13. H. B. Redfern, "Rudolf Laban and the Aesthetics of Dance," *British Journal of Aesthetics* 16, no. 1 (1976); idem, "The Place and Use of Language in Dance Appreciation," *Collected Papers in Dance*, vol. 3 (London: NATFHE Dance Section, 1984).

14. L. A. Reid, *Meaning in the Arts* (London: Allen and Unwin, 1969), chap. 1.

15. Eva Schaper, Chairman's Remarks, "The Critic and the Lover of Art," in *Linguistics Analysis and Phenomenology*, ed. W. Mays and S. C. Brown (London: Macmillan, 1972), p. 139.

16. Reid, *Meaning in the Arts*, p. 271.

HOWARD GARDNER

Toward More Effective Arts Education

Introducing the Four Elements

The major players on the arts education scene can be likened to the members of a newly formed string quartet. No matter how skilled each of the players may be individually, successful performance as an ensemble remains a formidable challenge. While realizing their individual parts properly, the players must learn to listen to one another, to pick up subtle cues of timing, attack, phrasing, etc., to arrive at the same—or at least concordant—interpretations of a piece and to blend these in a performance which makes sense not only to the players themselves, but also to their wider audience. When—for whatever reason—the players have hit upon the appropriate playing stances, the resulting sounds can be magnificent, but only careful working together over many years can ensure performances of a predictably high quality.

In incipient efforts to improve arts education, I've come to anticipate four separate players, or elements, on the scene. They may announce themselves overtly, or they may lurk in the background; but ultimately they must all be taken into account and synthesized if the effort is to succeed. To begin with, there are the *philosophical* notions of arts education: What is the purpose of teaching the arts, how are the arts construed, how do they relate to the rest of the curriculum and to the rest of society? Next, there are *psychological* accounts of learning in the arts: What is the student like, how can teachers work effectively, what are the effects of particular media of instruction, how does one evaluate success or failure? A third component entails the *artistic practices* of the past: What sorts of things have been done (for whatever reason); which kinds of settings have been favored; who are the masters, the students, the expected audience? And the final component—particularly complex in any industrialized society—is the *ecology of the educational system*: the assigned curricula, the school administration, processes of certification and licensure, the decision-making processes. Certainly, these four elements interact with and sometimes blend into one another; and a given component might be assigned under one interpretation to one element (say, philosophy) or to another (say, psychology). But in one way or another, concordantly or discordantly, these four voices will be heard.

. . . Project Zero was conceived—and in fact named—over twenty years ago in an attempt to understand, and ultimately to improve the quality of, arts education in our society. To say that at least some of us were naive about the complexity of the arts education scene is neither to criticize nor to compliment us—but that naivete has long since vanished! Many different histories of our Project can be written, reflecting the perspectives of the various participants and of the two major working groups. As it happens, a history which stresses our respective relationships to each of the four elements of arts education proves particularly relevant to my present theme: efforts to improve education in the arts.

The Elements at Project Zero:
The View from the Development Group

Building on the work of earlier philosophers, and particularly of founder Nelson Goodman, much of the work at Project Zero during the early years was concerned with discovering a viable *philosophical basis* and working out some of its implications for psychological and educational purposes.[1] It has proved epistemologically cogent and empirically suggestive to view trafficking in the arts as the handling of various symbol systems, such as language, picturing, gesturing, or music. Indeed one might think of the arts as involving the use of certain sets of symbols in certain ways—for example, attending to fine details in a symbolic pattern or apprehending the expressive potential of a particular symbolic configuration. On this view, an individual who would participate actively in the artistic process must learn to "read" and "write" in these different symbolic systems. And so arts education can be usefully viewed as the imparting of literacy skills in the area of artistic symbolization.

This apparently simple formulation turns out to be surprisingly productive. On the one hand, it supplies a clear direction—if not a metric—for effective arts education. To the extent that an individual becomes literate with a given symbol system in the arts, to the extent that he or she can productively perceive, create, or reflect within that system, one may assume that arts education has achieved some success. The Goodman formulation also avoids certain problems which have plagued conceptions and programs of arts education. While none would deny the import of issues of artistic value and merit, these prickly issues can be bypassed for many educational purposes. One need not make a decision about the overall merit of a work in order to understand its import, impact, or mode of functioning. By the same token, a focus on artistic symbolization makes it possible to demystify artistic processes. Whatever the role of inspiration, mystery, or emotional catharsis in the arts, these are much less readily dealt with in education than the regular and systematic (if somewhat less provocative) processes of symbolic cognition.

In our own work in the "Development Group" at Project Zero, we elected early on to examine the development in normal (and later, in gifted) children of various symbol-using capacities in art.[2] In what might be termed the *psychological* phase of Project Zero, we examined the steps through which children pass as they master various components of different artistic symbol systems: how they learn to appreciate style in different art forms; how they come to apprehend metaphor and other forms of figurative language; how they incorporate into their own fledgling works those expressive components which confer power and significance upon artistic symbolization. To be formulaic about it, we sought to cross the Goodman taxonomy of different symbolic systems and processes with the developmental approaches fashioned by Jean Piaget[3] and other cognitive-developmental psychologists. The story of our principal research approaches and topics has been related in many places . . . and so it need not be rehearsed in any detail here.

Still, even as we have confessed our naivete above, it is worth spending a moment to consider the various ways in which our view of artistic development has been altered over two decades and as a consequence of several dozen studies of children engaged in artistic activities. At first, like any fledgling research team, we had hoped to document a simple linear story of artistic development, one which would obtain across all art forms and all normal children, one which could take its place along the seemingly straightforward saga of moral development or the development of logical thinking. It was not to be so. (Nor, instructively, did it prove to be so in these other areas of development.) One can summarize our various realizations in the following succinct statements:

1. Development of skills in one artistic symbol system, say music, occurs in a systematic way, but the facts of such development cannot simply be applied to other artistic systems. In fact, each artistic area exhibits its own characteristic developmental paths.[4]

2. Rather than thinking of cognition as developing "of a piece," it is more accurate to view the intellect as having a number of separable components. We speak of the development of several distinctive "intelligences," each with its own peculiar trajectory. Whether an intelligence—like linguistic or bodily—is put to an artistic use turns out to be a personal or cultural decision, not an absolute imperative.[5]

3. Even as these intelligences develop in distinctive ways, they also have specific representations in the human nervous system. The various human symbolic competences can be mapped, at least roughly, onto different brain regions, across the two cerebral hemispheres, and within these cortical regions as well. Project Zero has pioneered in the study of cortical representation of different artistic symbolic skills.[6]

4. In some areas of development, children may simply get better with age, but this simple formula proves inadequate, and to some extent erroneous, in the arts. Indeed, in a number of ways, children before the age of seven display behaviors and proclivities which are closer to those of practicing artists than do youngsters who are in middle childhood.[7]

5. It is possible to put forth a sketch of prototypical artistic development in particular art forms, but there will be significant individual differences even among normal children. Thus, in the course of acquiring drawing skills, some children will focus on contours or patterns of specific objects, while others will rely on preestablished schemas or conventions.[8] Children with unusual talent or pathologies may follow still other courses. And the course of development may once again differ in cultures which are remote from one another.

6. Even as there are different courses of development in the productive sphere, there are separate developmental sagas which govern skills of perception, reflection, and critical judgment. Oftentimes, as in other developmental domains, perceptual capacities are more sophisticated than productive skills, but there are also some instances where production can be precocious.[9] The orchestration of perceptual, productive, and critical skills turns out to be a complex undertaking.

While it could be readily extended, this list of findings should give a feeling for the kinds of concerns which the development group has pursued and the kinds of conclusions to which we currently subscribe. Our area of study is still in its infancy, but it would not be inappropriate to claim that we have put forth an initial developmental psychology of the arts, one which can now be pitted against competing formulations.

But a developmental psychology is not a pedagogy of the arts. It soon became apparent to us—and our critics were quick to remind us—that what happens "naturally" in the course of development is in no way equivalent to what *can* happen, given a particular educational regimen or in light of the messages embedded in a given cultural setting. Developmental factors may set a kind of upper bound on what can be mastered at any particular time, but certainly the crucial factor in artistic achievement is the quality of education. If we were to move from philosophy and psychology to education proper, it was necessary for us to consider the relationship between developmental and educational factors—between development and learning.

Initial Forays into Education

It would be a gross caricature of Project Zero's history to contend that our philosophical and psychological studies were ever all-consuming. Indeed, from its earliest days Project Zero has been involved in a variety of ways in educational concerns. Under founding director Nelson Goodman, a memorable series of lecture-performances was staged for the Boston community in the late 1960s. At the same time, members of the staff undertook a rather detailed survey of ongoing effective arts-educational programs. This study not only familiarized us with the facts—and the conditions— of American arts education; it also gave us a preliminary feeling for the kinds of approaches which are usually successful and for those which are not. Thus, for example, we observed that the stated goal of a program was an unreliable guide to its overall quality or even to what was actually done from one day to the next: philosophical statements sometimes loom in splendid isolation from day-to-day practice. On the other hand, a tremendous amount of educationally effective insight might by conveyed "on the scene," in a manner akin to coaching, even by individuals who were notably inarticulate about what they were doing or why they were doing it.

Over the years there have been many other involvements, indeed forays far too numerous to mention, ranging from participation in the planning of radio and television programs in arts education to

studies of effective museum education to the staging of pilot programs of artistic training in local public schools. To my own mind a
particularly memorable experience was the assembling outside of
Boston of some thirty arts teachers from all over the nation who
had been singled out for the excellence of the arts programs in their
local schools. Once again, these teachers differed enormously from
one another on almost every dimension, and certainly in terms of
their articulateness. But what joined them was incredible dedication to their task; a studied indifference to "negative signs" from
uncaring colleagues or administrators; the capacity to integrate personally significant messages and themes into their pedagogy and
their work; and a desire to provide means of expression and communication, as well as clear-cut skills, to all students, and perhaps
especially to those who do not stand out in the traditional academic subjects.

But informative and even bracing as such forays may be, they
cannot substitute for a more intensive and longer-term involvement
in the arena of education. Project Zero might have elected to remain
primarily an "ivory tower" undertaking, tolerating occasional flirta-
tions with practice. In recent years, however, we have felt an ever-
stronger urge to collaborate with practitioners in arts education and
to become involved in projects located in the schools. We hope that,
as a consequence of two decades of research, we have something to
contribute; and we are quite certain that we have much to learn
about the two elements of arts education which until now have not
constituted a primary focus of our inquiry: effective artistic practices and the ecology of the educational system.

Project Spectrum and Arts Propel: Two New Initiatives in the School

In our observations of American schooling we have been struck by
the relative neglect of artistic intelligences and artistic education. The
"prototype" in most educational environments remains the identification, cultivation, and rewarding of two forms of intelligence—linguistic and logical-mathematical talent. Those blessed with that
combination of intelligence are virtually guaranteed a positive experience in the schools, while those exhibiting poor performances in
these two intellectual areas are destined to have a frustrating school
career and, in too many cases, a flawed conception of self.

Two collaborative initiatives that we have recently undertaken have
grown out of our work in the theory of multiple intelligences and

our dedication to the improvement of education in the arts. One, Project Spectrum, undertaken in conjunction with David Feldman of the Eliot-Pearson Children's School at Tufts University, is concerned particularly with preschool education. It has as a principal goal the devising of new means for assessing the intellectual proclivities of young children, and especially those proclivities which lie outside of standard academic areas. Increasingly, Spectrum has also emerged as a model of curriculum in the preschool area.[10]

The second effort, Arts Propel, a coventure with the Educational Testing Service and the Pittsburgh Public Schools, is an attempt to develop reliable means of assessing artistic potential and achievement in junior and senior high school children. We hope that these new means of assessment will be useful both to school teachers and to college admissions officers as a means of broadening their conceptions of student achievement.

Project Spectrum is built on two assumptions. First, that as young as the age of three or four, children differ from one another in systematic ways in the kinds of intellectual proclivities they exhibit. Second, the optimal way in which to assess—and to cultivate—these proclivities is to provide ample opportunities for youngsters to explore materials which engage their intellectual strengths.

Accordingly, working with teachers in a classroom at the Eliot-Pearson Children's School, we have created a rich environment consisting of puzzles, games, expressive media, instruments, activities, "nooks," and other paraphernalia which should engage various intelligences and combinations of intelligences. A large proportion of these materials is drawn from the arts—an appropriate tack at any age, but particularly so during the early childhood years. By watching the children as they interact with these materials during "free play" and by monitoring their behaviors as well under more controlled conditions, we secure information on the intellectual propensities of these children. We also are assessing their working styles.

At the conclusion of the year, we summarize our findings in Spectrum Reports, brief essays which seek to portray the landscape of the child's mind. Coupled with this description are suggestions of the kinds of activities which might engage the child further—at home, in school, and in the wider community.

Conceived of initially as a means of assessment, Spectrum has increasingly become an approach to curriculum. We feel that, at this early point in development, the provision of rich opportunities for exploration, invention, and transformation constitutes the optimal educational approach. When children hesitate to become involved with our materials, we provide special scaffolding; and when children are precocious, we propose more systematic training. But by and large, our developmental findings suggest that this is a time for self-initiated discovery and mastery.

A few years later, the time has come for more active intervention in the child's learning. We believe, nonetheless, that much in the ambience of the Spectrum classroom atmosphere ought to be preserved. Perhaps there can be a kind of "trickle-up" process, whereby aspects of Spectrum can also permeate the elementary grades. Indeed, a "Key" elementary school, based in part on Spectrum and multiple-intelligence concepts, is currently in operation in Indianapolis. Not surprisingly, its architects are arts teachers; and, without question, such a school is hospitable to the arts.

But schools and school systems which welcome the arts are a rare commodity on the contemporary American scene. The original purpose of our second initiative in the schools—Arts Propel— was to assess artistic potential, much in the way that IQ or SAT instruments are *designed* to assess scholastic potential. But we soon discovered that it was virtually impossible to assess artistic potential: most American children and adolescents have so little artistic training that one has to start from scratch. Thus, once again, what began as an assessment endeavor has come to resemble a curricular undertaking.

Based on our own studies of practicing artists, of effective arts education, and of children developing in the arts, we have arrived at a particular perspective on arts education. Arts Propel is an acronym which seeks to capture the principal components of an arts education: production, perception, and reflection. In our view, which contrasts in certain respects with that of the Getty Trust, production must remain central in arts education and particularly so among precollegiate students. The heart of any arts-educational process must be the capacity to handle, to use, to transform different artistic symbol systems—to *think with and in* the materials of an artistic medium. Such processes can occur only if artistic creation remains the cornerstone of all pedagogical efforts.

Yet production alone is not enough, at least not enough in the current cultural ambience. Nor does it suffice—as it once did—for a teacher simply to be a good practitioner of an art form. No, on our formulation the ability to effect discriminations, to perceive artistically distinctive features, is a necessary partner in artistic competence. So, too, is the capacity to reflect upon the arts, upon one's own goals and methods in artistic production, and upon the means and aims of other artistic practitioners. And so, in our Arts Propel conception, there is a constant dialectic among production, perception, and reflection, with each step informing and enriching the others.

How does Arts Propel work? There are two important and related components. On the one hand, we have devised richly textured tasks in several art forms—music, imaginative writing, and drawing—which call upon the skills of production, reflection, and perception. In one task in the visual arts, for example, students begin with the perceptual task of discriminating an original of the *Mona Lisa* from fakes of various degrees of persuasiveness; this perceptual task leads to a set of reflective exercises and also to productive experiments in handwriting and calligraphy. To take another example, this time from music, students begin by rehearsing a piece of music, but use this activity as a springboard for effecting various kinds of aesthetic discriminations and for reflecting upon what makes for a stunning or a lackluster performance.

Clearly, it should be possible—though it may not be easy—to arrive at means of assessing success at these various projects. Indeed, we can to some extent adapt the scoring systems developed in earlier empirical work at Harvard Project Zero. The greater challenge will be the development of assessment techniques for the second prong of Arts Propel—the collection of student portfolios.

Portfolios are familiar to observers of art education, because most professional schools require aspiring students to present a collection of their best work. We have greatly expanded the notion of the student portfolio. In our version, we are interested not primarily in the final or the best works, but rather in the processes and the components of the student's growth over significant periods of time. Thus the portfolios for which we are calling consist of notes on the gestation of a work; successive drafts, models, and reformulations; journal entries about one's learning, including reflections on exercises and projects; fine-grained tracings of the steps in a single work as well as broader surveys of the development of a theme over the course of a semester or a year.

Collecting these portfolios should be a relatively straightforward undertaking; but arriving at a reliable and effective means of evaluating the portfolio will be a formidable challenge. How, after all, does one reduce dozens or even hundreds of pages to a manageable but still representative sample and a succinct score or description? We are currently exploring a number of approaches which include self-descriptions and evaluations; scoring the number of different attacks which a student makes on a problem; the variety of ways in which a theme is revisited; the extent of interplay among productive, perceptual, and reflective components; the evolution of ideas over a significant period of time; the ability to introduce personal elements in an effective manner, and the like. Some of these approaches can be quantitative, but many will need to rely on subjective impressions, interjudge reliability, or "holistic" scoring methods.

Even if our attempts to boil down a portfolio to a precise cipher or predicate are not wholly successful, the effort will not necessarily be unworthwhile. In our own view, the very practice of assembling a portfolio, in which the development of one's own artistic thinking can be captured, may constitute an extremely important and valuable educational exercise. (Indeed, it has been a mainstay of one of the most successful of contemporary alternative schools—the Prospect School in North Bennington, Vermont.) Portfolio-centered education may provide a counterexample to the amassing of rote knowledge which many mistake to be the purpose of secondary education; it may bring students into closer contact with their own feelings and goals; it may provide a unique experience of exploring a theme or issue in great depth, an experience which is close to vanishing in the fast-paced America of today. Not least, from our own parochial perspective, it can provide a model of how productive, perceptual, and reflective elements—which certainly mesh in the mature artist—can come together in the artistic learner as well.

Conclusion: The Enduring Rehearsal

Until now, hugging our scholarly heritage, we have described our ideas with relatively little attention to the facts of implementation. Even as we have moved from the experimental laboratory to the Spectrum or Propel classroom, we have written as if there were no autonomous culture with which to deal—no school environment which could serve as a hospitable host, or as a skeptical spectator, or a formidable foe.

But of course, this rhetorical ploy embodies a fiction. Schools and school systems are among the most enduring of American institutions and, as nearly every student of the American educational system has pointed out, they are conservative institutions, slow to change, virtually impervious to radical alteration. Nor is this stead-

fastness a dysfunctional feature: few institutions can cope with radical change, and, given the superficiality of most educational fads, a
healthy skepticism is probably a desirable trait.

There is no royal road to success in affecting American education, but many roadmarks to ensured failure. In Project Spectrum
and in Arts Propel we seek to avoid these pitfalls. While we do not
hesitate to put forth and defend our own ideas, we have sought
to understand the issues and concerns of teachers and administrators, to listen to their own ideas, to engage in a dialectic of give-and-
take where we are learning as well as sharing our own insights.
If we are fortunate, what will eventually emerge is a revised notion
of each project. This reconceptualization should reflect the legitimate interests and concerns of all the participants and therefore
stand a greater possibility of achieving some success—and of being
on the mark!

Speaking after the Battle of Britain, Winston Churchill cautioned
his fellow citizens, "We are not at the end." Then he proceeded to
add, "We are not even at the beginning of the end. But we are at
the end of the beginning." If the goal of Project Zero is to be realized—if we are to witness and foster the improvement of arts education—we must be prepared for a very long engagement. Certainly
it will be less dangerous than war—in fact, it ought at least on occasion to be fun. But it will be a difficult and long-term endeavor.
Re-embracing the opening metaphor of a string quartet, I see the
collaboration among the elements less as a rehearsal leading to a
final performance than as a continuing open rehearsal. As the players get to know one another better, the resulting renditions should
prove increasingly effective and enjoyable. We hope that efforts in
Spectrum, Arts Propel, the Indianapolis Key school, and other similar ventures will come to exhibit these qualities.

Speaking about his own profession, the great economist John
Maynard Keynes once declared, "The ideas of economists and political philosophers, both when they are right and when they are
wrong, are more powerful than is commonly understood. Indeed,
the world is ruled by little else. Practical men, who believe themselves to be quite exempt from any intellectual influences, are usually the slave of some defunct economist."[11] I would not be so bold
as to make analogous assertions about any area of educational
thinking, and yet I think that Lord Keynes had a point. The ideas of
Project Zero, and of others who have thought about arts education,
are potentially important. Having had the luxury of developing
these notions over the past two decades, we feel it is now incum-

bent upon us to try to introduce them to the wider community. Perhaps, as we collaborate with artists, teachers, and students, as we seek to combine psychology and philosophy with educational practice in active school environments, we will produce some works which merit the rapt attention of others.

NOTES

The work in this essay has been supported by the Ahmanson Foundation, the Rockefeller Brothers Fund, the Rockefeller Foundation, and the Spencer Foundation. I am grateful to these agencies for their generous and flexible support of our work.

1. Nelson Goodman, *Languages of Art* (Indianapolis: Hackett, 1976); Howard Gardner, Vernon Howard, and D. N. Perkins, "Symbol Systems: A Philosophical, Psychological, and Educational Investigation," in *Media and Symbols: The Forms of Expression, Communication, and Education*, ed. D. Olson (Chicago: University of Chicago Press, 1974), pp. 27–56; Nelson Goodman, D. N. Perkins, and Howard Gardner, *Summary Report* (Cambridge, Mass.: Harvard Project Zero, 1972).

2. Howard Gardner, *Art, Mind, and Brain: A Cognitive Approach to Creativity* (New York: Basic Books, 1982).

3. Jean Piaget, "Piaget's Theory," in *Carmichael's Manual of Child Psychology*, vol. 1, ed. Paul Mussen (New York: Wiley, 1970).

4. Howard Gardner, "Artistic Intelligence," *Art Education* 36, no. 2 (March 1983): 47–49.

5. Howard Gardner, *Frames of Mind: The Theory of Multiple Intelligences* (New York: Basic Books, 1983).

6. Howard Gardner and Ellen Winner, "Artistry and Aphasia," *Acquired Aphasia*, ed. M. T. Sarno (New York: Academic Press, 1981).

7. Howard Gardner and Ellen Winner, "First Intimations of Artistry," in *U-shaped Behavioral Growth*, ed. S. Strauss (New York: Academic Press, 1982).

8. J. Shotwell, D. Wolf, and H. Gardner, "Styles of Achievement in Early Symbolization," in *Symbol as Sense: New Approaches to the Analysis of Meaning*, ed. M. Foster and S. Brandes (New York: Academic Press, 1979), pp. 361–87.

9. E. Winner, P. Blank, C. Massey, and H. Gardner, "Children's Sensitivity to Aesthetic Properties of Fine Drawings," in *The Acquisition of Symbolic Skills*, ed. D. R. Rogers and H. A. Slobada (London: Plenum Press, 1983).

10. U. Malkus, D. Feldman, and H. Gardner, "Dimensions of Mind in Early Childhood," in *The Psychological Bases of Early Childhood*, ed. A. D. Pellegrini (Chichester, U.K.: John Wiley, 1988).

11. C. Hession, *John Maynard Keynes*, (New York: Macmillan, 1984), p. 286.

PART FIVE

_____

Teaching and Learning in Aesthetic Education

Introduction

Among the aims of liberal education are the inculcation of dispositions to express and defend one's views rationally and to respect the ideas of others in a critical spirit of give-and-take. Such objectives explain why, in the previous section, Redfern insists that aesthetic education should develop the capacity for critical reflection about art and why she is dubious about assigning the responsibility for aesthetic education to professional artists who tend to favor their own predilections.

Yet critical reflection about art needs to be guided by relevant considerations and these are what E. Louis Lankford provides in his "Principles of Critical Dialogue." Well aware of the pedagogical concerns which preoccupy the educational theorist, Lankford discusses four principles that take into account the importance of a teacher's having not only a conceptual understanding of art, but also a knowledge of relevant contexts of instruction, forms of critical discourse, and characteristics of learners. Such knowledge allows the teacher and student to move back and forth from one method of art criticism to another depending on purposes, contexts, and personal backgrounds.

The character of critical discussion about art is further discussed by David W. Ecker and E. F. Kaelin in "Levels of Aesthetic Discourse" which, once again, is an excerpt from a larger analysis that must be read in its entirety to be fully appreciated. Talk about art, the authors point out, ranges from descriptions of aesthetic experiences of art objects and events at the lower rung of their ladder to increasingly theoretical analyses at the higher rungs. The aesthetic facts of the lower rungs, moreover, provide the data for critical higher-level generalizations. Although the object of critical discussion is constituted by the explanatory apparatus preferred by a writer, not all critical models are relevant to perceiving and describing a work's artistic expressiveness and significance. In this connection the authors mention some fallacies to avoid. The import of the authors' remarks is, however, quite evident: teachers should know what they are talking about as well as the level at which they do so. The research implications of Ecker and Kaelin's analysis should be equally apparent.

Having set out principles of critical dialogue and indicated possible levels of discourse in critical talk about art, Smith's "Teaching Aesthetic Criticism in the Schools" indicates what can be involved in teaching the young to develop a knack for aesthetic judgment, understood by Smith as encompassing a number of acts—e.g., description, analysis, characterization, interpretation, and evaluation. For pedagogical purposes Smith suggests breaking these acts down into aesthetic exploratory criticism, which discovers a work's qualities and meanings, and aesthetic evaluative criticism, which defends aesthetic judgments with appropriate reasons. Smith's account of the conventional wisdom about art criticism assumes Lankford's principles of dialogue and operates at several rungs of Ecker's and Kaelin's ladder of discourse; that is, it gives attention (moving from the bottom up) to the phenomena of observation, to criticism itself, to analysis of critical discourse (meta-criticism), and to theory that controls critical activity (meta-theory). Art critics do not, of course, proceed in the formal or orderly manner suggested by Smith, nor need teaching adhere to it; but however it unfolds, responsible criticism must derive its claims from observed phenomena and ground its judgments in description and interpretation. The more teachers themselves know how to do this the better they can teach critical skills to their students.

The previous three selections concentrated mainly on the visual arts, which admittedly is the principal bias of the editors of this collection. Aesthetic considerations, however, extend across the arts, and the following selections emphasize the contributions of film, music, literature, and dance to aesthetic education, most notably in the context of developing critical reflection about art. Thus in "Ten Questions about Film Form" George Linden remarks that while the enhancement of enjoyment of films may be primary, enjoyment itself must become reflective if we are to savor a film's full quality. Linden combines genetic, intuitive, and structural methods of art criticism in order to do justice to the complexity of films. The pedagogical utility of asking questions is now well established and readers should have no difficulty applying Linden's questions to recent films. Certainly a film that answers affirmatively all ten questions is likely, as Linden suggests, to be good if not necessarily great.

Continuing the quest for an understanding of quality and excellence in the arts and aesthetic education, which is a leitmotiv of the essays in this volume, Bennett Reimer's "Criteria for Quality in Music" accents four criteria—craftsmanship, sensitivity, imagination, and authenticity. Such criteria are helpful not only for thinking about the nature of excellence in art and performance, but also for deciding on curriculum principles of selection and for reflecting about teaching and learning. Reimer contrasts better with poorer exemplifications of his criteria by showing what counts as mastery of materials in contrast to shoddy execution. For example, he discusses sensitive exploration of feeling and its obverse, moral fiber in an artist's work and its absence, and a vivid and an impoverished imagination. Reimer thinks that far from being a mystery the criteria of quality in music are quite apparent. And he leaves no doubt that aesthetic education involves choosing and aiming for the best.

Vernon A. Howard's "Useful Imaginings" assumes that the major aim of aesthetic education is the cultivation of the imagination through the development of relevant dispositions. His remarks about the uses of imagination and the learning of dispositions follow a discussion of a master lesson in singing in which Howard makes a number of observations about the relations of technique and artistic expression and how becoming artistically competent reveals important similarities to becoming scientifically literate, a view that reflects the thinking of Nelson Goodman's essay in section 2 of this volume. After describing four uses of the imagination, Howard suggests imagination may be stretched by having students imagine the level of performance desired, by their trying out new things during the course of instruction, and by their imitating models.

Since writers often recommend that aesthetic education should include the study of visual, literary, and performing art, the question arises whether a theory of aesthetic education can assume a common model for the engagement of such different arts. In "The Aesthetic Transaction" Louise M. Rosenblatt suggests that a reader-response model has relevance not just for the study of literature but for the other arts as well. As we have indicated before, the keys to a writer's thought are the distinctions it makes, and central to Rosenblatt's transactional theory are those between efferent and aesthetic reading and between the text and the object of evocation. Rosenblatt explains that while any text, or comparable phenomena in the other arts, may be taken efferently or aesthetically, only the aesthetic stance is appropriate to certain things because of the ways they encourage the creation of an object of evocation. "Object of evocation" means the quality of the experience lived by the reader during the reading of a text, and in a special sense this object is the real literary work of art. The text figures as only one part of the transaction; the others are the reader, the time of the reading, and the reader's background. Efferent reading, in contrast, does not require the creation of an object of evocation. Its aim is mainly cognitive and seeks to extract meanings that may be used in further reading or study. While efferent considerations have a place in aesthetic transactions, they become relevant only through the way they fuse with more distinctively aesthetic considerations. Once Rosenblatt's somewhat unorthodox usage is understood—her object of evocation, for example, resembles descriptions of aesthetic experience—it becomes apparent that her model has general applicability. Further, though she construes the text as merely part of the aesthetic transaction, she does not go as far as some recent literary theory (e.g., deconstruction) in completely diminishing the authority of the text.

The emphasis on critical appreciation characteristic of this section is further evident in "The Analysis of Dance" by Janet Adshead and her associates, a group of British theorists of the performing arts. Assuming that before we can fully appreciate a dance performance we must know just what there is to be appreciated, Adshead et al. adopt a scheme devised by R. A. and C. M. Smith in order to locate and explain various aspects of dance and the skills involved in describing, analyzing, interpreting, and assessing dance form. It might be said that the chart indicates some of the preconditions for taking an aesthetic stance toward dance, an art form that certainly encourages doing so. The authors are careful to point out that their scheme is only for purposes of identifying aspects of dance and does not necessarily imply a procedural order of analysis.

If, as many contributors to this volume think, the purpose of aesthetic education is to develop in the young the ability to understand what is aesthetically worthwhile in art, then it is important to know how the young acquire such understanding. Significant progress has been made in understanding the stages of children's creative abilities and now Michael J. Parsons, in "Stages of Aesthetic Development," asks if the aesthetic, appreciative responses of the young also exhibit an orderly development. Taking his lead from cognitive developmental psychology and the philosophy of Jurgen Habermas, Parsons posits differences among empirical, moral, and aesthetic understandings, and attempts to discover what is distinctive about the latter. On the basis of his studies he discerns five stages of aesthetic growth within three general stages of human comprehension. The stages, only briefly mentioned in the article reprinted in this collection, are more fully discussed in Parsons's other writings (for which see his references). Important to note about Parsons's theory of stages is its normative conception of adequacy. Later stages of aesthetic understanding are better than earlier ones; they are more adequate for sensing what is important in art and for grasping its peculiarly aesthetic meanings. Accordingly, it becomes possible both to detect and assess aesthetic development and to intervene positively in it. Parsons provides an important contribution to aesthetic understanding and his achievement is indispensable for further work in cognitive studies in aesthetic education.

As in previous sections, it is possible to interrelate the several contributions just discussed. The goal of a critical appreciation of art remains constant, as does the emphasis on excellence and quality. The goal of aesthetic understanding (Parsons) provides a context in which we can see the relevance of the other selections. For example, in order to further the young's capacity for aesthetic transactions with works of art (Rosenblatt), teachers must have a knowledge of the principles of critical dialogue (Lankford) and of possible levels of discourse (Ecker and Kaelin). Such knowledge will then help them to teach relevant concepts of aesthetic criticism (Smith) and to realize the need to know the conceptual character of each art (Reimer, and Adshead et al.), the teaching of which should rely heavily on the asking of relevant questions (Linden).

E. LOUIS LANKFORD

Principles of Critical Dialogue

When critics or teachers talk about a work of art, they are doing so in assumed and implied contexts. For instance, a teacher speaking with advanced art students might assume that they are familiar with certain painting techniques, that they understand what is meant by visual balance and perhaps recognize major styles of modern Western art. The teacher adjusts the vocabulary accordingly and makes casual references to concepts that in other circumstances would require considerable explanation. A critic who remarks that a painting has "an aura of mystery" implies that this is a quality worth noticing. In the critic's estimation, "an aura of mystery" is a characteristic of the work which serves to distinguish it and contributes to its value. While differing contexts might not change the intensity of an audience's response to a work of art, the character of the experience would certainly be different. If the teacher had deemed it appropriate to speak at a more elementary level, or the critic had used the phrase "utterly confusing," one might imagine how different would have been the course of critical dialogue.

The Need for Limits

What we choose to bring into critical talk about a work of art affects how the work is understood and appreciated. Guidelines exist in the form of methods of art criticism to help direct the course of dialogue by directing the attention of viewers to specific aspects of a work. Problems can be built into solutions, however. Although a method may solve the problem of how one might explore the expressive properties of a work of art, it does not usually provide for variations among viewing audiences in the application of that method. Nor do methods generally deal with the question of an object's suitability for criticism; yet varied challenges by contemporary artists make identifying art objects for review no simple matter.

Interpretation is a common element of most methods, but interpretive criteria are often vague; to wit, what information is allowable in critical dialogue? Furthermore, educators are regularly faced with the problem of how best to work subsidiary goals alongside primary goals when art criticism is practiced in the classroom.

What are the limits of critical dialogue? What is appropriate critical discourse? What ought we consider prior to applying a critical method? What is necessary to really effective art criticism? I would like to propose four principles that determine in large measure the limits of critical dialogue. Strictly speaking, it is impossible to set exact limits on what may or may not be properly admitted to criticism, at least so long as artists continue to stretch perceptual possibilities through new art forms. Ultimately, critical contexts must be determined on a case-by-case basis. But an understanding of certain considerations fundamental to criticism can help create a context in which effective dialogue can take place. The principles themselves do not restrict the healthy open-endedness of talk about art. We must always be wary of recommendations that lead us to force square artworks through round perceptions. Instead, the principles are designed to suggest a consistent pattern of preparation for criticism.

Four Principles of Critical Dialogue

1. *A concept of art must determine the suitability of an object for criticism.* Ostensibly, if the term "art criticism" is to be properly applied, the object of criticism should be a work of art. Elsewhere I have argued that the question of artistic objecthood is ancillary to aesthetic expressiveness.[1] Even so, critics and teachers are occasionally faced with the challenge of defending the inclusion of an object in the study of art to a skeptical audience. It does little good for someone to proceed through a method as an academic exercise when the object under investigation has already been rejected as unsuitable, that is, as an object so remote from the viewer's concept of art that it seems little more than nonsense. This is seldom a problem with traditional forms of art like drawing and painting. It becomes an issue of major proportion when the object constitutes a radical departure from commonly recognized art forms. Giant curtains draped across valleys, strange monoliths rising from the desert, men and women who perform instead of paint—these are viewer puzzlements whose existence requires explanation before critique.

It is not my intent here to launch into a treatise on the theory of art, but it does make sense to recognize the importance of a concept of art to critical dialogue. Establishing the status of an object as art can alleviate uncertainty and pave the way for criticism. Criteria for acceptance will vary according to the theory or concept applied. Dickie and Sclafani[2] have suggested that the theory of art can be divided into three types, each of which has multiple variations: essentialistic, antitheory or open-concept, and concepts that depend on social institutions more than on properties of objects. By accepting one point of view the critic is making a decision to apply given criteria when selecting objects for examination. Or the decision may be an eclectic one, resulting perhaps in greater flexibility at the expense of consistency.

In any case, even if the concept of art is judged unimportant in relation to a concept of aesthetic experience, it is that initial passage of an object into the realm of art that warrants its examination in the ways and means of aesthetic criticism, as has been indicated in the methodologies of Broudy,[3] Kaelin,[4] and Smith.[5]

2. *A commitment to a context of relevant dialogue is necessary to effective art criticism.* Generally speaking, a context of relevant dialogue is composed of two overlapping elements: directives for perception and restraints on critical judgment. For example, one widely held directive is that any property of a work of art may have a bearing upon the meaning of the work. It is therefore improper to exclude arbitrarily one corner of a painting from critical examination and description. A widely held restraint is that a critical judgment must be supported by adequate reasons; that a simple statement of preference does not constitute sound judgment.

Plunging into dialogue without some sense of what is relevant and what is tangential or irrelevant can result in confusion, conflict, and inconsistency leading to weak critical syntheses. If we return to the question of what information we can bring into dialogue, we can see that the reply will provide a context of relevance by which we may interpret works of art.

To illustrate the importance of this principle I would like to examine briefly two popular approaches to art criticism, labeled "intrinsic criticism" and "contextual criticism" by Stolnitz.[6] Contextual criticism leads viewers to consider a work of art in terms of a range of referents extending beyond the visible structures of the work into areas of social and artistic origination and influence. Usually, this includes the cultural milieu and environment surrounding the creation of the work, biographical circumstances of the artist, and the apparent evolutionary or revolutionary character of the artwork in relation to the history of art.

Criticism of contextualism usually centers on the possibility of dialogue ranging too far from the unique characteristics of a work of art. Other arguments are that historical information is often piecemeal and that images and symbols take on new meaning through the passage of time. Artists are also recognized for their ability to perceive the world in peculiar ways, thus knowledge of culture will not fully account for artistic production.

Intrinsic criticism has as its focus the properties and qualities of the work of art. As exemplified in the work of Ecker and Kaelin,[7] the value and pertinence of critical dialogue is weighed against its ability to reveal what and how a work of art actually communicates. For dialogue to be relevant, it must be bracketed within the context of a publicly perceivable object, namely, the work of art itself. Criticism of this type involves identifying visual elements and their relationships and discovering how these visual structures affect the way we feel and how they contribute to the meanings conveyed.

Criticism of the intrinsic focus can come from two directions. For aesthetic educators, there is the concern that avenues of appreciation may be barricaded by overly restricting what may be included in class discussions. Students whose normal behavior is to dismiss Abstract Expressionism might have their interest piqued by tales of flamboyant modern artists and revolutions in the art world.

For critics, it is difficult to assess precisely what can be brought to an interpretation of a work. Is it misguided when discussing *Guernica* to reveal that a Basque village had suffered saturation bombing? Is Picasso's message so global as to render specific references picayune?

Clearly, not even a well-worked-out context of relevance is beyond question. Decisions must always be reached based on an interpretation of the context of relevance as applicable to the circumstances of the moment. But either of the approaches described would still be preferable to a haphazard one. Either can provide a well-grounded and evenhanded standpoint regarding works of art. There are advantages and disadvantages offered by each of these seemingly contrary strands of criticism. If it is not entirely possible to have the best of both worlds, it should be possible to capitalize on shared interests. The next two principles can help to clarify some of these so that harmonization of the two approaches can to some extent be achieved.

3. *Goals of art criticism must be established before the application of a method.* Whether criticism is accepted at its simplest level as "talk about art"[8] or a more expansive goal is adopted, such as "the criticism of life in the furtherance of humane values,"[9] the knowledge that something identifiable and worthwhile will be accomplished

through critical dialogue acts as a motivation and ultimately forms a sense of closure. Goals may be broad enough to encompass the ends of both contextual and intrinsic approaches, e.g., criticism is a means for enriching experience of artworks by making perceptions more discriminating and comprehension more thorough. But broad goals, particularly in educational situations, are supplemented by secondary goals or conjoined with other goals that have a direct bearing on critical proceedings.

It is not unusual for those in aesthetic education to seek to develop in students a keener perception of art as a social phenomenon. It would not seem unreasonable, then, that a critical discussion of a satiric engraving by William Hogarth would include references to early eighteenth-century London. A great deal of information about period morals, politics, and social customs could be used to help satisfy the social goal as well as meet the demands of contextual and intrinsic criticism. Only if the references did not serve to illuminate the perceptible properties of the engraving would the canons of intrinsic criticism be violated.

Multiple goals could certainly alter the emphasis placed on aspects of criticism. An educator seeking to develop empathetic sensitivity in students might stress the kinesthetic impressions evoked by an Italian Futurist painting. The same painting would be a study in the dynamics of line, rhythm, and color for a class learning principles of design. Provided other aspects of the work—symbolism, for instance—were not altogether ignored, neither teacher would be guilty of doing an injustice to the work, nor of bastardizing the process of criticism. The character of the critical experience would be adjusted to meet the demands of the educational arena in which criticism was taking place. Such shifting emphases are not only justifiable but natural and unavoidable. The perceptions of a critic are always shaped by precedent and critical priorities.

It would be counterproductive if goals were misaligned or misrepresented—if, for instance, a purely sociological account of Hogarth's works were given in lieu of aesthetic criticism, when criticism was the objective. But when goals are properly identified and thoughtfully balanced, critical dialogue can proceed with greater clarity and to maximum advantage.

4. *Characteristics of the participants should be ascertained prior to critical dialogue.* Every good critic and educator is aware that participants enter into dialogue with certain levels of experience, knowledge, and aptitudes relative to the subject at hand. Language is best geared to

a level that is at once readily understood yet intellectually challenging. It is important to be cognizant of the effect on art criticism these variables have, not only in terms of the complexity of vocabulary used, but also in terms of the relevance of statements made.

Suppose a critic made the statement, "This painting, while not by Picasso, exhibits many characteristics similar to Picasso's style of Analytic Cubism." For those familiar with Analytic Cubism, the statement functions as more than just a comparative remark; it is a signal to search for and recognize abstract forms depicting singular objects from multiple viewpoints, collage techniques, or a monochromatic color scheme. The concept of style is used as a shortcut to describe properties of the work of art. In this regard such references work in the service of both intrinsic and contextual criticism.

The effect on those unfamiliar with Analytic Cubism would be quite different. The same statement would function as a lesson in style, diverting attention away from characteristics of the work of art in particular and leading into speculative generalizations about Picasso's manner of painting. It is likely that such a move would be questioned in terms of its relevance for critical methods and goals.

In either case, the direction of critical dialogue could be altered by succeeding statements. "The painter was a disciple of Picasso" follows a decidedly contextual line, since it does not refer to qualities of the work of art itself. The statement "Like Picasso, the artist uses geometric planes, strong diagonals, and pronounced textures to form a complex pictorial space" would carry weight in both contextual and intrinsic contexts.

It is probably correct to say that the greater the art knowledge and experience of participants, the greater the potential for harmony among critical approaches. Knowledge of terms, techniques, styles, history, and culture can be learned outside of the context of critical dialogue but later may be applied toward the understanding and appreciation of works of art through the practice of art criticism.

Summary

In this essay I have attempted to demonstrate the need for guidance in critical dialogue beyond that offered by methods of art criticism. Values and concepts carried into criticism, even when filtered through the framework of a method, strongly affect how a work of art is perceived. By outlining four principles of critical dialogue, I hoped to suggest a consistent pattern of preparation for criticism which could, in turn, create a context in which effective critical dialogue can occur. In the process of realizing these principles, it is possible to reconcile to some extent contrasting approaches to art criticism.

NOTES

1. E. Louis Lankford, "A Phenomenological Methodology for Art Criticism," *Studies in Art Education* 25, no. 3 (1984): 151–58.

2. George Dickie and Richard J. Sclafani, eds., *Aesthetics: A Critical Anthology* (New York: St. Martin's, 1977), pp. 2–3.

3. Harry S. Broudy, "A Common Curriculum in Aesthetics in Fine Arts," in *Eighty-second Yearbook of the National Society for the Study of Education* (Chicago: University of Chicago Press, 1983), pp. 219–47.

4. Eugene F. Kaelin, *The Philosophy of Aesthetics: A Phenomenological Approach* (Saratoga Springs, N.Y.: Empire State College, 1973).

5. Ralph A. Smith, "Teaching Aesthetic Criticism in the Schools," *Journal of Aesthetic Education* 7, no. 1 (January 1973): 38–49.

6. Jerome Stolnitz, "The Educative Function of Criticism," in *Aesthetics and Criticism in Art Education*, ed. Ralph A. Smith (Chicago: Rand McNally, 1966), pp. 364–72.

7. David W. Ecker and Eugene F. Kaelin, "The Limits of Aesthetic Inquiry: A Guide to Educational Research," in *Seventy-first Yearbook of the National Society for the Study of Education* (Chicago: University of Chicago Press, 1972), pp. 258–86.

8. Edmund B. Feldman, "The Teacher as Model Critic," *Journal of Aesthetic Education* 7, no. 1 (January 1973): 50.

9. Smith, "Teaching Aesthetic Criticism," p. 38.

DAVID W. ECKER & E. F. KAELIN

Levels of Aesthetic Discourse

In order to present a synoptic view at the start, we shall arrange the orders or levels of discourse that may be associated with any knowledge claims concerning the existence or interpretation of aesthetic objects. A quick glance at figure 1 will reveal that each higher level of discourse has as its object of reference either one or more, perhaps all, of the strata located beneath it. This stratification will

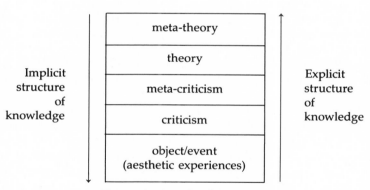

Figure 1. Levels of discourse

be useful to outline the limits of the various roles or professional attitudes, various techniques and methods proper to each of these, and finally the routing necessitated for checking any truth claims made at any one level. The orders of knowledge discriminable within the diagram will vary depending upon our point of departure beginning, for example, from either the top or the bottom of the "ladder." From any superordinate position, the warranted knowledge claims of a subordinate stratum will be taken as implicit, whereas the implicit knowledge of the subordinate strata is raised to the level of explicitness at that level of discourse. This means, in effect, that if too many rungs of the ladder are missing and if one's aim is to achieve explicit knowledge of aesthetic objects, then "one just can't get there from here."

To begin at the bottom, aesthetic inquiry must be grounded, as any other would-be scientific investigation, in the data of observation. But it matters greatly which data. Ultimately, all theorists who would also be practitioners must be able to point out the facts referred to in their discourse, or, in Peirce's terms, to devise a system of indexical terms to "tie theory to nature." The facts of aesthetic experience, qua aesthetic, must therefore constitute the data for aesthetic theory. In their attempts to meet this primary condition of referential adequacy,[1] some aestheticians have gone beyond the facts of actual response and substituted the data of other disciplines as explanations for the existence of aesthetic objects. Cases in point are George Santayana[2] and, in some of his unwary moments, D. W. Prall.[3]

Naturalistic explanations of aesthetic objects, however, are reductionist in that they attempt to explain the occurrence of aesthetic data in terms of natural—read "physical," "physiological," "biological," or, most often, "psychological"—phenomena. Thus, color is associated with light waves and their various physical properties, tones with sound waves and their properties, and so forth. Since such physical properties do not enter into the psychologically unique response centers of stimulated organisms, quite obviously this discourse is located at the level of theory in our scheme, and is in fact notoriously unrewarding for any inquiry occurring at a lower stratum of activity, notably that of criticism, in which critics merely give reports on the qualities they have experienced. Moreover, since it gives them no indication of how to look at the phenomenal object before them, critics have some ground for complaining against this sort of empty-headed empiricism.

For an example of physiological theory which preempts the place of straightforward critical response, consider the statement of George Santayana, who writes:

> The eye, by an instinctive movement, turns so as to bring every impression upon that point of the retina, near its center, which has the acutest sensibility. A series of muscular sensations therefore always follows upon the conspicuous excitement of any outlying point. The object, as the eye brings it to the center of vision, excites a series of points upon the retina; and the local sign, or peculiar quality of sensation, proper to each of these spots, is associated with that series of muscular feelings involved in turning the eyes. These feelings henceforth revive together; it is enough that a point in the periphery

of the retina should receive a ray for the mind to feel, together with that impression, the suggestion of a motion, and of the line of points that lies between the excited point and the center of vision.[4]

Clearly, this is physiological theory with the slimmest of ties to the phenomenal character of aesthetic experiences. Moreover, should any practicing critic be seduced by the blandishments of these naturalistic abstractions, we may be convinced that he has been deluded by a true, but unfortunately irrelevant, knowledge claim. Knowledge of the function of the rods and cones of our visual apparatus is certainly available; and, moreover, we can be assured that if they do not function, we will see nothing. But what it is that we have seen once they have been stimulated goes unelucidated in the naturalistic explanation.

On the other hand, critics, who sometimes are known to have used their eyes, use ordinary language to describe what they have seen; but even they may be deluded by a doctrine of historical development of styles or modes of expression and couch their explanations in the theoretical terms of historical analysis. We may call this the art-history fallacy of aesthetic explanation. Compare the experience of Picasso's *Night Fishing at Antibes* . . . with the historian Levitine's account of it:

> In spite of the distortions and abstractions, the artist's approach cannot be explained away as a mere "play of form." Thus, since *Night Fishing* contains a recognizable subject, as well as an intriguing manipulation of form, and is—at least from this point of view—a painting *comme les autres*, one may perhaps be justified in submitting it to the trials of a study of filiation—a typical artifice of art historians.
>
> Picasso's theme shows a degree of kinship with a variety of well-known "fishing subjects," ranging from Raphael's *The Miraculous Draught of Fishes* (Victoria and Albert Museum) to Copley's *Watson and the Shark* (Boston Museum of Fine Arts). However, this kinship is superficial. In a less obvious, but far more significant way, Picasso's composition appears to be more closely related to a lesser known work of an earlier tradition: *The Bathers*, a seventeenth-century anonymous Dutch painting in the Louvre.[5]

Just as obviously, as in the case of an appeal to physiology, this move is a snare and a trap enticing the critic to switch roles with the historian, whose specific mode of inquiry is located properly at the level of theory. In short, aesthetics as traditionally practiced, science, and history—all have a legitimate interest in aesthetic objects, but none has been a successful substitute for perspicuous criticism or authentic appreciation. One simply cannot bypass the stage of defensible art criticism.

Good critics speak in ordinary language, and when they communicate they call our attention to the phenomenal properties of the natural object. This is the process by which two centers or worlds of human experience are, as we have said above, to communicate. And the degree to which this communication takes place is a measure of the expansion of the shared contents of experience as each partner in the communication moves from the state of scepticism to ultimate self-conscious assurance in the contents of his knowledge. The only restriction we should like to place on this process is that the critic's audience test each critical assertion against the appearance in his own experience of the designated phenomenal properties. This is the task, along with some metacritical reflections, assumed by the late Douglas N. Morgan in his criticism of Picasso's *Antibes*:

> Picasso never wholly deserts our world. He plays upon and against our historic expectation-patterns. But the people he makes—while surely people and not mere symbols—are *pictorial* people, people to be seen and not sympathized with. As pictorial, they are not really distorted at all. They are exactly the kind of people they were created to be. They don't look "wrong"—they look "right." They are not "misshapen"; they are correctly shaped, in their pictorial context. These boys and girls have no antecedent history against which to speak of "distortion." They are what we see them to be, no more and no less.[6]

In a similar vein, it is one thing to mention that the *Guernica* is a mural-sized painting (11'6" × 25'8"), that its creator was Picasso, even that it was done in only one dimension of color-value (black, white, grays), still another to perceive the frightening explosiveness of the jagged forms and the way in which they express the destructiveness and consequent horror of modern warfare. . . . The language of the first description is physicalistic and value neutral; of the second, expressivistic and necessarily value laden.

The distinction drawn here, between the natural object as it has been formed by the artist and the created "object" that is a synthesis of its phenomenal properties, has likewise been the source of some confusion. Recall the argument between Mary McCarthy and Harold Rosenberg. Her insistence that only paintings hang on walls, and not human gestures, indicates to us that she was referring to the physical object manipulated by carpenters (in crating it), by movers (in shipping it), and by curators (in hanging it). Rosenberg, on the other hand, insisted that the phenomenal properties of action paintings viewed by him disclose a pattern of human gestures made in forming the object. The confusion laid out in these terms shows how there was no argument taking place between the two concerning the nature of criticism, but only about what in theory is to count as an aesthetic object. From Rosenberg's point of view, the task of the critic is to look upon the work as an action perpetrated by the artist:

> At a certain moment the canvas began to appear to one American painter after another as an arena in which to act—rather than as a space in which to reproduce, re-design, analyze or "express" an object, actual or imagined. What was to go on the canvas was not a picture but an event.
> The painter no longer approached his easel with an image in his mind; he went up to it with material in front of him. The image would be the result of this encounter.[7]

This description of the working stance of practicing artists, then, becomes a prescription for the way in which it is proper to view the work so produced. As such, the description is critical; the prescription, metacritical.

Anyone who takes the confused interchange between Rosenberg and McCarthy as an argument may be said to have committed the fallacy of discursive displacement, which English-speaking philosophers refer to rather dully as "a category mistake." Attending to one's discourse in order to avoid the category mistakes of discursive displacement immediately places one at the higher level of discursive usage. If the mistake occurs in criticism, the corrective stance is always to be found in metacriticism; if in theory, then at the level of metatheory. The only assurance, however, that metacriticism or metatheory, whose one-distance removal from a primary discursive level allows it to describe the functions of language at that level, will allow us to correct any mistakes made there, derives from the logical properties already implicit within the primary discursive levels; and the primary discursive levels themselves have significance only in the degree to which their assertions exhibit empirical adequacy. Thus criticism and theory must be both true and relevant.

In other words, there is no infinite regress in the explanation of aesthetic explanations because criticism and theory are grounded in fact. Metacriticism and metatheory are themselves grounded in the logical structures of the language used in criticism and theory. In this way all discourse having any relevance to aesthetic inquiry is grounded either in fact or in the uses of language to refer to fact. The present inquiry, constituted by a use of language concerning all uses of language relevant to aesthetic fact, may be viewed—indeed must be—as an empirical investigation of two differing but related sets of fact: first, the phenomenal appearance of aesthetic objects, and, second, the language or languages that may be used to account for their appearance.

If we are right in our interpretation of the expression, the structures of language levels related to the primary experiences of aesthetic objects constitute the relevance of the "structure of knowledge" (or its theory) for continued educational research within the domain of aesthetics proper. Given the fact that we have located at this point five levels of significant institutionalizable activity, ranging from the creation and appreciation of art to criticism or theory and from there to metacriticism or metatheory—all of which return us to our basic experience of these facts as the ultimate warrant for any knowledge claim concerning them—there would seem to be nothing more that might significantly be said on the subject. And if this is true, as we hope it is, educational researchers need not look beyond this schema to conceive an area of research but must look, instead, within it.

NOTES

1. David W. Ecker, "Justifying Aesthetic Judgments," *Art Education* 20 (May 1967): 5–8.

2. George Santayana, *The Sense of Beauty* (New York: Modern Library, 1955).

3. D. W. Prall, *Aesthetic Judgment* (New York: Thomas Y. Crowell, 1929), and *Aesthetic Analysis* (New York: Thomas Y. Crowell, 1936).

4. Santayana, *Sense of Beauty*, pp. 90–91.

5. George Levitine, "The Filiation of Picasso's *Night Fishing at Antibes*," *Journal of Aesthetics and Art Criticism* 22, no. 2 (Winter 1963): 172.

6. Douglas N. Morgan, "Picasso's People: A Lesson in Making Sense," *Journal of Aesthetics and Art Criticism* 22, no. 2 (Winter 1963): 169.

7. Harold Rosenberg, *American Painting Today* (New York: Horizon Press, 1965), p. 25.

RALPH A. SMITH

Teaching Aesthetic Criticism in the Schools

The Aim and Nature of Criticism

The ultimate aim of criticism in an open society is the criticism of life in the furtherance of humane values. To be sure, this is a revered and perennial aim of criticism, but the anti-intellectual temper of the times demands its reiteration. Another way to put this aim is to say that criticism strives to assert a measure of informal control over the quality of thought and feeling in a society. It is an exception to the general revulsion against authority that we still honor this function of criticism in scientific and technological domains. We do not want bad theories and bad engineering, and we are particularly insistent on maintaining better than minimal health standards, the safeguarding of which is not entrusted to amateurs. Yet this function of criticism is resisted in the aesthetic domain. Here just about anything goes, with superficial thought and feeling having free rein. But then, it might be asked, what's wrong with that? In the highly specialized era in which we live shouldn't there be at least one sphere of human activity in which persons can freely express their ideas and opinions, one realm of human enterprise in which expertise is not required?

These questions are not without point and I have no intention to be high-handed and dismiss them. At the same time, I think it must be acknowledged that aesthetic opinions are not always consistently held. It is not uncommon to hear persons assert in one context that art is a matter of personal taste or that all beauty is in the eye of the beholder, and in another, say, television or films, unequivocally deplore violence or pornography. Standards, then, are often appealed to; not everything is thought to be a matter for any kind of taste. Accordingly, I do not think we can afford to be indifferent either about the peculiar excellences and significances of works of art or about the kinds of attitude that should be taken toward them, however attractive the temptation not to take thought on this variety of experience.

If the ultimate aim of criticism is the criticism of life in the furtherance of humane values, the task for educational theory is to frame proximate aims of criticism that will connect with ultimate aims after schooling. We should not, of course, expect schools to effect a high level of professional critical performance; that, after all, is a lifetime goal for professional critics themselves. Rather, we should be concerned with a level of performance that is capable of achieving an intelligent interpretive perspective,[1] a capacity to perceive, understand, and appreciate works of art with quasi-professional skill. I think that a concept of criticism which divides into two basic sets of activities—into what may be called *exploratory aesthetic criticism* and *evaluative aesthetic criticism*—can help create the conditions for the kind of enlightened critical performance envisioned here as one appropriate outcome of aesthetic education.

Exploratory criticism may be described as an aid to and a means of sustaining aesthetic experience. Evaluative criticism may be called critical communication carried on in behalf of a given critique; that is, having both aesthetically experienced a work of art and provided an estimate of its goodness (or poorness), we communicate our account and defend it if challenged to do so. Each of these two basic types of criticism, in other words, performs a distinctive function.

Exploratory Criticism

By exploratory criticism, then, we shall mean those techniques and procedures that are helpful in realizing the aesthetic value of works of art. Such endeavor does not necessarily imply strong evaluative judgment. Rather, the central task is to ascertain an object's aesthetic aspects as completely as possible. Judgment in the sense of ascribing merit or pronouncing a verdict is temporarily suspended in favor of as full a view as possible. The complex entity that is a work of art cannot be immediately apprehended and thus repeated viewings are required. One must probe and explore a variety of elements, particularly their associations and suggestions, attend now to this and now to that, sense intensity of dramatic import, see aspects in one light and context and then in others, and so forth. In the early stages of aesthetic learning such probing activities will be practiced much more consciously than later when by bent of critical habit objects can be rendered meaningful more quickly.

It should be underlined at the beginning that while critical activity can be methodized and guided by some general principles, there are no hard-and-fast critical rules which, if patiently followed, will guarantee that all that can be seen in a work of art will in fact be experienced. As an aid, however, criticism is of considerable assistance and can be divided into the overlapping phases of *description*, in the sense of relatively straightforward noting of the more literal aspects of objects; *analysis*, which attends carefully to the interrelations of sensuous elements noted in description; *characterization*, which marks the peculiar nature of a work's aesthetic qualities; and *interpretation*, an effort to construe overall meaning.

Again, exploratory criticism does not imply strong evaluation, although a critical sense is not completely absent even in straightforward description: some minimal critical decisions must be made about what is worth singling out for attention. Still, there is an important difference between an effort intended to achieve a relatively neutral account of a work's properties, which may serve as the basis for strong evaluation or critical verdicts, and aesthetic evaluation, which has already formed a judgment and is concerned to communicate and defend it.

Description

In the effort to discern as completely as possible the character of a work of art, it is helpful to identify and name its major components. An exhaustive inventory is not necessarily called for, although it is well to remember that in art little things can make big differences. Such identifying and naming should include not only elements of subject matter (e.g., the objects in a still life) but also an object's major areas or formal divisions. The noting of representational and formal aspects may enable later analysis and characterization to decide whether subject and form are congruent or in conflict with each other, conditions which may affect overall interpretation of meaning and assessment of merit.

It is difficult to specify in advance all that a person needs to know in order to see a work effectively, but we can assume that in the case of serious works a knowledge of art history and aesthetic theory will stand one in good stead. Perhaps our guide in this respect can be Kenneth Clark. In *Looking at Pictures* he writes that "if I am to go on looking responsively I must fortify myself with nips of information . . . and the value of historical criticism is that it keeps the attention fixed on the work while the senses have time to get a second wind."[2] In different terms, Clark appeals to what Arthur

Danto calls a sense of an artworld,[3] an extensive knowledge of the history and theory of art.

Descriptive knowledge of the foregoing sort is often disparaged because appreciation courses are said to get arrested at this level. I suspect this charge is not always well founded, but doubtless it attests to confusion about the kinds of knowledge relevant to understanding art. Instruction that stops with literal description obviously falls short of what is singularly important in works of art. But this is not being proposed here; description is but a phase that leads on into more distinctively aesthetic territory.

Analysis and Characterization

The activity of analysis involves discerning much more closely the ways in which elements noted in description dispose themselves into a variety of forms and patterns. Thus subtle analogies as well as contrasts of color and shape may be detected, as may progressively differentiated themes. Formal analysis can be quite complicated and demanding, but there is no escaping it in the case of complex artistic artifacts.[4] Again, just how much of it should be done at a certain age or grade level is a relevant pedagogical question. It should probably be used cautiously in the elementary grades lest learners become too self-conscious about the dissective mode of attention that typifies analysis.[5] But used skillfully, analysis can lead even young minds to synoptic vision.

One cannot analyze for long, however, without noting the dramatic character of an element or relationship. Relationships are always certain kinds of relationships: elements clash or fuse harmoniously, appear in mutual or uncertain accord, attract or repel. Analysis thus tends to involve the characterization of elements and relations.

With the introduction of the term "characterization" we note a problem with critical language, if only to help explain the way critical terms are being used here. I said that we may characterize a relationship as jarring or harmonious. I could have said that we interpret, describe, or even that we evaluate it as such. For to say that "X elements jar" or "X elements harmonize" may be value judgments that X is good or bad *because* elements jar or harmonize. On the other hand, "jarring" or "harmonious" may be nonnormative descriptions which indicate that something simply *has* one or the other of these qualities. In short, it seems that we interpret as we see, that a characterization is occasionally an interpretation, and that an interpretation can sometimes be both a description and an evaluation. Such vagaries of language usage, however, should not divert attention from the fact that it is often possible to distinguish among a range of critical acts. A few words now about the properties of characterizing terms.

Setting aside those noncontroversial descriptive terms whose referents are relatively clear (e.g., "The still life contains a pipe, playing cards, and vase" or "The film is in color and deals with romantic love"), there are terms taken from nonaesthetic contexts and used in aesthetic situations to characterize works of art. It is thus one thing to say that elements are square, equidistant from each other, or converge toward the horizon line, but quite another to say they are strong, forceful, antagonistically engaged, or cast about in an atmosphere of free-floating anxiety. Whether certain elements are forceful or antagonistically engaged can be legitimately disputed, and more than one characterization of the same elements may be acceptable. But unless a work of art is radically ambiguous, it is unlikely that its pervasive quality can be both, say, turgid and lyrical. As in judging people, it is also possible to *mis*characterize elements, to be mistaken about an object's qualities, as I think the writer was who said that from Mondrian's late 1930 compositions "there emanates a mathematical harmony that has the delicacy of precision instruments, the sensitivity of radio activity, and the power of Diesel engines."[6]

A second property of characterizing terms is what was earlier called their occasional evaluative import: "X is graceful or disjointed" may convey a value judgment that X is good or bad because graceful or disjointed. But again, it may also simply assert a nonnormative description of an object's quality. When there is doubt about the meaning of critical statements there are a number of things one can do (e.g., the activities which comprise close textual analysis), but if textual analysis fails all one can do is to ask the artist, if he is available and willing to talk, what he meant. And, of course, even artists' remarks are not necessarily a final court of appeal.

Another point about such terms is their widespread use in critical talk. It is occasionally thought odd that human qualities are ascribed to inanimate material things, but it is in fact quite natural and it would be sterile discourse indeed that tried to get along without metaphorical description.[7] The displacement of sensory impressions from one sense modality to another is called synesthesia; it implies that works of art can look and feel the way human experience does.[8] And in numerous instances there is no good reason to doubt it.

Interpretation

Analysis and characterization phase into interpretation of overall meaning. Interpretation represents a kind of summary judgment arrived at by calling on all the pertinent knowledge, experience, and sensitivity a critic can bring to bear. But though overall interpretation depends on the variety of local meanings discerned in the work, interpreting is not simply adding them up to get the right meaning. There is no system of aesthetic arithmetic. The interpretation of Cézanne's *Card Players* as an "image of a pure contemplativeness without pathos,"[9] for example, grows out of local interpretations of the main figures whose "intent but not anxious" moods, "gravity of absorbed attitudes," "intense concern," and "progressive stabilization and detachment" are apparent. But, again, growing-out-of is not a simple additive process. Rather, local meanings fit or accord well with the larger one,[10] and it is a highly cultivated sense of aesthetic fittingness rather than a keen feel for discursive logic that is operative in aesthetic interpretation.

In brief, there can be variability among logically compatible interpretations of the same work; the sticky issue arises in the case of logically incompatible interpretations. Here I am saying that Cézanne's *Card Players* cannot be interpreted to mean both "pure contemplativeness without pathos" and "turbulent agitation without chaos." One meaning must be wrong, for the work is not that indeterminate or formless. The possibility must be held open, however, that new experience may turn up a more relevant, better-grounded interpretation.

An interpretation delivers the meaning of a work of art. Meaning may also be construed as the *content* of a work, in distinction from its materials, form, and subject matter.[11] Content, that is, implies an import which emerges from the interanimation of materials, subject matter, and form. Whether in Michelangelo's *Captive* or Delacroix's *Jacob Wrestling with the Angel*, subject matter and materials can be said to have been transfigured resulting in both instances in dramatic images of primordial struggle.

Evaluation and Aesthetic Argument

Up to this point exploratory criticism (description, analysis, characterization, interpretation) has been suggested as a set of techniques a learner can use to perceive an object as completely as possible. It is perhaps apparent, however, that once an object has been carefully described, analyzed, and so on, an appraisal of its worth or goodness has also been made or is at least strongly implicit in the detailed explorative account. The language of exploratory criticism, in other words, is typically normative. As indicated earlier, we describe, analyze, and characterize and at the same time, prize, appraise, and estimate.[12] Still, what criticism does in trying to render an object visible or aesthetically intelligible is in certain respects different from what it does in backing up interpretations and evaluations.

What it does in the latter case is aesthetic argument, which as here stipulated assumes that a strong critical evaluation of an object has already been made. If asked to justify his evaluation a responsible critic ought to be able to argue in favor of his assessment. This he can do by *re*describing, *re*analyzing, and so on, what he has already noticed for himself. He thus attempts in aesthetic argument to persuade others that the object is in fact reasonably seen, heard, or taken in the way his interpretation and judgment have stated. He may do all of this with quite an armament of verbal and nonverbal critical techniques. Indeed the resources a critic can use are practically limitless. Verbally, he may resurvey the same area with interesting variation, that is, point out once again both nonaesthetic and aesthetic features and how they are linked; or he may vivify with simile and metaphor, compare and contrast, reiterate and variegate, and so on. Nonverbally, he may draw on a repertoire of bodily gestures and facial expressions, which can also be effective tools of persuasion.[13]

Criticism in Action

It is now time to give body to this discussion. Meyer Schapiro's account of one of Cézanne's paintings of Mont Sainte-Victoire may be taken to illustrate criticism in action. After commenting on the importance of this mountain peak in the artist's life—Cézanne, it is said, repeatedly painted it to help externalize his own internal strivings and desire for repose—Schapiro presents his account of the painting, comparing it along the way, as critics are wont to do, with other paintings of the same subject matter by the artist.

> The stable mountain is framed by Cézanne's tormented heart, and the peak itself, though more serene, is traversed by restless forms, like the swaying branches in the sky. A pervading passionateness stirs the repeated lines in both. Even the viaduct slopes, and the horizontal lines of the valley, like the colors, are more broken than in the picture in New York. The drawing and brushwork are more impulsive

throughout. Yet the distant landscape resolves to some degree the
strains of the foreground world. The sloping sides of the mountain
unite in a single balanced form the dualities that remain divided,
tense, and unstable in the observer's place—the rigid vertical tree
and its extended, pliant limb, the dialogue of the great gesticulating
fronds from adjoining trees that cannot meet, and the diverging
movements in the valley at the lower edge of the frame.

It is marvelous how all seems to flicker in changing colors from
point to point, while out of this vast restless motion emerges a solid
world of endless expanse, rising and settling. The great depth is built
up in broad layers intricately fitted and interlocked, without an apparent constructive scheme. Towards us these layers become more
and more diagonal; the diverging lines in the foreground seem a
vague reflection of the mountain's form. These diagonals are not perspective lines leading to the peak, but, as in the other view, conduct
us far to the side where the mountain slope begins; they are pro-
longed in a limb hanging from the tree.

It is this contrast of movements, of the marginal and centered, of
symmetry and unbalance, that gives the immense aspect of drama to
the scene. Yet the painting is a deep harmony built with a wonderful
finesse.[14]

What do we have here? It may, I think, be called an instance of
aesthetic evaluation and argument.[15] Schapiro has explored the
painting, estimated the degree of its excellences, and presented
readers with an account they themselves may use in attempting to
realize the aesthetic value of the painting. It is aesthetic argument
in the sense that it is highly evaluative and persuasive; the account
invites the reader into this remarkable field of aesthetic value.
What, more specifically, is the content of Schapiro's critical account?

First, a description that noted merely representational elements—the mountain peak, foreground area with viaduct, house,
prominent tree, valley opening to the right—would obviously fail to
highlight what is most worth seeing in Cézanne's painting as a
work of art. It is not until some of its very special qualities and
relations are indicated and characterized that we begin to perceive
the manner in which the painting's sensuous elements are interest-
ingly disposed, or to see the painting's vivid qualities by virtue of
such dispositions. Thus Schapiro indicates the variety of ways in
which surface design and design in depth organically unite. He explains, for example, how the distant background tends to resolve
the strains and dualities of the foreground activity. He invites viewers to see the "majestic" mountain peak, "traversed with restless
forms, like the swaying branches in the sky," a "passionateness"

pervading the repeated lines in both, and limbs from trees which, though not touching, can nonetheless be seen as a "dialogue of the great gesticulating fronds." And he concludes that the resolution of formal analogies and oppositions gives an "immense aspect of drama to the scene."

If one examines Schapiro's critical statements carefully, one sees that they provide support for the belief that evaluative statements about a work's aesthetic goodness can be backed up with statements about its degree of formal unity, complexity, and dramatic intensity.[16] In slightly different terms, the qualities Schapiro singles out are special embodiments of such critical criteria. And it is believed by certain theorists (e.g., Beardsley) that the standards of unity, complexity, and intensity are in fact used to a considerable extent by the community of critics.

What must be discerned in a critic's account if one is interested in discovering his standards is not only the object (or parts therein) he has rated or evaluated but also his reasons for saying something is good or excellent (or the opposites of these). The norms or standards to which he appeals may be contained in or implied by the stated reasons. For example, a critic may say "X is good because of its tightly structured form" (in which case the standard appealed to is unity), or "X is good because of the great variety of detail" (complexity), or "X is good because it is delicate and graceful" (in which case the standard appealed to is degree of intensity).

More frequent, perhaps, are overall assessments that incorporate a number of these ratings, reasons, and norms; for instance, "Though it is structured rather loosely, X is good because its abundance of finely articulated details lends it an air of grace and delicacy" (in which case the standards appealed to are unity, complexity, and intensity). Or, as Schapiro could have said about the aesthetic space of *Mont Sainte-Victoire*: "The great depth, though seemingly without constructive scheme, assumes dramatic significance when its relational elements are seen to be intricately fitted and interlocked." Once again, the trinity of distinctively aesthetic standards appealed to by critics tends to be unity (e.g., "X is well organized, formally perfect, and has an inner logic of structure and style"), complexity ("X is subtle, imaginative, and rich in contrasts"), and intensity ("X is vivid, forceful, and full of vitality" or "X is tender, delicate, and ironic").[17]

The following diagram may be helpful in isolating the major components of a critical evaluation.[18] In a complete appraisal it is possible to isolate (1) the object of evaluation, or value object,

(2) the rating of the value object with a value term, (3) the reason why the object has a certain value, and (4) the standard, which is explicitly stated in or implied by the reason (3). To the extent to which a reason (3) and a standard (4) are present, they provide support for the critical judgment (2).

value object ◄─────────── rating(s)	
(1)	(2)
(3)	(4)
reason(s) ◄─────────── standard(s)	

Consider Schapiro's account of Cézanne. The value object (1) is obviously the painting *Mont Sainte-Victoire*. A general rating or value term (2) like "good" or "great" is not used by Schapiro, although he does use "marvelous" at one point and we can imagine him also using "remarkable" or "magnificent." The reason (3), at least in part, why the painting is marvelous or magnificent has to do with its "immense aspect of drama." What kind of critical reason is "immense aspect of drama"? It seems to imply the aesthetic standard of intensity, and thus we may place "intensity" at (4). If Schapiro had said "The landscape is marvelous because of its remarkable intensity," then the aesthetic standard appealed to would have been contained in instead of implied by his stated reason.

A single critical standard is, of course, not always sufficient to support an evaluation, and a final verdict will usually embody a careful weighing of merits and demerits as measured by a number of standards, not only distinctly aesthetic norms but also cognitive and moral ones. In selecting works for study in schools it might be well to select works valuable for aesthetic, cognitive, and moral reasons. How much the cognitive and moral values of art should be stressed is, of course, a legitimate pedagogical question.

I have made no reference to the role of creative activities in developing critical capacities. Such activities obviously have a place; no one is likely to be able to realize the aesthetic value of works of art without having had a fling at some making and doing. The early years and elementary grades are the time, I think, to get this kind of feeling for the shape, sound, and touch of things, along with, to be sure, some "nips of information." What we are learning about the intellectual development of the child seems to accord with this suggestion. It is during the early years that he is forging those cognitive powers and concepts that in later years he will refine and come to understand more formally.[19] The secondary grades (7–12) and the years afterward are the ideal time for the kind of aesthetic education I have discussed.

NOTES

1. A conception of general education that builds interpretive perspectives on significant domains of human experience may be found in Harry S. Broudy, B. Othanel Smith, and Joe R. Burnett, *Democracy and Excellence in American Secondary Education* (Chicago: Rand McNally, 1964), chaps. 3, 4.

2. Kenneth Clark, *Looking at Pictures* (New York: Holt, Rinehart and Winston, 1960), pp. 16–17.

3. Arthur Danto, "The Artworld," *Journal of Philosophy* 61, no. 19 (October 15, 1964): 571–84.

4. The classical analysis of form is found in DeWitt H. Parker's *The Analysis of Art* (New Haven: Yale University Press, 1926), chap. 2. See also D. W. Gotshalk, *Art and the Social Order*, 2nd ed. (New York: Dover, 1962), chap. 5; Monroe C. Beardsley, *Aesthetics: Problems in the Philosophy of Criticism* (New York: Harcourt, Brace, 1958), chaps. 4, 5; and Thomas Munro, *Form and Style in the Arts* (Cleveland: The Press of Case Western Reserve University, 1970).

5. C. L. Stevenson, "On the 'Analysis' of a Work of Art," *Philosophical Review* 67, no. 1 (January 1958): 44–45.

6. Charmion Wiegand, "The Meaning of Mondrian," *Journal of Aesthetics and Art Criticism* 2, no. 8 (Fall 1943): 70.

7. Frank Sibley, "Aesthetic Concepts," *Philosophical Review* 68, no. 4 (October 1959): 421–50, and "Aesthetic and Nonaesthetic," *Philosophical Review* 74, no. 2 (April 1965): 135–59. Both articles contain systematic discussions of aesthetic judgment and critical activities.

8. E. H. Gombrich, "Visual Metaphors of Value in Art," in *Aesthetics and Criticism in Art Education*, ed. R. A. Smith (Chicago: Rand McNally, 1966), pp. 174–75. See also Carroll Pratt, *The Meaning of Music* (New York: McGraw-Hill, 1931), pp. 150–215.

9. Meyer Schapiro, *Paul Cézanne* (New York: Harry N. Abrams, 1952), p. 88.

10. For a discussion of the relations between micro-meanings and macro-meanings, see Monroe C. Beardsley, *The Possibility of Criticism* (Detroit: Wayne State University Press, 1970), pp. 44–61.

11. Virgil C. Aldrich, *Philosophy of Art* (Englewood Cliffs, N.J.: Prentice Hall, 1963), chap. 2. Aldrich suggests that the question of meaning in art is best paraphrased as "What are we to look for in the work of art?" (p. 92).

12. As Aldrich says (ibid., pp. 88–89), "actually, description, interpretation and evaluation are interwoven in live talk about art, and there is a delicate job distinguishing them. But for philosophy of art it is possible to

make some useful distinctions in view of some real logical differences in the living language. So we picture description at the base, grounding interpretation, which is on the next level up, and evaluation, which is on top."

13. Sibley, "Aesthetic Concepts."

14. Schapiro, *Cézanne*, p. 74.

15. It might also be called a verbal report of aesthetic exploratory criticism. The report, however, is highly evaluative and persuasive and as such may also be construed as an argument for seeing the painting in the manner indicated by Schapiro. This is a somewhat special use of "argument" but one that I think is permissible. Another critic who took issue with Schapiro's account would reasonably do so by providing his own account of the painting. This is the way critics seem to argue with each other. For an instructive essay on the role of persuasion in aesthetic argument, see Brian S. Crittenden, "Persuasion: Aesthetic Argument and the Language of Teaching," in *Aesthetic Concepts and Education*, ed. R. A. Smith (Urbana: University of Illinois, 1970), pp. 227–62.

16. Beardsley, *Aesthetics*, chap. 10; and "The Classification of Critical Reasons," *Journal of Aesthetic Education* 2, no. 3 (July 1968): 55–63.

17. Beardsley, *Aesthetics*, p. 462.

18. This is a somewhat modified version of the method used to diagram classroom evaluative ventures in B. Othanel Smith et al., *A Study of the Strategies of Teaching* (Urbana: Bureau of Educational Research, University of Illinois, 1967), p. 163.

19. See R. A. Smith, "Psychology and Aesthetic Education," *Studies in Art Education* 11, no. 3 (Spring 1970): 20–30, and Charles W. Rusch, "On Understanding Awareness," *Journal of Aesthetic Education* 4, no. 4 (October 1970): 57–79.

GEORGE LINDEN

Ten Questions about Film Form

My problem is one of estimation. An aesthetic of film should not only provide one with a perspective for perception. It should also advance guidelines for judgment. Though the enhancement of enjoyment may be primary, enjoyment itself must be brought to the reflective level if the object is to be savored in its full quality. It is creative vision which we aim to engender. This implies an ability to draw distinctions between appetite and taste.

I need not dwell on the sad state of given film criticism. Most of it has been written by studio flacks or newspaper hacks. Both are out to sell something. Neither group regards film as an art. Though there has been some serious viewing and writing about film, close examination shows that even most of this degenerates quickly into morality or sociology. What is needed is to approach judgments of film from an aesthetic point of view. Such a point of view should be artistic, explicit, and precise.

Traditionally, there have been three approaches to art criticism: the genetic, the intuitive, and the structural. The genetic phase emphasizes the factors which went into the production of the work. Its aim is often to be pseudo-scientific and merely descriptive. Hence it attempts to explain how the work came to be what it is by describing its antecedent conditions. These conditions may be revealed objectively or subjectively. An objective genetic approach will emphasize previous works, derivations, and materials. Objective geneticism quickly becomes art history. Subjective geneticism dwells on the psychological makeup of the creator. Subjective geneticism often becomes merely biography or speculative psychology. Both types of genetic criticism move away from the work at eye and tend to ignore the phenomenon before us.

The intuitive approach to art criticism is a precipitate of romanticism. Its aim is to clarify the work or elucidate it through "sympathetic penetration and vivid adumbration."[1] The critic with this stance thus identifies with the work and attempts to articulate the foreground, not the background. Such an approach is basically im-

manent. When it strives for objectivity, it loses the force of vividness and often becomes a mere reporting of salient features. When
subjective, it may provide vivid insights, but it tends to degenerate
into idiosyncratic enthusiasm warped by the peculiar hang-ups of
the critic. With either emphasis, the intuitive view displays a dangerous tendency to simplify and engage in the apotheosis of the director. Film, however, is extremely complex and is the product of
many hands and eyes. Hence a more comprehensive and specific
perspective appears appropriate.

A third approach, the structural, is advocated by D. W.
Gotshalk.[2] This perspective incorporates the other two and attempts
to be more systematic and general. It establishes a general structure
of intrinsic centers of value: materials, expression, form, and function. It then examines whether these four aspects, besides exhibiting intrinsic values for perception, also cooperate to enhance,
reinforce, and reveal each other. The structural approach, being
both comprehensive and specific, appears to be particularly suited
to the analysis of a phenomenon as complex as film. The structural
approach, properly used, can be both objective and subjective.
Since film is an objective/subjective phenomenon, structural evaluation is a fitting activity. The viewpoint of the structuralist, however,
tends to be static. But film is a dynamic phenomenon. It is an attempt to project organized aural/visual movement in the absolute
timelessness of the present. The structural viewpoint does not
appear completely adequate for the analysis of such ephemeral
epiphanies.

Since the genetic approach to criticism is not always applicable
and quickly becomes art history, since the intuitive approach can be
vivid but limited, and since the structural approach would give us
general rules and standards which would be helpful but not necessarily apply to a dynamic form such as film, I propose to combine
all three approaches and to provide ten practical questions one can
ask concerning a film. I do not claim these questions are exhaustive.
I do hope they are helpful.

1. *Is the projected world pictorially plausible?* This is basically a question of unity and one is asking whether the film exhibits coherence,
consistency, and depth. The important point is: is the film coherent
with *its* situation? This is not a demand for realism, but merely that
the work be consistent with itself in such a way that everything that
is necessary is included and nothing that is needed is left out. It is
the demand that there be no contradictions without purpose for the
whole. *Beauty and the Beast* and *The Cabinet of Dr. Caligari* are highly

stylized and artificial. But the world presented by them is true to its conditions. The same may be said of *Miracle in Milan* for the exaggerated shots are true to the ironic and satirical theme.

Films may diverge from pictorial plausibility by being flashy or cliché. Being too flashy—technique for the sake of technique—is a characteristic of most films by Godard and Richard Lester. *Joanna, More, The Strawberry Statement,*[3] and *Move* all violate this criterion. All of them display flashy technique and pictorial composition which is often dazzling, but the dazzle serves no purpose. It adds no depth to character or meaning nor does it advance the theme of the film. To say that the photography is cliché is to say that it is not adapted to *this* film and hence is inappropriate. The opening sequence of *They Shoot Horses Don't They?* is lyrical cliché.[4] Since the rest of the film is tight and harsh, the lyrical opening doesn't fit the tone of the whole. Nor does it fit the form. The opening of *Shoot Horses* is a flashback. All other flashes in the film are flash-forwards except the quick cut to the horse as Gloria is killed at the end. The initial use of the flashback followed by a series of flash-forwards is disorienting. It reverses our initially established expectation and works unnecessarily against the structure of the film. The ending of *Bob & Carol & Ted & Alice* is an unwarranted romantic extension taken from *8½*. It was an attempt to add portentous meaning to what was basically light comedy. The psychedelic parties in *Midnight Cowboy, More, Bob & Carol & Ted & Alice, Diary of a Mad Housewife,* and *The Magic Garden of Stanley Sweetheart* are clichés of the with-it generation which could be cut from the films with little or no loss at all.

Pictorial plausibility may also be extended to the relations of character and situation. One may ask whether the situation of the character is consistent with his stance. Dialogue in *The Strawberry Statement* leads us to believe the hero a poor boy who worked hard to get in college and has to save money carefully. Yet his apartment is so filled with electronic gear that one almost thinks he is living in a broadcasting studio. The unremitting agony and harshness of *They Shoot Horses Don't They?* substantiates the toughness and resiliency of Gloria. It is puzzling, then, when she chooses suicide.[5] Another puzzle is where she got the gun or, if she had it, how she hid it all the time. Yet the intelligence, clarity, and strength of the whole is such that these minor defects do not ruin the film. In many weaker films they do. *A Man Called Horse* does not have its authenticity improved by the addition of Anglo-Saxon *Crest*-cleaned squaws.

As far as plausibility of character is concerned, one rule might be: look to the margins. If the background characters, the secondary and tertiary characters are strong, consistent, and well developed, the chances are it's a good film.

2. *Does this seemingly real world really seem?* Another way of putting this in experiential terms is: was the experience intensively stable? Does the film alter your way of looking at things? Were you engaged while watching it to such an extent that its images and rhythms became infectious? Again, one is not asking for realism. What one is looking for here is expressive power. *Singin' in the Rain* has a cliché plot and much camp photography. Yet its striking visuals and its high spirits, good humor, and elegance are such that one walks a little lighter and his heart dances with joy. When one walks out into the street, the sky seems bluer than blue and people are somehow lovelier. The eliciting of the extraordinary beauty of ordinary people is a basic quality of *Adalen 31;* when the film is over one wonders at the visual beauty of people he meets. On the other hand, the brooding objectivity and care of *Jules and Jim* make the outside world appear gray and complicated. A fine film not merely changes our mood, it changes our way of looking at things. One might call this the criterion of more/less. If the world outside the theater *looks* different when you leave it, the film was probably a fine film. If the rhythm of the film requires a durational span to drain from your consciousness and body, then the film was probably a fine film. If the outside world looks like *less of a place to be in*, it was probably a fine film. It presented the existential movement in its immediacy.

3. *Is the experience always fresh?* This is really a question of depth or thematic articulation and variation. Most films one has no desire to see again. Whatever was there you got the first time. But the fine film is so rich in pictorial and ideational content and nuance that, while you were whelmed, or even overwhelmed, you wish to see it once more. And when you have a second and a third and a fourth viewing you find it is even richer. The more you see it, the better it gets, and the more you see in it. *La Strada, 8½, Wild Strawberries, Citizen Kane* are all films of this type.[6] Yet the experience is always fresh and exhilarating. The first encounter with these films may have been sheer shock. They were so different from anything else, so self-complete that one did not know how to take them, and one is stunned. Yet in re-viewing them, they become more and more delightful. Film is so complex that, like a person, you have to live with it a while to get to know it. But unlike human relationships,

familiarity breeds neither contempt nor boredom. On the contrary, the greater familiarity with a fine film, the greater the delight renewed.

4. *Did the visuals and aurals work together?* In a fine film, the aurals and the visuals will work together either by complementation or by contrast. If they "split," it is probably a poor film. What I mean is this: if all you can remember after the film is over is the music, it was probably a poor film. The obtrusive blare of music in *The Magnificent Seven* and *Guess Who's Coming to Dinner* worked against the visuals. The music was so majestic and blatant, while the visuals were either unrelated or overwhelmed, that all one could remember was the music. In fact, a film may have fine music in it and, on first remembrance, you may have difficulty not only recalling what the music was but whether there was any at all. Two examples would be *The Graduate* and *Easy Rider*. In both, the visuals and audios worked so well together that one experienced them as unities, not as separate parts.

While the normal use of music in film is to fill sonic gaps or to underline the emotional substance of the visuals, it may also be used for structural echoing or reverberation. Thus in *Alexander Nevsky*, image and pitch are reinforcing structures. In Hitchcock's *Psycho*, on the other hand, music is used as pitch but not as pitch-structure and thus it strikes directly on the nerves. What I have in mind here is the scene where Norman comes barreling down the stairs and the music screams. Since there is no other music in that sequence and since it is direct and aural assault, one feels musically had.

Music can also be used as counterpoint or as inversion of the visuals. This often takes the form of irony. Thus one has musical themes playing ironic contrast *against* the visuals in *Scorpio Rising*. The same thing is true at the beginning and ending of *Dr. Strangelove*. Notice, by the way, how much more skillfully music is handled in *Strangelove* than in *On the Beach*. The "Waltzing Matilda" in the latter is so incessant that one has the feeling that Stanley Kramer is making a career of providing background visuals for foreground music. In one of his better uses of music, *Strangers on a Train*, Hitchcock uses "Ain't We Got Fun?" as ironic counterpoint to impending death. Hitchcock also displays fine use of music in *The Man Who Knew Too Much*, where it functions both as a plot device and as a means of increasing the tension of theme. In general, film accommodates itself best to "thin" music. Hence the opening Handel of *Bob & Carol & Ted & Alice* almost seems too much. And, at any rate, it is a cliché taken from Buñuel,who uses it to greater ironic depth effect in *Viridiana*. Neither the visuals nor the aurals nor both together should appear derivative, cliché, or otiose.

5. *Does it move?* Does it seem to last a short time regardless of the actual projected time? Or does it drag?[7] And if it drags, why? If a movie doesn't move, if it is merely a series of stills, it is probably a poor film. Sheer quickness of cutting or motion, however, is not enough. There must also be movement in depth. That is, movement should be more than merely surface agitation and should be appropriate to the situation. It is appropriate for comedies to move at a sprightly pace and drama and tragedy to move slowly. In both cases, however, movement should go *from* something and *to* something—for some purpose.

Motion is the disruption of stability and the change toward goal. Hence the rhythms of the film should be appropriate to the articulation of the sequence and the thematic whole. In *Petulia*, the jumpy rhythm works against the depth theme, though not as disastrously as in *The Knack*. Joseph Losey's late films, on the other hand, hardly move at all, but dwell. Some of Antonioni's and Bergman's films may be said to be almost static. What is necessary here is not merely motion, but directed motion. What is necessary is progressive development. What is necessary is growth and the emergence of perceived value.

6. *Is it merely a recorded stage play?* While the overuse of camera movement, editing, and technique can be distracting, the sheer static recording by a stationary camera produces non-film. Even though D. W. Griffith proved this point long ago and it was brilliantly expanded by Pudovkin and Eisenstein, one still sees films which are merely visual recordings. If we rule out such camp anti-films as Warhol's *Sleep* or *Empire*, we can still find films which are themselves static or still. In some cases the advance of technique was so inadequate that nothing else could be done. When sound was introduced, for example, film as a visual phenomenon almost died. Thus the early Marx Brothers' films such as *Animal Crackers* are peculiarly static.

But one might say the same thing of *Dutchman*. *Purlie Victorious* is slightly more of a film. But again what one has is a highly reverent recording of a stage play, and the camera does nothing. If the camera does nothing, the film does nothing. Reverence for drama, then, may be one reason for a film to slow down and become a non-film. In this case dialogue dominates and nothing happens on the screen. Another reason for this failing may be adulation of ideational content.

Film is not something primarily thought. It is something perceived. Hence a philosophic debate may be intellectually fascinating, but it is not film. Critics have recently rated *My Night at Maud's* as an excellent film. I would agree with them that it is excellent. I would disagree that it is a film. One might call it a fine exercise in moral decision, a subtle philosophic tract, an ironic contemplation of the accidents in life which befall a fixated personality, an interesting ethical drama, or any number of other things. But to call it a film is to falsify its nature. One becomes simply weary of reading subtitles. Perhaps it should be called a projected short story. In any case, in *My Night at Maud's*, the camera doesn't do anything, very little happens, and the result is a non-film. Our admiration for it is ideational, not visual. There is very little to *see* in the "film."

7. *Does it make you see more?* D. W. Griffith said: "Above all, my task is to make you see." This a fine film will do. It will alter your visual perspective, elicit and make visible that which you have either never seen or have become so habituated to that you see it no longer. A fine film should be admired for its visual, not ideational force. By means of images, not thoughts or words, it should bring us to a new awareness, a new appreciation of our lived environment. It should reveal to us some of what it means to be human. But this revelation should be through its visual/aural monogram, not through preachment, dialogue nor ideational messages. We may admire some films because of their strong ideational content (*Strawberry Statement* is a case in point) but which we would not wish to see again. The poetic spell of their images is withered or shallow even though they contain strong social messages.

A film, on the other hand, which brings us to vision—or brings visions to us—is one which displays great re-visibility. One wishes to see it again and again. And each time one finds more, not less, in it. This high re-visibility will have a lot to do with its unity, its style, its subtlety and articulation of nuance, of course. If you want to see it again, it is probably a good film. Why? Because you feel, or maybe know, that on another viewing it will literally become better looking. A fine film shapes vision; it is concerned with the fusion of vision itself, and it teaches us new ways of looking besides showing us new things at which to look.

8. *Are its symbols natural to their situation?* Photographs, by themselves, are often ambiguous. In film, when photographs are used in sequence, they often serve as visual metaphors or symbols. If such visual metaphors are fresh and relevant to their situation, it is probably a fine film. What is said for the photography itself also holds for framing and tempo. The fast tempo of the train run in *High &*

Low or the forest run in *Rashomon*, the hand-held camera work in the battle scenes of *Dr. Strangelove*, the daguerreotype texture of the stop-shots in *Butch Cassidy* arise naturally in their context and are appropriate to it. On the other hand, the flying gulls or doves as symbols of freedom are simply visual clichés. The expression of life-force and freedom in the montage sequence of the man in the river in *Occurrence at Owl Creek Bridge*, however, is natural metaphor. Here we see the joy of bubbles, the spider in its dew-wet web, the sun glinting on the waters, the exuberant green of young plants opening. All of these are appropriate to the psychological and physical situation of the character. The beautiful shots of the young child with the bubbles at the end of *Adalen 31* arise naturally and unforced from the window-washing sequence. Then the quick cut to the grinding stones of the pulp mill is a striking metaphor of the resumption of work and the necessity which binds man to be, always, a partial loser.

Another way of stating this is: does the film in shot, frame, angle, sequence, or other part exhibit dominance? The camera is perfectly indiscriminate in what it will record, particularly with our new lenses and fast stock. Everything cannot be of equal importance if anything is to be of value. Thus there must be a hierarchy of relative values. There must also be modulation and selective emphasis. The images chosen must be of prime importance for this film and this context. Things are valuable only in relation, but relations cannot all be equally possible. Were this the case there could be no contrast, no meaning, and ultimately no growth exhibited in the film.

9. *Is somebody in charge?* Whether it is an actor, director, producer, or writer, has someone infused the film with intelligence, wit, sensitivity, and style? And are these written on the face of the work? Does the clarity of control, strength, passion, and insight of the controller come through? The person in control and the one who welds the work into a personal style is usually the director. So one might say, was the film directed? An editor, however, often performs the same function. But whoever it is, control must be exhibited in the work if it is to be a fine film. For the controlled expression of power is what is meant by grace or fineness.

If the theme of the film is humanized, personalized, filtered through the vision of the artist who was in direct control, it is probably a worthwhile film. The tension of controlled structure will be written on the face of the film—in the relations of the images to images and in the funding of those images into depth content. The work must exhibit hard choices, not easy ones. It must express commitment. To say that a fine work is passionate is not to say that it is necessarily partisan. *Potemkin* and *Z* are both passionate and partisan. *The Battle of Algiers*, however, though intensely passionate, is not partisan, at least not to either of the sides in the conflict. As arid as it is, *Last Year at Marienbad* is passionate in its insistence that all shots and sequences remain as "pure" (i.e., formal) as possible. Passionate intensity may often be bad politics and worse religion but it usually makes fine film. And if the director or editor has such intensity, he will usually also have care. Care not for himself, but for his work. Because it is his work which will become the ultimate center of value, not his own psychic expressions. If so, his work will be fine work.

10. *Is it indefinitely sentimental?* The recourse to sentimentality is often a sign of failing art. Sentimental works are usually poorly made since they are designed for effect, and the feelings felt by the creator are often felt weakly or are inarticulate, or both. Sentimentality is often a mark of failure of expressive power. It is used as a device to hide shoddy work.

Sentiment is the soft focus of human emotions. Even when intense, it lacks structure. Sentiment thus suffers from excess mass. It reveals itself in the work as formlessness or misplaced emphasis. Hence the real difficulty with sentiment is that it lacks precision. It lacks definition. This lack of definition indicates easy choices. Since its structure is defective or broken, sentiment is imprecise. It is also romantic. Sentiment is an uncompressed feeling-mass which has not been given its proper and relevant limits. If this lack of definition is emphasized, sentiment becomes sentimentality. Basically, sentimentality is the exploitation of the audience at the expense of the medium. It is design aimed at arousing emotions not in the presentation. The sentimental film-maker hedges his bets by appealing to a precedent emotion on the part of his audience and arousing them to react in a way not embodied in the work. Hence his film becomes inauthentic.

A recent example would be *Cool Hand Luke*. *Cool Hand Luke* is half of a good film. Up until Luke's last escape from the chain gang, the Christ symbolism of the film is either muted, ironic, or oblique. This is counterpointed by humor. In the last escape, however, the director blatantly exploits the symbolism by having Luke's companion rush up and fall before him on his knees in the "Gethsemane" sequence. From then on, the characters and the film lose their authenticity as one shot of explicit symbolism is piled on another. This reaches its nadir as Luke is sacrificed in a church with the window frame acting as his cross. This was a singularly unperceptive and exploitative end for a man who was capable of singing "Plastic Jesus" in reaction to the death of his mother. The camera work, the lighting, and the music are all hyped to key on the Christ symbolism. Though some may think Luke's end is glorious, the film's end is dismal.

Sentimentality in film is a *visible* phenomenon. The harsh camera lens becomes soft, and the images caress and become tender when applied to that most expressive of all objects: the human face. Thus does Doris Day become the perpetual girl next door. Her face is not lined. It does not reveal all of the terrible, marvelous, and trivial events which have left their traces behind. On the contrary, her image is *limned*. Her face floats in a romantic aura like a marshmallow in a cup of warm chocolate. Sentimentality may be more than mere technique; it may become thematic substance. Hence one weeps so hard in a film like *The Blue Veil* or *Imitation of Life* that one literally can't see whether the film is any good or not. Of course, one may be weeping because he paid the admission price and not because the film is sad. It will usually be dismal, however.

This does not mean that sentiment is bad a priori nor that it should never be included in film. Sentiment can be handled in film and can be an integral part of it, if it is held within a strict form and not allowed to degenerate into sentimentality. *La Strada* is a sentimental film but held within the strict form of a half-fantasy world. The feeling and sentiment of *The 400 Blows* are deep but are held within a strict form and strong visual circumstance. *Elvira Madigan* and *Adalen 31* are both lyrical and sentimental. In *Elvira Madigan*, the lyricism is transmuted into romance without mawkishness. In *Adalen 31*, the lyrical romanticism is used to counterpoint a hard theme: a strike and death. Too often, however, we are faced with sentiment as an emotional cop-out and not as thematic variation or as transmuted style.

These, then, are my ten questions: (1) Is the projected world pictorially plausible? (2) Does this seemingly real world really seem? (3) Is the experience always fresh? (4) Do the visuals and aurals work together? (5) Does it move? (6) Is it merely a recorded stage play? (7) Does it make you see more? (8) Are its symbols natural to their situation? (9) Is somebody in charge? and (10) Is it indefinitely sentimental? Some of these criteria are genetic, some intuitive, some structural. Some are negative and some positive. No one can guarantee that they will fit all films. Nor even that if they fit any given film it would consequently be a masterpiece. But if a film were to fulfill them all, I am confident that it could be judged a good film if not a great one.

NOTES

1. D. W. Gotshalk, *Art and the Social Order* (New York: Dover, 1962), p. 174.

2. Ibid., p. 175ff.

3. The opening sequence of *The Strawberry Statement* is a dazzle of perspectives which might be entitled "101 ways to view a shell." Somehow, character and plot are lost in the shuffle.

4. The opening sequence of *They Shoot Horses Don't They?* is a pastiche of *Black Beauty, The Biscuit Eater,* and *The Pawnbroker.* Such a sentimental pastiche is false whipped cream on a hard cake.

5. In the book, Gloria's recurrent self-destructive cynicism is pounded home. In the film, she is merely cynical and tough, not suicidal.

6. An interesting contrast to make would be between two films by the same director and some of the same actors. Notice how thin *The Great Dictator* becomes on second viewing, while *Modern Times* or *The Gold Rush* are infinitely enchanting. The ideological preachment of *The Great Dictator* inhibits its visual and filmic inventiveness and hence its richness.

7. Curiously, a recent film with the (ironic) title of *Move* is ineptly static. Though the theme and substance are objective moving and the subjective "movement" of the hack writer's acceptance of his family situation, though all this is displayed with flashy editing and camera work, the film is virtually dead. It exhibits no development, no growth. One constantly expects something meaningful, but there is no closure. It goes nowhere.

BENNETT REIMER

Criteria for Quality in Music

Few issues in arts education are as central—and as vexing—as that having to do with the use of high-quality examples for study and performance. How can we be sure that the works of art we present to our students are exemplary of their particular genre and style and of the arts as a whole? We may sometimes want to use an awful example to make a specific point, but usually we hope to choose works that, because of their excellence, are likely to be deeply experienced in the present and to provide guidelines for quality in the future. Taking into account the age of our particular students and the amount of sheerly technical complexity they are likely to be able to handle, how do we select our examples with confidence that they are good or great or, at least, not bad?

The first principle to consider in this matter is that the goodness of an art work depends on the quality of its form. By form I mean all the forces in a work of art that make it a unified, dynamic phenomenon. Many works have a particular form—rondo, ballad, epic, etc., but my use of the word is broader than that. Form is the process, moment to moment, by which a work is created and experienced. It is the "how" a work of art becomes and is, not the "what" that it is. The "meaning" of a work of art is always a function of how it is formed, never of what it depicts or says. A work with trivial subject matter—a painting of sunlight on a pond, or a poem about stopping in the woods for a moment on a wintry night, or a short story about a suburban cocktail party—can, by the power of its expressive form, plunge us profoundly into feeling. On the other hand, a work with the most profound subject matter will, if it is superficial in form, be trivial and meaningless. This is the message of the famous comment by the theologian Paul Tillich that "There is more presence of ultimate reality in an apple by Paul Cézanne than in a picture of Jesus by Heinrich Hoffman."

Now we are confronted by a central question: exactly how does an artwork achieve excellence of form? This is hardly an academic question for those people responsible for decisions about the arts in education, for without a clear answer there are no clear guidelines for our choice of art, the performance of art, or the involvement of our students. Our profession demands that the choices we make be discriminating ones, and the communities we serve assume with some confidence that the art used in their schools will be appropriate for children to experience. These requirements, I would suggest, can only be met by using art of intrinsic aesthetic excellence; that is, excellence of expressive form.

There is a popular assumption that the quality of art cannot be defined—that excellence in the arts is merely a matter of taste, and, as we all know, in a democracy everyone's taste is equal in value to everyone else's. Further, *de gustibus non est disputandum.* It follows, in this view, that what people like us choose for our students and how we present what we choose are strictly a function of our own personal taste, which is no doubt in conflict with that of at least some people in our communities who then regard our taste as faulty if not perverse.

I want to argue that the criteria for excellence in art are in fact well known and can be applied with a high degree of discrimination by people who are trained to do so. Of course, subjective judgments are involved and *must* be involved. In that, the arts are no different from a great many other fields in which informed, educated, expert subjective judgments are essential; fields such as medicine, psychology, social work, pastoral work, and on and on. In all these endeavors subjectivity must be applied, but there is a great big difference between ignorant subjectivity and refined subjectivity. In the arts, as in everything else humans do, there is no substitute for knowing one's stuff, and knowing one's stuff includes conscious awareness of the criteria upon which we base our judgments about art and its performance—that is, the criteria upon which our taste has been developed. Further, I believe that our responsibilities in arts education include that we educate our students about those criteria, so they understand what guides us and also so they can use the criteria as guides for their own judgments.

While the literature on judgments about art, the literature of aesthetic criticism, is vast and complex, I would suggest that a workable base of operations can be built on just four criteria for establishing the quality of an artwork and, in the case of the performing arts, its performance. These four are 1) craftsmanship, 2) sensitivity, 3) imagination, and 4) authenticity. While one can spend a lifetime exploring all their theoretical and practical implications, I want to try to give enough of a sense of what each means that they can be used as bases for further thought and action.

Craftsmanship is the expertness by which the materials of art are molded into expressiveness. Each art has its own unique material—sound in music, movement in dance, language in poetry, the various visual media in the visual arts, and so on. These materials, as all materials, resist. That is why art requires materials—to set up a situation in which resistance must be encountered. The creative act in art consists precisely of a confrontation with resisting material, in which a resolution of the resistances is achieved through the use of skill, sensitivity, and imagination. The depth of resistance, the degree of tension in the act of creation and therefore in the resulting work of art, is one major factor in the greatness of the work. No great work is achieved without great work. The materiality of art is the battleground, the field of forces, upon which the creative struggle takes place.

To struggle successfully, to win through to an expressive form, requires a high degree of skill in both knowing profoundly about the material and acting with mastery upon it. This is quite different from skill in the more everyday sense, which is basically an ability to do things with some degree of dexterity. Craftsmanship includes that but reaches a level in which the resisting material is so integrated within the self as to be shaped by a unity of mind, hand, and heart. I think that is why there is something almost spiritual about craftsmanship, something that so integrates our human powers that we feel elevated by it. Anyone who has ever achieved real craftsmanship in some aspect of his life knows its tremendous impact, its incredible satisfactions. So when we labor to refine our craftsmanship, by perfecting our skills, by deeply identifying with our chosen materials, by feeling out its expressive potentials, all of which require time and sweat and often frustration, we are not just pursuing dexterity—we are searching for creative communion with those materials, and to the degree we achieve it we have achieved craftsmanship.

Craftsmanship, like just about everything else, exists in degrees. At one end is virtuosity, and it is no mystery why we regard with awe the chosen few who display it. But at the other end are those moments we have all experienced when things come together—when our skill and our insight reinforce each other and we say about something we or our students have done or are trying to do,

"Hey, that's not bad." A song, a drawing, a little dance, a verse of poetry—all can embody the significance that craftsmanship gives when it is present. We must, when choosing art for use in education and when performing art as part of education, be deeply aware of the quiet shining through that shows that craftsmanship has touched the work. Such work touches us.

The absence of craftsmanship is signaled by shoddiness, by disrespect for material, by forcing material to do something rather than trusting it to do something, by skill that is devoid of heart—skill that manipulates rather than serves. Such work demeans us.

Knowing our stuff means having the skill to tell the difference.

The second criterion, sensitivity, has to do with the depth and quality of feeling captured in the dynamic form of a work. The function of art is to give objective existence to feelings, which, by themselves, are private and transitory. In order to transform feelings into something public and enduring, a medium is needed—something that will hold on to the fleetingness of subjective experiences and give them outward being. The materials of art do precisely this. Sounds, movements, colors, shapes, the interplay of human forces as in a play or a novel—all of these are the public counterparts of private subjectivities. As artists shape their materials into form, they are at one and the same time giving shape to their feelings.

What they are *not* doing is "expressing" those feelings. To express feeling requires no artistic shaping. A baby crying, a child having a temper tantrum, an adult shouting at someone in anger or crying with joy or jumping up and down with excitement, are truly "expressing their feelings." In fact, if we sense that instead of giving vent to the feeling they are having, they are making some conscious decisions about how to do so by assessing the effect they are having and changing their behavior accordingly, we then are immediately suspicious that they are not just expressing—they are being artful. And our response is to wonder what they're up to.

Artists are up to something. Not something manipulative as we might suspect of those who are seemingly expressing their feelings but are not really. What artists are up to is the *exploration* of feeling—the probing of possibilities for feeling to develop, and extend, and repeat, and fade out, and fade back in, and be combined with another, and still another, and then change just a bit in a variation, and then dramatically transform itself into a new feeling, and then reappear as it first existed, and on and on until the journey of feeling brings itself to a close and the creative act is finished.

It is precisely because artists are not giving vent to a feeling they are having but are building up an expressive complex of developed feelings that we are able to judge the success or failure of the result. We cannot judge as good or bad or fair a person who is truly expressing his feelings. Would we say "that baby cries very well," or "only moderately well," or that "lady is screaming with good craftsmanship," or "she's screaming O.K. but I heard a lady screaming much better the other day"?

Every time an artist acts on his material he makes a decision. Thousands of such decisions are made for every painting or poem or film or play. The decisions are made on the basis of some overall plan: a lyric poem, say, has certain ways to do what it does; a requiem mass can do certain things but not other things, and so forth. They are also made on the basis of what just happened in the unfolding work, what might therefore happen now, what it might lead to happening a little later. Sensitivity is the "in touchness" an artist has with the developing, forming feelings, so that he can make ongoing decisions that ring true, that convince, that grasp us by their expressive power. Some works move us a little—they take us on a pleasant journey of feeling that we enjoy. Some works plunge us so deeply into complexities of feeling and intensities of feeling that we emerge from the experience profoundly changed. All works of art that are sensitively created have the potential to touch our feelings—to take them on an adventure, small or large, that deepens our sense of self.

The absence of sensitivity is betrayed by works in which the obvious overwhelms the subtle; in which the surface of feeling is offered rather than challenges to feel more deeply. The world is full of art so-called that gives immediate gratification of feeling, that condescends to our subjectivity rather than expanding it. Such art cheapens our sense of ourselves.

Knowing our stuff means being sensitive to the difference.

The criterion of imagination deals with the vividness of an art object and its performance. Most of our lives, moment by moment and day to day, is lived at a fairly placid emotional level (although there are those days that all hell seems to break loose and we feel like we're living inside a Wagner opera). At the everyday level we may, if we're fortunate, feel a general peace, a sense of ongoing satisfaction and pleasure with ourselves and what we're doing. That's fine—that's our need for tranquility. But we also need, from time to time, to make contact with the depths of which human experience is capable.

Art reaches for the depths. It may not try to reach very far. A Strauss waltz, say, or a Neil Simon comedy, or a light opera, isn't intended to plunge us into the deepest reaches of feeling. But even when the intent is modest, as in such works, success requires an out of the ordinary experience. We must, no matter how small or how limited the work of art, be to some extent captured by it, at least for a moment and at least to a degree of feeling that dips us a bit below the surface. Imagination in a work of art is what captures our feelings.

To be captured, something must grab us. When we expect a thing to happen, and it happens, we often move right through the experience without noticing it. It's when we're led to expect something and it does *not* happen, or it happens in a way we did not foresee, or it only happens after several unexpected deviations have occurred—that's when we begin to pay attention. Artists constantly strive to get us to pay that kind of attention. They are experts in setting us up, and then, by making a decision we would not have expected them to make, grasp our feelings and force us to respond. It may be the smallest change from the expected—that change is what gets us.

At every moment in the creative act, whether it consists of composing a piece of music or painting a landscape or writing a poem, craftsmanship and sensitivity combine to guide decisions that are also, to some extent, imaginative, that do not follow through in a straight, undeviating line of expectation but reach for the original solution, the unexpected event, the novel twist and turn, the unfolding of events that pull us, as we follow them, to feel more deeply because we cannot entirely predict the outcome. Great works of art present such challenges to our feelings by their richness of imagination—sometimes the audacity of their imagination—as to shake us to our foundations. Every good work of art, no matter how simple, must have enough originality to vivify our feelings, to bring them to more vibrant life. All such works, across the entire spectrum from the modest to the profound, enliven our experience.

When imagination is absent or is insufficient, a work of art betrays us. We go to it for vividness. What we get is the docile, the prosaic, the uninspired, the cliché. Many so-called artworks, whether through timidity or literal mindedness, have the opposite effect on us than art exists to have; they depress our feelings rather than excite them. Such art at best leaves us untouched. At worst it deadens us.

Knowing our stuff means being alive to the difference.

The final criterion for quality in art, authenticity, raises the issue of morality. This is among the most confused topics in the entire realm of aesthetics, and I cannot pretend to be able to unravel it in the context of this article. But I do want to make a few points. The major one is that morality in art, as with meaning in art, has little if anything to do with the nonaesthetic content of art, with the statements art may contain or actions it may depict or events it may tell about or opinions it might offer about the world and its workings. For art all such content is raw material and as such is neither aesthetically moral or immoral. It is how the material is treated that makes the difference. A novel or a play, for example, may be filled with lust and violence and war and greed and betrayal and every other problematic behavior of human beings and yet be profoundly moral nevertheless, such as Tolstoy's *War and Peace* or Shakespeare's *Hamlet*. On the other hand a work may be full of sweetness and light yet have the effect of degrading our humanity: I think of some dime-store pictures we've all seen of Jesus in day-glo colors on black velvet.

What, then, is morality in art? Simply put, it is the genuineness of the artist's interaction with his materials in which the control by the artist includes a giving way to the demands of the material. As much as an artist shapes his material, his material shapes him. The material of art takes on its own life as it begins to be shaped, making its own requirements which must be felt by the artist. To the degree the artist responds honestly, not forcing his materials to do his will but creatively interacting with the dynamics that have been set in motion, to that degree he is acting morally. It is when an artist ignores the unfolding interplay, or bypasses it in order to achieve something external to the needs of the developing feelings in the creative act, that he has violated his art and thereby corrupted it. As John Dewey says,

> If one examines into the reason why certain works of art offend us, one is likely to find that the cause is that there is no personally felt emotion guiding the selecting and assembling of the material presented. We derive the impression that the artist . . . is trying to regulate by conscious intent the nature of the emotion aroused. We are

irritated by a feeling that he is manipulating materials to secure an effect decided upon in advance.[1]

In art that is immoral. What it produces is art so-called that displays sentimentality rather than sensitivity, the surface appearances of feeling rather than its underlying vitality. An honest work takes us wherever it goes—to the unpleasant as well as the pleasant. No matter—it will, by virtue of its fidelity to its inner needs, ennoble our humanity. A dishonest work forces us to a foregone conclusion. We arrive at it with a nasty taste in our mouths—we know we've been used. Our feelings yearn for honesty, not for sentiment. We are honored by the genuine, no matter how tough to take. We are humiliated by the fake, in art as in everything else.

Knowing our stuff means respecting the difference.

An important implication of these ideas has to do with styles of art. Never before in history have so many styles existed simultaneously in each art. There is no "modern music"—there are many "modern musics." There is no "modern poetry"—there are many styles of poetry, each equally viable and with an equal claim to our attention. And so on for all the arts. So as we survey the incredible richness and diversity of artistic styles available from our own times, and all the artistic styles available from past times which are alive and well and continue to be relevant for modern sensibilities, the problem of choice becomes severe.

One aspect of choice is appropriateness for the specific educational objective being planned, and for that aspect it is necessary to deal with particular programs of instruction, which cannot be done here. But since the criterion of appropriateness must always include the prior criterion of intrinsic quality, the characteristics of quality I have suggested can indeed be of assistance. The major point to be made here is that each style in an art must be judged on its own terms. It is fruitless to deem any particular style of music, say, as inherently more or less worthy than any other style. Once deciding that style a or b or c or x is appropriate for a particular educational context, the criteria for quality must be applied to examples within that particular style. Every style, including the ones we are most used to in education, has examples on a continuum from excellent to poor. The obligation here is very clear—to know our stuff so well that we always aim for the best and choose the best no matter the style. Given the complexity of such an obligation, our task is not an easy one, but then, no one promised us a rose garden.

The criteria for quality I have proposed for judging art apply in an additional way: they are the bases for judging the work we do as aesthetic educators. What makes us good at what we do? I would suggest that our craftsmanship at our work is a major factor for our success, and that an important part of craftsmanship for us is being aware of and articulate about the criteria we use for judging the quality of the arts we choose. I would also suggest that our sensitivity, both to the expressive values of the arts we deal with and to the expressive potentials of the students we deal with—their abilities to participate actively in artistic expression and to share deeply in aesthetic impression—will be crucial for our impact. Our imagination—our ability to challenge, to vivify, to enliven the experience of art for students—is a factor they depend upon, and depend upon week after week after week. We are the continually flowing fountain of energy that shuns the routine, avoids the easy solution, argues for giving a bit *more* than what everyone expects, so that teaching and learning in the arts will include the delight of freshness. And our authenticity—our devotion to the highest standards of quality, subject to the particular social and educational contexts in which we work—is the bedrock upon which authentic arts education can be fostered.

Put in this way our task is formidable indeed. But it is also a challenge that can provide a lifetime's satisfactions. For underneath the specifics of doing well what we have chosen to do is the knowledge we have that our efforts are connected directly to one of the deepest of all human needs, the need for aesthetic nourishment by the power of good art.

NOTE

1. John Dewey, *Art as Experience* (New York: G. P. Putnam, 1934), p. 68.

VERNON A. HOWARD

Useful Imaginings

A primary use of imagination is as mediator between means and ends. Seldom do we learn anything so complex as playing a musical instrument or interpreting music in a fixed and final way. Both technical and interpretative abilities admit of indefinite refinement. Technical skills cultivated by drill are embedded within higher-level capacities requiring constant attention to detail, judgment, and choice. And even drill at some point requires close scrutiny of how exercises are to be done, what constitutes correct performance of them, and why one does them. Ultimately, such diagnostic judgment is a matter of calibrating techniques and skills already mastered to ever-changing circumstances and new performance demands. . . .

The estrangement of means and ends is a double estrangement: of means without dreams (drudgery) or of dreams without means (fantasy), neither of which is the name of success. In imagination we learn to connect them up in ways that enable us to realize our dreams. That in turn requires a discipline of the mind as much as of the body through practice. To parody Kant, imagination without practice is empty; practice without imagination is blind.

A second and even more fundamental use of imagination in performance is to hold ends-in-view within a continuum of ends and means. What that Deweyan mouthful means is that our performance techniques and objectives co-vary under the pressure of changes and challenges foreseen and unforeseen. Means and ends require continual, mutual reevaluation as one's abilities and understanding grow. Or, to put it another way, our original performance objectives change as our facilities to realize them improve.[1] Improved facility at the keyboard, for example, enables one not only to perform a musical passage up to some preconceived (given) standard of phraseology, but also to reconceive the phraseology itself— to project a new standard.

Ends and means-in-view can both be proximate or final: building facilities like keyboard fluency or performing publicly up to or beyond standard, finger drill or dress rehearsal. But only as ends and means are "taken in," made part of one's intelligent response repertoire, do they form a continuum, that is, escape being mere rote responses or a "bag of tricks."

With the exceptions of commands, recipes, and drill manuals, ends and their means-in-view are not simply read off from either tradition or from the situation at hand. Rather, they are held in imagination as directives (rules and routines) and frequently revised therein as changing circumstances demand. In effect, imagination allows us to adjust our acquired know-how and techniques to particular cases and even to revise them or transfer them to new realms of application.[2]

A third function of the imagination in performance is to promote a spirit of inquiry: to enable us to change our course of action according to what we learn from our mistakes; in other words, to revise. Even the humblest finger drills are trial-and-error "experiments" the significance of which is entirely lost if we cannot measure our mistakes against our goals. Nothing in the behavior itself tells us what we ought to be doing or how. Rather, the remembrance of things just past is held up in comparison to the desired ideal, with the aim of closing the gap through successive approximations, as something possible to do.

Part of the essential discipline of practice is to remember and to compare ruthlessly, trial after trial by reference to a standard clearly conceived—in effect to *take care*. It takes time and much effort to learn how to care in the sense of critically heeding one's moment-to-moment efforts. Yet such caring is the first lesson of practice; for without it, practice degenerates into mere repetition, drudgery without correction or direction.[3] The implicit distinction here is between critical foresight and mere preconception of slavish adherence to habit or routine. Only in imagination can we confront past experience with present challenge by holding ends-in-view as well as the past in re-view. In so doing, imagination focuses the whence and the whither of our efforts in critical overview, supporting the will by showing a way.

Finally, imagination plays a crucial role in the assimilation and growth of personal standards of performance. It's easy to admire virtuosity at a distance in blissful ignorance of what makes it possible (a prime source, incidentally, of appeals to amorphous "creativity," "inspiration," "gifts," "talent," and the like). It's far more difficult to understand it, or to take such virtuosity as a personal goal, break it down into digestible bits, and to "keep the flame" while enduring all the pain. In *Artistry* I half humorously described such an apprenticeship as follows:

> Nearly anyone who takes the trouble to look into this book can recollect labors of love or loathing at the keyboard, at the drawing board, in the exercise studio, or on the playing field. The sheer drudgery of it all as measured against the evolving vision of mastery is perhaps one of the most daunting, humbling experiences known to us. Long periods of Sisyphean despair punctuated at intervals by the elation of small accomplishments, the wagering of one's talents against the odds of perfection, the feeling that pain and failure are one's only reliable companions, such are the moods of ambition when subjected to a hard discipline. The pathos of the quest for mastery is amusingly captured in baritone Louis Quilico's mock prayer: "Dear God, you gave me a voice, I didn't ask for it. So help me!" At the opposite extreme, one imagines another version: "Dear God, I asked for a voice. You didn't give it to me. So help me to practice!" Whatever the speed of learning or the proportion of one's "gifts," the fact of practice—the necessity of honing one's talents—remains.[4]

And I would go further: whether we are concerned with music "appreciation" or conservatory training, one equation remains constant: namely, that the ideas and the ideals of music (or of virtually anything worth learning, for that matter) go hand in glove. It's what we refer to colloquially as "getting the feel" or "the hang" of something, be it a slice of performance strategy, a sense of what is going on in opera, or, equally important, a feel for the appropriate methods of inquiry into such matters.

To develop such "feeling," it is not enough to learn the skills and techniques of inquiry or of performance alone. To be able is not necessarily to be willing, or conversely.[5] One needs also to acquire the disposition to use the techniques of inquiry or performance. That is what it means to connect means to ends-in-view. It is a question not only of identifying the task but of identifying with it.

Now it is far easier to teach definite skills than it is to teach dispositions, just as it is easier to teach someone how to balance a checkbook than to inculcate the value of thrift. The one is a question of particular facilities, the other of character and personality. Yet both are required if learning in any domain is to be more than a futile exercise. But how are dispositions, the values and ideals of a discipline, taught?

I am tempted here to take the Socratic way out and say that they cannot be taught, not because they aren't learned somehow, nor because they are unspecifiable, but because they have to be felt and absorbed as aspirations as well as known. That is the "aesthetic" face of all sustained learning and inquiry: the personal thrill of achievement and growth under the aegis of an ideal. Not until the task becomes mine does it come alive in thought and action.

How, then, are such dispositions learned? At the risk of gross oversimplification, I would point to three familiar ways in which we identify ourselves with a quest. First, from dreams, usually engendered by early "exposure," a pure fantasy of oneself doing that— wanting to run like Carl Lewis, to sing like Pavarotti. Whether such dreams remain Mittyesque depends upon opportunity and instruction, not to mention such subtle personality factors as having a nose for reality and a tolerance for scrutiny.

Second, dispositions just as frequently emerge from discovery through instruction itself, from the often surprising discovery of personal competencies or potentialities revealed in trying something new. As mentioned, there is an inherent thrill (or positive reinforcement, if you prefer) in realizing that one can do something well, even at rudimentary stages. Whether one is willing to endure the subsequent pain of instruction depends upon not only the strength of one's personal vision, but also upon the availability of critical support.[6]. . . Without something larger than one's ego at stake, the burden of exposure would be unbearable.

Third, and most broadly, I am inclined to say that dispositions (positive or negative) are mostly learned by example: from the people we admire or loathe; from teachers who drill, explain, and inevitably demonstrate in their own persons what it is to be and to do that; from observing with increasing acuity (and independence) the accomplishments of others. The experience becomes self-sustaining when at last one learns to learn unassisted from close scrutiny of others' achievements. In that way, even a bad performance by a great virtuoso becomes the occasion for critical appreciation and self-instruction.

In all of this the imagination sustains critical hindsight and foresight, not so much as a matter of "inspiration" as of control within a means-ends continuum linking the necessary skills to the propelling disposition to do well. I hasten to add that as teachers we are not responsible for everything (good or bad) that happens within so complex a nexus of forces. The point bears mentioning as caution against the teacher's hubris of taking undue credit or blame for the learner's success or failure. Suffice to recall that learners have their responsibilities, too, and that every learner of any age brings innumerable preformed habits and dispositions to the task, some of which, sadly, may be intractable. Fortunately, the old cliché about the will finding its way often reverses itself; where a way can be found, so usually can the will.

The Basics of Creativity and Critical Thinking

As an offshoot of the "back to basics" movement in recent years, a great deal has been made of creative and critical thinking. An immense literature of uneven quality has grown up around the topics of creativity and critical thinking, enough to justify describing them as "movements" in educational pedagogy and research. Among works of lasting significance in both fields I would mention inter alia those of Perkins,[7] McPeck,[8] Nickerson,[9] Csikszentmilhalyi,[10] and Scheffler.[11] A forthcoming book of my own deals with both creative and critical thinking in the context of writing.[12] Notwithstanding the fierce attention devoted to these topics, certain thoughtless trends about thinking are rife and worth avoiding, especially where the arts are concerned.

A legacy of nineteenth-century faculty psychology was the "faculty curriculum" which was supposed to develop certain mental and moral traits: literature and the arts for the sensibilities, logic and mathematics for the intellect, sport and military training for character, and so on. Similar assumptions also riddle the common nonsense about creativity and critical thinking wherein the latter are construed as supervenient mental capacities—kinds of super skill—consisting of specifiable subskills. Each, in other words, comes with its own special "bag of tricks." The latter are often assumed to be exhaustive of the super skill; that is, not merely necessary but sufficient.[13] Hence, learn "synectics" or "lateral thinking" and ye shall be creative! Learn logic (or some variation thereof) and ye shall be a critical thinker! Nobody of course subscribes to these views as just stated, but they lurk in the background as a hidden agenda, as yet another instance of the wistful wish to achieve high ends by fixed means.

Add to this muddle the further too common assumption that creativity and rationality occupy separate mental domains, and the historical circle is nearly complete. Among the adjectives presumably staking out the domain of the creative: spontaneous, intuitive, subjective, personal, imaginative, inspired, expressive, emotional, associative. A similar, contrasting list circumscribes the domain of the critical: rational, logical, factual, truthful, disciplined, objective, public, precise, linear, testable, and the like.

And to complete the circle: what subject areas reflect these dichotomous domains? Why, those are the arts and sciences respectfully, with the humanities loosely mediating between leaning now toward "knowledge" (history, philosophy) and now toward "self-expression" (poetry, painting, and, of course, music). And so one dichotomy engenders another, the one distorting our view of mental processes, the other our views of art, science, and the humanities.

Such a simplistic and misleading scheme alienates even as it misrepresents, leaving us confused as to what art and science are, what they do as symbolic constructions, what the complex relations among them are, and what it takes to do them well. It is a short step from here to labeling the presumed domains of "knowledge" and of "self-expression" as "basics" and "frills," respectively. Obviously, this happens time and again in public debates over educational priorities with disastrous and vexing results for art and science instruction alike.

This is not the place to reply to epistemic prejudices except to note that any of the adjectives occurring in the one list above could as easily occur in the other. . . . And by the same token, an unimaginative, uncreative science is a contradiction in terms.

If truth is cheap in science, emotion is more often a means than an end in both art and science. One pursues a problem in physics or philosophy out of felt curiosity that is logically shaped. At the same time, to play "expressively" or, more generally, to express emotion through art is not merely to indulge in depression, joy, or passion. It is, rather, a discipline of the emotions to learn how to use and explore them through the symbolic constructions of art. Otherwise, a shout is as good as a symphony.

And that brings me to the central point of this discussion; namely, that music education is education of an understanding that ranges from physical dexterity, to emotive discovery, to perceptual insight, to pattern recognition, to associative hunches, to logical argument—in no particular order and in every combination. Moreover, small acts of imagination mediate the many ways of understanding throughout, from running scales to public performances, from merely hearing to learning listening. If not alone in developing and continually calling upon these capacities, music is, at the very least, a vast and diverse arena for their highest exercise. Such an understanding is not only of music and what it does or means in and of itself, but of what it reveals about ourselves, about our own and other times, and about the many worlds of culture. Becoming educated about music is to create the conditions of music educating us in turn.

Clearly, I am assuming that such understanding, however cultivated by whatever subjects or experiences, is a "good thing," perhaps the best thing that we can expect of an education that is liberal (in the original sense of liberating from ignorance) and humane (also in the original sense of probing our humanity). So what justifies the pursuit of understanding in any of its forms? My all too brief answer is, nothing, or perhaps everything. Or, in Goodman's words, "The point of having leisure time, of a decent moral climate, of prosperity beyond basic need, lies in what these can help make possible. The plays, the music, the mathematical physics, and painting, and sculpture do not pose the question 'Why?'; they answer it."[14]

Refrain

Nothing in what I have been saying here runs against the many differences of method, purpose, symbolic construction, sensory modality, or meaning to be found among artistic, humanistic, and scientific disciplines. Rather, my purpose has been to suggest (hardly to prove) how they serve a common aim of understanding while pursuing specifically very different ends-in-view. Neither should I want to leave the impression that any epistemic philosophy will ever summarily say "what it all adds up to"; for that would be to destroy the many different ways of understanding a many-faceted world. As Martha Graham is purported to have said, "If I could say it, I wouldn't bother to dance it." Still, I hope that the foregoing remarks shed some light on how the imaginings of music contribute to the growth of understanding, including, perhaps especially, those exact, revealing little imaginings like the "smelling of a flower."

NOTES

1. John Dewey, *Art as Experience* (New York: G. P. Putnam, 1934), pp. 45–47.

2. Vernon A. Howard, *Artistry: The Work of Artists* (Indianapolis: Hackett, 1982), p. 135.

3. Ibid., pp. 160–64.

4. Ibid., p. 157.

5. Israel Scheffler, *Conditions of Knowledge* (Chicago: Scott, Foresman, 1965), pp. 19–20.

6. The notion of critical support is crucial for understanding apprenticeship relationships of the kind discussed herein. Yet nowhere to my knowledge is its role in the personal growth of disciplinary values examined. An odd oversight considering the amount of attention that educators have devoted to the so-called problem of "motivation."

7. D. N. Perkins, *The Mind's Best Work* (Cambridge: Harvard University Press, 1981).

8. John McPeck, *Critical Thinking and Evaluation* (New York: St. Martin's, 1981).

9. Raymond S. Nickerson, *Notes about Reasoning* (Cambridge: Bolt, Beranek, and Newman, 1982).

10. Mihaly Csikszentmihalyi, *Beyond Boredom and Anxiety* (San Francisco: Jossey Bass, 1975).

11. Israel Scheffler, *Of Human Potential* (London: Routledge and Kegan Paul, 1985).

12. Vernon A. Howard and J. H. Barton, *Thinking in Writing* (New York: William Morrow, 1986).

13. McPeck, *Critical Thinking and Education*, p. 8.

14. Nelson Goodman, *Of Mind and Other Matters* (Cambridge: Harvard University Press, 1984).

Louise M. Rosenblatt

The Aesthetic Transaction

Postulating relevance to all the arts, I shall attempt to present, in necessarily abbreviated form, a model of the relationship between the reader and the text. Although I shall not be able to do justice to my transactional theory as a whole,[1] my answer to the problem of "literariness" or "poeticity"—i.e., of "the aesthetic" in "literature"—has implications, I believe, for aesthetic education in general.

The term "transactional" signals a basic epistemological concept: John Dewey had early noted the paradigmatic shift in science from Cartesian dualism, which saw human beings as separate from nature, to a post-Einsteinian sense of human beings in a reciprocal relationship with their environment. Since "interaction" has acquired the dualistic implication of separate, already defined entities acting on one another, Dewey suggested "transaction," to indicate a reciprocal, mutually defining relationship in which the elements or parts are aspects or phases of a total situation or event.[2] Language—to use an example especially important to my argument—should not be seen as a self-contained, ungrounded, ready-made code of signifiers and signifieds, but as embodied in transactions between individuals and their social and natural context. The physical signs of a text (aural or visual) have acquired meaning, have become words, in a triadic relationship, involving, as C. S. Peirce phrased it, sign, object, and interpretant, or, as the psychologists phrase it, sign, object, and "organismic state."[3] The sense of a word is not simply its public, lexical meaning but "the sum of all the psychological events aroused in our consciousness by the word."[4] For the individual, the verbal signs carry both public, socially accepted, decontextualized linkages between sign and object, and private, kinaesthetic, affective, cognitive colorings.

Reading is a transactional process that goes on between a particular reader and a particular text at a particular time, and under particular circumstances. All of these factors affect the transaction. The reader does not approach Shakespeare's text in order to uncover an already defined entity, *the* meaning, *the* literary work of art. The physical text is simply marks on paper until a reader transacts with them. Each reader brings a unique reservoir of public and private significances, the residue of past experiences with language and texts in life situations. The transaction with the signs of the text activates a two-way, or, better, circular, stream of dynamically intermingled symbolizations which mutually reverberate and merge.

Central to this process—and usually ignored—is what William James termed "selective attention." We are constantly engaged, he pointed out, in "choosing" from all that is offered by the moment-to-moment transaction with the environment.[5] During the transaction between reader and text, what is brought into awareness, what is pushed into the background or repressed, depends on where, on what aspects of the triadic symbolization, the attention is focused. Some impulsion, no matter how vague at first, some principle, whether conscious or unconscious, is required to guide selection from the multiple potentialities resonating between the reader and the signs on the page. Possibilities open up concerning diction, syntax, ideas, subject, themes, linguistic and literary conventions, in short, concerning a tentative framework or guiding principle of selection. Each additional choice signals certain possibilities and excludes others, satisfies or frustrates earlier expectations, thus shaping, testing, and revising, not only the developing structure of meaning, but also the selective principle itself. If symbolizations arise that cannot be assimilated into the emerging synthesis, a complete rereading and revision may occur.

Selection and synthesis thus become fundamental activities in the making of meaning. A complex, to-and-fro, self-correcting transaction between reader and verbal signs continues until some final organization, more or less complete and coherent, is arrived at and thought of as corresponding to the text. The "meaning"— whether, e.g., poem, novel, play, scientific report, or legal brief— comes into being during the transaction.

The sketch of the basic reading process presented thus far has not, however, specified what differentiates the reading process that results in a scientific report from the reading that produces a poem or novel. The traditional notion that the difference inheres in the text alone overlooks an essential and overarching component of the guiding selective impulse in any reading—the adoption of a "stance" toward what is being aroused in consciousness. Stance determines whether selective attention will focus predominantly on the public, lexical aspects of meaning, or whether the focus will broaden to permit attention to the matrix of personal overtones, kinaesthetic states, intellectual or emotional associations. Since both aspects of the sense of words are usually involved to some degree, stance regulates, one might say, the proportion or "mix" of public and private aspects of meaning opened to the selective, synthesizing, organizing process. And "proportion" implies a continuum: every reading event falls somewhere on a spectrum covering what I term the "predominantly efferent" and the "predominantly aesthetic" stances.

The kind of reading in which the focus of attention is predominantly on what is to be retained *after* the reading event I term "efferent" (from L. *efferre*, to carry away). An example at the extreme efferent end of the continuum is the mother whose child has swallowed a poisonous liquid and who is hastily reading the label: She ignores, pushes into the periphery of attention, everything except the barest public referents of the verbal signs, constructing the directions for action as soon as the reading ends. Nearer the center of the continuum, admitting more of the personal aspects of symbolization, but still instances of predominantly efferent reading, would probably be readings of a newspaper, a history textbook, or a legal brief. Given the efferent stance, meaning emerges from an abstracting-out and analytic structuring of the ideas, information, directions, conclusions to be retained, used, or acted on after the reading event.

The predominantly "aesthetic" stance, covering the other half of the continuum, designates an attitude of readiness to focus attention on what is being lived through in relation to the text *during* the reading event. Welcomed into the center of awareness are not only what the words point to, their public referents, but also the rest of the triadic symbolization, the qualitative aspects associated with the verbal signs and their referents. "Organismic states" receive attention. The sounds of words, their rhythmic repetitions and variations, may be listened to in the metaphoric "inner ear." Inner tensions, sensations, feelings, and associations accompanying images and ideas may color imagined scenes, actions, and characters. The experienced evocation is felt to be the poem, the story, the play corresponding to the text. This lived-through "work," this "evocation," is what the reader "responds to" as it is being called forth during the transaction, and as it is reflected on, interpreted, evaluated, analyzed, criticized afterwards.[6]

Any text can be read either efferently or aesthetically. Hence "literariness" or "poeticity" cannot be said to reside in any traits of the text alone. If the text of Shakespeare's Sonnet 70 is to be read as a poem, an aesthetic stance is required: Admitted into the center of selective attention must be, of course, the referents of the particular words, but the shutters must be opened wide to admit also their experiential aura. There will be no dearth of ideas and of logical relationships, yet they will be inextricably interfused with their lived-through, qualitative colorings and textures.

If, however, the purpose is to classify the metaphors or analyze the syntax, or even to give a "literal" paraphrase, attention would have to be withdrawn from the inner experience in order to place in the center of attention the mainly public aspects of meaning. The purpose of accumulating evidence for a verifiable result would require the efferent stance. The reader would be selectively matching the symbolizations against some classificatory criteria for the metaphors, some linguistic system for the syntax, or generally accepted "literal" meanings of the verbal signs for the paraphrase.

The text of a weather report, say, is equally open to either predominant stance. A reader might efferently arrive at a practical prediction of rain, or might shift to an aesthetic stance, attend not only to the referents but also to the sound and rhythm of the words, to their qualitative and associational overtones, and live through, evoke, a "pop" poem.

Readings of the same text, as well as of different texts, may fall at different points on the efferent/aesthetic continuum. My reading of Shakespeare's Sonnet 70 may fall nearer the middle of the continuum—i.e., attend more closely to the structure of ideas, and logical relationships among metaphors, than my reading, say, of the text of a lyric from one of the plays. But my aesthetic readings of the Sonnet 70 text itself at different times may also vary in this way. Similarly, my readings of a Darwin text might be either predominantly efferent or aesthetic, or might vary in their emphasis on awareness within, say, the efferent range.

Despite the fact that each reading brings into play a different "mix" of elements, dominant stances are clearly distinguishable. Someone else can read a text efferently for us, and report or summarize the results. No one else can read a text aesthetically for us; no one else can experience the aesthetic evocation for us.

Emphasis on the reader and the reader's stances does not deny the importance of the text. Both the text and what the reader brings to the transaction are essential to, will contribute to, the poem or story or play that crystallizes out, that is evoked, during the transaction. The evocation is the "object" of response, interpretation, and evaluation. The reader, returning to consider the text in the light of the evocation, may discover much in the signs of the text that may have been overlooked, may find that elements in the experienced evocation have no linkage with, have been projected onto, the text, because of attitudes, assumptions, ignorances, brought to the transaction. The reader may become self-critical, and seek a new, more rewarding or more valid, transaction.[7]

The aesthetic transaction, as presented here, should not be confused with formulations that continue the old dualistic approach. Descriptions of "the aesthetic attitude" or "the aesthetic approach" as variously inhering, e.g., in sensory contemplation, in nonvolitional contemplation, in intense concentration of attention ("absorption in the object"), or psychical distance, usually leave extremely vague "the object" of the contemplation or attention. The text itself tends to assume that role. Again, those who find "literariness" or "poeticity" or "the aesthetic" in the autonomy of the literary work—the message for its own sake—offer mainly a negative criterion, absence of external purpose, and, identifying work or message with the text, fall back on formalistic efferent analyses of the text. Similarly, those who directly find the aesthetic to reside in textual traits such as deviations from normal syntax, metaphor, linguistic and literary conventions, or fictiveness, do not recognize that such signs can be read either efferently or aesthetically.

When we speak of a text as "expository" or "poetic," as "discursive" or "nondiscursive," as "scientific" or "literary," understanding of the reading transaction will prevent our accepting the implication that these terms describe qualities inherent in the texts themselves. Such terms may indicate the presumed intentions of the authors as to the stance they wish their readers to adopt. "Competent" readers do usually seek clues in the text as to the author's intention—unless the readers have some other purpose for the particular reading. Or such terms applied to a text may express a judgment as to whether the text would best reward an aesthetic or an efferent reading—when, for example, we rate a text as a poor novel but a useful source of sociological information.

"Aesthetic stance" and "aesthetic transaction" are not evaluative terms. They can apply to the reading of a comic book or the text of *Paradise Lost*. Only after we establish the kind of transactions involved, the kind of "object" evoked, can we apply a fully appropriate set of evaluative criteria. We can make explicit the criteria that lead us to say that the *Paradise Lost* text offers potentially greater rewards for an aesthetic reading, but that also implies a transaction with a particular kind of reader. Problems arise when the stance and the criteria of value applied are not appropriate to the situation—as when political arguments are read aesthetically or poems are read literally.

The teaching of literature has suffered from failure to recognize that "the literary work"—the object of interpretation, appreciation, analysis, criticism, evaluation—is the evocation lived through by the reader-critic during the transaction with the text. Precisely because the efferent/aesthetic continuum is not understood, students are not helped to develop the habit of adopting a stance appropriate to the particular reading event. Children are given "stories" but are asked questions that reward an efferent reading. "Literature" courses in school and college present "good" and "great" texts, but the student's attention is weighted toward what will be required *after* the reading. With traditional concerns of the literary critic, the literary analyst, and the literary historian as models, the "study of literature" has tended to hurry the student reader away from the evocation, to focus on efferent concerns: recall of details, paraphrase, summary, categorization of genres, formalistic analysis of verbal techniques, "background knowledge" and literary history. Such matters *may* help students to think self-critically about their evocations, but the teaching is self-defeating if the students have had only a vague, hasty experience bordering on the efferent and must rely mainly on the teacher's or critic's secondhand accounts of their experience.

Curriculums and classroom methods should be evaluated in terms of whether they foster or impede an initial aesthetic transaction, and on whether they help students to savor, deepen, the lived-through experience, to recapture and reflect on it, to organize their sense of it. In the light of such awareness, students can discover how the new experience, the evoked literary work, relates both to the text and to their earlier experience and assumptions; they can become self-critical and hence grow in capacity to evoke and to criticize. Centered on the personal transaction, traditional concerns—validity of interpretation, criteria of evaluation, historical perspective—can then provide frameworks for thinking about literary works of art.

The transactional theory, the concepts of the efferent stance and the aesthetic stance, apply to the other arts as well as "literature." To say that from earliest childhood the individual should be helped to develop the full potentialities of language, public and private, is to say that the efferent and the aesthetic are necessary alternative approaches to all experience. The transactional relationship between reader and text is, despite the differences in medium, paralleled in all the arts.[8] The artifact, e.g., painted canvas or shaped marble, can become part of the whole spectrum of efferent and aesthetic transactions. We may approach the artifact efferently, seeking some publicly verifiable fact, such as its size, or (closer to the middle of the continuum) some detail of technique or subject as evidence that will identify the type or the artist. Or we may adopt a predominantly aesthetic stance and broaden our focus of attention to include the qualitative impact, a selective awareness and synthesis of inner states related to perception of the artifact. Again, the lived-through evocation can be reflected on and interpreted; we can return (efferently, it may be) to the artifact to see what details or aspects involved may help to explain or justify the evocation.

Education in the other arts has shared with the teaching of literature a tendency to hurry students into mainly efferent concerns. They have been led to concentrate on the "public" aspects of the artifact, what can be pointed to in, e.g., the identification of subject, analysis of technical or stylistic detail, or attribution of biographical or historical "periods." Important though these may be, they should not obstruct the live circuit between perceiver and artifact. The student should be helped to pay attention to the interfusion of sensuous, cognitive, and affective elements that can enter into the process of selective awareness and synthesis. No matter how limited or immature, this can provide the basis for growth. Aesthetic education should be rooted in the individual aesthetic transaction.[9] The student thus can be helped to bring increasing sensitivity and sophistication to the evocation of "works of art," and can learn to bring to bear ever wider contexts for their interpretation and study.

NOTES

1. Limitations of space prevent my treating the many theoretical questions that arise. Please see Louise M. Rosenblatt, *The Reader, the Text, the Poem: The Transactional Theory of the Literary Work* (Carbondale, Ill.: Southern Illinois University Press, 1978), and *Literature as Exploration*, 4th ed. (New York: Modern Language Association, 1983).

2. John Dewey and Arthur F. Bentley, *Knowing and the Known* (Boston: Beacon Press, 1949), p. 69ff and *passim*.

3. Charles Sanders Peirce, *Collected Papers*, vols. 3–4, ed. Charles Hartshorne and Paul Weiss (Cambridge, Mass.: Harvard University Press, 1933) 3.360. See also Elizabeth Bates, *The Emergence of Symbols* (New York: 1979),

p. 66. The relationship of the printed to the spoken word cannot be treated here, but does not affect the basic point about the triadic symbolization.

4. Lev S. Vygotsky, *Thought and Language*, ed. and trans. Eugenia Hanfmann and Gertrude Vakar (Cambridge, Mass.: MIT Press, 1962), p. 8.

5. William James, *The Principles of Psychology*, vol. 1 (New York: Henry Holt, 1950), pp. 242, 245, and chap. 9, *passim*.

6. I originally used the term "instrumental," but found that, as in the solution of a problem in "pure" mathematics, absence of a practical or external purpose did not rule out what I here term the "efferent" stance. And, of course, we have the familiar instance of the mathematician shifting to the aesthetic stance and sensing the "elegance" of the process itself.

As for the term "aesthetic," I trust that the transactional context and the definition of the two stances counteract its diverse usages.

7. What the student brings to the transaction is as important, educationally, as the character of the artifacts studied. The assumption is not that any evocation "goes," but that if there is to be growth, it must build on, expand, and if necessary modify the perceptual habits, the sensitivities, the assumptions, that are the residue of past transactions in life and in art.

8. The text, as a set of signs that are part of a semantic system, can be more easily dissociated as an artifact from the aesthetic evocation than can a painted canvas or a bronze statue, which seem so much more *the* work. The semiological situation is similar, however, as the many studies in perception demonstrate. See "Coda: Literature as a Performing Art," in Rosenblatt, *Literature as Exploration*; Rosenblatt, "Act I, Sc. 1: Enter the Reader," *Literature in Performance* 1, no. 2 (1981).

9. This brief exposition could not deal with the transaction between author and text, or artist and artifact. We can at least recall that the author is the first reader of the text. The potential role of the production of such artifacts in the education of the student of literature or art is another of the many implications of the transactional theory to be explored.

JANET ADSHEAD, VALERIE A. BRIGINSHAW,
PAULINE HODGENS & MICHAEL ROBERT HUXLEY

The Analysis of Dance

General concepts which may apply to many kinds of dance are useful, but as soon as one considers a specific dance, the range of components required for analysis is reduced because of those very characteristics that make one dance style distinct from another. In describing, discerning, and naming the elements of movement, it quickly becomes convenient to use shorthand phrases which summarize and name a particular kind of movement (i.e., clusters and complexes). In time, phrases such as "pas de basque" become the verbal currency of one style of dance, and it becomes unnecessary to explain them after the initial learning stage.

In the same way, the abstract symbol system used to notate a dance is a reflection of the range of movement used and its analysis. The same problems exist here over the generality and specificity of coverage required by any one dance form. Through several centuries, attempts have been made to devise a notation system, but for our purposes of charting dance as art in the twentieth century, we need consider only the two in which the dance repertoire is written, that is, Labanotation/Kinetography Laban and Benesh notation. Although both systems claim to be comprehensive in the sense of being capable of notating any kind of movement in a variety of settings in addition to dance—athletics, medical analysis, and animal behavior—their use in actual practice is indicative, among other things, of their perceived value within the dance realm. Further, although both systems have been used to notate ballet as well as modern dance, the Benesh system is used more for the former and Labanotation for the latter. Labanotation is, in fact, used for a greater range of purposes and styles of dance than is Benesh.

The Chart

In drawing up the chart in relation to dance, we have taken and adapted the Smiths'[1] first two categories of skills and concepts but not the categories of anticipated difficulties.

Before describing briefly each stage of the chart, it is crucial to note that what is presented is a basis for the analysis of dance. The chart provides a structure and framework through which important elements of the dance might be located; it does *not* necessarily imply a particular order of events to be followed in the process or method of analysis. Users of the chart may enter it at different points depending on their interest, e.g., interest in a particular dancer's role, a prevalent dynamic stress, a recurring motif—in other words, *how* one uses the model depends on *what* it is one wishes to study.

The progression from stage one to stage four of the model is hierarchical in the sense that the final evaluation of the dance rests on an interpretation having been made, which in turn relies on the recognition and characterization of the genre, the subject matter, and its treatment in the dance. This recognition and characterization are the consequence of perceiving relations of various kinds among sections of the dance and assessing their relative importance. This in turn is possible only in terms of the objectively available features of the dance, its movement components and qualities in the presentational setting. A strict hierarchical structure is not maintained within each stage of the chart.

The stages of the chart are interdependent: each stage describes a skill or related group of skills, first of discerning, describing, and naming components of the dance; second of discerning, describing, and naming relations among components of the dance and recognizing their comparative importance; third of recognizing and characterizing the dance statement or meaning in order to interpret the dance; and fourth of appraising and judging in order to evaluate the dance.

The skills of column one are related to the concepts of column two in that the nature of the dance itself provides the structure of concepts, and the skills are then used in relation to these very specific concepts. Of course one can describe, discern, recognize, and characterize many things. The conceptual structure appropriate to the subject tells us what, in the case of dance, we are attending to.

Stage 1 of the chart sets out the basic components of dance. These components are units of movement, for example, a single step taken by the right foot that is small and moves in a forward direction (relative to the body of the dancer) with lightness and at a quick pace. The simultaneous occurrence of such components forms a cluster of movement elements. It is possible to analyze movement in greater depth and from a variety of standpoints, whether anatomical or

1.	Skills	2.	Concepts
1.1	discerning, describing, and naming components of the dance	2.1	components
		2.11	*movement*—whole body or parts—including actions, gestures, and stillness, e.g., steps, jumps, turns, lifts, falls, locomotion, movement in place, balances, positions
		2.111	spatial elements
		2.1111	shape
		2.1112	size
		2.1113	pattern/line
		2.1114	direction
		2.1115	location in performance space
		2.112	dynamic elements
		2.1121	tension/force—strength, lightness
		2.1122	speed/tempo
		2.1123	duration
		2.1124	rhythm
		2.113	clusters of movement elements—simultaneous occurrence of any of 2.11, 2.111, and 2.112
		2.12	*dancers*
		2.121	numbers and sex
		2.122	role—lead, subsidiary
		2.123	a cluster of elements concerned with dancers—simultaneous occurrence of 2.121 and 2.122
		2.13	*visual setting/environment*
		2.131	performance area—set, surroundings
		2.132	light
		2.133	costumes and props
		2.134	clusters of visual elements—simultaneous occurrence of any of 2.131, 2.132, and 2.133
		2.14	*aural elements*
		2.141	sound
		2.142	the spoken word
		2.143	music
		2.144	clusters of aural elements—simultaneous occurrence of any of 2.141, 2.142, and 2.143
		2.15	*complexes*—simultaneous occurrence of elements of clusters and/or clusters, i.e., any grouping of 2.11, 2.12, 2.13, and 2.14.

A Chart of Skills and Concepts of Dance—Stage 2

1.	Skills	2.	Concepts
1.2	discerning, describing, and naming relations of the dance form	2.2	form
		2.21	*relations according to components*
		2.211	relations within and between movements, e.g., within and between spatial and dynamic elements and clusters of movement elements
		2.212	relations within and between dancers, e.g., within and between numbers, sex, and roles of dancers and clusters of elements pertaining to dancers
		2.213	relations within and between elements of the visual setting/environment, e.g., within and between the performance area, light, costumes, and props and clusters of visual elements
		2.214	relations within and between aural elements, e.g., within and between sound, the spoken word, music, and clusters of aural elements
		2.215	relations within and between complexes (see 2.15—Stage 1)
		2.22	*relations at a point in time*, i.e., any combination of 2.21
		2.221	simple/complex
		2.2211	likenesses/commonalities
		2.2212	differences/opposition
		2.23	*relations through time*, i.e., between one occurrence and the next, e.g., between one movement and the next or one dancer and the next resulting in named relations (canon, fugue, ostinato, etc.) and general categories (elaboration, inversion, etc.)
		2.231	exact repetition/recurrence
		2.232	alteration of one or more components and/or clusters
		2.233	addition or subtraction of one or more components and/or clusters
		2.234	alteration of the order of events

		2.24	*relations between the moment and the linear development* (at a point in time and through time), i.e., relations accounting for particular effects which depend to some extent on a specific moment(s), e.g., emphasis by means of accent, reinforcement, focus, climax
1.21	recognizing the comparative importance of relations within the dance	2.25	*major/minor/subsidiary relations*
		2.251	complexes, strands, units, phrases, and sections in relation to each other
		2.252	complexes, strands, units, phrases and sections in relation to the total dance form
		2.253	the total web of relations

biomechanical; but it is suggested here that detail beyond this level of analysis is unlikely to be commonly used in choreographic or performance analysis or in the appraisal of a dance. The categories are not all-inclusive, but they can, in principle, be extended in depth to the minutest movement. Greater detail may, for example, be required by the notator.

To extend the example, the step described might be performed by two female dancers who take, respectively, a major and a subsidiary part in the total dance. The two dancers perform the step in the stage area limited by three large mobiles lit by a wash of blue color and placed in a triangular formation with one at the back of the stage and one at either side. Words are spoken off-stage at the same time that random sounds are produced by the clicking of parts of the mobiles against each other.

The purpose of this example is to demonstrate the several types of clusters, that is, the simultaneous occurrence of movement elements (2.11) performed by dancers (2.12) in a visual (2.13) and aural (2.14) setting. These simultaneously occurring elements and clusters form a more complicated unit that we term a complex (2.15).

Stage 2 of the chart analyzes varied types of relations that may exist within the total web of relations in a dance. Relations may be of a number of types, e.g., those seen at a specific moment, as in a photograph or when a film is stopped. *Relations at a moment* may suggest a large amount of movement through many strands of action which interweave in a spatial design, vary in dynamic quality, and are performed by a number of dancers who relate to each other in different ways. In contrast, relatively little movement may be apparent (in quantity), and what movement there is may be clearly directed toward a specific point, while the various strands of action may reinforce each other through echoing the spatial design or dynamic of movement. The parallel here is with harmonic/chordal analysis in music based on a vertical structure.

Under this category of relations sustained at one moment, the possibilities of what is related to what form a vast complex. The same possibilities are present in the category of *relations through time*, with the addition of all the relations that accrue from one moment following another. Essentially, relations through time involve a linear or contrapuntal analysis in which movements, dancers, as well as aspects of the visual and aural setting are considered in relation to each other from the preceding moment to the next; consequently, one complex is related to another following it in time.

Although the general term "development" is a tempting one to refer to progress through time, it is fraught with differing nuances of meaning. We have instead named particular relations through time resulting from the use of such choreographic devices as ostinato or canon. Fundamentally, any one component or cluster or complex may be sustained as it is, may be repeated from one moment to the next, or may be altered in a number of ways, for example, by adding new elements or by taking away something that was formerly there. The possibilities are endless.

Relations between a particular moment (vertical analysis) and the linear (contrapuntal) development through time may account for the emphasis on certain parts of the dance by reinforcement, directing attention to a climactic point, or highlighting areas of the dance. The recognition of units of the dance, whether these are phrases with a parallel in music or chunks that hold together in other ways, reveals relations between sections of the complete work and leads to a consideration of the dance form as a whole. The total dance form might then be related to the visual environment or to the relative importance of certain clusters or complexes of elements throughout the work. Several different lines of development may be continuing, with one of them predominating, all of them being in balance, or one resulting from another.

Thus at Stage 2, the dance form (2.2) may be analyzed according to the components that are related (2.21), that is, the movements, the dancers, the visual and aural components, clusters, or complexes. The total form may also be seen in terms of occurrences at any one moment (2.22) or through time (2.23) or through a further relationship of the moment to the linear progression (2.24). In consequence, certain sections of the dance may reveal strands that recur many times or relatively minor events or highlighted moments that occur only once (2.25). It is the recognition of these complexities and the acknowledgment of the relative importance of different parts that allow an interpretation to be made.

Stage 3 attempts to locate elements that contribute to the recognition and characterization of genre, style, and subject matter and that lead to an interpretation of the dance. It necessarily draws on

---

A Chart of Skills and Concepts of Dance—Stage 3

1.	Skills	2.	Concepts
1.3	interpreting, recognizing,	2.3	interpretation
	and characterizing the	2.31	*genre*, i.e., a particular form of dance, e.g., ballet, modern dance, stage dance
	dance statement/meaning	2.311	general style, i.e., a distinctive example of a genre: ballet—preromantic, romantic, classical, modern; modern dance—pretraditional, Central European, traditional, contemporary, postmodern; stage dance—tap, musical, jazz, cabaret
		2.312	a distinctive choreographic style, e.g., Ashton, Balanchine, Tetley, Graham, Hawkins, Cunningham, Robbins
		2.32	*subject matter*
		2.321	content, e.g., "pure" movement, a story, a theme, a topic, an idea
		2.322	treatment of the subject matter, e.g., representative, narrative, literal, dramatic, mimetic, lyrical, expressionistic, impressionistic, abstract, symbolic
		2.33	*quality, mood, atmosphere*, i.e., aesthetic descriptions of clusters, complexes, relationships, phrases/sections, and the whole dance
		2.34	*artistic statement/meaning*
		2.341	relationships between 2.31, 2.32, and 2.33

the preceding two stages in that they describe the components of the dance in relationship and thus offer a structure for marking the observable features of the dance. The terms "genre" and "style" are open to a variety of meanings, as is evident in the literature of the arts; their use for purposes of this article is explained below.

The recognition of the *genre* (2.31), that is, the requirements and characteristics of a particular form of dance—e.g., ballet, tap, jazz—is crucial to a valid interpretation. It would be simply inappropriate to make statements about tap dancing using criteria of appraisal relevant to ballet. This recognition of genre is derived directly from 1.1 and 1.2, since each form of dance is a particular selection from the total available range of movement possibilities and relationships, made in a way that produces a distinctive statement. Genre is recognizable as jazz dance or modern dance by its use of specific kinds of movement.

The *style* of a dance is recognized by the manner of expression used in that dance. For example, Graham, Hawkins, and Humphrey are all modern dance choreographers of the same era. Yet there is no danger of confusing a dance choreographed by one with that by another, as each choreographer has developed a distinctive expressive style.

The way in which the *subject matter* is dealt with makes it in some ways a subsection of genre. It involves recognition of certain general characteristics of the treatment of subject matter (2.31)—including, for example, abstraction, representation, and impressionism—that may have currency across the arts. Aesthetic descriptions of quality, mood, and atmosphere (2.33) derived from complexes and from sections of the total dance form are backed up by statements of the relative importance of sections/themes identified in the previous stage. Understanding and expression of the "artistic statement" and "meaning" of the dance are dependent upon the sum total of these three stages.

Stage 4 is concerned with evaluation, that is, with appraising and making judgments. The effectiveness and appropriateness of the dance are assessed with reference to discrimination among parts and between parts in relation to the whole, to the way in which the material is presented and structured, and to the characterization of specific complexes and units as meaningful, all taken in relation to the question of genre and style. It then becomes possible to say whether a given dance is a good dance of its type, i.e., within the particular genre and style. The dance may be more or less convinc-

A Chart of Skills and Concepts of Dance—Stage 4

1.	Skills	2.	Concepts
1.4	evaluating, appraising, and judging the dance	2.4	evaluation
		2.41	*choreography*
		2.411	appropriateness and effectiveness of genre—general and choreographic style, subject matter—content, and treatment in relation to quality, mood, atmosphere, and meaning
		2.412	appropriateness and effectiveness of this dance vis-à-vis other dances which have similar characteristics
		2.42	*performance*
		2.421	appropriateness and effectiveness of a particular performance of the dance in terms of technical competence and the interpretation given
		2.422	appropriateness and effectiveness of other interpretations of the dance
		2.43	*response and appraisal*
		2.431	appropriateness of the response—liking/disliking, reasons offered and substantiated
		2.432	validity of other appraisals, of the critical response of others

ing in these terms. Certain criteria, canons, and standards are implicit in different kinds of dance, and the dance may be judged effective in this light.

It may be the *choreography* that is evaluated (2.41) and/or a particular *performance* of it (2.42), in terms of both the skill exhibited in the performance and the interpretation offered. The performance may be compared with others of the same work. Further, the *response* to the dance may be evaluated (2.43).

In many ways, the individual response is the most important aspect of the entire enterprise, since it is the raison d'être of the dance as well as the spectators' reason for looking at it. Works of art are seen to be of value when they move the spectator and offer a heightened experience. It is our contention that everything in the chart leads to this response and, in turn, is derived from it. We would argue that an informed response is the ultimate aim of dance studies in the context of aesthetic education. For most students, this response will occur in watching dance and for some also in making or performing.

Within aesthetic education, the purpose must be to come to appreciate and understand the dance more fully. One's own response may be limited, and illumination may occur through studying the responses of others. The study of critical writings reveals reasons for the appraisals offered, and these reasons are given in relation to visible, objective features of the work. Interpretations placed on a group of such features may vary to some degree, but in order to arrive at a considered judgment, the reasons for an interpretation can be examined and validated by reference to the dance itself.

Some Notes on Interpretation

The notion of "interpreting" the dance (Stage 3 of the chart) perhaps needs some amplification, since the word can be used in a number of rather different ways, e.g., with reference to different parts of the act of performing or to various people involved in the performance. The *member of the audience* may place a certain interpretation on a particular performance in the sense of the meaning(s) derived. The educator and student are also spectators and respond in the same way the audience does, but they may apply more analytic procedures to the work in their attempt to arrive at a considered statement of its significance. At the other end of the continuum from the casual spectator, the professional critic interprets the dance in a particular way and passes on that interpretation by means of impressionistic, descriptive, or reasoned statements about the dance.

From a rather different point of view, the *dancer* offers a particular interpretation of the dance through the way in which he or she performs it. The dancer's interpretation does not reflect idiosyncratic mannerisms but a fully thought-out approach to the performance of the dance. It is precisely this which the critic or scholar attempts to locate in comparative analyses of different performances. At the level of interpreting a work as a whole, one might consider whether the Royal Ballet's performance (interpretation) of Tudor's *Dark Elegies* offers an interpretation similar to that of the Ballet Rambert. Anyone who has seen both or who merely has read the critics on the subject would know that contrasting interpretations were being offered by these companies, which substantially affected the judgments made of the work.

The choreographer is in the unique position of *making* the dance and therefore of determining, through specific structure and form, the range of possible interpretations. The choreographer will, by linking this particular set of movements in this particular way, set a boundary for the validity of any one interpretation.

The basis upon which *all* these kinds of interpretation rest is, however, the observable features of the dance, that is, the movement components, the dancers, the setting and accompanying aural elements, and the clusters, complexes, and relations which they form (2.1, 2.2). Interpretive statements are not plucked from the air but are rooted in one or more particular realizations of the dance in which pertinent features can be located. In consequence, reasons can be adduced for the statements made.

Clearly, when the director of a performance is also its choreographer, one might assume congruence between the interpretive and choreographic roles; but as soon as someone other than the choreographer brings a performance into being, elements of a different or alternative interpretation may enter. In time, if the dance remains in the repertoire, a number of different directors will produce the dance, and a number of different interpretations will be available for enjoyment, illumination, and study. It is an important area of dance performance analysis to locate those aspects of different performances that are crucial to success, that is, those that appear consistently as opposed to those that change. For example, costume is often a variable, and a parallel might be a Shakespeare play performed in modern dress. Some universality of meaning overrides these changes or is perhaps highlighted by them. One might argue that for a dance to remain the same dance, some core of meaning must remain constant—as is the case with some pieces of music that are still perceived as artistically significant years after their contextual surroundings have changed, many of their performance features have altered, and their performance is purely a reconstruction from a score.

Both the critic and the performer/director require knowledge that goes beyond the levels of analysis identified here. The possession of an artistic background, which illuminates any dance, is relevant, as is familiarity with the medium and with specific styles and genres within the medium. Acquaintance with other instances of performance of the same work and study of its score also contribute to an understanding of any one interpretation of it.

Summary

The chart of skills and concepts for dance demonstrates agreement with, and offers practical support for, the basic assumptions upon which the original chart was constructed. The "aesthetic domain" of dance has been clearly laid out in terms of skills and concepts for what the Smiths term "skillful probing" and "full participation." In effect, the use of the chart may provide a means by which a more informed response to and a deeper experience of dance may be made possible and in consequence a more discerning dance public may be created.

NOTE

1. R. A. and C. M. Smith, "The Artworld and Aesthetic Skills: A Context for Research and Development," *Journal of Aesthetic Education* 11, no. 2 (April 1977): 124.

MICHAEL J. PARSONS

Stages of Aesthetic Development

The idea has long been familiar that our creative abilities in the arts move through a number of developmental stages. There are several accounts of this development,[1] and its general character is well known. This knowledge has of course had considerable influence on art education. It has long seemed plausible to me that our appreciative abilities undergo a similar development. In this paper I want to generalize from work that I have been doing and argue that there is a place for a cognitive developmental approach to aesthetic response. That approach takes further the cognitive trend in the psychology of the arts, fills a gap in cognitive developmental theories, and could be helpful to art educators.

Recent work in the psychology of the arts has stressed the cognitive character of abilities connected with the arts.[2] Arnheim's work[3] has been influential in this connection. Howard Gardner[4] and Project Zero[5] have done a number of well-known studies of the origin and development of various skills and abilities; these studies in general treat the arts as symbol systems. There are other recent studies on the development of early symbolic skills,[6] influenced especially by Werner and Kaplan.[7] These studies in general investigate especially the earliest ages.

There have been several attempts to use cognitive developmental theory to understand responses to the arts. Machotka[8] argued that the appreciation of realism in paintings marks a developmental stage because it requires the ability to compare the representation with the reality, and this in turn requires the Piagetian stage of concrete operations. He studied the reasons given by children of various ages for judgments of paintings and showed that indeed the age at which realism is typically preferred is also the age at which concrete operations typically become possible. Gardner[9] argued that such an approach would not be fruitful beyond the youngest ages because the appreciation of art does not require more than concrete operations (though maybe criticism does). But, with Winner and Kirchner,[10] he also showed that people's understandings of where

art comes from do fall into three stages of development. And, somewhat further afield, Gablik[11] has argued that the history of art can
be organized into three major stages corresponding to Piaget's three
main stages of cognitive thought.

A more full-scale cognitive developmental theory of aesthetic development would obviously be sympathetic with this trend. But in
my view such studies are based on a conception of cognition that
is not really hospitable to the arts. They assume that there is only
one cognitive domain—the "Piagetian" one of empirical-scientific
knowledge. This means that there is only one stream of cognitive
development and that development in the arts must be a kind of
application of Piaget's findings. Put another way, one could say that
while they take a cognitive approach to the arts, they do not ask
what is specific to the arts—what kind of cognitions they mediate. I
find this unduly limiting, because it does not allow us to get close
to what is aesthetic about aesthetic response or to questions of aesthetic value. An alternative is to take seriously the view that aesthetic meanings are *sui generis* and that responding to works of art
is different from responding to other kinds of objects. This is the
view of the philosophical tradition going back to Kant, a tradition
that divides human cognition into three basic kinds: the empirical,
the moral, and the aesthetic. One contemporary version of this
tradition that has influenced me in particular is the work of
Habermas,[12] who argues that the three are different because they
are concerned with three different worlds: the outer world of nature, the social world, and the inner world of needs and desires.

If aesthetic meanings are different in kind from empirical and
moral meanings, they will be expressed in distinctive concepts.
Aesthetic thought will have its own concerns and structures, its
own problems and ways of supporting judgments. An analysis of
aesthetic development will focus on the development of these
specifically aesthetic concepts and judgments. There are well-
known theories of development of empirical-scientific and moral
concepts and judgments in the work, respectively, of Piaget[13] and
Kohlberg.[14] It seems an obvious thought that there may be a parallel development of aesthetic thinking. James Mark Baldwin[15] is the
only one to have tried to work this thought out in detail, though he
thought of it more as an enterprise in logic than in evidence.

It may be worth pointing out, parenthetically, that the cognitive
focus does not deny the importance of the emotional side of aesthetic experience. Rather, it denies the value of the distinction in
this case. Our cognitions and our emotions are intricately related in

aesthetic response. The way we understand a painting influences our feelings, and our feelings guide our understanding of it. In general, cognitions give shape to emotions and for this reason are the better focus for developmental analysis.

One of the virtues—and difficulties—of this approach is that it takes value issues seriously. Because it is developmental, it must arrange our understandings of art in a sequence of increasing adequacy. It presupposes that some responses to a work are to be preferred to others because they more adequately grasp the qualities of the work. The stages of development must reflect this situation because they will make possible increasingly adequate responses. Each stage will rest on a better understanding of art and use it to interpret paintings more adequately. An account of these stages therefore must be normatively oriented: it will consist largely of an account of these successive understandings and of how and why they are more adequate.

The approach also has the advantage of connecting with the body of established cognitive developmental theory and thus of relating the discussion of particular skills and concepts in a more comprehensive theory of development. It can also connect aesthetic development with a more basic psychological development. Each successive new understanding of art is related to a new ability to understand the perspective of others. This is because perspective-taking is the common theme of cognitive developmental theories. One could argue that they all assume that cognitive development is achieved through the realization of our naturally social being. We move from an initial state of egocentrism to one of autonomous sociality; and furthermore this movement can be divided into three major levels, in the aesthetic as much as in the moral and empirical domains.

In each domain we begin in the same cognitive state. We are born small, without language, with native reflexes but without concepts or categories, subject to an unorganized plenty of sensory stimuli. Though we are socially oriented, we are unable to distinguish self from others. We are aware only of what appears to us and not of what appears to others; and we are subject only to our pleasures, pains, and perceptions. From this beginning we construct an understanding of the world, including the world of art; we do this by gradually becoming aware of the presence of others, by learning their language and sharing their admirations. At this level we are able to appreciate the sensuous beauties of paintings, the skills of manipulation, the values of representation, the interest of subject matter, and the stereotypes of beauty and ugliness. We take the norms involved for granted, as if they were facts established by perception. We do not distinguish interpretation from perception, nor the aesthetic from other kinds of experience.

At the next level we are more fully members of our society, living its achievements from the inside, sharing its values, grasping its intentions. Cognitively we can take the point of view first of individual others and then of the society as a whole. This enables us to transmute the joys and stresses of our biological impulses into a wider world of publicly meaningful appreciations. We can understand art as the expression of subjectivity, appreciate the expression of a wide range of difficult emotions—the violent, the ugly, the tragic; and later find meaning in the formal aspects of paintings, in style, genre, and social and historical context. We are aware of our own subjectivity, understand that we interpret what we see, distinguish facts from values, and find art criticism helpful.

The third is the level of autonomous judgment—the "post-conventional" level, as it is often called. The basic point here is that we make our judgments more in light of good reasons and less in light of socially current opinions. We can criticize in a reasonable way the values and categories of our society and, what is the same thing, examine our own experience for the influence on it of stereotype, habit, and idiosyncratic factors. In this way we can more relevantly respond to the actuality of the work and more adequately grasp its qualities. At the same time we can raise questions about both our own and the work's values. Indeed, we can see the purpose of art as raising questions about perception and value, reformulating accepted needs and norms, and helping us reach a better understanding of our inner nature. This is individual independence of thought, but it is not the less social for that. The criticism of established values—in society as well as in the art world—has the implicit goal of improving them, of reaching an unachieved but possible consensus based on reason.

My own work[16] has focused on responses to paintings and fleshes out this skeletal structure with an account of the development of a number of concepts with which we think about paintings. It further divides these three levels into five stages and analyzes the movement from one to another in particular responses to particular paintings. I assume that one could work out similar accounts that focus on any of the other art forms.

In focusing on the cognitive, the approach is of course also in harmony with current emphases in art education on the cognitive and the disciplinary. And because of the advantages mentioned above—that it can deal with aesthetic value issues and connect with an established psychological tradition—it may be quite useful to educators. It coincides in particular with the needs of the movement to establish art as a serious school study dealing with aesthetic understandings. It presumes that aesthetic development requires significant interaction with artworks and hard work struggling with them. Because, like all cognitive developmental theories, it is a cognitive conflict approach, it suggests that the best works to spend time with will be those that are difficult enough not to be comfortable, and easy enough to be accessible. Moreover, it offers some general explanations and predictions of what will be suitably challenging at different stages, and some guidelines for selecting such works in particular cases. For example, one could say that in general works expressing strong but difficult emotions are educationally profitable for children who are beginning to operate at the beginning of the second level mentioned above.[17] So one could identify the aesthetic topics that would likely be worth discussing with such children.

In the same way, it appears that the idea of style is understood differently at different stages, and a serious consideration of its historical significance is likely to be useful only later in the second level. Style in paintings is understood first only as behavior due to habit or whim; though an artist's style can be identified, it is essentially meaningless matter of fact. Later it is understood as the characteristic mood or feeling of the artist, and only after that can it be seen with its art-historical meanings of the echo of one work in another. Only at this latter stage does it seem worthwhile teaching "style" deliberately. In general, the theory could suggest how various aesthetic themes and concepts are likely to be understood by different groups and which are most likely to succeed educationally.

For teachers, a scheme of cognitive development offers the possibility of understanding in a new way how their students construe aesthetic concepts and what kind of cognitive problems they have with them. This opportunity to understand students may be its most important contribution. But it also offers, from the cognitive developmental tradition, some basic strategies for dealing with these problems, strategies that may be summarized in the slogan "challenge and support." And finally it may provide a way of evaluating the success of educational programs, because it allows the assessment of student improvement in regard to the central educational concern—the grasp of what is aesthetically valuable in works of art.

NOTES

1. For example, J. H. Di Leo, *Young Children and Their Drawings* (New York: Brunner/Mazel, 1970); H. Gardner, *Artful Scribbles: The Significance of Children's Drawings* (New York: Basic Books, 1980); R. Kellogg, *Analyzing Children's Art* (Palo Alto, Calif.: Mayfield, 1969).

2. For a lengthier overview of this trend and of the accompanying trend in art education, see R. Smith, "The Changing Image of Art Education: Theoretical Antecedents of Discipline-based Art Education," in R. A. Smith, ed., *Discipline-based Art Education: Origins, Meaning, and Development* (Urbana: University of Illinois Press, 1989), pp. 3–34.

3. R. Arnheim, *Art and Visual Perception* (Berkeley: University of California Press, 1954); and *Visual Thinking* (Berkeley: University of California Press, 1969).

4. H. Gardner, *The Arts and Human Development: A Psychological Study of the Artistic Process* (New York: Wiley, 1973). See also essays collected in his *Art, Mind and Brain: A Cognitive Approach to Creativity* (New York: Basic Books, 1982).

5. See, e.g., D. Perkins and B. Leondar, eds., *The Arts and Cognition* (Baltimore: Johns Hopkins University Press, 1977); and *Harvard Project Zero: Basic Abilities Required for Understanding Creation in the Arts* (Cambridge, Mass.: Graduate School of Education, Harvard University, 1974).

6. For example, N. Smith and M. Franklin, eds., *Symbolic Functioning in Childhood* (Hillsdale, N.J.: Lawrence Erlbaum, 1979).

7. H. Werner and B. Kaplan, *Symbol Formation* (New York: Wiley, 1963).

8. P. Machotka, "Aesthetic Criteria in Childhood: Justifications of Preference," *Child Development* 37 (1966): 877–85.

9. Gardner, *The Arts and Human Development*.

10. H. Gardner, E. Winner, and M. Kircher, "Children's Conceptions of the Arts," *Journal of Aesthetic Education* 9, no. 3 (July 1975): 60–77.

11. S. Gablik, *Progress in Art* (London: Thames and Hudson, 1976).

12. For example, in pp. 8–42 of J. Habermas, *The Theory of Communicative Action*, vol. 1, trans. Thomas McCarthy (Boston: Beacon Press, 1984).

13. J. Piaget, *The Science of Education and the Psychology of the Child* (New York: Orion Press, 1970).

14. L. Kohlberg, *Essays on Moral Development*, vols. 1 and 2 (San Francisco: Harper and Row, 1981).

15. J. M. Baldwin, *Thought and Things: A Study of the Development and Meaning of Thought*, vol. 3 (London: Swann, Sonnenschein and Co., 1914; reprint, New York: Arno Press, 1974).

16. M. Parsons, *How We Understand Art: A Cognitive Developmental Account of Aesthetic Experience* (New York: Cambridge University Press, 1987).

17. See M. Parsons, "Talking about a Painting: A Cognitive Developmental Analysis," *Journal of Aesthetic Education* 21, no. 3 (Spring 1987): 37–55.

Bibliographic Note

In addition to the references cited in the essays in this volume and in this note, mention should be made of a number of bibliographic sources and relevant journals. The first systematic attempt to identify the literature of aesthetic education, including references to philosophical aesthetics, was the Office of Education–University of Illinois Philosophy of Education Project directed by Harry S. Broudy. This project was not restricted to aesthetic literature but identified topics and sources across problem areas of education and the disciplines relevant to them. See Harry S. Broudy, Michael J. Parsons, Ivan A. Snook, Ronald D. Szoke, *Philosophy of Education: An Organization of Topics and Selected Sources,* University of Illinois Press, 1967; Christiana M. Smith and Harry S. Broudy, *Philosophy of Education,* Supplement, 1969; Ronald P. Jeffrey, *Philosophy of Education,* Supplement, 1971. The latter was available from the office of *Educational Theory* for a short period of time, but no longer. Some copies, however, probably found their way into libraries. This project produced a number of anthologies, including Ralph A. Smith, ed., *Aesthetics and Problems of Education,* University of Illinois Press, 1971.

Another extensive review of the literature may be found in a number of bibliographic pamphlets in the Central Midwestern Regional Educational Laboratory (CEMREL) materials located in the archives of the University of Illinois Library at Urbana-Champaign. For a comprehensive listing of CEMREL's publications, see Stanley S. Madeja with Sheila Onuska, *Through the Arts to the Aesthetic,* St. Louis, CEMREL, 1977, 137–41.

Other efforts to keep track of the philosophical and theoretical literature may be found in R. A. Smith, "The Philosophical Literature of Aesthetic Education" in *Toward An Aesthetic Education,* Music Educators National Conference, 1971, 137–90; "Educational Aesthetics Today" in Margaret Gillett and John A. Laska, eds., *Foundation Studies in Education: Justifications and New Directions,* Scarecrow, 1973, 326–54; and "The Changing Image of Art Education: Theoretical

Antecedents of Discipline-based Art Education," in *Discipline-based Art Education: Origins, Meaning, Development*, ed. R. Smith, University of Illinois Press, 1989, pp. 4–34. Though not restricted to a discussion of the theoretical literature, Smith has also surveyed recent trends in "Arts Education in the United States, 1960–1983: A Personal View," *Educational Analysis* 5, no. 2 (1983): 89–101, a British publication. A condensed version, "Two Decades of Politics and Arts Education," was published in the *Journal of Aesthetic Education* 16, no. 3 (Fall 1982): 5–14.

Contributions by British writers to the literature of aesthetic education may be found in a number of reports of conferences held on aesthetic education: Daphne M. Tribe, ed., *Aesthetic Education: Freedom and Imagination*, Derby Lonsdale College of Higher Education, 1981; Alan Simpson, ed., *Aesthetic Education and the Problems of Assessment and Evaluation*. Didsbury School of Education, Manchester Polytechnic, 1980; Joan W. White, guest editor, "Aesthetic Education Conference 1980—Roehampton Institute, Southlands College," *Journal of Aesthetic Education* 15, no. 3 (July 1981); Alan Simpson, guest editor, "Homerton College Aesthetic Education Conference 1982," *Journal of Aesthetic Education* 18, no. 1 (Spring 1984); and Janet Hauton, *Aesthetic Education and Creativity*, Bishop Grosseteste College, Lincoln, 1984.

A curriculum publication series of six volumes edited by Malcolm Ross is also helpful for gaining a sense of contemporary British thinking about aesthetic topics. See *The Creative Arts*, Heinemann, (1978); *The Arts and Personal Growth* (1980); *The Aesthetic Imperative* (1981); *The Development of Aesthetic Experience* (1982); *The Arts: A Way of Knowing* (1983); *The Aesthetic in Education* (1985), all published by Pergamon, Oxford and New York. A brief bibliography of aesthetics and aesthetic education can also be found in H. B. Redfern's *Questions in Aesthetic Education*, Allen and Unwin, 1986, 111–18.

The British National Association for Education in the Arts has published a number of monographs in their *Take-Up* series; e.g., David Aspin, *Objectivity and Assessment in the Arts: The Problem of Aesthetic Education* (1984); Peter Abbs, *English as an Arts Discipline* (1985); *Agenda for the Arts* (January 1986); and John Blacking, *Culture and the Arts* (August 1986). A recent publication is Peter Abbs, ed., *The Symbolic Order*, Falmer, 1989.

The literature of philosophical aesthetics and aesthetic education may be followed in three journals: the *Journal of Aesthetics and Art Criticism*, published by the American Society for Aesthetics; the *British Journal of Aesthetics*, the journal of the British Society for Aesthetics, published by Oxford University Press; and the *Journal of Aesthetic Education*, published by the University of Illinois Press. The American Society for Aesthetics has also published *Cumulative Index: Volumes I–XXXV, 1944–1977*, ed. John Fisher, 1979; and *Supplement to the Cumulative Index, Volumes XXXVI–XL, 1982*, 1982. See also Allan Shields, *A Bibliography of Bibliographies in Aesthetics*, San Diego State University Press, 1974. *The Philosophical Index* also prints annotated references on aesthetics and aesthetic education.

Other helpful bibliographies, though not restricted to the philosophical literature, may be found in Clarence Bunch, ed., *Art Education: A Guide to Information Sources*, Gale Research, 1978; Stephen Mark Dobbs, "Research and Reason: Recent Literature and Ideas in American Art Education," *Curriculum Theory Network* 4, nos. 2–3 (1974): 169–91, a special issue devoted to curriculum in art; and Stanley S. Majeda, *Arts and Aesthetics: An Agenda for the Future*, St. Louis: CEMREL, 1977, Part 2.

Contributors

RALPH A. SMITH is Professor of Cultural and Educational Policy in the Department of Educational Policy Studies at the University of Illinois at Urbana-Champaign. The editor of the *Journal of Aesthetic Education* since its inception in 1966, he has, in addition, edited *Aesthetics and Criticism in Art Education: Problems in Defining, Explaining, and Evaluating Art; Aesthetic Concepts and Education;* and *Discipline-based Art Education: Origins, Meaning, and Development.* He has also authored *The Sense of Art: A Study in Aesthetic Education* and *Excellence in Art Education.* He is currently general editor of a series titled The Disciplines and Art Education: Contexts of Understanding, and the co-author, with Albert William Levi, of the series' first volume titled *Art Education: A Critical Necessity* (in press).

ALAN SIMPSON is a former Chair of Art and Design Education at Didsbury School of Education, Manchester Polytechnic. He is a member of the Executive Committee of the British Society of Aesthetics and has organized national conferences on aesthetic education and lectured on aesthetics and art education in the United States, Hungary, Poland, and West Germany. His articles have appeared in *The Aesthetic in Education* (ed. M. Ross), *The Eidos of Art* (Poland), the *Journal of Philosophy of Education,* the *British Journal of Aesthetics,* the *Journal of Art and Design Education,* and the *Journal of Aesthetic Education.* He has exhibited his work as a practicing artist, and his ceramics are in collections in Great Britain, the United States, and Australia. He has recently taken early retirement.

PETER ABBS is Lecturer in Education at the University of Sussex where he is a co-director of the M.A. course Language, the Arts, and Education and director of the Postgraduate Certificate in English Curriculum Group. He has authored a number of volumes, including *Autobiography in Education; Reclamations: Essays on Culture, Mass-Culture, and the Curriculum; English within the Arts,* and edited *Living Powers: The Arts in Education.* He has also published two volumes of poetry, *For Man and Islands* and *Songs of a New Taliesin.*

JANET ADSHEAD has been a Leverhulme Fellow in Dance and is currently M.A. Course Tutor at the University of Surrey. She has written *The Study of Dance,* co-edited *Dance History: A Methodology for Study,* and edited *Dance*

Analysis: Theory and Practice. She has also edited a number of national and international proceedings on dance education, and her articles have appeared in such journals as *New Dance, Physical Education,* and the *Journal of Aesthetic Education.*

DAVID N. ASPIN, formerly Professor of Education at University of London King's College, is now Dean of the Faculty of Education, Monash University, Melbourne, Australia. He has been involved in numerous symposia and conferences on education and the arts and was a major contributor to the influential Gulbenkian Report, *The Arts in Schools.* His articles have appeared in several books and educational journals, including the *Journal of Philosophy of Education,* the *Journal of Art and Design Education,* and the *Journal of Aesthetic Education.*

MARGARET P. BATTIN is Professor of Philosophy in the Department of Philosophy at the University of Utah. A past president of the Pacific Division of the American Society for Aesthetics, she is the author of *Ethical Issues in Suicide* and is one of four editors of *Puzzles About Art: An Aesthetics Casebook.*

MONROE C. BEARDSLEY (1915–85), one of the most influential philosophers of art of the mid-twentieth century, taught philosophy first at Swarthmore College and then at Temple University. He served as president of the American Philosophical Association and the American Society for Aesthetics and was a Fellow of the American Academy of Arts and Sciences. Among his major works are *Aesthetics: Problems in the Philosophy of Criticism, The Possibility of Criticism, Aesthetics from Classical Greece to the Present: A Brief History,* and *Philosophical Thinking,* with Elizabeth L. Beardsley.

DAVID BEST is a Research Fellow in the Philosophy Department at the University College of Swansea, United Kingdom. Among his recent books are *Expression and Movement in the Arts* and *Feeling and Reason in the Arts.* He is a frequent speaker at national and international conferences and congresses.

VALERIE A. BRIGINSHAW is Head of Dance at West Sussex Institute of Higher Education, Chichester, England. Her research interests include dance and ideology, feminism and dance, and postmodern and new dance. She has recently written "Copeland's 'Objective Temperament' Revisited or Do We Really Know What Postmodern Dance Is?" She is also conducting research for a television program and a series of videotapes supported by education packs that document British new dance.

HARRY S. BROUDY is Emeritus Professor of Philosophy of Education at the University of Illinois at Urbana-Champaign. His writings have had a major impact on thinking about such educational problems as teaching as a profession, the role of the arts and humanities in the curriculum, and the nature of general education. Among his important publications are *Building a Philosophy of Education, Exemplars of Teaching Method, Enlightened Cherishing: An Essay on Aesthetic Education, The Real World of the Public Schools, Truth and Credibility: The Citizen's Dilemma,* and *The Uses of Schooling.*

GILBERT A. CLARK is Professor and Coordinator of Art Education and holds a joint appointment in Gifted and Talented Education at Indiana University. With Enid Zimmerman he has published *Art Design: Communicating Visually, Educating Artistically Talented Students*, and *Understanding Art Testing*.

DONALD W. CRAWFORD is Professor of Philosophy at the University of Wisconsin–Madison and the editor of the *Journal of Aesthetics and Art Criticism*. He is the author of *Kant's Aesthetic Theory* as well as a number of essays that have appeared in such collections as *Essays in Kant's Aesthetics* and *The Philosophy of Immanuel Kant*. He has also published numerous articles in philosophical journals, including the *Journal of Aesthetics and Art Criticism* and the *Journal of Aesthetic Education*.

MICHAEL D. DAY is Professor of Art and Head of the Art Education Program at Brigham Young University. He has been active in a number of national and state curriculum development projects and is a specialist in curriculum evaluation. Two of his case studies were published in *Art History, Art Criticism, and Art Production: An Examination of Art Education in Selected School Districts*, and he is one of the authors of *Children and Their Art*, now in a fourth edition.

MARCIA MUELDER EATON is Professor of Philosophy at the University of Minnesota and the author of a number of volumes, including *Basic Issues in Aesthetics*, *Art and Nonart*, and *Aesthetics and the Good Life*. She is also a frequent contributor to the *Journal of Aesthetics and Art Criticism* and other philosophical journals.

DAVID W. ECKER is a Professor of Art Education at New York University where he teaches courses in aesthetics and arts education. His recent interests include the educational application of the tenets of phenomenology and the problems of multicultural education. He has contributed chapters to such volumes as *Arts and Aesthetics: An Agenda for the Future* and *Philosophical Redirection of Educational Research*, and is the co-editor, with Elliot W. Eisner, of *Readings in Art Education*.

R. K. ELLIOTT is Reader Emeritus in the Philosophy of Education of the Institute of Education at the University of London and current editor of the *Journal of Philosophy of Education*. He has also been a lecturer in Philosophy at Birkbeck College of the University of London and a Professor of Education at Birmingham University. His articles and essays have appeared in numerous publications, including the second edition of *Philosophy Looks at the Arts*, edited by Joseph Margolis.

HOWARD GARDNER is Professor of Education at Harvard University, Research Psychologist at the Boston Veterans Administration Hospital, and Adjunct Professor of Neurology at the Boston University School of Medicine. He has authored several volumes, including *The Arts and Human Development*, *Developmental Psychology*, *Frames of Mind*, and, most recently, *To Open Minds: Chinese Clues to the Dilemma of American Education*. He is also co-director with D. N. Perkins of Harvard Project Zero, a basic and applied research unit in the arts and arts education.

NELSON GOODMAN is Emeritus Professor of Philosophy at Harvard University. One of the major philosophical thinkers of our time, his work on symbolic systems has had a major influence on aesthetic thinking, especially his *Languages of Art: An Approach to a Theory of Symbols, Ways of Worldmaking,* and *Of Mind and Other Matters.* He has also written *Problems and Projects, Fact, Fiction, and Forecast,* and, with Catherine Z. Elgin, *Reconceptions in Philosophy.*

MAXINE GREENE is William F. Russell Professor in the Foundations of Education at Teachers College, Columbia University, and the author of *Existential Encounters for Teachers, Teacher as Stranger, Landscapes of Learning,* and *The Dialectic of Freedom.* A past president of the Philosophy of Education Society and the American Educational Research Association, she is a distinguished lecturer and has contributed to numerous aesthetic education projects. Her work at Lincoln Center in New York City has inspired similar efforts at other performing arts centers throughout the country.

W. DWAINE GREER is Associate Professor of Art at the University of Arizona. He has been active in state, regional, and national curriculum activities and was formerly director of the Southwestern Regional Laboratory (SWRL) aesthetic education program in Los Angeles. He has served as director of the Getty Institute for Educators on the Visual Arts and is currently directing the Getty Center for Education in the Arts diffusion project. His articles have appeared in such journals as *Art Education, Studies in Art Education,* and the *Journal of Aesthetic Education.*

PAULINE HODGENS lectures in dance and aesthetics of dance at Roehampton Institute, London, in B.A./B.Ed. programs. Her research interests lie in the area of interpretation of artworks and the conceptual problems to which these give rise. She is the author of an annotated bibliography on aesthetics and dance and of analyses of two works in Janet Adshead, ed., *Choreography: Principles and Practice,* and of a further work to accompany a video recording of Davies's *Rushes* (published by the National Resource Centre for Dance, University of Surrey).

VERNON A. HOWARD is a philosopher of education and the arts and co-director with Israel Scheffler of the Philosophy of Education Research Center at the Harvard Graduate College of Education. A professional singer who performs in lecture/recitals, he is also the author of *Artistry: The Work of Artists,* and, with J. H. Barton, of *Thinking on Paper.*

MICHAEL ROBERT HUXLEY is Head of Dance at Leicester Polytechnic, England, where he teaches dance history, choreography, and performance. His written work includes an analysis with Ramsay Burt of British new dance in M. Febvre, *La danse au defi,* and he has published in Adshead and Layson, eds., *Dance History,* as well as in *New Dance* and *Ballet International.*

E. F. KAELIN is Professor of Philosophy at the Florida State University, Tallahassee, and is the author of *An Existentialist Aesthetic, Art and Existence, Heidegger's "Being and Time": A Reading for Readers, The Unhappy Consciousness: The Poetic Flight of Samuel Beckett,* and *An Aesthetics for Art Educators.*

E. LOUIS LANKFORD is Associate Professor of Art Education at the Ohio State University and the author of numerous articles on aesthetics and art education in such publications as *Studies in Art Education, Art Education,* and the *Journal of Aesthetic Education.*

ALBERT WILLIAM LEVI (1911–88) was, at the time of his death, David May Distinguished University Professor Emeritus in the Humanities at Washington University. Among his important works are *Philosophy and the Modern World; Literature, Philosophy, and the Imagination; Humanism and Politics; The Humanities Today;* and *Philosophy as Social Expression.*

GEORGE LINDEN is Professor of Philosophy at Southern Illinois University at Edwardsville. He is the author of *Reflections on the Screen* and has published numerous articles in such journals as the *Journal of Aesthetics and Art Criticism* and the *Journal of Aesthetic Education.*

HAROLD OSBORNE (1905–87) was the founder and longtime editor of the *British Journal of Aesthetics.* At the time of his death he was also the president of the British Society of Aesthetics. His major publications include *Aesthetics and Criticism, Aesthetics and Art Theory: An Historical Introduction, The Art of Appreciation,* and *Abstraction and Artifice in Twentieth-Century Art.* He also edited *The Oxford Companion to Art* and *The Oxford Companion to the Decorative Arts.*

MICHAEL J. PARSONS is Chairman of the Department of Art Education at Ohio State University and the author of *How We Understand Art: A Cognitive Developmental Account of Aesthetic Experience.* His articles have appeared in such journals as the *Journal of Aesthetics and Art Criticism, Educational Theory,* and the *Journal of Aesthetic Education.*

H. BETTY REDFERN is a freelance lecturer in the fields of education, aesthetics, and the arts. A former teacher of literature, music, dance, and physical education, she has written *Concepts in Modern Educational Dance; Dance, Art, and Aesthetics;* and *Questions in Aesthetic Education.* She currently resides in Cumbria, United Kingdom.

BENNETT REIMER is John W. Beattie Professor and Chairman of the Department of Music Education at Northwestern University. He is the author of *Philosophy of Music Education* and *The Experience of Music,* and his articles have appeared in numerous journals, including the *Music Educators Journal, Design for Arts in Education,* and the *Journal of Aesthetic Education.*

LOUISE M. ROSENBLATT is Professor Emerita of English Education at New York University and the author of *Literature as Exploration* and *The Reader, the Text, and the Poem.* She has also contributed essays to such journals as *Re-*

search in the Teaching of English and a number of anthologies, including *Developing Literacy.*

ROGER SCRUTON is Professor of Philosophy at Birkbeck College of the University of London and the author of numerous volumes, among them *Art and Imagination, The Aesthetics of Architecture, The Politics of Culture,* and *The Aesthetic Understanding.* His inaugural lecture at Birkbeck College lamented the neglect of aesthetics in modern philosophy and argued a strong case for a revival of interest in aesthetic experience and aesthetic education.

Index